Interpretations of Conflict

Interpretations of Conflict

ETHICS,

PACIFISM,

AND THE

JUST-WAR

TRADITION

RICHARD B. MILLER

The University of Chicago Press / *Chicago and London*

Richard B. Miller is assistant professor of religious studies at Indiana University.

The University of Chicago Press, Chicago 60637
The University of Chicago Press, Ltd., London
© 1991 by The Trustees of Lake Forest College
All rights reserved. Published 1991
Printed in the United States of America

00 99 98 97 96 95 94 93 92 91 5 4 3 2 1

Library of Congress Cataloging-in-Publication Data
Miller, Richard Brian, 1953–
  Interpretations of conflict: ethics, pacifism, and the just-war tradition / Richard B. Miller.
    p. cm.
  Includes bibliographical references and index.
    ISBN 0-226-52795-6 (cloth). — ISBN 0-226-52796-4 (paper)
    1. War—Moral and ethical aspects. 2. Pacifism. 3. Just war doctrine. 4. Deterrence (Strategy) I. Title.
  B105.W3M55 1991   91-3044
  172'.42—dc20   CIP

♾ The paper used in this publication meets the minimum requirements of the American National Standard for Information Sciences—Permanence of Paper for Printed Library Materials, ANSI Z39.48-1984.

for Barbara and Matthew

Contents

Acknowledgments   ix

Part One: Preliminary Investigations

Introduction: Pluralism and Moral Discourse   3
The Lure of Self-Reflexivity
Proceeding down the Low Road
Terms for Interpretations of Conflict

1   Prior Intimations and Current Questions   16
The Presumption against Harm
Adumbrations and Approximations
Nonmaleficence and Levels of Moral Discourse
From Convergence to Further Inquiry

Part Two: Roman Catholic and Protestant Approaches

2   The Just War and Civil Conflict: Changing
Paradigms in Roman Catholic Social Ethics   53
Moral Grammar in Transition
The Classical Paradigm
The Modern Paradigm: The Just War
The Modern Paradigm: Civil Conflict
Justice, Friendship, and Otherness

3   Catholic Pacifism in the United States: Ethical Pluralism and
the Problem of Tradition   76
Elements of a Pacifist Ethic
Rights-Based Pacifism
Eschatological Pacifism
Iconoclastic Pacifism
The Problem of Tradition

4   Pacifism and Just-War Tenets: How Do They Diverge?   106
The Point of Convergence
Theological Criticisms of Just-War Tenets
Ethical Criticisms of Just-War Tenets
From Divergence to Convergence

5   A Protestant Protest and Transvaluation   125
The Protestant Principle
Repentance and Conventional Discourse about War
The Objectivity of God's Sovereign, Immanent Activity
The Transformative Tension between Theology and Ethics
A Repoeticization of War

Part Three: The Problem of Nuclear Deterrence

6   Love, Intention, and Proportion: Paul Ramsey on the
Morality of Nuclear Deterrence   147
Deterrence, Pacifism, and the Just War
Agape, War, and Moral Discourse
Morality and Nuclear Deterrence
Intention: Thin or Thick?
Conclusion

7   The Morality of Nuclear Deterrence: Obstacles on the
Road to Coherence   168
Conventional Approaches to the Morality of Deterrence
The Success Thesis
The Just-War Thesis
The Anticipatory Thesis
The Argument from "Supreme Emergency"
The Exceptionalist Thesis
Conclusion

Part Four: Practical Reasoning and Public Discourse

8   History, Moral Discourse, and the Problem of Ideology   193
History: Didactic or Ideological?
The Grammar of American Exceptionalism
Comparative Justice and the Law of Nature
Intertextualism and Nonsectarian Pacifism
Rationalization and Counterideology

9   On Duty, Virtue, and the Interpretation of Conflict   224
Plurality and Ambiguity
Phronesis, Memory, and Nonmaleficence
Against Realism and Confessionalism
Can Pacifists and Just-War Theorists Tell a Just War?

Epilogue: Pluralism and Irony   245
Notes   247
Index   289

Acknowledgments

This book could not have been written without the company of old and recent friends, all of whom helped me develop and refine the arguments found herein. Charles L. Garrettson III, James N. McKean, Claire McKean, Ash Nichols, and Kim Nichols provided me with more than a few chances to clarify my ideas; to them I owe no small debt of companionship, spirited debate, humor, and affection. David Boeyink, Lois Daly, Terence Martin, Jr., Robert Orsi, Joseph Rautenberg, William Schweiker, Mark Kline Taylor, Mary Jo Weaver, Charles Wilson, and Henry Veatch read various sections of this book and provided numerous suggestions along the way. Daniel Boucher and Sara Pike performed valuable service as research assistants during the initial stages of my writing. Stanley Hauerwas, John Langan, and David H. Smith meticulously reviewed an earlier draft of the entire work and pointed to several weaknesses, some of which I doubtless failed to emend. James Childress, Charles Curran, Francis Schüssler Fiorenza, and James Gustafson have provided invaluable moral and intellectual support; they remain exemplars of erudition, clarity, and rigor.

I would also like to thank my students at Indiana University, who allowed me to sharpen my ideas in the context of the classroom. I could not have envisioned several sections of this book had it not been for their curiosity, tenacity, and intelligence.

I am likewise indebted to the Lilly Foundation, whose support during the summer of 1989 enabled me to write the bulk of Chapter 8, and the National Endowment for the Humanities, whose Summer Stipend in 1990 provided the freedom to carry out final revisions of the entire manuscript. I am grateful to Patrick Olivelle for providing release-time from teaching during the fall of 1988. Departmental colloquia in the spring terms of 1988 and 1990 enabled me to refine sections of chapters 2 and 8, respectively. Generous grants-in-aid from the Office of Research and the University Graduate School, and the Dean of the Faculties at Indiana University likewise hastened the completion of this work. Jenny Mobley and Kevin Adkins were indispensable in assisting with the technological details for producing the manuscript. Alan Thomas and Randolph Petilos of the University of Chicago Press saw to this project's conclusion with grace and efficiency. Salena Fuller Krug scrupulously edited the manuscript and called my attention to more than a few stylistic infelicities.

Some material in this work has been published previously, although it appears here in expanded form. I wish to thank the editors of the following journals for their kind permission to use materials for several chapters: Chapter 4 originally appeared as "Christian Pacifism and Just-War Tenets: How Do They Diverge?" *Theological Studies* 47 (September 1986): 448–72; chapter 5 originally appeared as "H. Richard Niebuhr's War Articles: A Transvaluation of Value," *Journal of Religion* 68 (April 1988): 242–62 (© 1988 by The University of Chicago; all rights reserved); chapter 6 first appeared under the same title in the *Journal of Religious Ethics* 16 (Fall 1988): 201–21; and chapter 7 likewise appeared under the same title in *Horizons* 15 (Spring 1988): 21–42. Where I cite the work of others, I have chosen to leave exclusive language intact, despite my aversion to such language.

Finally, I owe no small debt to Barbara Klinger for her affection, wisdom, intellectual acuity, and transformative wit, and to Matthew Miller for his infectious exuberance.

R.B.M.
Bloomington, Indiana
August 1990

PART ONE

PRELIMINARY INVESTIGATIONS

Introduction:
Pluralism and
Moral Discourse

The Lure of Self-Reflexivity

Contemporary ethics, including religious ethics, is troubled by the problem of its own mission. What, precisely, is the nature of moral inquiry? How should ethicists carry out that inquiry? What problems ought to be at the top of an ethicist's list? On what (or whose) authority may an ethicist speak? What impact should the ethicist seek, either in the professions or in the public realm at large? What do we say about those ethicists whose professional or public impact is negligible? What is the difference between religious and philosophical ethics? How might we compare the morality of different religious traditions? Mirroring widespread self-reflexiveness in the humanities, ethicists debate the nature of their mission as much as, if not more than, the specific moral problems that once fueled ethical reflection. In a self-reflexive mode, the inquiring ethicist is the subject of his or her inquiry.

These questions have emerged in the context of cultural pluralism, in which rival accounts of the right and the good bid for our allegiance. And, as Karl Mannheim argues, pluralism is a function of massive social forces, especially the forces of democratization. Once the horizontal mobility of classes was accompanied by rapid vertical mobility, social conditions became ripe for a conflict of worldviews, previously separated in static, hierarchical societies. According to Mannheim, "it is with these clashing modes of thought, each of which has the same claims to representational validity, that for the first time there is rendered possible the emergence of the question, . . . how is it possible that identical human thought-processes concerned with the same world produce divergent conceptions of that world?"[1]

Among ethicists, pluralism has produced several problems. If "the same world can appear differently to different observers,"[2] how can we agree about what is right or good for everyone? How is it possible to overcome differences, to arrive at some basis for consensus? To what extent does a search for consensus require us to sacrifice our particularity, our specific identities? If this search requires us to convert to someone else's web of belief before we converse, in what sense can genuine agreement ever occur? If we fail to convert to another's web of belief, are our moral disagreements finally intractable? In the context of pluralism, ethicists have been thrown back on their heels. Given widespread disagreement about the right and the good, ethicists tend self-reflexively to ask, In what consists the future of moral inquiry?

One set of responses to these questions proceeds along what I shall call the high road, conceiving the adjective in descriptive but not congratulatory terms. Those who travel the high road address the question of place and perspective in a culture of moral differences. I call the road "high" because it proceeds above the terrain of discrete moral problems concerning the justification of right or good action. It leads to an Olympian vantage point, from which we may survey the conditions for successfully carrying out ethical inquiry. Those who travel along this road search for the source of our moral knowledge, raising questions that are sociological and epistemological.

The high road is very wide. Proceeding along it are four distinct paths, or efforts, to develop ethics in an age of turbulent social change, the end of static hierarchies, and the clash of perspectives about moral truth. Each path marks an attempt to answer the question, Where do we get our moral information, our values, our sense of obligation, our vision of the good life? Is our moral information provided by some common source, allowing us to get beyond our other differences?

On one side of the high road are those for whom ethical information is provided by the common fund of "nature." Epistemologically, *nature* refers to a body of ethical wisdom available in principle to all rational persons, irrespective of historical, religious, or cultural backgrounds. To travel along this path we must proceed away from cultural particularity toward a readily available body of ethical data.[3] Substantively, *nature* refers to an objective set of ends or goals, toward which human action is innately inclined. Such ends are unmediated by the symbols of culture or history; rather, they are inherent in human nature itself.

Reference to human nature can operate both descriptively and prescriptively in this first approach: descriptively, as an account of what it means to flourish as a member of the human species, to participate in a larger human essence; prescriptively, as a standard against which to measure the direction of human purposes. To act immorally in this approach is to be "inhuman." Further, human flourishing includes the exercise of human reason, and insofar as such flourishing is rational it is discernible to others involved in rational inquiry. Along this path, trafficked heavily in Catholic ethics, we might overcome pluralism by attending to the requirements of human well-being, confident that *well-being* denotes a set of objective goods accessible in principle to human reason, regardless of cultural location.

Moving alongside this path, traveling in roughly the same direction, is a second group: those for whom ethical knowledge must not only be objective but also detached, proceeding from a "view from nowhere." Agnostic about the reality of shared human ends, this approach views the mission of ethics largely in constructive terms, where ethical rules and terms are invented according to the constraints of disinterested rationality. Epistemologically the goal is to construct procedures of epistemic neutrality, to imagine a place in which the effects of local knowledge, individual preferences, or special relations are deferred. So John Rawls and Alan Gewirth would have us proceed. For these authors, cultural particularity lies on the other side of the "veil of ignorance" or provides the material from which to excavate the a priori conditions of human action. Substantively, their goal is to arrive at ethical terms freed from implication in any specific set of goods or preferences. Epistemic neutrality thus provides a secure foundation or Archimedean point from which more specific ethical criteria may be developed. Here we can overcome pluralism by developing procedures for effacing differences at the outset of our ethical theory. Such procedures are premised on the belief that detached rationality is sufficient for constructing criteria for justice and moral consistency.[4]

Counterposed to these two groups, traveling in the opposite direction, are those for whom ethical knowledge must begin from somewhere, since moral perception and action occur in particular times and places. Dissatisfied with attempts to invent morality from the ground up, those on this side of the high road conceive of ethics as an "inside job," rooted in the constraints and opportunities furnished by our locales. The general goal is to replace *Moralität* with *Sittlichkeit,* echoing Hegel's critique of Kantian formalism. According to this view, ethical inquiry should proceed within, not away from, those communities whose moral beliefs shape our vision. Given this direction, the source of ethical knowledge is relative to history, community, and tradition.

On this side of the high road two paths are becoming well-worn. Those traveling a more deeply worn path insist upon the particularity of all knowledge and the concomitant imperative to adhere to the legacy of one's tradition. This view rejects reference to nature as woefully abstract and dismisses epistemic neutrality as enshrining modern liberal beliefs about human autonomy. The alternative to abstractions or autonomy is found by returning to the idea that traditions and communities shape moral perception. According to this approach, then, the rationality of tradition replaces the tradition of rationality, exorcising from us the "Cartesian anxiety" underlying our quests for secure foundations and Archimedean points.[5]

In its most extreme form, commitment to one's tradition outweighs, perhaps eliminates, the idea that our traditions may include moral ambiguities. And, freed from the peril of ambiguity, ethics becomes confessional, a kind of ethical positivism. For authors like Stanley Hauerwas and John Howard Yoder, the truths of one's religion or culture serve as a beacon to other travelers; the mission is less to overcome differences than to be truthful to the beliefs that make one different. If those truths lead nowhere, the failure lies with the listener, not the speaker. Epistemologically, this approach is unabashedly relativistic: ethical beliefs are obligatory only within distinct webs of belief or cultural languages.[6]

Those bearing down less stridently along this same side of the high road, seeking to avoid the horns of objectivism and relativism, argue that the mission of ethics is social criticism, seen as an interpretive endeavor. Like nature, invention, and confession, interpretation has epistemological and substantive dimensions. Epistemologically an interpretive approach differs from reason aimed at ends, disinterested rationality, and confessionalism by making "the linguistic turn." The linguistic turn, as David Burrell notes, "ought not to be construed as a determinate method so much as a peculiar quality of attentiveness to language, and how our employment of language shapes our inquiry."[7] Those who make the linguistic turn require us to examine our moral grammar and the ambiguity therein. By their account, the plasticity of language allows us to find new moral meanings, new possibilities for ethics, in traditional resources and vocabularies. So, for example, to defend the new idea of religious freedom, modern Catholics (belatedly) drew on an account of the natural law, the same law with which Catholic teaching once condemned religious liberty; similarly, Martin Luther King, Jr., drew on familiar American beliefs in equality and freedom to defend the new idea of civil rights. In both cases the result was simultaneously to conserve and revise cultural beliefs, exploiting the polyvalence of moral meanings to clear the way for a new vision. Substantively, the goal of an interpretive approach is to assess cultural trends, movements, practices, attitudes, or policies by drawing from a reservoir of inherited moral language. Ethics from an interpretive point of view is inescapably intertextual, finding new wine in old wineskins. In this way Michael Walzer argues for the practice of social criticism, using Israel's prophets to illustrate how religious and moral grammar might be exploited during cultural crises.[8]

Contrary to these four efforts in contemporary ethics, in this book I will proceed down the low road of ethical inquiry (again the adjective is descriptive, not evaluative). My mission is to address pluralism by arriving at a basic value about which evidence shows widespread cultural acceptance, and then to return to some discrete problems that have traditionally fueled ethical reflection. By *evidence* I mean compatibility with philosophical arguments (like those developed along the high road), compatibility with Western religious beliefs, and general cultural assent. The road is low for two reasons: first, because it remains close to the terrain of specific moral issues, issues less rarefied than the problem that ethics is to itself in an age of self-reflexivity; second, because it proceeds in the direction of *actual* ethical pluralism surrounding the moral problem under consideration, not the notion of pluralism conceived in the abstract. Rather than settle questions about pluralism in advance of detailed ethical inquiry, this study will immerse itself in rival ethical approaches to a tangible set of issues. Proceeding along the low road, this work will invoke the idea of a "tradition" not as some reified category, but as a distinct moral idiom with corresponding practices and occasions for debate.

In this book I will remain close to the terrain of specific moral problems and actual ethical pluralism by examining several questions posed by war according to the moral vocabularies of pacifism and the just-war tradition. In Western ethics these idioms presently shape our interpretations of conflict, providing the grammar of moral value and judgment in times of international strife. Moreover, ethical issues surrounding war and peace can be addressed by beginning from an insight shared by both of these vocabularies. Despite their differences (one providing qualified permission for war, the other prohibiting war), both vocabularies share a bias against violence. This bias establishes a general suspicion about recourse to war, expressed as a presumption against the use of lethal force. Soon I will examine how this bias constitutes a point of convergence between pacifism and just-war tenets. I will also examine various approximations of this convergence to uncover a range of issues meriting further analysis, problems about which pacifists and just-war theorists can have mutual concerns.

In order to get such an analysis moving, I will take as axiomatic James Childress's argument, namely, that the common ground between pacifism and just-war ideas, their presumption against the use of force, can be expressed as the duty of nonmaleficence.[9] Both vocabularies begin with an intolerance of cruelty and harm, voicing compassion for those who suffer. At the very least, such a presumption establishes a heavy burden of proof for those who wish to justify war. This insight has brought pacifists and just-war theorists to recognize that even though they may finally disagree about whether certain wars can be justified, they still have enough in common to warrant careful ethical analysis and discussion. Further, it has led members of both camps to recognize their mutual abhorrence of suffering and cruelty. It has also led them to recognize that their ethics are not wholly incommensurable in a culture worried about moral pluralism and incommensurability. But little has been done to develop the implications of this shared insight, or to carry forward an exchange between both camps around a common set of interests.

This book is designed to carry forward that conversation, joining pacifists and just-war theorists around a mutual set of concerns, or problems, or questions. To that end I will use Childress's idea of sharing common ground as the point of departure for this book. The shared duty of non-maleficence is meant to call attention to a point of convergence between these two moral vocabularies about war. I spend some time talking about how pacifism and just-war tenets can be joined by nonmaleficence in order to initiate the work of putting these two traditions together in conversation. It is also the case that reference to nonmaleficence will function heuristically to open up new interpretations of Western grammar about war and peace. So the overall goal of the book is to develop the implications of nonmaleficence for the ethics of war, and to point to *further* terrain that can be explored by representatives of both pacifist and just-war traditions. To this latter end we will explore the relation of justice and order, the ethics of civil disobedience, the suggestive tensions between pacifism and just-war tenets, the problem of self-righteousness in moral discourse about war, the ethics of nuclear deterrence, and the problems surrounding ideology and public discourse. This book is not an extended argument about nonmaleficence, although we will explore its relevance for moral discourse about war in several places. The larger goal is to show how pacifism and just-war tenets can be joined around several theoretical and practical issues.

The title of this work is meant to suggest that, of the four approaches to ethics proceeding along the high road, my own view comes closest to the last. I move toward such a position in the last two chapters by discussing the requirements of moral rhetoric and practical reasoning, although I know that the source of ethical knowledge merits fuller treatment than I have given here. More complex theories about the proper mission of ethics, strategies of interpretation, and the nature of cultural meanings direct the ideas of these pages to a higher road and require another book, perhaps more than one.

Proceeding down the Low Road

The chapters herein form less a single monograph, with a beginning, middle, and conclusion, than a set of essays, four of which I originally wrote out of narrowly focused interests. I have revised and expanded those essays for inclusion here. Each of these chapters might be read independently of the others, yet I have brought them all together under the claim that pacifism and just-war tenets share significant common ground or common problems. This ground will be surveyed by placing these moral vocabularies in dialectical relation to each other. Heeding a general suggestion by Alasdair MacIntyre, I will develop a "conversation between traditions, learning to use the idiom of each in order to describe and evaluate the other or others by means of it."[10] Out of this dialectical conversation I will direct attention to a host of theoretical and practical problems that vex, or ought to vex, pacifists and just-war theorists alike.

While there has been a spate of works about the problems of war and peace, several features make this book anomalous according to the paradigm of "normal" research in ethics today.

First, by raising theoretical and practical issues pertinent to both pacifism and just-war ideas, this work introduces a new ethical approach to the problem of war and peace. Most previous approaches view these traditions as mutually exclusive. I wish to show that much work can be done by developing the implications of the point of contact between pacifism and just-war tenets. To that end, I will show how this convergence suggests material for further analysis, preparation for which I provide in chapter 1.

Second, this work will not proceed in a linear direction. That is, I will not proceed inductively, tracing the historical progress of moral discourse about war from classical forebears until today. Nor will I move deductively, applying moral criteria to special problems posed by nuclear technology, terrorism, or liberation movements. Instead, the directions within and between these chapters militate against either horizontal or vertical linear movements, because I will follow the traces of divergence, otherness, reversal, protestation, antinomy, discrepancy, obstacle, counterideology, and dialectical tension in Western grammar about the morality of war. One underlying premise of the analyses found here is that linear approaches fail to uncover more subtle meanings and terms that structure Western discourse about war. Proceeding dialectically from an initial point of contact will open up new meanings in our moral vocabularies, providing interpretations and posing questions that have gone undeveloped in the ethics of war and peace.[11]

Third, this book will challenge much of the conventional wisdom about war and peace in ethics today, especially Christian ethics. While relying upon the previous works of others, I will depart from, and often refute, standard interpretations of violence, war, and peace. The issues about which I will speak are as follows.

In chapter 1 I will examine the convergence between pacifism and just-war ideas, the idea that both share a common moral bias against the resort to lethal force. I will begin by discussing five versions of that convergence (the Augustinian, Thomistic, modern Protestant, contemporary Catholic, and practical convergences), including a critique of each. I will then draw upon Henry David Aiken's taxonomy of moral discourse to amplify the way in which a bias against violence may be understood in the ethics of war. Specifically, I maintain that the duty not to harm is not only an ethical notion, on which pacifism and just-war ideas are based; it is also a postethical idea, implying compassion for those who are victims of harm, a bias against suffering, an intolerance of cruelty. Using Aiken's argument I extend the implications of nonmaleficence beyond the terms according to which it has been used in discourse about war. I then return to the five other forms of convergence to show how they furnish the subject matter of the remaining chapters of this book.

Chapters 2 through 5 will explore how a point of contact between pacifism and just-war traditions might shape interpretations of Roman Catholic and Protestant ethics. In chapter 2 I will show how a moral presumption against harm can be understood in Catholic ethics in light of the moral value of order and classical beliefs about civic friendship. Contrary to the widespread notion that justice is the chief principle in just-war theory, I will argue that order has a relative priority over justice in Catholic thinking about violence, often requiring individuals or groups to suffer injustice rather than disturb the wider social order. A bias against violence is conditioned by the status of order; one may be required to suffer injustice if order would otherwise be jeopardized by violence on behalf of justice. In this way I show how the value of nonviolence (in the form of suffering an injustice) is intelligible in Catholic ethics.

In chapter 3 I will follow a trajectory out of the previous chapter, amplifying one way in which a bias against violence has developed in contemporary Catholicism. I survey the rich pluralism of Catholic pacifism, classifying the variety of recent Catholic pacifism in three types: "rights-based pacifism," "eschatological pacifism," and "iconoclastic pacifism." Then I will examine each type, seeking to clarify their bases, methods, duties and goals, social visions, and notions of political obligation. I close by discussing some unresolved issues facing Catholic pacifism today, drawing on a facsimile of just-war tenets to structure the ethics of civil disobedience and pacifist dissent.

In chapter 4 I will turn the tables and show how pacifists would resist efforts to inform some of their ethical concerns with reference to just-war criteria. To that end I will survey the various criticisms of just-war ideas by contemporary pacifists. After examining differences between pacifism and just-war tenets, I then identify more dimensions of their convergence, dimensions which shed additional light on the ethics of war. The goal is to show that the point of convergence is both more troublesome and more suggestive than recent ethical theory might have us believe.

Chapter 5 will focus attention on the allegation that pacifists and nonpacifists share the common temptation to exaggerate their own importance. To that end I will examine one effort in recent Protestantism to relativize the value of pacifist and nonpacifist discourse. Do we not inflate the importance of this-worldly concerns by arguing about the morality of statecraft and political life? Protestants often address this question by insisting that God's sovereign rule of history is vastly more important than temporal endeavors—however praiseworthy those endeavors might be. Yet for many Protestants this belief poses the danger of evacuating religious discourse of ethical relevance, since it directs our attention away from history toward transhistorical, otherworldly concerns.

With this problem in view I will examine the neglected work of H. Richard Niebuhr on war. Writing in response to the Manchurian crisis and the Second World War, Niebuhr developed a Protestant protest against conventional ethical attitudes, providing theological bases for self-criticism as an ongoing requirement in moral discourse. I want to show that his critique of pacifism and nonpacifism is designed not to reject those points of view, but to purge them of the possibility of self-justification and moral conceit. This critique produces an approach to war focusing on the duty to attend especially to the needs and the suffering of the innocent on either side of battle.

Chapters 6 and 7 will explore an issue relevant to pacifists and just-war theorists, namely, nuclear deterrence. Insofar as deterrence is designed to prevent the outbreak of war, its goals are convergent with any ethic cautious about recourse to lethal force. But this does not mean that deterrence is automatically sanctioned by traditional canons about statecraft and war. To examine the problems posed by nuclear deterrence, in chapter 6 I will assay Paul Ramsey's influential attempt to conceive of a moral nuclear deterrent according to his account of responsible statecraft. I show that Ramsey might have avoided problems in his justification of deterrence if he had embraced the kind of interpretation of just-war criteria I develop in chapter 1, based on Childress's point of convergence.

In the subsequent chapter I will extend the range of my criticisms of deterrence to include a wider body of attempts to justify its moral tenability. With pacifists and just-war theorists in mind, I enter into dialogue with the U.S. Catholic bishops, David Hollenbach, Michael Walzer, James Sterba, and Gerald Mara, examining obstacles to their confidence in the morality of nuclear deterrence.

Chapters 8 and 9 will shift the focus to problems of practical reasoning and public discourse about social conflict. In chapter 8 I raise the question, What does it mean to use history in moral discourse? I address that question by critically examining efforts to use historical materials as a resource for the ethics of social conflict today. Focusing on the cultural effects of history, I will call attention to American mythology about violence and war, especially the belief in the United States as a savior nation. My goal is to assess the merits and problems of ideology in moral reasoning among pacifists and just-war theorists alike.

In chapter 9 I address the problem of forming judgments about the morality of war within the framework of just-war criteria. Although pacifists and just-war theorists may disagree about the morality of war in general, both can rely on just-war tenets to assess the relative morality of particular wars. Thus, a common interest in practical reasoning and criteria for public discourse occupies an important place within each of these two traditions. Yet, given the plurality of criteria and the variety of just-war theorists in contemporary social ethics, how can just-war tenets provide a framework for public debate? In response to this question I argue that the skill of practical judgment, what Aristotle called *phronesis*, must supplement the duties of the just-war tradition to mediate between theory and application. Drawing from the insights of virtue ethics, I develop a notion of *phronesis* as historical and hermeneutical, in which interpretation guided by memory is central to moral reflection. Here I seek to show that moral discourse about war in the public realm requires a dialectical relation between just-war duties and the virtue of practical reasoning.

Terms for Interpretations of Conflict

Although pacifist ideas and just-war tenets should be common coinage in our moral grammar today, their precise meanings are often uncertain and more frequently unknown. Throughout this work I will presume familiarity with these vocabularies.

By *pacifism* I mean two general claims. First, *pacifism* denotes a negative moral position—"antiwarism"—the moral prohibition of war. Pacifists sometimes, but not always, ban all forms of killing, including individual self-defense. My focus will remain more restrictive than this latter, wider, prohibition, since antiwarism more accurately defines the ethics of pacifism.[12] Nevertheless, much of the just-war tradition begins by justifying individual self-defense, as if that justification refuted the pacifist rejection of war. When I discuss just-war ideas in chapter 1, then, I will have to include just-war theorists' attempts to justify both individual killing and the resort to war, since many within that tradition have seen these two justifications as inseparable.

Second, *pacifism* denotes a positive moral position, the imperative to "seek peace." By this positive injunction pacifists typically mean building harmonious relations, reducing tensions, developing pacifist virtues, reconciling oppositions, or reordering political arrangements according to the goals of nonviolence.

The just-war tradition provides a justification for the limited use of force in war. Several reliable historical studies trace the development of this tradition, and I shall not rehearse that history again here.[13] The basic idea of just-war morality is that for the good of the community it may be necessary to defend present members, and the conditions for membership, from outside threats. Whether such a defense is permissible or morally imperative is a nuance about which contemporary just-war theorists equivocate, but the logic of just-war tenets can easily include the latter, stronger claim.

Just-war criteria include a number of complex terms and distinctions. Despite this complexity, however, the objective of this tradition is deceptively simple: to distinguish some forms of killing (war) from murder, and to keep the killing in war from becoming murderous. It is the attempt, in short, to classify some human acts as morally acceptable, and to assign limits beyond which those acts become unacceptable. Killing is murder when it intentionally extends beyond the agents of aggression or oppression, or when such unintended but foreseen deaths in war are disproportionate to values being defended. Killing is not murder when it is confined to those who have seriously threatened the well-being of the community, or when accidental deaths are proportionate with the values being defended.

Over the course of its long history, the just-war tradition has developed on two pillars, the *jus ad bellum* and the *jus in bello*. The former is designed to answer the "when" or "whether" question: When, if ever, is resort to lethal force justified? The components within this pillar consist of several moral criteria, the satisfaction of which justifies recourse to war. The latter is designed to answer the "how" or "methods" question: What methods are morally acceptable once recourse to war has been justified? Here the idea is that the justification for entering war does not extend to all methods in war: the ends do not justify the means. *Ad bellum* criteria define the terms for justification, while *in bello* criteria set the terms for limitation. Various interpretations of these criteria and their relation have emerged over the centuries, but no adequate understanding of this tradition is possible without reference to both pillars of just-war ideas.

In the next chapter, as I have indicated, I will draw pacifism and just-war tenets together by claiming that each presumes a bias against violence. Here I will suggest how this presumption ought to affect the manner in which *ad bellum* and *in bello* criteria are interpreted and ordered. *Ad bellum* criteria include the following:

1. *Just cause:* Just cause is designed to call attention to the *occasion* in which justifiable war occurs, those instances when we are permitted or required to use lethal force. War is justifiable as a defense against outside dangers: threats to innocent life, conditions for the community's future, and basic human rights. War is not justifiable as an exercise of revenge or domination. According to classical formulations of this criterion, war was also justifiable to vindicate justice, to avenge wrongdoing. Such notions have less currency today, but they might be justified by the claim that to avenge wrongdoing is necessary as part of a general, long-term need to defend one's borders or one's sovereignty.

Recourse to war is subject to further ethical qualifications, which comprise the remainder of just-war criteria.

2. *Competent authority:* This criterion precludes resort to war by private individuals, allowing only those who are responsible for the public order to declare war. This criterion presumes, moreover, that criteria of

political legitimacy have been satisfied. In cases of revolution a government may lose its legitimacy. Authority is then transferred to other representatives of the community.

3. *Right intention:* Right intention refers to the legitimate goals of using lethal force, not merely the psychological state of the aggrieved party. Such goals are typically confined to self-defense or protection of innocent life. This criterion prohibits lust for cruelty and vengeance in combat, and proscribes the use of force to acquire control over an adversary. In the aftermath of war, this criterion permits us to establish stronger conditions of peace than those which preceded war. In this way the criterion of right intention would be robustly carried out. Given the presumption against harm, it would seem only appropriate to seek such peaceful conditions—if only to reduce the likelihood that war will recur.

4. *Last resort:* Also reflecting a moral presumption against harm, this criterion holds that all peaceable means of settling disputes within reasonable reach of the relevant authorities must be exhausted before resort to war is justifiable. If successful defense of a just cause is reasonably possible according to nonviolent methods, then there is a moral obligation to use them.

5. *Relative justice:* This criterion holds that no state may act as if it possesses "absolute justice," that neither side may claim a monopoly of justice in defense of its cause. Rather, the justice is relative, especially given the problems of measuring justice objectively in the drama and passion of war.

6. *Proportionality:* Within the orbit of *ad bellum* criteria, proportionality requires one to ask, Will the prospective suffering, the costs incurred in war, be commensurate with the overall values that are being defended? Is the war, in moral terms, worth risking? What losses to ourselves and the world community can be sustained given the values in defense of which war is being fought?

7. *Reasonable hope for success:* A corollary of proportionality, this criterion excludes reckless or futile fighting in defense of a cause. Although it may at times permit us to defend very noble values against tremendous odds, its general purpose is to prevent irrational uses of force.

In bello criteria, establishing the moral limits to the use of justifiable force, are two:

1. *Discrimination:* This criterion, the shorthand for which is "noncombatant immunity," prohibits the intentional attacking of civilians. This criterion has not one, but two, key distinctions. The first, more obvious distinction draws a line between combatants and noncombatants. *Combatant* denotes anyone who is materially cooperating with the war effort, posing an objective threat to a community's political and social order. The second distinction draws a line between intentional (i.e., purposeful) and foreseen, but unintentional, effects of an act.

According to the logic of these distinctions, intentional attacks against noncombatants are tantamount to murder. Such attacks are directed against innocent people, where *innocent* serves as a military or political, but not necessarily moral, term. The foreseen, unintentional loss of life *passes* the test of discrimination but is subject to moral scrutiny entailed by the second *in bello* criterion, proportionality.

2. *Proportionality:* This principle requires us to measure, in a rough-and-ready way, the foreseen, unintended losses against the values that are defended in a particular act of war. At this level of analysis we are required to think about the morality of specific tactics: Is the good that is being pursued or defended commensurate with the unintended losses that may reasonably be expected? Tactics are immoral when the foreseen, unintended loss of life is incommensurate with the defended values, even if those tactics are discriminate. In an age of lower-yield nuclear weapons, whose employment may pass the initial test of discrimination but may lead to an uncontrollable level of violence, the principle of proportionality has assumed added relevance in moral discourse about war.[14]

Although the just-war tradition has proven remarkably durable over the past fifteen centuries, its merits as a moral vocabulary are now in question, especially given the perils wrought by war in the modern age. With such developments in mind, ethicists of various affiliations have heeded the Second Vatican Council's mandate "to undertake an evaluation of war with an entirely new attitude."[15] In that same spirit I will examine pacifism and just-war tenets, endeavoring to amplify their meaning, their relation, and their resources for dialectical inquiry. In so doing I will continue to proceed down the low road of ethics, resisting an approach to ethical inquiry from the vantage of Olympian heights. Along the way, I will proceed with concrete issues and real versions of pluralism clearly in view.

O N E

Prior Intimations and
Current Questions

The Presumption against Harm

In Western ethics our vocabularies about war are framed by the problem of justifying injury, especially killing.[1] This problem is sharpened by the general belief, widely embraced in Western culture, that persons deserve respect, perhaps even care in times of need. Such beliefs place strong presumptions against harm or injury, often expressed in the feeling of horror toward cruelty, or compassion for those who suffer. In Western religious ethics the problems of injury and killing are complicated by the belief that life is sacred, that God alone is sovereign over life and death. Together with the commandment not to kill and the commandment to love one's neighbor, these cultural and religious beliefs raise several difficult questions: Is it possible to obey these commandments and injure another individual? Can we reconcile killing, especially killing in war, with the belief in life's sanctity, the requirements of respect, or the virtue of charity?

Answers to these questions in Western ethics are guided by a fundamental bias against violence, enshrined in the general duty not to harm. Although this bias has been widely recognized over the centuries, its importance has received unprecedented attention in contemporary approaches to the morality of war. According to James Childress, the duty not to harm constitutes a point of convergence between pacifism and just-war tenets. However much it may seem that pacifism and just-war ideas are incommensurable (the former banning war, the latter justifying limited war), pacifists and just-war theorists actually share a common starting point: a moral presumption against the use of force. Using W. D. Ross's language of prima facie duties, Childress shows how pacifism and just-war tenets converge. The duty not to kill or injure others (nonmaleficence) is a duty within each approach. For the pacifist nonmaleficence is an absolute duty admitting of no exceptions, at least in the context of war. For the just-war theorist nonmaleficence is a prima facie duty. Such duties are usually binding but may be overridden in exceptional circumstances, particularly when innocent life or human rights are at stake. According to Childress, the phrase prima facie "indicates that certain features of acts that have a certain *tendency* to make an act right or wrong claim our attention; insofar as an act has those features it is right or wrong. But our actual obligation depends upon the act in its wholeness and entirety."[2]

A prima facie duty is one for which there are compelling reasons to act. This means that such a duty is obligatory, unless it clashes with another duty.[3] Prima facie duties are not absolute but place the burden of proof on those who wish to override them when they conflict with other duties, "in virtue of the totality of . . . ethically relevant circumstances."[4] Accordingly, prima facie duties point us in the direction of what is presumptively correct for moral behavior. But what is finally correct may differ, depending on a thicker description of the situation in question.

For the just-war theorist, war poses those "ethically relevant circumstances" in which the duty of nonmaleficence conflicts with other duties, and in which nonmaleficence may be overridden by the obligation to protect oneself or others from aggression. In such a situation nonmaleficence must give way to other, more pressing obligations, which may include acts of harm. At the same time, however, to override a prima facie duty is not to abandon it. Such duties continue to function in the situation or in the subsequent course of action. That is, a prima facie duty leaves "residual effects" or "moral traces"; after overriding such a duty our conduct must be affected by it. The subsequent course of action should approximate as closely as possible the imperatives or values inscribed in the overridden duty.

In the context of war, such residual effects have subjective and objective dimensions. At the subjective level, the subsequent course of action ought to entail not moral guilt, but at least regret. At the objective level, the duty of nonmaleficence exerts "pressure" on the conditions and methods of war. War must be a last resort, pursued for the ends of peace, declared by a competent authority, carried out by limited means, etc. Our acts of harm must be moderated by the reservations enshrined in the duty not to harm, and the criteria of the just-war tradition specify such reservations. In this way, Childress reconstructs the logic of the *jus ad bellum* and the *jus in bello* without departing from his central point, namely, that pacifism and just-war tenets share a common presumption against the use of force.[5]

Nonmaleficence, then, provides the basis for an overlapping but not strict consensus between two rival moral vocabularies about war.[6] Pacifism and just-war tenets do not run on parallel tracks but are like contiguous curves, sharing a common point before moving in divergent directions. Reference to this overlapping consensus, moreover, underscores the mutual need pacifists and just-war theorists have for each other. As Childress remarks, "Just-war theorists need pacifists to remind them of their common starting point: the moral presumption against force and war. And pacifists need just-war theorists to provide a public framework for debates about particular wars and for the restraint of the practice of war."[7] The divergent directions of pacifism and just-war tenets are the result, in part, of the type of duty structuring nonmaleficence (absolute or prima facie, respectively), determining whether and how it is related to other duties.

Although Childress's insight is relatively recent in the ethics of war, direction has been provided for him by a subtle undercurrent in moral discourse from Augustine to the present day. In the next section I will examine intimations of the idea that pacifism and just-war tenets share a point of contact: the Augustinian convergence, the Thomistic convergence, the modern Protestant convergence, the contemporary Catholic convergence, and the practical convergence. Each of these accounts foreshadows Childress's insight, and each provides material about which I will speak in subsequent chapters. Yet it is also true that these adumbrations suffer from important defects. After critically examining each of these convergences, in the third section I will sharpen the idea of nonmaleficence as a point of contact between pacifism and just-war tenets, seeking to amplify its internal structure, its implications, and its merits for moral discourse about war. In the final section I will spell out how prior intimations of Childress's insight provide material to be pursued in more detail in chapters 2–9. These intimations prepare us for a point of convergence that is both substantive and heuristic: substantive, because it is a value shared by each approach; heuristic, because it opens the door to new interpretations, suggesting uncharted terrain along which to travel. And in exploring such terrain, we may begin to map an area on which pacifists and just-war theorists may join their interests in the dialectic of conversation.

Adumbrations and Approximations

Augustine compresses his position about the morality of violence in a comment about killing as a form of defense. About such killing, he writes, "I do not approve of this, unless one happen[s] to be a soldier or public functionary acting, not for himself, but in defense of others or of the city in which he resides, if he act[s] according to the commission lawfully given him, and in the manner becoming his office."[8] The *Augustinian convergence,* distilled in this citation, joins pacifism and just-war tenets by requiring pacifism at the level of individual relations and just wars in the arena of social relations. Moreover, both pacifism and just-war morality, as we shall see, are held together by Augustine's notion of peace-as-order. Strange as it may seem to contemporary attitudes, Augustine prohibits individual self-defense by invoking beliefs about the order of our attachments, the orientation of our affections. Moreover, Augustine argues that war serves peace if the goal of war is to restore order, the *status quo ante bellum.*

Augustine adumbrates more recent versions of the convergence between pacifism and just-war tenets, especially when he writes that peace among people relies on "the observance of two rules: first, to do no harm to anyone, and, secondly, to help everyone whenever possible."[9] Nonmaleficence—expressed in the mandate of Matt. 5:38 to "resist not evil"—supports one portion of the Augustinian position (individual pacifism, "do no harm to anyone"), while care for others supports the right to use violence in their defense (a just war). Augustine and Childress recognize a conflict of duties, in which the duty "to help everyone whenever possible" might require some forms of harm. This conflict requires both authors to draw on some distinctions to relativize the force of nonmaleficence. For Augustine, however, this relativization turns not on a theory of prima facie duties. Instead, Augustine relativizes the duty of nonmaleficence by restricting its range of application, drawing on distinctions about objects of defense, types of acts, and forms of authority.

Augustine's first restriction, based on different *objects of defense,* prohibits self-defense but requires "the defense of others or of the city in which [one] resides." Moreover, Augustine's prohibition of self-defense requires total nonresistance to evil, not nonviolent resistance.[10] Here Augustine relies on some basic anthropological assumptions, developed obliquely in a treatise devoted not to killing and war but to biblical hermeneutics, *On Christian Doctrine,* and in *On the Freedom of the Will.*

In his hermeneutical essay, Augustine presumes a fundamental dualism about the self, arguing that the value of one's neighbor, made of body and soul, is greater than that of one's own body.[11] It follows that I may risk my life for the neighbor or the city, but not for myself. Since the value of the neighbor is greater than that of my body, I may risk my body for another's body and soul. Moreover, the value of my body does not provide sufficient reason for me to repel an attacker, jeopardizing another's body and soul, in individual self-defense.

In his treatise on the will, Augustine observes that individuals may very well be legally free to kill in self-defense, but they are scarcely free from a moral point of view. Those who kill in self-defense, he argues, act for "those things which can be lost against their will and which . . . ought not be loved at all."[12] Among those things that can be lost against one's will is mortal life, life in the body. To defend the body against attack represents a disordered set of attachments, ranking our attachment to mortal life above the value of the immortal soul and the value of the neighbor. Inordinate attachment to ephemeral goods jeopardizes one's virtue, understood in terms of a well-ordered character. About life in the body, Augustine writes that "there may be a doubt on the part of some as to whether it can be taken away from the soul when the body is destroyed. But if it can be taken away, it is worthless; if not, there is nothing to fear."[13] Augustine thus draws upon a dualistic anthropology, distinguishing body and soul, to establish a hierarchy of values.

Augustine's argument also draws on his theology of history, where human history and eschatology are distinct but not wholly divorced. Human history provides not our final home, and its values ought not serve as the final measure of human actions. Rather, the eschatological promise of salvation ought to affect the shape of human conduct during this historical pilgrimage. In this way Augustine holds together the moral and the salvific dimensions of human existence in his theological ethics. Taken together with his dualistic anthropology, Augustine's theology of history yields the following position: It is better in this life to suffer bodily harms than to blemish the soul in defense of the body, disordering one's affections and endangering one's eschatological destiny.

Augustine also restricts the force of nonmaleficence by distinguishing between *interior* and *exterior* actions. Emphasizing the role of intentions and affections in morality, Augustine states, "The sacred seat of virtue is the heart."[14] When violence is necessary in defense of others, the command to "resist not evil" makes reference not to "a bodily action, but an inward disposition."[15] Accordingly, the soldier may act in a manner "becoming to his office," without malice or vengeance, and in keeping with biblical teaching. Love, virtue, and killing are reconcilable at the level of individual action, since love and virtue have been divorced from visible, tangible acts carried out against others.

Finally, the force of nonmaleficence is restricted to *private* individuals, not *public* officials or those acting on their behalf. Central here are beliefs about how nature assigns roles and duties for the preservation of order. For Augustine, "the natural order which seeks the peace of mankind ordains that the monarch should have the power of undertaking war if he thinks it advisable, and that the soldiers should perform their military duties in behalf of the peace and safety of the community."[16] Those who act under the authority of others, Augustine argues, are less inclined to act out of passion, or disordered affections, than those who take the law into their own hands.[17] The law of nature requires us to seek right order and harmony, about which public authorities are responsible, and for which war may be a necessity. Thus, the prohibition of violence does not obtain for the soldier, "if he act[s] according to the commission lawfully given him." Indeed, because the soldier is commissioned by such authority, his actions are blameless.[18]

The duty of nonmaleficence, enshrined for Augustine in the biblical mandate to "resist not evil," is thus circumscribed by distinguishing between realms of morality in three ways: self/other, interior/exterior acts, and private/public authority. Augustine restricts the force of nonmaleficence by confining it to the first term in each of these pairs. Taken together, these distinctions produce an ethic which, among other things, prohibits private individuals from using force either in self-defense or to protect their neighbors from harm. Rather, private individuals are to summon public authorities for protection and rescue. None of these distinctions is original, having emerged in Christian sources as early as the second century.[19] Yet under the power of Augustine's influence these distinctions assumed unprecedented authority, providing the framework for the subsequent, and more systematic, just-war criteria in medieval and reformation ethics: just cause (defense of *group* safety); proper intention (peaceful *interior* orientation of the subject); and proper authority (*public* officials, not private individuals).[20]

But what is perhaps more important than the historic place of Augustine's argument is the logic according to which he holds together the private individual's duty of nonresistant pacifism and the soldier's duty to resist aggression in a just war. The key to this convergence lies in an overarching theory of the meaning of peace. Peace, for Augustine, is not the absence of violence, but tranquillity, concord, a set of properly ordered relations within or between human beings. At the level of individual existence, peace is "ordered repose of the appetites," a harmonious agreement between cognition and passion.[21] Peace also tempers the body and facilitates a healthy relation between body and soul. The "instinctive aim of all creatures," peace is a law of nature, the condition of our very being.[22] At the level of social existence, the aim of peace is ordered fellowship with others, the "tranquillity of order, . . . the assignment of things equal and unequal in a pattern which assigns to each its proper position."[23] Peace of the Heavenly City—"the only peace deserving of the name"—consists in "the perfectly ordered and completely harmonious fellowship in the enjoyment of God, and of each other in God."[24]

Earthly peace—the peace of temporal, mortal, existence—is vulnerable to the vagaries of pride and avarice, the chief causes of war. War, says Augustine, is a consequence of sin, a "necessity" in our earthly condition. But as a necessity war is also a remedy for sin, for it is the duty of the wise sovereign to wage war, the end of which is the restoration of peace.[25] The real evil of war is not war itself, or death and injury, but the "love of violence, revengeful cruelty, fierce and implacable enmity, wild resistance, and lust for power."[26] It is generally to punish these things that just wars are fought.[27] Seen in this light, war is justified to restore right relations. Wars are full of horror and cruelty, and all should acknowledge these realities with grief.[28] But grief is not guilt and, for Augustine, a just war is the servant of peace, not its opposite.

Peace-as-order, then, provides the framework in which Augustine joins the duty of individual, nonresistant pacifism with the soldier's duty to resist aggression. In either case, the chief question is whether physical injury contributes to or diminishes the right relations required by order. Injuring another individual in self-defense represents disorder: the agent wrongly values those things that can be lost against his or her will, ranking the temporal above the eternal. Those who act in self-defense have disordered attachments, misdirected affections, a morally weak character. Further, private self-defense and protection of third parties disturb the hierarchical civil order sanctioned by the natural law. Hence, private acts of defense are tantamount to vigilantism, usurping the authority of public officials who are commissioned to protect the common good. Moreover, the public official's failure to injure another in defense of the neighbor or the community represents a refusal to restore right relations between groups. Failure to act would leave those relations disordered, lacking the kinds of repairs provided by just acts. Neither nonresistance nor war, then, has moral meaning independent of Augustine's wider conceptual system. Peace-as-order furnishes the "point of contact" for Augustine's moral theology about war, the initial starting point from which individual (private) and social (public) morality proceed in divergent directions.[29]

Implicit in Augustine's distinction between private and public morality is an attitude about the relative value of bodily life, understood in individual and corporate terms. Augustine establishes fewer prohibitions for protecting the body politic than for individual, "private" bodies (e.g., ourselves and our neighbors) because the problem of attachment appears to him to be greater in the latter case than in the former. Augustine's position thus includes the judgment that our attachment to bodily, mortal life is a greater danger for individuals in relation to themselves and their neighbors than it is for public officials who act on behalf of the collective body. Hence, the community may be protected with methods that are morally inappropriate for individuals.

It is also the case that, for Augustine, the relative peace and order of political life is necessary for individuals who are destined eventually to enter the Kingdom of God. Accordingly, a greater amount of disorder is tolerable for corporate bodies than for individuals; the "relative peace" of communities may include a measure of disorder, which finds no parallel with the requirements for individual, internal concord. Individuals, not communities, must worry about their salvation. Consequently, there ought to be greater concerns about individual disorder than about collective disorder. A measure of collective disorder is acceptable in Augustine's account under the assumption that members of the City of God, individuals on a pilgrimage toward their final home, need some civic and material conditions to pursue their lives of virtue.

Hence for Augustine we have a complex formula for understanding the relation between private and public morality. On the one hand, these moralities diverge insofar as they include different assumptions about the value of "bodily" life, different worries about "bodily" discord, and different moralities of "bodily" protection. On the other hand, however, these moralities are held together by the idea of peace-as-order: When assessing the dangers of private or public violence, Augustine asks us to consider whether injuring another contributes to or diminishes right relations required by order.

Yet the convergence that peace-as-order provides for Augustine's position is not without its defects. The most pressing difficulty is one of internal coherence: Augustine overlooks the fact that individual self-preservation is necessary for defending the neighbor within the community. If one may assume, as Augustine surely did, that the individual is part of a larger social whole, then the duty of nonresistant pacifism at the level of "private" morality deprives the neighbor of an agent of defense. Stated conversely, self-defense only for public persons—soldiers and public officials—may deny the neighbor other sources of protection. The problem lies, then, in reconciling the implications of Augustine's first permission of violence (to protect the neighbor) with the last restriction he places on violence (public authorities only). Self-defense by "private" individuals might be morally justifiable on the grounds that it is ordered finally to the neighbor's defense. Such a justification would include the premise that it is not unrealistic to think that people can act in self-defense without an inordinate attachment to their own bodily lives. It could also include the judgment that the danger of inordinate attachment to mortal life is negligible when measured against the benefits one can provide a neighbor or loved one who is threatened by a maleficent intruder. This judgment would thus allow private individuals not only the right to defend themselves, but also the right to assist, perhaps with force, third parties who are victims of harm, especially when it is improbable that reliable public officials will arrive when necessary. Requiring individual, nonresistant pacifism at the level of private authority subverts the duties that derive from one's relations with the neighbor. Nonresistant pacifism overlooks the positive moral aspects of those instrumental measures—like self-defense or the protection of the innocent—necessary to fulfill duties to others. If we and our loved ones are being attacked, are we serving order if we confine our response to summoning the police? Whose order?

The *Thomistic convergence* relies less on a "point of contact" from which individual and social morality diverge than on a general moral presumption against violence. This presumption places a moral pressure on the structure of Thomas's discourse about how violence ought to be carried out by private individuals or public authorities. Augustine's most systematic follower, Aquinas constructs his views about the morality of killing in light of an account of the order of charity. Thomas's three criteria of the just war—just cause, competent authority, and proper intention—reflect Augustine's threefold strategy for restricting the application of Matt. 5:38, the biblical expression of the duty of nonmaleficence. But in synthesizing Aristotelian philosophy with Christian beliefs, Thomas assigns even greater positive force to the "natural" as an epistemological and substantive basis for moral discourse than we find in Augustine. As a result, Thomas is able to justify individual self-defense as a dictate of the natural law, thus overcoming an obstacle internal to Augustine's theory.

Aquinas develops his version of a presumption against violence in his discussions of charity, homicide, and war. According to Thomas, charity toward the neighbor follows from the requirement to love God, since "what we ought to love in him is that he be in God."[30] But it is also the case that, in the order of charity, we may love ourselves more than we are to love our neighbors. Both the self and the neighbor may participate in the divine good, but the fact that the self "participates in the divine good is a more powerful reason for loving than the fact that another is associated with him in this participation."[31] About love of the enemy, Thomas states that charity never requires that we love our enemies "precisely as enemies," because such love implies "loving evil in another," contrary to charity itself. Further, charity never absolutely requires that we love our enemies individually, because such a love would be impossible, beyond the limits of human finitude. Nevertheless, charity does require that we love our enemies as to their nature, in general, because the genus of neighbor-love includes enemies as a species. Moreover, charity requires that "we should be prepared to love even a particular enemy," a love that is "required as an attitude of mind . . . if real necessity arise[s]."[32] Love of one's enemies, then, is neither accepted nor rejected unequivocally. Rather, for Thomas the "nature" of the enemy as a human person requires an attitude of generic benevolence, thus prohibiting acts which only vindicate justice against others in violent confrontations.

Aquinas's discussion of killing in self-defense is nothing more than a specification of these claims about the proper ordering of self-love, neighbor-love, and the love of enemies in response to injustice. His discussion of killing, in short, is part of his casuistry of charity. And in this discussion, Aquinas develops the crucial distinction between intended and unintended effects of a moral act. When we are victims of aggression, Thomas argues, we may never *directly* or *intentionally* injure the attacker as a means of self-defense. But this does not rule out self-defense altogether. Preserving ourselves may be lawfully intended because self-preservation derives from natural inclinations, enshrined in the natural law. It also coheres with the order of charity, as we have seen. If injuring another is foreseeable, it must remain "beside" the intention (*praeter intentionem*), an accident of the act. Laying the seeds for the principle of double effect, Thomas says that "an act of self-defense may have two effects: the saving of one's own life, and the killing of the attacker." The intention to defend oneself is lawful, "because it is natural for anything to want to preserve itself in being as far as it can."[33] About the injury to another we may feel regret, but we are not morally guilty, so long as our intention conforms to the duty of self-preservation.

Thomas thus departs from Augustine's argument for nonresistant pacifism by confining the duty not to harm other persons to the realm of intention. In other words, Augustine prohibits self-defense in a private individual's outward action, and restricts the force of Matt. 5:38 to the realm of intention only in the case of publicly authorized violent deeds. Aquinas, in contrast, permits self-defense in a private individual's outward action, so long as that individual abstains from disordered intentions.

Thomas's proscription of direct harm in self-defense means that there should be no moral difference between how an assailant may be injured and how innocent people might be harmed in cases of accidental injury. In *both* cases injury may never be done intentionally, even though the objects of violence—assailants and innocents—are different. The order of charity allows only indirect, accidental injury. In this way Thomas crafts his own version of a presumption against violence. Without such a presumption, Thomas would be committed to the notion that direct harm of an assailant is just, that injury may be intended to vindicate justice. Without such a bias against violence Aquinas would be able to distinguish the harm permitted against aggressors from the harm permitted against innocent people. But Aquinas refuses to draw such a distinction because charity transforms justice. To be sure, the demands of charity do not eclipse the demands of justice and the duty of self-preservation because for Aquinas the order of nature is not destroyed by grace. Instead, charity produces a bias against violence, precluding all forms of intentional harm, even against the attacker in justified self-defense.

Thomas's bias against violence is also enshrined, albeit subtly, in his discussion of the use of violence by a soldier in war. Following Augustine on this point, Aquinas *does* allow that it *is* legitimate for a soldier intentionally to slay an opponent in a just war: "Killing in self-defense in this sort of way is restricted to somebody who has public authority to do so. . . . This is exemplified by the soldier who fights against an enemy."[34] While this apparent concession to the necessities of war seems to contradict Thomas's prohibition of intentional killing in individual self-defense, he justifies the soldier's act if it is commissioned by a higher authority. Since the higher authority commissions the war, the soldier does not, strictly speaking, take the sword. Following a medieval presumption on behalf of authority, Thomas writes, "If a private person uses the sword by the authority of the sovereign or judge, or a public person uses it through zeal for justice, and by the authority, so to speak, of God, then he himself does not draw the sword, but is commissioned by another to use it, and does not deserve punishment."[35]

Operating behind Thomas's version of this medieval presumption on behalf of authority is the Aristotelian understanding of fourfold causality: peace is the final cause, authority is the formal cause, the sword is the material cause, and the soldier is the efficient cause in the just war. The fact that the soldier may kill intentionally, then, is *evacuated* of any moral content because the soldier is only the efficient cause. The soldier may not attempt to quench a cruel thirst for vengeance, but he need not worry about the morality of intentional killing, since the real agent in war, the formal cause, exists higher up in the chain of command.

The effect of this argument is to *restore* the presumption against violence that is apparently compromised when Thomas grants the soldier the right intentionally to injure an opponent. Thomas's notion of soldiers as efficient causes suggests that his discussion of killing another in self-defense, individual homicide, provides an analogy for evaluating the acts performed by the *authority*—the formal cause—in a just war. And, although Aquinas permits public authorities intentionally to kill particular agents who attack the body politic, it remains the case that such killing must be referred to the common good, which is being defended against a collective foe. This means, among other things, that charity transforms justice insofar as authorities are required to do *more* than give belligerents their just due in the form of retributive attack. Charity requires that other demands be included as well, namely, the duty to insure that one's own citizens are not victims of sin or aggression. When the public authority orders his intention to the common good in such acts, that intention is shaped by charity.[36] Accordingly, intentional acts of harm must be subsumed under goals broader than vindictive aims.

Aquinas's notion of the public authority as the formal cause of a collective endeavor also suggests that we include in our ethics a judgment about what a leader may (and may not) intend to do to another corporate body. One consequence of this suggestion is that we are asked to see enemies in individual and corporate terms. The permission to harm enemies intentionally pertains to individual bodies, not a collective body or the conditions by which it sustains a common existence. Thomas would thus have grave moral doubts about wars which, as a means of self-defense, aim intentionally to undermine the conditions of an enemy's collective life.

If Aquinas's reasoning about the ethics of homicide can be viewed as analogous with the case of the public authority's resort to violence, two implications thus emerge: intentional harm must be ordered to the defense of the community, not the vindication of justice alone; and harm to the conditions of an enemy's corporate life must remain beside the authority's intention, an accident of acts on behalf of collective self-defense.

The presumption against violence within this Thomistic approach is also developed in light of the demands of preserving order, about which I will speak in detail in chapter 2. Here it is sufficient to note that the presumption against harm derives from a general benevolence owed to all persons, and that this presumption is enshrined in the subtle restrictions Thomas places on (1) the intention in individual conflict and (2) the intention of authorities when they mandate violent acts in defense of the community. Aquinas thus suggests parallels between the morality of defending the individual, private body and the morality of defending the corporate body, since both moralities would permit "bodily" harm only if it is foreseen but unintended, or if it is ordered to ends beyond the limits of vindicating justice.[37]

Despite the fact that Thomas may overcome the problem of Augustine's theory, however, another problem emerges when his medieval presumption in favor of authority is considered today. To evacuate the act of soldiering of moral content, placing the onus of morality higher up in the chain of command, defies our contemporary sense of professional responsibility. Soldiers are rightly expected to exercise moral judgment, to draw moral boundaries, to be more than "efficient causes" in the overall structure of a war. Blind obedience has been replaced by expectations of prudence, character, and moral agency. From the Nuremberg trials to the My Lai massacre, reference to the chain of command no longer suffices to acquit soldiers of moral atrocities. The paternalism present in the Thomistic convergence—and, for that matter, in Augustine's work— has given way to a more complex mixture of obedience and freedom.

The *modern Protestant convergence* focuses on the sovereignty of God, thus diminishing the importance of pacifism or just-war tenets by stressing the belief in God's sovereign rule over all human actions. The idea is to insist that orientation to God is more important than the moral or practical exigencies of human affairs. Such an orientation, called the "Protestant principle," protests against the possibility of exaggerating the importance of worldly aspirations, however noble they may be.[38]

The first sustained version of this convergence was developed in a relatively unknown work of the Calhoun Commission, "The Relation of the Church to the War in the Light of the Christian Faith," in 1944.[39] Chaired by Robert Lowry Calhoun, this commission included some of the most prominent representatives of midcentury American Protestantism: John Bennett, H. Richard and Reinhold Niebuhr, Georgia Harkness, Roland Bainton, John McNeill, Wilhelm Pauck, and Angus Dun, to name a few. The commission's chief objective was to address the theological and ethical dimensions of the Second World War, to examine "the nature of Christianity and . . . what this means for the Church in a war situation."[40] One goal of the document, then, was to furnish "specific guiding judgments" for Christian action, a "body of working insights" rather than an ethical code. Cautious about arriving at certitude in moral judgments, the authors insist that they cannot supplant "enlightened conscience by prescribed rules."[41]

The Calhoun report reflects a characteristically Protestant approach to ethics in several respects: in its emphasis on the sovereignty of God in human history; in its attention to the fiduciary dimension of human experience, about which objects of loyalty are central; in its notion of experience as morally ambiguous, precluding security and self-righteousness on either side of battle; in its notion of the religious community as herald to the outside world; and in its reliance on history rather than nature as a source of ethical wisdom. This last feature leads the commission to affirm pacifism and just-war tenets for historicist reasons, as part of the historical deposit of the Christian tradition. Moreover, this version of Protestantism was liberal and Calvinistic: liberal because its theology linked the activity of God to the processes of nature and history, proceeding outside a supernaturalistic frame of reference; Calvinistic because its interpretation of war joins an understanding of divine activity with the self-knowledge of human agents in war.

The epistemological point of view in the Calhoun report exemplifies what James Gustafson calls "perceptual intuitionism," which "involves an interpretation of the events and actions in the light of not only such political and other concepts as pertain, but also in the light of religious beliefs and theological principles."[42] Emphasis lies not on applying a rule to a situation, but on interpreting the situation and discerning the fitting response in light of religious beliefs and practices. Accordingly, the report embarks upon a task that is simultaneously interpretive and theological— an exercise that H. Richard Niebuhr called "inner history."[43] Inner history for the Calhoun Commission combines two questions: What is going on? What is God doing in the war? The symbolic framework guiding the interpretation, moreover, is explicitly trinitarian, drawing upon traditional beliefs in God as Creator, Redeemer, and Sanctifier. Viewing human action in relation to this divine activity, the commission thus emphasizes humans as creative moral agents, sinners in need of redemption, and subjects of moral and religious renovation.

That God is sovereign creator in the war means that God "is maintaining invincibly an order that men cannot overthrow," that "the existence of every situation depends on the creative energy of God's will."[44] Reference to God as creative ground includes a general acknowledgment of "orders of creation" to underscore God's creative will as the condition for human action. Yet the Calhoun report eschews any systematic use of natural theology or natural law morality to develop its ethics.[45] Instead, the authors place their emphasis on the ordering activity of God. *Ordering activity:* the term suggests dynamism and historical relativity rather than unchanging natural essences. God does not will the war in any direct sense, but God does will the conditions of creativity, responsibility, and interdependence within which humanity carries out its warring activity.

According to the commission's theological views, the notion of God as sovereign redeemer follows almost as a corollary to the notion of creative ground. The idea is not that God "judges" humanity from some supernatural vantage point, but that a breach in the order of creation brings disaster upon us all. War is the product of human wickedness, the exercise of pride and idolatry, faithlessness and lethargy. The effect of these acts, the fury of war, confirms "the existence and inescapability of divine law." Indeed, war itself is the exercise of divine judgment, a punishment immanent in the process of history itself. "It is not God's will that war shall come upon mankind," the commission avers, "nor that it be regarded as a suitable instrument for good."[46] Rather, war vindicates the divine law by revealing that our resistance to that law redounds to our ill, that we reap what we sow. So the commission remarks, "Divine judgment is not vengeful. It is inexorable."[47]

Yet the commission likewise holds out hope for transformation and renovation in war, changes in human conduct interpreted as the effect of God's sanctification. Among such gifts are "reinforced strength and courage, sharpened insight and self-forgetfulness, steadfast patience and serenity and joy, invincible security." In such changes there is evidence of the power of life to overcome division and death, the "miracle" issuing "in human life transformed, redirected, with new dimensions in which to grow."[48]

Seen in these theological terms, then, war is a "crucifixion," a tragic event in God's providential ordering of history. As H. Richard Niebuhr had argued in a series of provocative articles in the early 1940s, these authors maintain that war is a crucifixion in the sense that "the burden of suffering is not distributed according to guilt and innocence, but that all suffer, even the best."[49] So the commission asks rhetorically, "Can we say that the men killed in battle, or the refugees driven out to wander and starve, or the children who die in bomb shelters or blockaded famine areas are vicarious redeemers of our time?" The Calhoun report does not equate the war with the Christ event, but it does insist that the symbol of the cross sheds light on "the meaning of this present struggle." Repoeticizing war in light of their confessional symbol, the commission members "see that the spirit in which suffering and death are confronted can make them vehicles of life for many rather than merely of loss."[50]

The chief problem posed by the war, then, is not ethical but interpretive, although this hermeneutical aspect has important fiduciary and ethical implications. Central to the task of the Calhoun report is to clarify the events of the war, to define their moral meaning. Without a proper descriptive frame of reference, it suggests, fellow Christians will misconstrue the real stakes in war. The danger is that Christians will thus restrict their loyalties to national or military necessities. Narrow, nationalistic loyalties among Christians, the commission fears, will only mirror worldly divisions in the war itself. Doubtless the commission has in mind the problem of cultural Christianity, in which religious beliefs baptize secular attitudes and institutions. As the commission remarks, "In practice, both individual Christians and organized churches, Roman Catholic, Orthodox, or Protestant, have become so deeply involved in national or cultural loyalties that when serious conflicts arise, their loyalty to a universal Church and to fellow Christians of other countries or cultures is often subordinated, if not temporarily extinguished."[51] The evil of total war results from our tendency to exaggerate finite objects of allegiance, elevating the survival of a nation or culture above all else. One goal for individuals and groups, then, is to widen the moral horizon in which war is to be interpreted. Within a more expansive frame of reference, the nation "is one member of a world society in which diverse and cultural patterns exist in a wider human context."[52]

It is only after the interpretive implications of this Protestant theology are developed that the commission introduces conventional ethical categories into its report. For without a wider frame of reference, the authors suggest, conventional ethical categories will go awry, reinforcing the particular loyalties of people in conflict rather than the objective realities of the events themselves. Ethics must be postponed to a later moment, after theological interpretation has set the parameters for evaluation. Only then do the authors turn to traditional Christian attitudes toward war, drawing upon the typology of holy war, just war, and pacifism, which Bainton would later develop in a more comprehensive historical survey.[53] Presently, the document notes, the first of these attitudes is on the wane, while the second and third have drawn closer together. In this way the commission constructs its convergence of pacifism and just-war tenets, the first systematic effort of such kind in American Protestantism.

The commission develops its point of convergence from an interpretation of war as a morally ambiguous affair, in which clear moral options are available to neither side of battle. Many Christian pacifists are aware of the "self-sacrificing heroism of men and women who are giving their lives in an effort to check the spread of tyranny," while other Christians participating in the war "are no less clearly aware of the depth of evil both in the conduct of modern war on either side and in the national behavior on all sides."[54] We err by interpreting war as an arena of stark moral differences, in which right and wrong have been carefully charted, and where saints and sinners are clearly visible. Rather, the commission notes, the justice in war is relative, not absolute, leaving neither side with a monopoly on righteousness.

Reference to relative justice is now a commonplace in moral discourse about war, although it seems to have less of a place among pacifists than in just-war theory. Relative justice requires us to interpret war cautiously and self-critically, since it implies that none of the participants can be wholly free of moral implication in the evils of war. Yet the problem with the Calhoun report is that the convergence of pacifism and just-war ideas, from which relative justice derives, is cast exclusively in Christian terms. The report gives the impression that neither tradition has analogues or equivalents in secular ethics. Nor is the content of pacifism and just-war tenets developed systematically. The convergence itself is cast in confessional terms, as a new moment in Christian ethics alone. Within a more self-consciously pluralistic culture, the religious exclusiveness implicit within this document—or its assumption of all-inclusiveness—is insufficient for moral discourse about war. Is the point of contact between pacifism and just-war tenets exclusive to Christian ethics? In suggesting an affirmative answer to this question, the commission fell prey to the same cultural Christianity to which it ostensibly directed its protest.

A second version of the modern Protestant convergence, developed by Karl Barth, represents an even more radical theological poeticization of war. For Barth, the ethics of killing must be framed by a highly confessional understanding of theological ethics, premised on obedience to the revealed Word of God, freely communicated in divine commands to individual consciences. Barth's method is controlled not by nature and its dictates—in sharp contrast with Aquinas—but by historical revelation, whose design is to reorder and sanctify natural inclinations. Yet for Barth, unlike for the Calhoun Commission, reference to historical revelation includes a supernaturalistic belief in God's agency. Such supernaturalism was designed to overcome what he considered to be accommodationism to secular culture in liberal Protestantism. For Barth, there can be no attenuation of the radical otherness of God, no constraints set by finite human expectations about the meaning of the divine Word. And, owing to the freedom of God from natural forces, historical processes, and human expectations, either pacifism or war may be commanded to individual consciences. The convergence of these conventional ethical approaches to killing and war lies, then, in the sovereign freedom of God.

Barth's account of divine freedom does not mean, however, that humans are subject to divine caprice, left without ethical moorings or benchmarks. About matters of killing, ethical decisions are guided, prepared, or directed—but never absolutely dictated—by the sixth commandment of the Decalogue, "Thou shalt not kill."[55] For Barth such biblical commands are never absolute, for moral absolutism constrains divine freedom and eclipses the possibility of novelty in history. But they do provide provisional, tentative indications about the direction that responsible human action is likely to take.

Barth's use of the sixth commandment resembles other versions of the convergence between pacifism and just-war tenets in that he, like Aquinas, constructs an ethic premised on a strong presumption against the use of force. Yet unlike Thomas's, Barth's presumption develops in a theory of spheres and boundaries rather than in an account of the requirements of charity in the normal course of life. Indeed, one distinguishing feature of Barth's approach is his claim that traditional approaches to war, be they pacifist or nonpacifist, fail to recognize the exceptional nature of killing and the even more marginal place of war on the terrain of human experience. Traditional approaches conceive of war as yet another problem for careful moral distinctions and casuistical methods. In failing to draw lines between typical moral problems and the boundary experience of war, traditional approaches fail to describe adequately the real problem at hand. As a corrective to conventional approaches we need a scrupulous biblical analysis of life and its limits, establishing uniquely strong presumptions against killing and war, especially war in its modern guise.

Drawing on various New Testament passages—Paul's reproof of Christians seeking legal redress (1 Cor. 6:1–11), Paul's statement that vengeance is left to God, not humanity (Rom. 12:17–20), and the Sermon on the Mount—Barth argues that nonresistant pacifism constitutes the rule of Christian ethics, from which killing can only be a rare exception. These biblical passages "declare the simple command of God which is valid for all men in its basic and primary sense, and which is thus to be kept until further notice."[56] All killing—abortion, euthanasia, self-defense, capital punishment, and war—lies on the "extreme margin" of moral existence, constituting an emergency that can be justified only by a command of God in a rare departure from scriptural testimony.

Within this biblical perspective, individual self-defense "seems to be almost entirely excluded." The presumption against such killing means that the agent must be vigilant and self-critical about the apparent morality of killing, open to alternatives to retaliation as a means of defense. Barth asks, "Ought we not at least to postpone, to put in second place, all the considerations which might finally lead us to the resolve to meet force with force?"[57] At the very least, killing must be the ultima ratio, available only after other means have been considered and perhaps used. Self-defense, then, "cannot possibly be the first word but only the tenth at the very earliest."[58] And even then violence cannot occur without a keen sense of its moral ambiguity, where "I have in fact to kill the killer before he actually becomes a killer, so that he is only responsible for the will to do it whereas I must bear responsibility for the actual deed."[59]

The effect of Barth's version of the presumption against harm, then, is to place a premium on the notion that individual self-defense must be a last resort, after all other peaceful measures have been examined. But for Barth there is more to be said about killing in self-defense. In keeping with his general method of annexing conventional ethical ideas after first developing his theological views, Augustinian and Thomistic ideas return to Barth's agenda, albeit in revised, "sanctified" form. When Barth considers the remote occasion when self-defense is justified, the first point is that God, not the human agent, commissions the act. Moreover, the act is one of obedience, not one in which the agent "throws himself afresh into the jungle struggle for existence in which the reviler is met by reviling." And the cause will not be one's own, "but that of the divine resistance entrusted to him."[60] Hence, Barth justifies violence in self-defense according to the conditions of authority, intention, and cause, each of which is understood with God, or God's purposes, as the sole referent. Those creaturely realities of human authority and intention, mediating for Augustine and Aquinas the implications of charity, are absent here. Killing is first and foremost a theological event for Barth—as is most of history—and the principal error of humanity is not that humans kill, but that they usurp the divine prerogative by authorizing human actions independently of the divine command. Those commands put violence at the edge of existence, and even at the edge, Barth's authorization of killing displaces the human by subordinating our action to providential purposes.

The moral reality of war leads Barth to move to even greater lengths to articulate the meaning and implications of violence as an ultima ratio. War exists on the "extreme zone" of human experience, at the limit of limits, requiring "even stricter reserve and caution than have been found to be necessary in relation to such things as suicide, abortion, capital punishment etc."[61] Writing after the advent of nuclear weapons, Barth maintains that modern technology discloses the true reality of war—that war has as its goal neither economic power nor the neutralization of forces, but the annihilation of peoples, "with neither glory, dignity nor chivalry, with neither restraint nor consideration of any respect."[62] Today whole peoples are ushered into combat. Thus, for Barth, there are no grounds for distinguishing between combatants and noncombatants; in the present age, "everyone is a military person."[63] This means, among other things, that war is a uniquely individual and personal decision, the morality of which cannot be settled by higher authorities within a "hypostatized" theory of political leadership. A "trial" for which there is "no match," the mass slaughter of war "might well be mass murder," the possibility of which "should not be seized like any other, but only in the very last hour in the darkest of days."[64]

Within the normal course of affairs, prior to the emergency wrought on the margins of life, the chief duty of the state is to fashion peace. Indeed, if there is any defect in pacifism beyond its ethical absolutism, Barth insists, it is that pacifists typically focus on the evils of war in the abstract, without reference to the so-called conditions of peace which precede war. The "real emergency" of today concerns the strengthening of peaceful conditions of existence, the goal of which is to expand further the sphere of normal, stable political relations.[65] With order and peaceful conditions as the state's first priority, the hope is that war will become even more extraordinary, more remote, among our options for settling differences.

War remains within the remote bounds of possibility for Barth under conditions that subsequently have been called, under the authorship of Michael Walzer, "the supreme emergency."[66] For Barth (and Walzer), such an emergency assumes that a state "can throw another into the wholly abnormal situation of emergency in which not merely its greater or lesser prosperity but its very existence and autonomy are menaced and attacked."[67] In these circumstances, "a nation can find itself faced by the question whether it must surrender or assert itself as such in face of the claims of the other. Nothing less than this final question must be at issue if a war is to be just and necessary."[68]

Such an emergency must not be understood, however, as a Barthian version of nationalism or survivalism. Rather, Barth wants to retain the idea that national autonomy may have a theological element, that "with the independence of a nation there is entrusted to its people something which . . . they are commissioned to attest to others." For Barth, values higher than the state's preservation are to be protected, values "more important than the preservation of the lives of those who are unfortunately trying to take it from them." In the situation when a nation is either directly attacked or summoned by treaty obligations, that nation may be directed by the command of God to use military force.[69] Indeed, the command must be obeyed unconditionally, irrespective of possible failure or military imprudence.[70] And, if war is pursued under the banner of obedience, "it is also ventured in faith and therefore with joyous and reckless determination."[71] In more traditional terms, war for Barth may have a "just cause," the defense of special values; it must be pursued unconditionally, even without a reasonable hope for success; and it need not be waged with reference to special limits or means.

Yet Barth's disregard for the question of limits in war raises serious problems for his argument. Combined with his assertion that today "everyone is a military person," Barth's position opens the door to the kind of wholesale destruction that his presumption against violence would seem to exclude. Surprisingly, no such exclusion or qualification is evident. Indeed, the kind of righteousness in faith to which Barth appeals in the "reckless determination" of war moves his position far beyond the rigors of pacifism or just-war tenets, closer to a view of war as religious crusade. At the limits of experience, moral limits seem to disappear; we not only leave the sphere of normal relations as we enter war, we go over the edge, leaving behind the presumptions and distinctions—like that between soldier and civilian—that ought to obtain. Is it self-evidently and permanently clear that children, the elderly, the homeless, and the sick are "military persons"? Does this mean that all institutions and facilities of the enemy nation, e.g., hospitals, schools, or farms, become military targets? Does the providential command of God deliver its recipients from the task of drawing distinctions, from the requirements of practical reasoning?

Barth's failure to address these questions unveils the chief flaw of his position: His presumption against violence fails to leave moral traces once it becomes necessary to override the duty not to harm or kill. As I will argue later against Walzer's use of the supreme emergency on behalf of nuclear deterrence, Barth's position eclipses the moral conventions that structure traditional discourse about war, abandoning those limits in the extreme zone of the supreme emergency. Barth's distinctive version of this problem can be traced to his method, which subordinates the moral to the salvific in a self-consciously theological system of thought. Usually this means that Barth will criticize and then annex conventional ethical ideas as moral benchmarks after placing them under the regime of the Word of God. But in the case of war the command of God nullifies rather than annexes the moral traces provided by the sixth commandment. Fortified with religious assurances under God's command, the Barthian Christian must embrace the belief that war is hell, a zone of human nihilism, where all distinctions must be abandoned. Is it not ironic that a position which begins with paeans for the "emergency of peace" concludes with a theological authorization for the fury of war?

The *contemporary Catholic convergence* permits pacifism and just-war tenets as equally valid options for individuals, but mandates just-war tenets for the morality of states. This view thus departs from a centuries-long rejection of pacifism in official Catholic teaching, developing a highly qualified version of the Augustinian convergence. Embracing the natural law conviction that it is the duty of the state to protect its citizens, both Augustine and contemporary Catholic teaching require the use of force to defend the community. The difference lies in the fact that contemporary Catholic teaching *permits* rather than *requires* a pacifist ethic for individuals, even when the state must go to war. And, as I shall argue in chapter 3, the pacifism endorsed by recent Catholic teaching stands closer to an ethic of nonviolent resistance than to Augustine's requirement of selfless nonresistance.

This convergence, whose roots lie in *The Pastoral Constitution of the Modern World* of the Second Vatican Council, has been refined in the ground-breaking pastoral letter of the U.S. Catholic bishops, *The Challenge of Peace: God's Promise and Our Response.* Following conciliar teaching on human rights, the bishops argue that both pacifism and just-war criteria "testify to the Christian conviction that peace must be pursued and rights defended within moral restraints and in the context of defining other basic human values."[72] In a way that would not satisfy all pacifists, Catholic teaching endorses nonviolence in light of the requirements of human dignity and rights, a "rights-based pacifism."

Within this framework the bishops devote special attention to the close relationship between pacifism and just-war tenets. They repeat virtually verbatim Childress's thesis when they argue that just-war criteria and pacifism "support and complement one another, each preserving the other from distortion."[73] Although the bishops eschew the language of prima facie duties, they embrace a facsimile thereof, arguing that church teaching "establishes a strong presumption against war which is binding on all; it then examines when this presumption may be overridden, precisely in the name of preserving the kind of peace which protects human dignity and human rights."[74] Indeed, any decision to go to war "requires extraordinarily strong reasons for overriding the presumption *in favor of peace* and *against* war."[75] And, for those states considering war, there are historical examples of successful efforts to defend nonviolently against aggression.[76]

Yet this nuanced recollection of Augustine opens the door to a nuanced version of the obstacle internal to Augustine's theory. Again the question concerns the precise relation between private and public morality, but with a different ethical twist: If the state has the moral duty to defend its citizens within the constraints provided by just-war criteria, then those pacifists who refuse to contribute to the national cause are morally delinquent for failing to cooperate in a collective moral duty. At the very least, the overarching principle of human rights should require pacifists to contribute in nonviolent ways to humanitarian needs. Yet it is not clear how much, or in what ways, the pacifist is permitted to dissent from a just war. The bishops address this issue only vaguely, repeating the endorsement of pacifism from *The Pastoral Constitution on the Church in the Modern World*. The council praises the practice of nonviolence, "provided that this can be done without injury to the rights and duties of others or of the community itself."[77] Following one trajectory out of this statement, the U.S. bishops encourage the study of methods of nonviolent defense and resistance.[78] But about the more specific duties of pacifists within a community engaged in legitimate defense the bishops are virtually silent. They seem to draw on a hypostatized notion of the state, in which the duty of the state is abstracted from the morality of individuals. And in this abstraction, the limits of the pacifist's rights in light of the state's duties are not specified. This discrepancy is unusual in Catholic ethics, in which rights and duties usually correlate rather neatly. But in the pastoral letter the precise relation between the ethic of nonviolence and the individual's responsibility to the state carrying out a legitimate defense remains unclear.[79]

A slightly different version of the contemporary Catholic convergence is developed by David Hollenbach, S.J. Like Barth, Hollenbach insists that the presumption against violence establishes a theory of exceptions as a basis for moral discourse about war.[80] Yet Hollenbach refuses to let go of traditional moral distinctions once war has begun, thus overcoming the chief defect in Barth's position. Moreover, Hollenbach's argument relies less on an account of spheres and margins than on a general theology of history, which sanctions pacifism and just-war tenets as equally valid options for individual consciences. Christians, Hollenbach states, exist "between the times" of the cross of Jesus Christ and the eschatological fruition of divine purposes. The memory of the former requires Christians to seek nonviolence and justice; hope in the Kingdom awaits the final consummation of these ideals. In the meantime, "an unresolved tension between justice and nonviolence continues to exist."[81] Pacifists and just-war theorists differ not about the grave importance of peace and justice, but only about the relative priority they assign to each.[82] Given this unresolved tension, theology supports both positions, allowing Christians to be faithful to their broad vision of history. Hence, pluralism about the morality of war is the "theological consequence of the incompleteness and partiality of *any* specification of the relation between the kingdom of God and the realities of history."[83]

Hollenbach then argues for preferring just-war criteria to pacifism in matters of public policy. His solution rests on determining which of the two approaches may find public approbation without excluding the other. The solution lies, in other words, not in a natural law theory about the duties of the state, but in an account of the functional requirements of pluralism. Of the two traditions, just-war criteria may be accepted without gainsaying the more stringent criteria of pacifism for individuals. A public policy premised on pacifist tenets, in contrast, would exclude just-war criteria for individuals, thus undermining the pluralism justified on theological grounds.[84] For Hollenbach, just-war tenets provide the outer limits beyond which no public policy may proceed, but within which a more stringent pacifist position remains open for individuals. Seen in this way, pacifism and just-war tenets are less like contiguous curves and more like concentric circles.

Hollenbach's theology "between the times" to embrace both pacifist and just-war tenets differs, then, from official Catholic teaching. The official position provides a relative and ethical endorsement of both pacifism and just-war thought: Each must serve the cause of human rights. Reference to human rights to endorse ethical pluralism *excludes* pacifists for whom the protection of human rights is untenable. The criterion of human rights, in short, provides the basis for accepting some forms of pacifism and excluding others. Hollenbach goes beyond this position by drawing on a theology of history to provide an unconditional and theological rationale for ethical pluralism. Moreover, because he does not draw on a theory of rights as a criterion for adjudicating between tenable and untenable forms of pacifism, Hollenbach provides a rationale for accepting versions of pacifism which Catholic teaching would not embrace.

Yet it is precisely on the issue of pluralism that Hollenbach's argument falters. Hollenbach's embrace of pluralism is too general to sort out specific ethical questions about the merits and requirements of pacifism and just-war criteria. It is hardly satisfactory to argue that just-war criteria have a privileged place in public policy because they, unlike pacifism, do not jeopardize legitimate pluralism. Such an argument appeals more to the function of a position than to its conceptual adequacy. Moreover, Hollenbach's embrace of pluralism is too general to specify the place of political and moral obligations of pacifists in a nonpacifist state; like the bishops, he fails to sort out the duties of pacifists when the state legitimately goes to war.

The *practical convergence* of pacifism and just-war tenets proceeds in a direction opposite to Barth's. While both Barth and various representatives of the practical convergence might agree that modern war, especially nuclear war, is hell, the latter conclude that such a judgment ought to confirm some of the more general prohibitions of war bequeathed to the West by pacifism. Here pacifists and just-war theorists converge at the practical judgment that modern war would be a nihilistic horror, far beyond the limits imposed by just-war criteria.

Representatives of the practical convergence can be found among pacifists and just-war theorists alike. In the 1960s, the noted Catholic pacifist James Douglass rejected just-war criteria as untenable, but he also held that just-war theorists had at least the theoretical resources to reject modern war as a form of indiscriminate violence.[85] Twenty years later, after the development of more sophisticated, lower-yield nuclear weapons, Hollenbach concludes that any use of nuclear weapons would violate the *in bello* criteria of discrimination and proportionality, as well as the *ad bellum* criterion of "reasonable hope for success."[86] Among Protestants, the most notable expression of the practical convergence is present in the pastoral letter of the United Methodist Council of Bishops, *In Defense of Creation: The Nuclear Crisis and a Just Peace*.[87] For the Methodist bishops, nuclear war poses the danger of uncontrollable warfare, contrary to the dictates of discrimination, reasonable hope for success, and proportionality. In language that goes well beyond previous arguments, the Methodist bishops base their position on the claim that creation as a *theological* reality remains in jeopardy in the nuclear age.[88]

Yet one problem with the practical convergence is that it lies entirely at one level of practical reasoning, confining its focus to the application of moral criteria to the case of modern war. The dangers of modern war, or a nuclear war, are massively important, the stakes of which can hardly be exaggerated. But it remains true that the practical convergence obscures theoretical and other practical issues that may be addressed by just-war theorists and pacifists alike. What is the theoretical relation between pacifism and just-war tenets? How might we trace their similarity and difference? What complaints about our contemporary moral landscape might representatives of both traditions share? What projects might join members of both groups? How might resources from one idiom help the other refine its claims? To answer such questions, the precise relation between pacifism and just-war tenets must be pressed further. In so doing we may refine these moral vocabularies and uncover a wider array of issues to which both pacifists and just-war theorists may speak.

Nonmaleficence and Levels of Moral Discourse

We can begin to amplify the convergence between pacifism and just-war tenets by drawing on a taxonomy of ethical discourse, developed in an important essay by Henry David Aiken.[89] According to Aiken, such discourse can be distinguished according to expressive-evocative, moral, ethical, and postethical levels. As we proceed from the first to the final level, we ascend to broader, more comprehensive terms according to which the prior levels can be made intelligible. Doubtless ethicists move back and forth between these levels in the art of developing an argument, violating the tidiness implied by Aiken's classifications. So, like most taxonomies this one needs the proviso that such classifications are heuristic, providing precipitates from fluid mixtures.

With the aid of Aiken's categories I want to broaden the range and clarify the procedures according to which pacifism and just-war tenets operate. Aiken's distinction between moral and ethical levels of discourse will sharpen the unity-and-difference between our two moral vocabularies about war. Further, using Aiken's insights will enable me to show how nonmaleficence shapes the morphology of just-war tenets. This discussion will also allow us to see how widely the currency of nonmaleficence circulates in contemporary religious and philosophical ethics, especially at what he calls the postethical level of discourse.

The first level of discourse about which Aiken speaks, the expressive-evocative, consists of "initial responses . . . of the unreflective, stock variety." On this most elementary level, we "express our passing feelings of favor or disfavor."[90] Here we voice our opinions, often casually or spontaneously, sometimes carelessly, before we refine those opinions upon reflection. Such opinions may vary in intensity and range of emotion, but they exist prior to rational, critical examination.

Critical reflection begins at what Aiken calls the moral level of discourse, in which there emerges "a problem of conduct and a problem for appraisal and ultimate decision."[91] At this level we are required to answer the "ought" question: What ought I or we to do? What is the proper expression of my individual character, or our group identity, in this instance? The moral level, often wrongly considered the only level at which ethicists operate, classifies acts or patterns of behavior as required, permitted, or prohibited for individuals or groups. Discourse here is situational, aiming to determine the appropriate behavior for a person or group in a particular context. We answer ought questions by using moral codes, passed along as part of a community's tradition, specifying "certain types of behavior which ordinary . . . persons within a given community would approve."[92]

At the moral level of discourse, pacifism and just-war tenets constitute distinguishable approaches to the problem of killing and war. Whereas the main goal of the just-war tradition is to classify some forms of killing as nonmurderous, the pacifist rejects such a classification. Each tradition, in short, answers the ought question of killing in war differently. Such differences at this moral level have led to the idea that pacifism and just-war tenets are mutually exclusive, although these differences are scarcely the last word about the relation between these two moral vocabularies.

The ethical level elevates moral inquiry to the plateau of objectivity and impersonality. Here we must defend the answers to the ought question in general, abstract terms by placing those answers under the control of a basic value, e.g., justice, freedom, nonmaleficence, benevolence, or self-perfection. In contrast to the moral level, the ethical level does not specify types of behavior or character appropriate to particular situations; rather, it furnishes a rationale according to which answers to the ought question gain intelligibility and coherence. Here we put our responses at the moral level under critical scrutiny. As Aiken remarks, the moral level is "directed to the solution of particular problems of conduct," while the ethical level is "directed rather to the organization, regulation, and correction of lower-order attitudes."[93] At the ethical level, then, we are to define procedural rules, clarifying the formal structure of virtues and imperatives.

At the ethical level the duty of nonmaleficence operates as a point of contact between just-war tenets and pacifism. Each vocabulary begins with the duty not to kill or injure others. Within pacifism, nonmaleficence constitutes an absolute duty; within just-war ideas, nonmaleficence is relativized by conflicting duties in the emergency wrought by war.[94] As a prima facie duty within just-war tenets, nonmaleficence is usually binding but may be overridden by competing duties, like the duty to protect human rights or innocent life.

Moreover, at the ethical level, procedural or formal questions obtain. In considering these two approaches to war, especially just-war criteria, the foremost formal question concerns the priority of nonmaleficence over other duties, e.g., the duty to protect other people from harm. According to the logic of prima facie duties, nonmaleficence is ranked higher than the duty to protect oneself or others, and is "trumped" by such a duty only in the emergency wrought by another's maleficence. Moreover, the duty to protect remains under the "pressure" provided by the duty not to harm, requiring at least the shadow of pacifism to loom over the subsequent course of action. How is it that nonmaleficence can enjoy this pride of place vis-à-vis duties to protect oneself or others?

The answer to this question lies in the difference between negative and positive duties. It is a commonplace in ethical theory to hold that, *in general,* the duty to refrain from inflicting injury (a negative duty) is stricter than the duty to protect ourselves or others from injury (a positive duty)—although this does not mean, as Phillipa Foot observes, that the latter is not a very strict duty itself.[95] Indeed, Western moral, religious, and legal conventions have all considered it more important to specify the harm we must not do to others than to stipulate the positive acts that we must carry out. Without this ranking of negative and positive duties, Sissela Bok argues, "everyone might be held responsible for all the accidents and deaths in the world from which they could conceivably have protected others." Without this ranking, in short, to carry out unharmful acts—moderate relaxation or recreation, for example—rather than to patrol city streets looking for victims of aggression would then be turned into culpable neglect.[96] Without such a distinction, moreover, we would consider it justifiable to harvest the organs of one person without his or her consent in order to keep ourselves or others alive. The fact that neither the duty to patrol streets nor the duty to harvest organs is imperative, all else being equal, is due to the primacy of nonmaleficence, a stricter duty than the positive requirements to protect oneself or others.

For the just-war theorist, nonmaleficence may be overridden in those situations in which others violate, or are about to violate, nonmaleficence, leaving oneself or others to lie victim to an aggressor's attack. Overriding nonmaleficence on my part, then, is warranted by the *prior or portending maleficence exercised by others.* It is the unwarranted violation of non-maleficence by a threatening party that occasions my duty to override nonmaleficence in defense of human rights and innocent life. The duty to defend or protect is relative to the situation in which victims lie helplessly in wait.

The fact that nonmaleficence enjoys a prima facie priority over the duty to protect oneself or others creates a complex structure for just-war tenets. Within the general structure of pacifism, nonmaleficence may serve as a first principle, from which specific moral decisions—answers to the ought question—may follow directly. But in just-war tenets the logic works differently. Rather than provide a reason for action which follows straightforwardly from the duty not to harm, just-war tenets furnish a rationale for violence that must *overcome* the presumptions established by the duty not to harm. Nonmaleficence as a prima facie duty means that the justified use of force must hurdle over the obstacles presumed in the duty not to harm, but those hurdles are not first principles. Moreover, as I have said, even after a prima facie duty is overridden, it leaves moral traces in the situation or in the subsequent course of action.

Just-war ideas developed along the lines of prima facie duties are structured by a conflict of duties, and once nonmaleficence is overridden it nonetheless casts a shadow over the remaining course of action.

Aiken calls the final and most general level of discourse the postethical level. Beyond this point no further ethical questions can be raised, for one is confronted with the most basic question, Why be moral? To Aiken, this question admits of no definitive rational solution. Rather, we must accede to the existentialist insight about moral life, namely, that "no purely logical or metaphysical 'reason' can bind a man to any obligation whatsoever," that only by "gratuitous decision" do we ever answer the postethical question. In order to move the will at all toward morality, Aiken concludes, a fundamental leap is necessary: "Decision is king."[97]

Yet at this level of discourse Aiken may have left behind one of his most fundamental insights, namely, the importance of tradition, ethical language, and communal values in moral experience.[98] Rather than embrace the individualist and decisionist resolution to the postethical question, it is also possible—and, in my judgment, more plausible—to refer to the customs of tradition and history, the deposit of conventional wisdom about our social relations, in order to address the question, Why be moral? True, reference to custom and culture may provide no surer rational warrant than does individual decision. But Aiken simplifies rather than amplifies the nature of moral experience by confining the place of custom to the second level in his taxonomy. Customs inscribed in cultural or religious traditions provide not only specific classifications and codes of action. They also provide the place through which the ethos of a culture "breathes," where more general, less articulate beliefs are enshrined. The beliefs of a culture and its religions, the less articulated "common sense," move the will to act no less, and probably more, than individual volition in which decision is king.

When seen as a datum of common sense, religious belief, or customary values, nonmaleficence attains a wide and suggestive range of metaphors to express its postethical meaning. Most basically, nonmaleficence suggests a bias against suffering, intolerance of humiliation, respect for human dignity, and compassion for those who are victims of dangerous powers beyond their control. The duty not to harm, then, suggests the duty to listen to the cries of pain and infirmity, to heed the lamentations of those who are agonized or alienated. It thus includes the mandate to hear alternative voices, to reckon with disturbing, disorienting, perhaps adversarial utterances: the elegies of those otherwise forgotten in the travails of history. Indeed, the duty not to harm is hardly intelligible apart from a general sense that injury is at least presumptively wrong, to which sorrow and mourning, if not guilt, are the appropriate responses. Without such a bias against suffering it would hardly make sense to respond to calamitous twists of fate as tragic and regrettable. Lacking sensitivity to suffering, in short, we would reside in a culture in which compassion is trivialized, reduced to a matter of taste or idiosyncrasy, held up as a supererogatory sentiment rather than a moral virtue.

At this postethical level, the duty of nonmaleficence in fact enshrines both a religious awe for the sacredness of life and a philosophical respect for human dignity and solidarity. Indeed, at this level it becomes possible to ascertain how, as Childress remarks, "the claim that injury and killing are prima facie wrong is . . . compatible with a number of philosophical and religious frameworks."[99] Nonmaleficence in fact enjoys a wide currency today. The duty not to harm and the intolerance of cruelty are firmly embedded in the vocabularies of Kantians, Aristotelians, postmodern critics of traditional moral philosophy, and recent theologians. Consider a few prominent examples.

Among Kantians, the duty not to harm follows straightforwardly from the critique of heteronomy and the second formulation of the categorical imperative, the duty to treat all persons as ends in themselves and not merely as means. Alan Gewirth, for example, provides one of the clearest formulations of this Kantian position. According to Gewirth, all persons have rights to freedom and well-being by virtue of the logical implications of human agency qua agency. To deny others freedom and well-being would be to act under the pain of contradiction, denying others those conditions for action required by our own action. For Gewirth, the general rights to freedom and well-being can be derived by first excavating the a priori conditions of action and then extending those conditions to all persons according to the principle of generalizability. And, since rights are claims that individuals have on each other, the rights of one party entail a corresponding set of duties, incumbent on others: "Human rights are requirements in the sense of justified demands against other persons, the Respondents. These have the correlative duties at least not to interfere with the Subjects' having the necessary goods of action, and in certain circumstances they also have the correlative duties to assist or see to it that the Subjects have these goods."[100]

In this context, then, the duty not to harm would be correlative with the right not to be harmed. Such a right would derived, like the right of freedom, by excavating the necessary conditions of human action and then generalizing the implications of such conditions to all people similarly situated. Without the right not to be harmed (which generates the duty of nonmaleficence incumbent on others) we would lack protection against encroachment or interference, necessary conditions of human agency. According to Gewirth, such a negative duty is prior to and stricter than positive duties, which generate moral expectations only when the situation permits.[101]

Within a teleological framework, in contrast, the logical order of rights and duties is reversed: rights are derived from the prior duty of self-perfection, the proper goal of human flourishing. So Henry Veatch constructs his retrieval of a natural law ethic. For Veatch, unlike Gewirth, rights are unintelligible without reference to objective interests that define the goals of human well-being. Argues Veatch, "Given the notion of an end or goal or perfection of human life that is determined by man's nature, it follows that the business of living, for a human being, must consist of an ongoing enterprise of trying to become and be simply what one ought to be. That is, because man's natural end is determined . . . by nature, that end will be obligatory."[102] Rights are those claims possessed by individuals, providing them with necessary conditions for acquitting the obligation of self-perfection. Veatch remarks, "My being under obligation to do thus and so implies that I have a right not to be interfered with or prevented from discharging my duty."[103]

Central to Veatch's argument is a variant of the ethical maxim, "ought implies can." This means that possessing the duty of self-perfection implies moral protection against others who might hinder one from realizing such a duty. Without such protection, the requirement to fulfill the duty of self-perfection would be beyond our reach.

In this teleological context, then, an argument on behalf of the duty of nonmaleficence would take the following form: If, as Veatch argues, the duty of self-perfection entails rights which protect us against interference, then the *right not to be injured* follows from the duty to pursue our perfection. For, without such a right, it would be absurd to insist on the imperative of self-perfection, or to create moral expectations accordingly. Moreover, given the principle of generalizability, the "right not to be injured" entails the "right not to be injured for all persons similarly situated." In this way Veatch is able to argue on behalf of the duty not to injure others, the duty of nonmaleficence, since the general right not to be injured generates the correlative duty, incumbent on others, not to harm.

Despite their different starting points, both Gewirth and Veatch argue from the conviction that we can build a bridge to social ethics after developing an understanding of the self, that we can develop a social morality according to basic premises about the requirements of human agency or human flourishing. They thus stand in stark contrast with the postmodernist theory of Richard Rorty, who seeks sharply to divide private from public morality. According to Rorty, there is no such thing as a self with constitutive dimensions "deep down," no a priori conditions of action nor a telos of human well-being. Thus, moral philosophies like those developed by Gewirth and Veatch are wholly misguided. Instead, Rorty would have us embrace the belief, traceable to Nietzsche and Freud, in the contingency of the self and ethics. Remarks Rorty, there is no humanity "with an intrinsic nature, an intrinsic set of powers to be developed or left undeveloped." Rather, Freud and Nietzsche require us to turn away from the notion of paradigmatic humanness to the recognition of "the idiosyncratic contingencies of our individual pasts, to the blind impress all our behavings bear." And if there is no intrinsic nature to the self, there can be no morality based on autonomy or self-perfection. Our morality, science, poetry are not "products of distinct faculties but . . . alternative modes of adaptation."[104]

Rorty's claims are designed not to jettison public morality altogether, but to sever its ties from metaphysical accounts of human nature. Social morality consists for Rorty in our capacity to remain sensitive to cruelty and suffering. For such sensitivity we need no theory of the self, no account of common and essential humanness as a foundation of human rights, no "wish to be kind to be bolstered by an argument." All we need is "a sense of a common danger," premised on the liberal belief that "cruelty is the worst thing we do."[105] We share with other humans not a common essence in which we can participate, but "the ability to feel pain."[106]

Rorty thus attempts to hold together a theory of the postmodern self with the possibilities for social ethics without building a philosophical bridge from the former to the latter. But his recipe for a public morality, novel as it appears, nonetheless trades on the same idiom central to my argument about pluralism and Western moral vocabularies about war. Rorty's account of what alerts us to others, "the ability to feel pain," is but a trope of the duty of nonmaleficence. Solidarity for Rorty is an expression of compassion or empathy for those who are vulnerable to humiliation, torture, or degradation, a form of horror in the face of cruelty. The duty of nonmaleficence, perhaps a less elegant trope, can be thus construed as a distillation of our moral vocabulary about suffering, one of those "platitudes which contextually define the terms of a final vocabulary currently in use."[107]

Doubtless solidarity, "the ability to feel pain," and the platitude of nonmaleficence are but secular versions of a prior theological vocabulary in the West. At the very least, these terms are now compatible with broad and diverse currents in secular moral philosophy. Yet for those who, unlike Rorty, refuse to forswear the vocabulary of religion, nonmaleficence has important theological resonances. In such a context the duty not to harm expresses a conviction that creation is a relative good and that injury or killing constitutes a loss to the general fabric of the divine creative design. As Barth recognized perhaps more clearly than any other theological writer, the problem of killing raises religious questions about usurping divine sovereignty over matters of life and death. For this reason, Barth places his discussion of killing and war in a volume devoted to the doctrine of creation. For Barth, the sixth commandment is but one expression of the general theological conviction that humans are not the final arbiters of life, that the sacredness of life establishes a firm presumption against harming other members of the created order.

Similar inferences about nonmaleficence can also be drawn from a reservoir of religious beliefs about salvation. In Western religion, soteriological language is defined as deliverance from a life that is in some sense lacking and vulnerable. As David H. Smith remarks, "If human persons were not alienated, alone, sick and starving—if human existence were not in some way deficient—then there would be nothing gained from communion with God."[108] In this general religious vein, then, the duty not to harm gains postethical intelligibility from beliefs about the promise of deliverance from the limited and fragile conditions of everyday life. If suffering were not at least a presumptive wrong, then the benefits implied by deliverance would make little sense.

The bias against suffering, cruelty, and injury, then, has currency with a variety of philosophical and religious outlooks. It coheres with several of what Rorty calls our final vocabularies, those postethical convictions beyond which we cannot proceed to justify our moral terms. Seen in this light, the duty not to harm provides what Rawls calls a "weak premise" for ethical inquiry, a noncontroversial starting point from which to build our moral interpretations.[109]

In a liberal culture, this bias against injury, cruelty, and suffering fails to draw distinctions between near and remote neighbors, familiar and unfamiliar, kith and stranger. Rather, nonmaleficence as a postethical value expresses nonpreferential compassion, an undiscriminating empathy for others. However, such nonpreferentialism is not designed to efface differences in culture, custom, class, language, race, or gender, bathing all persons under the soft and romantic light of "humanism." Indeed, as Kierkegaard well knew, the real danger to a culture's well-being occurs when it fails to define boundaries, to classify relationships, and to distinguish patterns of behavior.[110] Instead, the nonpreferentialism implied by this postethical account of nonmaleficence is designed to prevent such differences from becoming *differences of value,* ontological differences in which race, gender, or social background become differences of moral weight.[111]

From Convergence to Further Inquiry

Clarifying the duty of nonmaleficence and its implications in light of Aiken's taxonomy may seem all too abstract and esoteric, inching us up toward the high road, which I promised in the Introduction to eschew. However, the idea that pacifism and just-war tenets share a point of contiguity can be given further ethical substance, and can bring us to some more tangible moral issues, if we return to the problems found in the Augustinian, Thomistic, modern Protestant, contemporary Catholic, and practical convergences adduced above. Each of these problems allows us to see more clearly a range of issues about which pacifists and just-war theorists may have common concern, about which I shall soon speak in more detail.

Contrary to Augustine's views, a coherent convergence of pacifism and just-war tenets places some restrictions on pacifist ideas. Such a convergence makes it necessary to rule out nonresistant pacifism, requiring instead some forms of resistance. If there is a duty to protect others or the community (a just-war tenet), then there is a subordinate, relative, instrumental, but not insignificant duty to protect oneself. Self-preservation, in the form of either attack or nonviolent resistance, need not be a self-centered ethic, but can derive from the duty to protect the vulnerable neighbor.

The ethical position implied by this criticism of Augustine, requiring self-defense through some form of resistance, may take the direction of physical harm or nonviolent resistance. Either method can be ordered to the final goal of self-defense. This means that one key difference between just-war ideas and nonviolent resistance lies not, strictly speaking, at the level of intention or goal, since the intention of either must be at least instrumental self-defense. Rather, the difference lies at the level of methods, determined in terms of proportionality. While ordered to the same overall goal, just-war tenets and the ethic of nonviolent resistance diverge at the point where one must decide *how much* resistance is acceptable in self-defense. Those who embrace nonviolent resistance draw the line earlier than does the just-war theorist, arguing that to kill or physically to harm another person in self-defense is, in the final analysis, disproportionate. The just-war tradition draws the line later, on one side of which it is permissible intentionally to harm or kill attackers, but not those who are innocent of aggression.[112] The two approaches, then, do not differ about the morality of the goal or about the necessity of drawing limits, but only about *where* the limits are to be drawn.

Contrary to the Thomistic convergence, in which moral accountability is located high up in the chain of authority, a coherent account of the relation between just-war tenets and pacifism creates some moral expectations for those participating in a war. What may have distinguished pacifism from just-war tenets in the past—and what may distinguish the two camps today in the minds of many—is that for the pacifist war is an intensely moral and personal decision. To object to war puts one on the edge of the community, isolating the pacifist and sharpening his or her alien status vis-à-vis the rest. Such isolation no doubt intensifies the personal aspects of dissent, requiring fortitude and tenacity to resist the pressures of the collective will. The historic impressiveness of such tenacity has produced the idea that the pacifist is uniquely eligible to dissent from participating in war, an idea enshrined in earlier U.S. law prohibiting anyone but religious pacifists from objecting conscientiously to war.[113] But if the convergence of pacifism and just-war ideas has any merit beyond an esoteric level, then the question of war's morality should be a grave, personal, individual decision for all, participant and objector alike. And, such decisions are not only confined to the matter of participating in war, but also extend to the means of participation. One of the pressures placed by pacifism on moral discourse about war accentuates the gravity of the participant's accountability in the heat of warfare, requiring a complex mixture of obedience and moral freedom in the chain of military command.

For similar reasons it is necessary to reject the Barthian convergence. Barth's problem is a theological hyperextension of Aquinas's, in which the chain of command is located in the authority of God's sovereign will. In the emergency wrought by war, such authority evacuates the individual's need for the virtue of prudence, for drawing distinctions and defining limits. If the presumption against harm has any effect once it has been overridden, then it must leave moral traces, requiring the agents of war to be discriminating and prudent in the exercise of force.

Against the Calhoun Commission, I have sought to show the currency of nonmaleficence in a variety of contexts, moving outside any single religious point of view. The duty not to harm and the bias against suffering are compatible with but not exclusive to Christian tenets. Efforts to see the relation of pacifism and just-war tenets in such terms are likely to be more successful than the Calhoun Commission's attempt to resist cultural Christianity.

Contrary to the contemporary Catholic convergence, it is necessary to define more carefully the responsibilities of the pacifist given the constraints provided by the state's duty to protect its citizens against attack. Minimally, this would mean that the pacifist is obligated to contribute some form of assistance to ameliorate the ravages of war, to embody a bias against suffering in the form of compassionate, humanitarian work. The role of pacifists in war, then, would be understood as an alternative form of participation, not nonparticipation. Moreover, such a role would have no room for those who wish to obstruct a just war by, e.g., generating popular dissent or civil turmoil. Civic responsibility and civic virtue are expected of pacifists no less than of nonpacifists, prohibiting acts or programs whose intent is to obfuscate the cause of justice and the state's duty of justifiable, yet limited, defense.

Finally, against the practical convergence, it should be evident that the other convergences adduced above—despite their defects—raise a host of theoretical and practical issues for pacifists and just-war theorists to consider, beyond that of applying just-war tenets to the horrific possibility of modern war. The dialectical relation between pacifism and just-war tenets to be examined in this work, as described in the Introduction, can now be clarified in light of the issues raised by these prior accounts. Henceforth we shall proceed self-reflexively, but intertextually, by addressing a range of issues posed from *within* moral discourse about war.

The Augustinian and Thomistic concern for peace-as-order and the presumption against harm will be explored in the next chapter. There I examine how a bias against violence gains its intelligibility from the moral value of order, and how this approach draws from classical beliefs about civic friendship. Then I trace the shifts in conceptual schemes according to which a presumption against harm has been embraced in Catholicism, looking at the relation between justice and order in the hierarchy of Catholic values.

The modern Protestant convergence focuses theologically on the sovereignty of God and ethically on the notion of war as an extraordinary problem in moral experience. In chapter 4 I will join the notion of non-maleficence to the notion that war is an extraordinary affair on the landscape of moral life. There I will seek to show how the convergence of pacifism and just-war tenets along the lines of nonmaleficence is compatible with something like Barth's version of war as an ultima ratio, at the limit of limits. In chapter 5 I will examine theological belief in the sovereignty of God in the work of H. Richard Niebuhr, one of the architects of the Calhoun report and a critic of pacifists and nonpacifists alike during the 1930s and 1940s. Niebuhr's approach includes an important retrieval of a bias against suffering in interpretations of conflict, some aspects of which draw from the Augustinian convergence. Moreover, Niebuhr's Augustinian notions are appropriated in the nuclear context by Paul Ramsey, whose views I will examine in chapter 6. There I will return to my account of nonmaleficence and just-war tenets to provide a corrective to Ramsey's treatment of responsible statecraft.

The contemporary Catholic convergence embraces both pacifism and just-war criteria, allowing individuals to choose either option as a means of protecting human rights. Chapter 2 will show how this qualified embrace of pacifism gains intelligibility from the traditional value of order, as I indicated above. Chapter 3, on Catholic pacifism, will allow me to amplify my criticisms of Augustine's requirement of nonresistant pacifism, and to clarify what I mean about pacifists' duties during wartime. Contemporary Catholic applications of just-war criteria to public policy, moreover, will be central to my criticisms of efforts by the U.S. Catholic bishops and Hollenbach to justify nuclear deterrence, in chapter 7.

Perhaps more than the other convergences, the practical convergence raises the question of moral reasoning, which will serve as the chief topic in chapters 8 and 9. There I will try to answer several questions: Is it not the case that judgments about the morality of war rely on a prior interpretation of the meaning of war and its purposes? What, then, are the historical and hermeneutical aspects of practical reasoning for pacifists and just-war theorists engaged in interpreting the morality of conflict? How else might the duty not to harm be relevant to the interpretations of conflict, given the broader implications of nonmaleficence at the postethical level of discourse?

From the contiguous point of nonmaleficence we may now inquire further into the ethics of war, preparation for which is provided by Western ethicists from Augustine to the present day. To additional reflections on the moral caution about violence in discourse about war, and the terms according to which that caution is intelligible in Catholic ethics, we shall now turn.

PART TWO

ROMAN CATHOLIC AND PROTESTANT APPROACHES

T W O

The Just War and Civil Conflict: Changing Paradigms in Roman Catholic Social Ethics

> The problem is no longer one of tradition, of
> tracing a line, but one of division, of limits; it
> is no longer one of lasting foundations, but one
> of transformations that serve as new founda-
> tions, the rebuilding of foundations.
>
> > Michel Foucault,
> > *The Archaeology of Knowledge*

Moral Grammar in Transition

In the last chapter I briefly suggested that Aquinas develops a bias against suffering and the moral presumption against harm from the imperative to preserve order. I also suggested that this imperative provides a somewhat different basis for prohibiting violence than the restrictions placed on harming others owing to the virtue of charity. In this chapter I will explore in more detail how a moral presumption against harming others gains its intelligibility from the moral imperative to preserve order, especially civic friendship, in Thomas's thought and in contemporary Catholic social ethics. I will show that, contrary to the widespread notion that justice is the sole or chief principle in just-war thinking, order has a relative priority over justice in Catholic thinking about violence, often requiring individuals or groups to suffer injustice rather than disturb the wider social order. Evidence for this fact is available not in Catholic discussions of charity or peace, where ethicists have tended to focus their interpretations,[1] but in the logic that rules Catholic approaches to war and revolution.

Thomas is heir to a relatively well-developed body of thought about the morality of conflict between or within political regimes. The just-war tradition, with its origins in the work of Augustine, and medieval theories of tyrannicide, rooted in the writings of John of Salisbury, furnish prior rationales for using lethal force in emergencies between or within communities. Yet this traditional approach about the morality of violence is presently undergoing subtle stresses in official Catholic teaching, Latin American liberation theology, and less radical Catholic ethics in North America. Complex factors—ranging from the existence of sovereign states and nuclear capabilities in an increasingly interdependent world order, to explosive social unrest in the third world—have posed new problems, unforeseen by those who crafted, or worked within, the traditional paradigm in Catholic social thought.

Perhaps most notable about the ferment in Roman Catholicism is the fact that the values of justice and order, especially the order of friendship and peaceful unity, have undergone a subtle alteration, reversing the grammar that structures moral reasoning about war, peace, and violence. Recent discussions have brought large fragments of the classical paradigm to bear on modern problems only by altering the terms and priorities of the traditional framework. Murmurings of the traditional legacy remain audible, but they are now ruled in a new conceptual field. On the one hand, there is a basic caution about the use of force in official pronouncements about global order; on the other hand, there is a relatively permissive attitude among liberation theologians about the use of force on behalf of justice in civil conflict. Caution about war within the compass of just-war reasoning, coupled with a relatively open attitude about violence in civil conflict, reverses the attitudes and logic of the classical paradigm. Indeed, contemporary discussions of war between polities are framed by an account of global relations that echoes classical thinking about civil war, while the use of force in civil conflict today is conceived in terms similar to the background assumptions of classic just-war reasoning.

To clarify the terms of Catholic thinking on war and civil conflict, I will outline the basic structure of the classical paradigm by examining the moral logic of Aquinas on tyrannicide and war, focusing carefully on the nuances that distinguish his reasoning about tyrannicide from his treatment of the just war. I will then turn to contemporary discussions in Catholic circles to show how and why the classical paradigm changed. This change will explain how the modern paradigm introduces moral terms which give rise to two unprecedented emphases in recent Catholic social ethics: the morality of pacifism in discourse about just wars, and the immorality of acts of omission in assessments of civil conflict.

Moreover, as we shall see, in either the traditional or modern approaches to conflict, attitudes toward violence depend on how the enemy, "the other," is perceived in relation to the community. Generally, such attitudes depend on whether the unjust foe is connected with or alienated from the civil order. The willingness to use violence is directly proportional to the otherness, the cultural or political distance, of the unjust foe. And this relation between violence and otherness is scarcely new: it is deeply rooted in the classical paradigm about the use of force. This means that attitudes toward violence may change as we adopt a different vantage point toward those who are unjust. So throughout this chapter I will attempt to decipher the place of the other in relation to communal order and the effect of the other's presence on attitudes toward violence in Catholic ethics. I will then conclude by discussing the significance of otherness and order in relation to justice in Catholic thinking about social conflict.

The Classical Paradigm

Aquinas's work represents, more than any other medieval thinker's, the classical paradigm for thinking about war and civil conflict because he carefully distills medieval thought about the relation between law, morality, and political arrangements, and because his own contribution to the issue of tyrannicide became authoritative for future discussions. That his work assigns a relative autonomy to the discipline of political science in his theological system reflects strong currents in medieval culture, where political arrangements slowly gained autonomy from religious control.[2] Whether Thomas is rehearsing widespread medieval notions or thinking originally, however, his thought displays the tensions between justice and order when considering the use of force.

Aquinas places the problem of tyrannicide in the wider context of his theory of political life and the basis and limits of political authority. In these more general matters he articulates the medieval understanding of the role of the community and its relation to law, as well as the medieval preference for monarchy as the ideal form of rule.[3] Following Aristotle, Aquinas conceives of the polity as a natural institution, a product of native social inclinations, necessary for the perfection of human nature.[4] Thus, the polity is to be guided by the laws of nature, conceived as dictates of practical reason available in principle to all rational creatures. All law for Aquinas must be "an ordinance of reason, directed to the common good, and promulgated by the sovereign."[5] The natural law, promulgated by God, is inscribed in human reason, constituting a set of unchanging general principles against which to measure particular human laws, or positive law, promulgated by the monarch.[6] Indeed, the order of nature— the fact that all things are ordained to their respective natural ends—is an effect of God's rule, for "God is the cause of the entire order of things, and consequently He is the governor of the whole universe by His providence."[7]

As a product of human social inclinations, moreover, the secular polity clearly differs from its supernatural counterpart, the church. Thomas defines the church as a mystical body, a collectivity whose members extend across time, both past and future.[8] Although Thomas articulates a characteristically medieval outlook about secular polity, he stands outside those currents in later medieval thought which progressively conceived of the polity as a secular *corpus mysticum,* a sempiternal reality.[9] Rather, the polity for Thomas is a wholly natural reality, composed of citizens who coexist within the finitude of time.

Political monarchs are thus subject to the dictates of the natural law, especially the requirement that the sovereign is to protect the common good. For Thomas, the sovereign is above the law, *legibus solutus,* only in its "coercive force," since there is no higher authority to enforce the law's demands on an uncooperative monarch. But the sovereign remains subject to the law in its "directive force," its rational dictates, and every ruler worthy of the name will submit to it voluntarily.[10] Accordingly, about the Justinian dictum, "Quod principi placuit habet legibus vigorem" (whatever pleases the prince has the force of law), Thomas writes that, in order to have the nature of law, a command "needs to be in accord with some rule of reason."[11] Hence, for Aquinas the sovereign is absolute only in the strict legal sense, namely, that no higher human authority exists to impose legal obligation upon him.[12]

But this is not all there is to be said about immoral sovereigns, or tyrants. On the issue of the supreme limit of political authority—the tyrant who may, for moral reasons, be killed—Thomas develops a series of distinctions, found first in his *Commentary on the Sentences of Peter Lombard* (1252–56).[13] First, there is the tyrant whose title to the throne is defective (a usurper), either because the person is unworthy or because that person acquired power through violence and coercion of the citizenry. When ruled by an unworthy sovereign, Thomas notes, citizens are obligated to remain obedient because such defects are not impediments to legitimate authority, which derives finally from God. But the acquisition of power by violence and coercion is an impediment to legitimate authority, and individuals are free to reject such an authority unless it has become legitimate through subsequent public consent or intervention by a higher legitimate authority. In those cases when there remains no legitimate title, however, the usurper may be killed by an individual, as Cicero argues in *De Officiis* about the killing of Julius Caesar. About Cicero's argument, Aquinas concurs: "In such a case, one who liberates his country by killing a tyrant is to be praised and rewarded."[14]

A second form of tyranny, distinct from that of the usurper, is that of the sovereign who forfeits legitimate authority by abusing regal power. If the sovereign's commands are contrary to virtue, the citizen is not only free to disobey, but is obliged to disobey. If the sovereign's commands exceed the competence of his authority, the citizen is free to obey or disobey. But in neither case does Thomas provide a warrant for active public or individual resistance, understood as violent rebellion or tyrannicide. Thus, there are no final limits or restrictions for the tyrant who abuses rightful authority.[15]

In a subsequent discussion of tyranny, *On Princely Government* (1263–67), Thomas amends his position. Focusing exclusively on the tyrant who abuses rightful authority—one who "substitutes his private interest for the common welfare of the citizens"[16]—Aquinas provides a highly qualified justification for insurrection. According to Thomas, a moderate amount of tyranny may be tolerated, "at least for a time, rather than run the risk of even greater perils by opposing it."[17] Such risks include the danger of rousing the tyrant to greater savagery, breeding greater factionalism in the populace, or creating conditions for a new and even more severe form of tyrannical rule. It would be too dangerous, moreover, to allow private individuals to slay the tyrant because as a matter of fact it is "more common for evildoers than for just men to expose themselves to such dangers."[18] Allowing individuals the right to depose the tyrant would jeopardize the just ruler more often than the unjust ruler. Thus, unless the right to appoint the prince belongs to some superior authority, the solution to tyranny lies in some public check on the abuse of power, especially where the community elects the ruler for itself. A public assembly, representing the community, may either curb the tyrant's power or may depose the sovereign should no other remedy be available.[19]

What is noteworthy about *On Princely Government* is not that Thomas repudiates his earlier position, as is widely held, but that he *amplifies* his justification of civil conflict and insurrection.[20] In his earlier position, Thomas provides the right for an individual to kill a *usurper;* that he later provides the right for some public authority to depose the tyrant who *abuses* rightful authority marks not a repudiation, but an addition to his argument. True, Thomas does not argue on behalf of killing the tyrant-by-abuse, but he does open a door in *On Princely Government* that had been closed in his work. In the *Commentary on the Sentences* Thomas does not grant to anyone the right to depose the tyrant who abuses rightful power, while in *On Princely Government* he grants this right to a public authority of some kind. Accordingly, the correct formulation of Thomas's position, taking together both of these works, is as follows: The individual has the right, under strict conditions, to kill the tyrant-by-defect; a public authority has the right, under similarly strict conditions, to depose the tyrant-by-abuse.

These distinctions between usurpation and abuse, individual and public authority, and tyrannicide and deposition are left behind in the *Summa Theologiae*, II-II, Q. 42 (1267–72), Thomas's last and most compressed discussion of tyranny.[21] In response to the question, "Whether Sedition Is Always a Mortal Sin?" Thomas maintains that there is no sedition in disturbing an unjust regime, one that is conducive to the private good of the monarch rather than the common good.[22] Indeed, unjust laws are "acts of violence" committed against the community.[23] The *tyrant* is guilty of sedition, and disturbing tyranny is legitimate unless the "consequent disturbance be so excessive that the people suffer more from it than from the tyrannical regime."[24]

What is perhaps most notable about this last discussion is that, with most of Thomas's distinctions gone, the real subtext of his argument comes to the fore. That subtext, as I have suggested above, is the trade-off between the moral values of justice and order. Aquinas holds that, in instances of civil strife, it is imperative to tolerate some measure of injustice for the sake of preserving order. The value of unity and peace, the *ordo pacis,* constitutes a conservative value for Thomas, and a value to be conserved, because it is a condition for political existence. Indeed, sedition, the sin of the tyrant, is opposed to "that special good which is the unity and peace of a people."[25] When the populace rises up to depose the tyrant, there should be some proportion between the values that are jeopardized and those that might be gained. According to Aquinas, there are strong presumptions *against* the notion that the pursuit of justice in civil conflict is a sufficient reason for resorting to lethal force, all else being equal. Instead, the sovereign must be guilty of long-standing oppression: the order must be conserved, not jeopardized, by recourse to rebellion. And in cases in which oppression is *not* severe and long-standing, Thomas maintains that it will be better to suffer some injustice than to risk anarchy. Thus, it is only partially correct to hold that Thomas's treatment of tyrannicide is hedged in by the question of expediency, namely, whether tyrannicide would be an effective solution to oppression.[26] Rather, a moral tension structures Thomas's thinking, where honoring the demands of one value may jeopardize the demands of another. In matters of civil conflict, not all forms of injustice are to be punished or vindicated, but only those which are long-standing and finally intolerable, and only when disturbing an unjust regime will not undermine the peace and unity of the populace. When faced with unjust laws, one may be obliged to obey if obedience is necessary "to avoid scandal or riot." "On this account," Thomas remarks, "a person ought to cede his or her rights."[27]

The importance of order as a moral value and the concomitant imperative to suffer some injustice becomes clearer if we turn to Aquinas's well-known treatment of the just war. Thomas delineates three conditions for a just war: War must be declared by a competent authority; its cause must be just (self-defense, restoring rights and property, and avenging injustice); and peace, understood as the restoration of right relations, must be the intention of the belligerents involved in the war.[28] The logic here is that an act of violence is presumptively wrong, but not absolutely wrong without further description. Such an act receives its overall moral character—what Thomas calls its "moral species"—according to the goal to which it is ordered, within a set of circumstances.[29] For the sake of vindicating justice (goal) after one has suffered an attack (circumstances), the use of lethal force may have a commendable moral species, that is, a just cause. Moreover, conflicting parties in war are construed according to an ethical zero-sum game: As long as one side remains within the compass of Thomas's three criteria, relevant moral differences between two parties are absolute, for the *ad bellum* justification of one cause entails the (prior) injustice of the other.

It would seem fitting to view Thomas's argument about tyrannicide as a logical extension of his more general justification of a just war, since the conditions defined for war could pertain to violence *ad intra* as well as *ad extra*. Thomas could then simply transfer the terms for thinking about war to the case posed by the unjust sovereign. In both cases, Aquinas might add, harm is permissible if it remains beside the intention of those carrying out acts of violence, or if intentional harm against enemies is ordered to aims broader than vindicating justice alone. Aquinas would then appear to have crafted the ethics of individual self-defense, corporate defense *ad extra*, and corporate defense *ad intra* within a uniform logic. In all three cases, Thomas seems to reason by analogy about violence to individual and corporate bodies: Acts which are justified in terms of "bodily" self-preservation may include violence so long as the harm to others remains *praeter intentionem*, or is ordered by proper authorities to the common good.

Yet Aquinas's ethics of civil strife is in fact more complex than a reading from analogical reasoning might initially suggest. Insurrection differs from war in one very significant respect. In the case of war, Aquinas assumes that *order has already broken down* due to violence wrought by an alien force. As he notes, war is different from civil conflict in that war is waged "against an external enemy [*contra extraneos et hostes*], one nation as it were against another."[30] In contrast to sedition, war presupposes an *other*, one who stands outside, and seeks to subvert, the *ordo pacis*.

This fact of otherness, or this presence of radical *difference*, thus allows Aquinas to consider war in relation to justice without having to weigh the requirements of peace and unity. Since order has broken down, we are not obliged to calculate the proportion between the values lost to order and those gained on behalf of justice. In fact, violence is construed in the context of a just war as *restoring* the status quo of peace, which has been upset by a prior attack. The values of justice and order remain in principle here, yet the case of war allows the value of order to recede quietly as a competing term in Thomas's discussion of violence. And once order recedes, the direction of Aquinas's thought unveils the necessary condition that distinguishes war from insurrection. War, unlike tyranny, presupposes radical difference, carried on against an enemy from without. Doubtless, both the external foe and the tyrant are enemies of the common good. But the latter, unlike the former, commits sedition, which "is between mutually dissident sections of the same people."[31]

This value of order and its underside, the phenomenon of otherness, require Thomas to conceive of war and tyrannicide in subtly different terms. The values of order and unity of the polity require Aquinas to think about tyrannicide with hesitations and caution; the justice of civil rebellion is not unqualified, for such rebellion may implicate its agents in even graver dangers than those posed by the unjust regime. But these hesitations are absent when it comes to war. There are no competing values to consider, fewer cautions against resorting to force, and no injustices to suffer, because the presence of the other, the "external enemy," has destroyed the status quo of order. And, because order ceases to compete with justice, Aquinas may proceed without hesitating into a declaration of cause, authority, and right intention as conditions for a just war.

That Thomas is more cautious about the use of force in the case of insurrection than in war is a testimony to his indebtedness to Aristotle. Especially important is Aristotle's understanding of *philia*—or friendship, including kinship and civil fellowship—as a crucial element in political existence, and a rightful moral value as such.[32] Kinship and civil fellowship have value for Thomas—indeed, they are objects of "piety"—because our parents and our country are principles of our being, second only to God, who is the first principle.[33] Some neighbors, especially those who are kin and fellow countrymen, are special to us because they "are close to us by natural origin, from which they can never get away, since it is this that makes them what they are."[34] Friends are also necessary for the development of *eudaimonia,* to which the polity as a whole must be ordered. For Thomas as for Aristotle, civil order is a natural and moral good, necessary for human flourishing and a life of virtue. Given the value of civil fellowship, it is no exaggeration to say about Aquinas's notions of temporal life what Alasdair MacIntyre says about Aristotle's: "Civil war is the worst of evils."[35]

Equally important, moreover, is Augustine's influence on Aquinas's thinking about the value of concord and the dangers of conflict in political regimes. Following Augustine's remarks in *The City of God,* Aquinas defines peace as "the tranquillity of order" and concurs that peace is a goal toward which all things naturally tend.[36] For Augustine this tranquillity denotes the state of quiescence, which derives from properly ordered relations between individuals. Similarly, Aquinas understands concord as a fruit of charity, which "joins the hearts of many into one focal point."[37] For both Aquinas and Augustine the notions of tranquillity and concord establish a presumption against conflict, for conflict is a symptom of unsatisfied ambition, contrary to the elementary inclinations of nature and the infusion of charity. Conflict does not structure historical change or social relations as it does for more radical thinkers in modern Catholicism

Chapter Two

and contemporary ethics; rather, conflict signals the breakdown of order and peaceful unity. It is a symptom of human pride and disordered reason. Accordingly, Thomas prescribes caution when conflict infects the political community.

These Aristotelian and Augustinian elements lead Thomas to assign a moral value to life-in-community itself.[38] They also suggest an order of charity about enemies within and without the community. Enemies within the community, by virtue of the fact that they share a kinship of origin, are to be tolerated more than enemies from without. An order of charity is implied because the intramural enemy must be granted concessions that would be inappropriate in relation to the extramural enemy. Ties to the latter enemy are more remote, requiring what I called in chapter 1 an ethic of generic benevolence. While this benevolence entails a presumption against harm, it does not go so far as to tolerate injury to the body politic. Hence, Aquinas's order of charity entails a greater caution about resort to force *ad intra* than *ad extra*.[39]

Having noted the caution that distinguishes Thomas's treatment of insurrection from this discussion of war, we can now trace the convergence that unites them: Insurrection, like war, needs proper authority (the public assembly, in the case of the tyrant who abuses rightful power); its cause must be just, namely, the protection of the common good against a foe; and its intention must be ordered toward restoring public peace and repairing justice. But so long as the tyrant does not wholly undermine order, the use of force against tyranny finds insufficient justification in these three criteria, implicating insurrectionists in a wider set of moral evils than those perpetrated by the enemy, the unjust ruler. Seen in this way, Aquinas *does* reason like a good casuist, i.e., by analogy, from one ethical case about "bodily" violence to another. But as with all such analogical reasoning, it is important to be alert to similarities as well as to differences between cases, lest those differences be lost in a quest for ethical simplicity.

Excellent recent historical surveys show how this classical paradigm underwent slow but important permutations in the changing political, economic, and religious world of western Europe in the sixteenth and seventeenth centuries.[40] Both the emergence of the sovereign nation-state as a new center of political authority and the Protestant Reformation eroded the political and spiritual bonds of the Christian commonwealth, which Aquinas could take for granted.[41] Further, the discovery of the New World and the pillaging of native Americans created new moral problems, at least for those working in the classical paradigm, about the limits of violence against "heathens." In this new context, Vitoria shifted the emphasis of just-war thought from *ad bellum* criteria to a concentration on *in bello* criteria for limiting the use of force, especially against nonbelligerents.[42] Concurrently, among those considering the use of force against tyrants, the door was opened slightly wider than Thomas allowed in justifying the use of force in civil conflict: Mariana, a seventeenth-century Jesuit, argued that once the public authority has deemed the sovereign a tyrant-by-abuse, a private individual has the right to kill the monarch.[43]

These developments adumbrate contemporary discussions of war and civil conflict in Catholic ethics. But it is not until the twentieth century—especially with the emergence of nuclear technology, increased international trade, widespread insurrection in colonized regimes, and growing disaffection with Western capitalism—that the classical paradigm as a whole has undergone dramatic stress. It has been left to contemporary Catholics to radicalize the progressively cautious attitude about just war, and the progressively permissive attitude about insurrection, that emerged in the Spanish Scholasticism of the sixteenth and seventeenth centuries.

The Modern Paradigm: The Just War

The chief link between the classical and the modern paradigm in Roman Catholicism is provided by Pius XII.[44] Notable in this respect was Pius XII's attempt to place just-war considerations in a wider global framework, stressing the need for a more adequate structure to foster international community. Moreover, he reduced the number of criteria of the just cause from three (self-defense, restore rights and property, avenge injustice) to one: self-defense or defense of others being unjustly attacked.[45] Pius XII also qualified his permission of war with an additional moral consideration. Even a just war in self-defense, he writes, "must be waged at the risk of giving a free hand in international affairs to brute violence and lack of conscience." It is not enough, he concludes, "to have to defend oneself against just any injustice in order to justify resorting to the violent means of war. When the dangers caused by war are not comparable to those of 'tolerated injustice,' one may have a duty to 'suffer the injustice.'"[46]

Pius XII thus set in motion what was to become a notable development in subsequent Roman Catholic thought: caution about authorizing, in the name of justice, the recourse to war, given the constraints implied by the value of order—this time, international order. At the same time, however, Pius XII was emphatic that pacifism had no place in Catholic moral theology. It was left for the pontificate of John XXIII, the Second Vatican Council, and postconciliar writings to radicalize the caution and the background considerations that structure Pius XII's position about recourse to lethal force. The relevant texts are *Peace on Earth* (1963), *The Pastoral Constitution of the Church in the Modern World* (1965), and *The Challenge of Peace: God's Promise and Our Response* (1983).

Perhaps the most notable feature of *Peace on Earth* is John XXIII's emphasis on the importance of social relations, global order, and interdependence in human experience. The note is struck in the opening line of the text: "Peace on earth, which all persons of every era have most eagerly yearned for, can be firmly established only if the order laid down by God be dutifully observed."[47] Building on a theme he developed less systematically in *Christianity and Social Progress* (*Mater et Magistra;* 1961), John XXIII delineates four distinct sets of relations within the complex web of human experience: relations between individuals, relations between individuals and states, relations between states themselves, and relations between states and the entire international order. So important are these relations that John XXIII uses each of them as organizing rubrics in all but one of the major divisions of *Peace on Earth*. According to John XXIII, the entire global community is constituted by this network of interrelatedness and interdependence, and is to be ordered according to the dictates of the natural law. To underscore this point he uses the metaphor of the "human family" and the "universal common good" recurrently to define the social unit within which persons are to flourish according to the demands of human dignity.[48] He is also the first pope to address such a document not only to his fellow clergymen and members of the faithful, but "to all persons of good will," underscoring his ecumenical and global orientation.

The effect of John XXIII's ideas is to broaden Catholic vision, in accord with the trajectory set by Pius XII, in a truly global way. Yet operating in this paradigm is just the kind of tension between justice and order that led Aquinas to a relatively cautious position about civil conflict. With John XXIII's approach, war is now seen as a conflict that can seriously affect the wider fabric of global relations. Thus, it should not be surprising that one finds a relatively cautious attitude in *Peace on Earth* about the legitimacy of using lethal force on behalf of justice. As J. Bryan Hehir observes, *Peace on Earth* is alone among the recent papal documents in providing no explicit endorsement of the right of self-defense for peoples and states.[49] Rather, John XXIII writes, there can be "no doubt that relations between states, as between individuals, should be regulated not by the force of arms but by the light of reason, by the rule, that is, of truth, of justice, and of active and sincere cooperation."[50] While not gainsaying just-war reasoning, John XXIII emphasizes instead a wider framework for assessing the morality of violence between nations. Within that framework, tremendous weight is placed on the value of order, complicating the demands of justice as a rationale for recourse to lethal force.

Although John XXIII's virtual silence about just-war ideas and his overtures to the language of peace in *Peace on Earth* resonated strongly with increased pacifistic fervor in Catholicism during the early 1960s, neither his optimistic tone nor the structure of his argument can support a pacifist position, since war is not explicitly banned. Yet the ecumenism, optimism, and rhetoric of the document signaled an important change in

Catholic teaching and provided at least a muted opening to pacifist sentiments. And it is just this opening that is widened two years later in *The Pastoral Constitution,* the final document produced at the Second Vatican Council. Purporting to evaluate the problem of war with "an entirely new attitude," the authors cross the threshold approached by John XXIII by furnishing the first official sanction in Catholic teaching for pacifism as a legitimate option for individuals. The document praises "those who renounce the use of violence in the vindication of their rights."[51] Thus the council endorses laws which accommodate "those who for reasons of conscience refuse to bear arms, provided however, that they accept some other form of service to the human community."[52]

At the same time, *The Pastoral Constitution* provides a more explicit endorsement of just-war ideas than is found in *Peace on Earth,* albeit in an ad hoc, unsystematic way. The council document affirms the legitimate right of self-defense "once every means of peaceful settlement has been exhausted."[53] And the document draws, at least implicitly, on *in bello* considerations of discrimination and proportionality to condemn the use of weapons that inflict "massive and indiscriminate destruction, far exceeding the bounds of legitimate defense."[54]

This simultaneous affirmation of pacifism and just-war ideas is a recent development in Roman Catholicism and must be viewed in light of a new conceptual arrangement for thinking about war and peace. For *The Pastoral Constitution,* as for *Peace on Earth,* the problem of conflict is inscribed in an understanding of global community and the universal common good. The effect of this reconfiguration is to radicalize the notion of *philia* by uniting all persons within the common kinship of the "human family," thus eliminating the hidden feature of Aquinas's argument, the presence of otherness. For Aquinas, war presupposes an other, an "external enemy," who stands apart from the common good and threatens it from without. But by defining conflict in a vision of world order, modern Catholic teaching elides the notion of radical difference from the just-war framework. Thus, it becomes necessary to consider violence in a framework in which "the other" has been domesticated. Then we must recall the subtext of Aquinas's argument about insurrection, namely, that for the sake of order and peaceful unity it may be necessary to suffer injustice rather than risk further dangers to the community. The fact that pacifism has been endorsed within the framework of a reconstructed and expanded notion of human community is an outgrowth—not a linear or mathematically deduced product, but a product nonetheless—of modern Catholic thinking about violence within the trade-offs between justice and peaceful unity. For at the heart of much pacifist thinking is the conviction that, for the sake of moral values like that of peace, we may be required to suffer voluntarily rather than reciprocate an act of violence, however "just" that reciprocation may be.

These papal and conciliar texts on war and peace form tributaries of authoritative Catholic teaching that flow into the U.S. Catholic bishops' pastoral letter, *The Challenge of Peace*.[55] Moral caution about justifying the use of force, coupled with a concern for the moral value of order, is central to four key aspects of the text: the discussion of global interdependence, the endorsement of pacifism, the exposition of just-war ideas, and the moral analysis of nuclear deterrence.

In the third main section of the pastoral letter the bishops articulate a basic feature of Catholic social thought: All persons are united in one human family, "rooted in common creation, destined for the kingdom, and united by moral bonds of rights and duties."[56] They then complement that religious idea by referring to the empirical reality of increased political and economic interdependence throughout the globe. Their point is to provide religious and pragmatic reasons for identifying problems which transcend national boundaries, but which affect all peoples at least indirectly. For the bishops, traditional religious tenets and concrete facts converge at the notion that major global problems—e.g., worldwide inflation, environmental dangers, widespread unemployment—"cannot be remedied by a single nation-state approach."[57] Instead, it is now incumbent on world leaders to consider the tangible benefits of cooperation, to identify and pursue mutual interests. As such, the bishops place superpower antagonisms in the framework of an emerging world order where, for both moral and practical reasons, "states are called to interpret the national interest in light of the larger global interest."[58] Moreover, in keeping with the subtext of the Catholic emphasis on the moral value of order, the bishops' argument attenuates the sense of otherness that fuels superpower rivalry. True, the bishops clearly acknowledge "the differences between the two philosophies and political systems," observing that "diplomatic dialogue usually sees the other as a potential or real adversary." Yet the bishops underscore with greater emphasis "the irreducible truth . . . that objective mutual interests do exist between the superpowers," and that "the Soviet people and their leaders are human beings created in the image and likeness of God."[59] Correcting some of the optimism of *Peace on Earth,* the bishops adopt a more "realistic" perspective, calling for attention to the "concrete if limited" interests shared by the superpowers.[60] But their chief point, whether optimistic or realistic, theological or empirical, accords with John XXIII's vision: The growing interdependence of the globe, and the fact that there are no winners in a nuclear exchange, mandate "new structures of cooperation."[61]

World order is also related to the bishops' moral logic about war and peace. As they remark, the basic fact about human unity and interdependence "pervades the entire teaching on war and peace: for the pacifist position it is one of the reasons why life cannot be taken, while for the just-war position, even in a justified conflict bonds of responsibility remain."[62] Following the trajectory set by *The Pastoral Constitution,* the bishops explicitly affirm pacifism as a legitimate option for individual consciences. Yet, as I noted in the last chapter, the bishops take the relation between pacifism and just-war ideas one step further than *The Pastoral Constitution* by frequently citing a version of Childress's insight: a bias against violence, a moral presumption against killing, constitutes a crucial point of contact between pacifism and just-war tenets.[63] In other words, within a vision framed by the notion of global order and interdependence, the bishops explicitly underscore with technical moral language a caution about recourse to lethal force. They thus emphasize the positive merits of nonviolence and insist that just-war ideas begin "with the presumption *in favor of peace* and *against* war."[64]

This caution about the use of force within a vision of an interdependent globe is amplified in the bishops' explication of just-war ideas, especially the principle of relative justice. That principle, the bishops observe, "stresses that no state should act on the basis that it has 'absolute justice' on its side. Every party to a conflict should acknowledge the limits of its 'just cause' and the consequent requirements to use *only* limited means in pursuit of its objectives."[65] In direct contrast with the traditional paradigm, the moral differences between adversaries are now ruled in new terms—not as an ethical zero-sum game, for the differences between adversaries in the modern global context are relative, not absolute. As a result, it is necessary to consider the recourse to war cautiously, since "the external enemy" has now been conceived intramurally, domesticated in an enveloping global network.

Similarly, in the transition from their list of *ad bellum* categories to *in bello* categories of discrimination and proportionality, the bishops say that they will apply these terms *not only* as criteria for the means of warfare (which is the traditional mode of application), *but also* to the *jus ad bellum.*[66] As earlier papal and conciliar teaching had stated less explicitly, the bishops note that the destructive potential of modern weaponry requires us to weigh the prospective consequences of using lethal force (guided by *in bello* criteria) in the logically prior decision to justify recourse to lethal force (guided by *ad bellum* criteria). This means that the bishops are going beyond the limits implied by Pius XII's reduction of just causes from three to one (self-defense) and his worries about the effects of war on the international order. There is now yet another restriction to consider in calculating the *jus ad bellum:* As a condition for going to war, one must be reasonably certain, *prospectively,* that the methods of war will stand within *in bello* restrictions.

While caution in modern Catholic teaching about recourse to lethal force appears to draw on traditional criteria of justice in war, in fact it echoes the background considerations of Aquinas's treatment of civil conflict and insurrection. Thomas, we should recall, requires us to tolerate a measure of injustice for the sake of order. We may have to suffer some injuries to the common good rather than risk other, more mysterious, but potentially more harmful outcomes. Insurrection is not a moral zero-sum game in which one side's justice entails the other side's injustice, but one in which the entire political structure may collapse, contrary to the interests of all involved, under the weight of unanticipated anarchic forces. Similarly, the notion of world order reconfigures the problem of conflict so that now war ceases to be a moral zero-sum game. Instead, we should recognize that what may begin as a just war can easily escalate to a level of uncontrollable ferocity, of anarchy, taking down all parties involved.

This fear of radical disorder and anarchy lies behind the bishops' discussion of nuclear war, especially their treatment of using nuclear weapons in a first strike. The bishops insist that "the danger of escalation is so great that it would be morally unjustifiable to initiate nuclear war in any form." This judgment suggests that the dangers of anarchy following the initiation of nuclear war are so great that it would be better to suffer tremendous losses than to risk implication in a series of events whose direction may be unmanageable. It also leads the bishops to proscribe the first use of nuclear weapons, even if conventional methods of warfare are failing and the only option left is to cross the nuclear threshold during the course of a just war.[67]

The trade-off between justice and order likewise structures the final point to be examined here, namely, the bishops' treatment of nuclear deterrence. According to the bishops, nuclear deterrence can receive only temporary and highly qualified acceptance. The conditions of such acceptance are three: Nuclear deterrence cannot be linked to war-fighting strategies, for such strategies "encourage notions that nuclear war can be engaged in with tolerable human and moral consequences," thus weakening the goal of deterrence; nuclear deterrence must be detached from the quest for superiority in arms competition; and nuclear deterrence should be used "as a step on the way toward progressive disarmament."[68] These terms constitute a "strictly conditioned moral acceptance of nuclear deterrence."[69]

The bishops evaluate nuclear deterrence with a two-step method. They first evaluate various uses of nuclear weapons according to the canons of just-war ideas. They then argue, using the principle of moral equivalence of action and intention, that acts proscribed by just-war criteria may not be intended for the sake of deterrence. But more important than this method of analyzing deterrence is the bishops' muted confidence that nuclear deterrence has worked thus far to guarantee some measure of order in international relations, however imperfect that order might be. Although the bishops acknowledge that deterrence poses the threat of nuclear war, negative social and economic consequences, and the risk of further nuclear proliferation, they underscore more emphatically "the independence and freedom of nations and entire peoples, including the need to protect smaller nations from threats to their independence and integrity."[70] Construing nuclear deterrence as a source of order, the bishops are unable to deliver an unequivocal moral condemnation of deterrent threats. Indeed, the bishops seem to find the judgment of prior conciliar documents—that nuclear deterrence generates an imperfect peace, a "peace of a sort"—to be sufficient for providing a conditional acceptance of deterrence. They argue for tolerating the imperfect justice of nuclear deterrence, echoing Thomas's mandate to tolerate the unjust tyrant. In both cases there is the fear that greater perils might emerge on the horizon. According to the bishops, such dangers include the threat to individual national sovereignty—understood in other terms as nuclear blackmail—in the absence of deterrent threats. Moving hastily away from the "peace of a sort" of nuclear deterrence, without proper safeguards and negotiations, may implicate world leaders in even greater dangers to freedom and order than those posed by the present international system.

Modern Catholic social teaching thus reconfigures the problem of the just war according to a vision of global order and interdependence. From Pius XII through the U.S. Catholic bishops, modern Catholics now conceive of traditional just-war categories in a way that removes one crucial but subtle feature of the traditional approach, the principle of radical difference. Moreover, this reconfiguration introduces a notion that quietly recedes from the traditional discussion of war, the notion of order. For as we saw with Aquinas, traditional just-war reasoning construes the enemy extramurally, as the agent responsible for the breakdown of the status quo, the *ordo pacis*. In the modern period, given the grammar of the "universal common good," we are asked to construe our rivals intramurally, as co-members in an all-encompassing network of moral rights and duties, and to weigh the trade-offs between justice and order when considering recourse to violence. In the modern paradigm, then, Thomas's "external foe" has been domesticated and internalized, the value of order refuses to recede, and moral differences between adversaries are relativized. In this new context, MacIntyre's remark that "civil war is the worst of evils" now defines not the perils of insurrection, but the parameters of just-war reasoning in modern Catholic social thought. And within this configuration, pacifism now emerges as a legitimate moral option for individuals, for pacifism represents the willingness to suffer injustice on behalf of competing moral values.

It should come as no surprise, then, that the vocabulary of at least one recent Catholic pacifist draws from the vision of global order and interdependence. Raymond Hunthausen, archbishop and pacifist, writes that "in this 'new moment' in human history of which our pastoral speaks, our world citizenship has become a reality." Global citizenship establishes a higher moral law, relativizing the duty to obey the laws of any particular nation when those laws violate the interests of humanity. Civil disobedience, seen in this light, draws its moral sustenance from "an allegiance to all of the human family which goes beyond loyalty to the nation state." Hunthausen thus commends recent nuclear protesters who have carried out acts of civil disobedience against the weapons industry: "In order to become responsible to this higher law, we must face the irony that it has become appropriate to contravene lesser laws and accept the penalty." Both the United States and the Soviet Union, by developing vast nuclear arsenals, "have taken upon themselves a power wholly outside of the power proper to a nation state."[71] The vocation of peace, then, is cast not simply as a biblical mandate, but more notably as an imperative deriving from the universal common good. In this way Hunthausen draws out one trajectory of recent Catholic social teaching, radicalizing the imperative of nonviolence in light of the relative differences between the superpowers vis-à-vis the interests of humanity, viewed in a network of unity and interdependence.

The Modern Paradigm: Civil Conflict

Although moral grammar about civil conflict is not wholly devoid of elements of the traditional paradigm in modern Catholicism, for the most part that idiom is now shaped by the paradigm of liberation theology, developed chiefly in Latin America.[72] To liberation thinkers, traditional approaches to social ethics have proven to be yet another conservative ideology, in which ranking the value of order above that of justice only conceals oppressive neocolonial interests. Over and against traditional approaches, liberationists argue that it is necessary to unmask the suffering beneath the veil of order, to denounce the dependence of third world nations upon the first world, and to announce an alternative vision of "a more just and fraternal society," structured according to socialist ideals.

While this Catholic radicalism in Latin America has several representatives in recent decades, the most notable is Gustavo Gutierrez, whose book *A Theology of Liberation* continues to serve as the charter document for liberation thought.[73] For Gutierrez, it is essential to begin theological reflection in the context of Latin America with a clear notion of radical difference and division, especially the class conflict between rich and poor.[74]

According to Gutierrez, recent history in Latin America is marked by the discovery of the true "other" in Latin American society—the *anawim* or nonpersons, the "condemned of the earth"—those members of poor, marginalized classes and ethnic groups whose suffering constitutes the "underside" of history and society.[75] Growing out of popular struggles against economic oppression and political repression, liberation theology is an attempt to think within a new frame of reference, where solidarity with the poor is axiomatic for critical, committed reflection. This commitment to the poor, Gutierrez remarks, "creates a dividing line between two experiences, two epochs, two worlds, two languages in Latin America and thus in the Church."[76] In such a context, "class struggle is a fact, and neutrality . . . is impossible."[77]

Yet on Gutierrez's side of the dividing line there exists a moral idiom whose meaning stands within a lineage of biblical themes and Catholic social teaching about political and economic order. Central to that idiom is the principle of human dignity, the notion that all persons have moral worth and human rights irrespective of class, race, or gender. Specifically, Gutierrez draws upon *The Pastoral Constitution* and postconciliar church teachings, especially the Second General Conference of Latin American Bishops at Medellin, Colombia (1968),[78] all of which reflect a relentless concern for protecting and enhancing basic human rights. Accordingly, Gutierrez argues that material poverty is a "subhuman" condition, "inimical to human dignity and therefore contrary to the will of God."[79] His insistence that liberation thought be devoted to the "creation of the new humanity," one in which each person is able to assume control over his or her destiny within the concrete matrices of human experience, draws favorably from Paul VI's encyclical, *On the Development of Peoples*.[80] And Gutierrez's entreaty to respect the uniqueness of the Latin American reality, to resist any domestication of the Latin American context within a first world perspective, and to attend to local and cultural specificity is likewise echoed in the papal letter, *A Call to Action* (1971). In that text Paul VI claims that regional differences among people today make it "difficult . . . to utter a unified message and to put forward a solution which has universal validity." So, he continues, "it is up to the Christian communities to analyze with objectivity the situation which is proper to their own country."[81] Perhaps most important, both liberation thought and recent Catholic teaching affirm, with varying nuances, the same general premise, namely, that the pursuit of social justice is integral to the experience of religious redemption. Given these points, it is possible to justify a place for liberation theology within the broad currents of Catholic ethics, despite the tensions between it and more traditional approaches to social conflict.[82]

Clearly most of Gutierrez's work has been an attempt to trace the theological and epistemological implications of this commitment to liberation, leaving relatively short shrift to the more refined ethical problems surrounding revolution, e.g., the meaning of violence and its relation to conflict, intention, harm, revolution, and liberation. And, as if to express a momentary caution even about the theological implications of revolutionary praxis, Gutierrez insists that liberation thought is not a "theology of revolution," understood as a religious baptism of radical action. Rather, liberation thought requires "immersion" in and active solidarity with revolutionary struggle. Theologies of revolution, Gutierrez insists, are like the systems they seek to undermine in that both the system and the revolutionary theology still require some overarching ideology or conceptual legitimation, one that offers "a Christian justification for stances already taken."[83] Liberation thought, in contrast, seeks a more self-critical stance relative to historical praxis, where praxis is both prior to and consequent upon theology, in a complex spiral of commitment and critical reflection.[84]

This contrast means that liberationists do not wish to gainsay the legitimacy of revolutionary action. Instead, they prefer to commend a dynamic and reflective approach to such activity. Doubtless more important, however, is that Gutierrez accepts as virtually self-evident the justification of revolution. Indeed, for Gutierrez the rhetoric of class struggle is indicative of the current Latin American context, not a systematic moral analysis of the basis for revolutionary praxis. In this rhetorical and polemical vein, Gutierrez insists that it is necessary to engage in "real and effective combat" against the oppressors of the poor. Even the commandment to love one's enemies "presupposes recognizing and accepting that one has class enemies and that it is necessary to combat them."[85] The political goal of revolutionary struggle is the formation of a new, classless society, one in which "private ownership of the means of production will be eliminated."[86] And in order to achieve such a society, it is necessary to "struggle for the liberation of the oppressed," seeking to subvert "an order of injustice."[87]

Radical class division; conflict; the importance of local rather than universal solutions; historical praxis on behalf of the poor and dispossessed: these are cardinal features of the liberation paradigm. Within this new paradigm, moreover, the language of insurrection stands within an idiom that introduces one feature, the principle of otherness, and removes a feature that exerts a subtle pressure in the traditional approach to insurrection, the principle of order. With Gutierrez, to act in solidarity with "the other" is to grant the givenness of class difference and struggle, in which the marginalized classes are victims of forces over which they have no control. The liberation perspective presupposes a fundamental divorce between two economic classes, not unlike Thomas's notion of the "external enemy" in relation to the community under attack. With both Gutierrez and Thomas, a relative openness toward the use of violence coexists with the notion that violence has already occurred, that the *ordo pacis* has been undermined by some agent from without. This means that the cause of justice can be pursued without the qualifications normally required by considerations of peace and unity. Gutierrez echoes aspects of traditional just-war thinking—otherness and its underside, the breakdown of order—only to reconfigure them in the moral framework of class struggle and civil conflict.

For Gutierrez, the "external foe" does not introduce violence in any conventional sense, like that of physical aggression carried out by belligerent individuals or groups. Rather, he insists, the violence is "institutional."[88] Violence occurs almost invisibly, by the impersonal structures of Western capitalism on which Latin American societies depend, and which define the material conditions of human agency and well-being. The foe is more anonymous than the foe of just-war reasoning, and its methods are more systemic than the emergency wrought by an attack on the common good, traditionally construed. But in either the traditional approach to the just war or the modern approach to revolutionary praxis, the same vocabulary provides the moral basis for recourse to lethal force: human well-being has been violated by an extramural agency, and the structures of order are inadequate to resolve the conflicts between dramatically alienated interests.

We can further highlight how the modern approach toward civil conflict reconfigures the grammar of tradition by recalling the issues of violence and moral implication. According to the traditional approach to insurrection, there is a presumption against conflict given the classical notions of *philia* and peace as quiescence. Thus, as we have seen, Aquinas's justification of insurrection proceeds with caution; the perils of rebellion may implicate its agents in a wider and more dangerous train of events. For Gutierrez, in contrast, conflict is a fact of existence in Latin America, and *failure* to enter into the struggle, adopting a position of irenicism or neutrality against oppression, implicates the neutral agent in the injustices carried out in the status quo. Not to recognize the fact of class struggle "is really to put oneself on the side of the dominant sectors." The terms of difference reflect an ethical zero-sum mentality, where relevant moral differences are absolute. Hence, the question of class conflict is not "a question of admitting or denying a fact which confronts us; rather, it is a question of which side we are on."[89] For Gutierrez, then, conflict is not a disvalue, a symptom of restless ambition or disordered reason; rather, conflict is a stubborn reality in the context of Latin America, a fact of life within which ethical analysis must situate itself.

The approach to civil conflict within liberation thought thus reflects a paradigm shift in Catholic social ethics, reversing the terms and priorities inscribed in the traditional vocabulary about war and civil conflict. The fact that theories of revolution reverse traditional moral ideas is not altogether surprising—revolutions, after all, are designed to overhaul our conventional wisdom. But the precise nature of that shift merits some clarification. The reversal presented by liberation theology is not identical to that of a revolutionary eclipse of moral discourse, as described in Jon Gunnemann's provocative study of revolution and morality.[90] According to Gunnemann, modern revolutions are entirely disanalogous with the moral theory implied by just-war logic or the classical paradigm.

Revolutionary praxis, Gunnemann argues, seeks to overthrow the prevailing social order and moral ideology of the status quo; the postrevolutionary era promises a decisive break from the old order, creating an entirely new historical horizon for understanding evil and its antidotes. Accordingly, Gunnemann insists, it is profoundly difficult to establish a logic of justification for revolution "when it is this very logic that a revolution calls into question."[91]

Seen against the backdrop of this notion of revolutionary change, the reversal in Catholic liberation thought is both more and less dramatic than the relation between revolution and moral discourse in Gunnemann's account. On the one hand, liberation approaches to revolution in Catholicism fall short of genuine revolutionary novelty, because the terms of social critique draw from a well-established body of Catholic ethics about human rights, human dignity, and social justice. However novel they may seem, Catholic liberationists fail to escape intertextuality, their reliance upon a prior moral idiom. Reliance on such an idiom thus runs contrary to Gunnemann's claim that "the revolutionary, rightly or wrongly, perceives no moral community to which he can appeal, or at least no moral community that includes the enemy."[92] The tensions described by Gunnemann between revolutionary zeal and conventional morality are more characteristic of radical Protestant thinkers, for whom individual or social transformation is typically more apocalyptic than in Catholic ethics. Rather, it is more accurate to say about Catholic liberation theology that violence is openly countenanced on behalf of social justice as a necessity in a radically divided society, where divisions are a function of violence by alien powers and where "order" is achieved by massive political repression.

On the other hand, the paradigm shift of Catholic liberation theology is· more radical than in Gunnemann's account, because the new framework for social criticism inverts the moral categories according to which violence between groups has been classically understood. The radicality lies not in the fact that revolutionary zeal eclipses conventional moral categories, but in the fact that these categories undergo a *new discursive formation*.[93] That formation is new in two senses.

First, radical otherness constitutes a basic feature of moral discourse about social conflict. The foe has been externalized according to the radical class differences characteristic of dependent capitalism in Latin American societies. And, in contrast to the traditional paradigm about tyrannicide, the principle of order quietly recedes from view given the fact that what is now an "external foe" has subverted material structures of existence. Thus it is legitimate, indeed unavoidable, to tolerate some measure of disorder for the sake of establishing just relations.

Second, the moral problem facing the revolutionary is akin to that facing the insurrectionist within the traditional paradigm, but now the terms of the problem are reversed. Within the liberation paradigm, ethical implication in an immoral set of circumstances derives *not* from actions (on behalf of justice) that may imperil the social order, but from a *failure* to act on behalf of justice. The moral vocabulary of the liberation paradigm requires us to think about conditions in which disorder and radical divisiveness are facts of life, rather than specific emergencies wrought by the particular failings of a tyrant. These systemic realities are part of a context in which moral implication on one side or another is a condition of existence. And in this context, moral implication is now defined in terms of *inaction,* or acts of omission, rather than action, or acts of commission. Moral problems surrounding acts of omission are not new, but they have assumed unprecedented importance in Catholic social ethics given the terms governing liberation theology.

Justice, Friendship, and Otherness

Moral discourse about war and peace in Catholic social ethics, either in its classical or contemporary formulations, is structured by a tension between the value of justice and the imperative to preserve order, especially the order that inheres in peaceful unity. It remains to determine the significance of this tension for moral reasoning in Catholic social thought.

Although the notion that justice is the supreme virtue, prior to and regulative of all other duties and goods, has been widely embraced in recent ethical theory,[94] Catholic discourse about war and peace represents an alternative view, in which justice must compete with rival moral terms. Indeed, the imperatives of justice are qualified by the demands of community and *philia,* and become unqualified only where justice is designed to correct the morally diminished conditions in which order has broken down completely. Hence, as is evident in the traditional discussion of war and the contemporary discussion of revolution, the unqualified arrival of justice signals the absence of other, perhaps rarer, virtues of friendship and peace.

In this perspective, justice operates as a remedial rather than as an unconditionally valuable moral term. For, in each of the two paradigms, justice is invoked to repair an injured set of relations between people in a community. Reference to justice, then, is not a consequence of a hierarchy of virtues, defined in the abstract, but a consequence of those empirical circumstances in which peace has been undermined. And, in the most urgent formulations—when reference to justice is unqualified—those circumstances include the complete breakdown of order by a force from without.

As one outcome of this Catholic approach to war and civil conflict, in which the value of justice is remedial and circumstantial rather than absolute and unconditional, we cannot say in advance whether an increase in justice constitutes an overall improvement in social relations. On the one hand, an increase in justice may arise where before there was injustice and grave disorder. In this instance, of course, an overall moral improvement is clear. Such seems to be the perspective in the classical approach to war and the contemporary approach to civil conflict: justice is the virtue for reestablishing right relations, for repairing the social fabric now torn by an agent from without. Here we are required to tolerate disorder for the sake of justice.

On the other hand, however, an increase of justice can occur where before there was some measure of peace and friendship. Where there is such friendship, appeals to justice may disturb whatever measure of order sustains the status quo. Thus an overall moral balance might be diminished in those instances when it becomes necessary to invoke the demands of justice, because justice may increase less than order decreases. Such seems to be the perspective in the classical approach to insurrection and the contemporary approach to the just war: Vindicating the demands of justice against an agent from within might jeopardize the wider social order. Here we may be required to tolerate injustice for the sake of order. Hence a caution about using lethal force, however just that use might be.[95]

According to Catholic ethics the problem of violence between or within social arrangements is structured by an ethical tension. Within this tension, the justification for the use of force varies, depending upon the circumstances in which injuries have occurred. Central to understanding those circumstances is ascertaining whether *philia* envelops or distinguishes the relevant parties. Attitudes about using violence depend on whether the enemy is connected with or alienated from the civil order. The willingness to use violence is directly related to the otherness, the cultural or political distance, of the unjust foe. The range of *philia* thus defines the terms according to which differences between parties are to be understood, determining whether or not an agent of harm is to be tolerated. The construal of differences, the priorities of the classical paradigm, and the attitudes toward violence, all undergo a reversal as one proceeds from the traditional to the contemporary paradigm in Catholic ethics about just war, civil war, and peace. And in tracing this reversal we must follow the clues left by the classical legacy, especially where justice remains limited by rival demands of moral experience, the experience of constitutive attachments and civic fellowship.

T H R E E

Catholic Pacifism in the United States: Ethical Pluralism and the Problem of Tradition

Elements of a Pacifist Ethic

In the previous chapter I sought to show that a bias against violence in Catholic ethics, expressed as a moral caution about resorting to lethal force, can be uncovered by examining the trade-offs between justice and order. When the imperative to preserve order is given a relative priority over the imperative of justice, we may be required to suffer injustice, or at least tolerate its abuse. Further, insofar as the imperative to preserve order requires us to suffer or tolerate injustice, it opens the door to a fundamental tenet of nonviolence.

Unfortunately, however, my account of order, justice, and a moral caution about violence may oversimplify Catholic discourse about the tenets of nonviolence. Recently in Catholic ethics the bias against violence has crystallized in the form of pacifism, strictly understood as a prohibition of war as a means of settling conflict. Further, the various ideals, duties, and expressions of nonviolence, in Catholicism no less than in Protestantism (where pacifism has found its most hospitable place in Western religion), are pluralistic and ethically complex.

Catholic pacifists typically draw on a host of reasons somewhat foreign to the official Catholic embrace of pacifism at the Second Vatican Council. We can group this plurality into three types: "rights-based pacifism," "eschatological pacifism," and "iconoclastic pacifism." Types, of course, are only heuristic devices. When used in ethical analysis, they either bring together what appear to be different approaches, or help us sort out different moral attitudes within what seems to be a monolithic position.[1] The first type refers to pacifism as a means of promoting human rights and includes the official Catholic position; the second designates a pacifism shaped by an otherworldly orientation, unconcerned about political effectiveness and power; and the third designates a pacifism which seeks wholesale social reform, often with the aid of radical civil disobedience and ceremonial action. Each of these types, the patterns within them and the differences between them, will receive fuller treatment below.

Ethical complexity has remained beyond the analysis of those developing, or commenting upon, the pacifisms that now dot the Catholic landscape. Despite the flowering of pacifist witness and practice, especially in the United States, few ethicists have paid attention to the elements that comprise a pacifist ethic. For the most part pacifism as a social ethic has been viewed like vegetarianism in a meat-eating culture: it is an option available for those considering a choice, perhaps a noble ideal, a benign form of dissent. But from the viewpoint of official Catholic teaching, the analogy between cultural attitudes toward vegetarianism and pacifism as a social ethic is misguided. Catholic teaching places the liberty of conscience in a wider theory of rights and duties, which requires pacifists—unlike vegetarians—to honor debts that accrue to the social order by virtue of their dissent, as a requirement of social justice.

Conceptual clarity about the rights and duties of Catholic pacifism might be aided with reference to some basic terms about political obligation and social ethics. To that end I introduce here ten elements for a pacifist ethic, a set of distinctions useful for refining the moral framework in which pacifists typically operate:

(1) *Absolute/relative:* Is the *basis* for pacifism, providing the general rationale of the position, a matter of absolute principle? Is the prohibition of war an end in itself? Or is pacifism justified relatively, as an appropriate means to goals more general and more comprehensive than the elimination of war (e.g., ethical personalism, human rights, critique of militaristic ethos)?

(2) *Sectarian/transformationist:* Does the *social vision* or *goal* require pacifists to withdraw from society, as part of a utopia separated from the wider social order? Or does the pacifist seek to change existing social structures?

(3) *Self-sacrifice/harmonious relations:* Do pacifists *define peace* as self-sacrifice or as reconciliation between antagonistic parties? Those who emphasize self-sacrifice define peace as selflessness, which does not guarantee social harmony; those who emphasize reconciliation define peace in terms of social harmony, which does not always require selflessness. Are there limits to selflessness?

(4) *Individual/social:* What is the *range of obligation* of pacifism? Is pacifism permitted for individuals only, as an "option" that may be exercised by the free conscience, perhaps as a higher ethic? Or is it mandated for all persons, as a universal imperative?

(5) *Nonresistance/nonviolent resistance:* What are the appropriate *methods* of pacifist practice? Does the pacifist claim that *all* forms of

resistance are immoral, or does he or she permit some forms of resistance, those which conform to nonviolent methods? What counts as "nonviolent"?

(6) *Ad intra/ad extra:* For those pacifists who accept the methods of nonviolent resistance, against whom is resistance directed? Does the pacifist enjoin resistance as civil disobedience against prevailing authorities, or as a strategy of defense against outside aggression?

(7) *Direct action/indirect action:* What are the appropriate forms of *political action* for pacifists engaged in political protest *ad intra?* What methods of civil disobedience are commended? Does the pacifist call for the violation of unjust laws only, operating from the conviction that unjust laws fail to bind the conscience (direct action)? Or does the pacifist allow for symbolic forms of disobedience which may violate just laws, seeking not to reverse any specific law but to call attention to a more general set of problems or beliefs (indirect action)?

(8) *Submit/evade:* Considerations of political obligation affect judgments about the *consequences of legal disobedience.* If pacifists are arrested for violating a law, should they submit to civil punishment, or may they evade the penalties of the law? Does it make a difference to those who may decide to evade penalties whether the law in question is considered just or unjust?

(9) *Persuasion/coercion:* For those involved either in direct or indirect action, is the goal to educate by appealing to reason or conscience? Or is the goal to coerce, to force a change, regardless of the impact on the opponent or on public attitudes?

(10) *Conditional/unconditional exemption:* During conscription in war, nations may allow individuals the liberty of conscientious objection. Should those who exercise such liberty be required to perform alternative service? Or is the liberty to dissent unconditional? In the case of alternative service, what forms are appropriate and why?[2]

Many combinations of these terms are possible, at least in principle. For example, an eschatological pacifist might argue for social reform on relative grounds, call for nonresistance, and extend the range of obligation to individuals, with sectarian ideals, while another eschatological pacifist might argue for social reform on the same grounds, but may call for nonviolent resistance and extend the range of obligation to the entire society, with transformationist ideals. Moreover, in their various political activities, they may disagree about the forms of action, the legitimacy of coercion, and the limits of political obedience. Rights-based and iconoclastic pacifists might combine these elements in various ways, too.

In what follows I will explore the pluralism and complexity in contemporary Catholic pacifism, focusing on the United States. This focus is designed to narrow the analysis to manageable limits, although it is also true that Catholic pacifists in the United States have been some of the most influential exponents of pacifism in the Catholic community world-wide. In choosing to be more analytic and critical than historical, I will furnish a moral topography rather than a narrative of Catholic pacifism.

In the course of developing this topography I will clarify the elements listed above, when relevant, *within each type*. With Catholic pacifism "mapped" this way, a cluster of ethical, political, and practical problems will come into view. Despite the praise of nonviolence in official Catholic teaching, pacifism as defended and practiced by Catholics remains some-what anomalous, resisting the framework of a pacifist ethic provided by the Second Vatican Council and subsequent Catholic teaching. Exponents of pacifism have been unclear about the moral vocabulary authorizing their views, their understanding of political obligation, their practical methods, and their overall goals, to name a few. In several areas, Catholic pacifists have either ignored or broken away from pacifism as officially endorsed. As pacifists contribute more to Catholic social ethics, they will have to contend with a variety of problems posed by the importance and the details of tradition in contemporary Catholicism. And, as I hope to show, Catholic pacifists may ease their anomalous status by drawing on a facsimile of just-war tenets to structure their ethics of pacifist dissent. In so doing, they may sharpen the ethics of civil disobedience and political obligation in a culture of moral pluralism, helping us define a world of common moral interpretations to structure disagreement and debate.

Rights-Based Pacifism

The official Catholic embrace of pacifism, as I have indicated, is provided in the final document of the Second Vatican Council, *The Pastoral Constitution of the Church in the Modern World*. Reference to the merits of nonviolence are brief:

> We cannot fail to praise those who renounce the use of violence in the vindication of their rights and who resort to methods of defense which are otherwise available to weaker parties, . . . provided that this can be done without injury to the rights and duties of others or of the community itself.[3] . . . It seems right that laws make humane provisions for the case of those who for reasons of conscience refuse to bear arms, provided however, that they accept some other form of service to the human community.[4]

The first statement is directed chiefly to pacifists. Here the council affirms the liberty of conscience, the "secret core and sanctuary" of all persons in the depths of which echoes the voice of God.[5] Such liberty provides the moral space for embracing pacifism as an alternative to the historically dominant just-war tradition. Yet this liberty is qualified in at least three important respects, all of which draw from elements of a pacifist ethic.

First, consider the general justification of nonviolence. Central to the overall discussion of war and peace in *The Pastoral Constitution* are the notions of human dignity and human rights. Human rights, of course, are claims of an individual: claims to be protected from encroachment (negative rights) or claims to the elementary necessities of a decent human existence (positive rights). But the main point is that rights are objective claims, assigned to us qua human, regardless of whether we want those claims or not. Injustice is construed as the violation of those rights inherent in human nature. It follows that to permit such a violation when one can do otherwise is to be morally deficient in the protection of one's claims. Rights as objective claims produce the correlative duty of some form of self-defense. To permit the violation of one's rights when something can be done to protect them is inhuman, an act of moral delinquency.

In this framework of rights and the duty to protect them, the justification of nonviolence is relative, not absolute. The council praises nonviolence only in the context of the defense of rights, a defense that is seeking alternative methods. The council is *not* endorsing total nonresistant pacifism, for nonresistance would relinquish all methods of self-defense. In this respect, the council refused to embrace Augustine's requirement of self-sacrificial love, adopting instead the Thomistic notion that self-preservation is a dictate of the natural law, here cast in the language of human rights. In a rights-based framework nonresistant pacifism as a deontic judgment is morally deficient, for it fails to protect human rights. Nonviolence thus finds endorsement insofar as it can muster some resistance as a legitimate means to the end of self-defense.

Second, the liberty of the pacifist conscience is permitted only if it respects the rights of others. This means that the pacifist may be obliged to offer some defensive (albeit nonviolent) protection of others whose rights are in jeopardy by a third party. Further, respecting the rights of others has implications for the relation between the pacifist and his or her political community. Assuming that there are some just laws in a relatively just polity, pacifists no less than nonpacifists are obliged to obey them. The duty to obey just laws is a clear inference from the requirement not to injure "the rights and duties . . . of the community itself." One instance in which nonviolence would *not* be praised, then, would be an instance in which pacifists violate just laws in acts of civil disobedience. As I stated above, indirect action often takes this form of civil disobedience, to call attention to a wider set of social injustices or ethical beliefs. Indeed, to violate a just law for wider symbolic purposes, outside of a revolutionary setting, allows the ends to justify the means.[6] Thus, the council provides at least a muted proscription of indirect action, at least those forms which occur in a relatively just political context.

Third, because the council holds to the claim, central to the *jus ad bellum*, that war is a duty incumbent on government authorities "to protect the welfare of the people entrusted to their care,"[7] the range of obligation for pacifism is extended to individuals only, not entire communities. Reflecting one feature of the Augustinian convergence, the council distinguishes between private and public morality, mandating a just-war ethic for the latter. But as I stated in chapter 1, the council departs from Augustine by permitting rather than requiring a pacifist ethic for individuals. Moreover, inferences drawn from the second statement, cited above, qualify the moral shape of this individual witness.

The implied audience of the second statement is composed of policymakers who must make judgments in times of national conscription. Here the council excludes policies that permit pacifists to object conscientiously in war without performing some form of alternative service. Whether that service must be related to the overall defense against aggression, or whether it may be of a purely civilian type, the council does not say. But it seems clear that the prerogative of dissent has limits, about which two aspects of Catholic teaching are morally relevant.

First, given the Catholic justification of war, to protect human rights, it is reasonable to infer that the council would not censure policy-makers for expecting pacifists to make some contribution to a legitimate form of collective self-defense, e.g., ambulance driving, fire watching, caring for those rendered homeless by war, policing areas after bombardment to protect from looting.[8] Such alternative service, even if not formal cooperation in the war effort, is still a form of participation and solidarity with those in the community who suffer in war, and often on behalf of war. Leaders of a morally legitimate war ought to require at least as much while allowing others to dissent. Indeed, assuming that a war is a morally legitimate exercise of self-defense, a duty of self-preservation and protection, pacifists are morally delinquent in failing to aid and abet if they absent themselves from the collective moral effort.[9]

Second, in assessing the requirement of alternative service, one must consider the more general framework of Catholic ethics, in which rights and duties are generally correlative. To permit the pacifist to dissent from the protection of the community from which he or she enjoys civil benefits would be a violation of fairness. Given the fact that other persons take risks on behalf of the community from which they derive benefits, pacifists make exceptions of themselves if they withdraw totally from efforts to preserve the community. Absent any risk at all, pacifists are vulnerable to the charge that their liberty of conscience comes at a price of moral exceptionalism. Pacifists who fail to shoulder social burdens appear to be free riders, persons who enjoy the advantages of civil life without doing their share to uphold it. But if alternative service is a duty concomitant to the prerogative of dissent, then the problem of exceptionalism may disappear, or at least be eased to tolerable levels. Alternative service as a condition of pacifist dissent might be construed as a form of repayment of debts, an attempt to redress an imbalance of civic responsibility given the general requirements of fair play and political obligation.[10]

Given these last two considerations, official Catholic teaching provides general contours for expecting pacifists to abide by the requirements of civic virtue in the form of voluntary, alternative service during times of national conscription. Such expectations are intelligible either as part of the duty of legitimate collective self-defense, or in light of a more general theory of political obligation.

A final inference about pacifism may be drawn not so much from the literal sense of the two passages from *The Pastoral Constitution* as from the general ethical assumptions of the document as a whole. As I have indicated, the ethical terms in *The Pastoral Constitution* draw from the assertion of human dignity, which yields an account of positive and negative rights. Moreover, rights are correlative with duties to protect those rights, within limits. And it is to the means of permissible defense that this final inference pertains.

If the belief in human rights entails the requirement to protect those rights, and the individual is nonetheless permitted to adopt the pacifist stance of nonviolence, it follows that the pacifist is required to order his or her intention toward the goal of self-defense. In this respect official Catholic teaching resembles the general lines of my criticism of the Augustinian convergence in the first chapter: nonviolence, not nonresistance, is permissible for pacifists. According to Catholic teaching, pacifists are no different from those committed to the just war, at least in terms of the morality of ends: Both groups must order their resistance to the same end, namely, the defense of individual and communal rights. The difference between the pacifist and nonpacifist concerns the matter of drawing the line beyond which self-defense assumes immoral *means*. Specifically, beyond the limit of nonviolent resistance, the pacifist is allowed to judge the means to be disproportionate to the end of self-defense. A pacifist judgment of proportionality would conclude that the disvalues of the means (killing another) outweigh the values pursued as ends (self-defense). Concerning this claim, a claim about means, not ends, official Catholic teaching permits individuals to disagree.[11]

Judgments about means, as these may divide pacifists and nonpacifists, also bear upon an important element in a pacifist ethic, the question of self-sacrifice. As I stated above, self-sacrificial nonresistance as a deontic judgment is incompatible with an ethic understood in terms of rights and the correlative duty to protect them. But nonresistance is not ruled out of this approach altogether. Rather, self-sacrifice or nonresistance is permitted once a reasonable amount of resistance is *first* offered. If after mustering some form of nonviolent resistance the pacifist is nonetheless "up against the wall," he or she is then allowed to say, "Beyond this I cannot go. I must now yield to aggression." In this respect, nonresistance is a judgment of proportionate reason when one is left to choose between harming others or being harmed.

When examined in its details, then, the official Catholic embrace of pacifism qualifies a pacifist ethic in light of the demands of justice: the justice of self-preservation and protection of others as objective moral ends; the fairness of political obligation and civic duty, which exclude moral exceptionalism on the part of pacifist witness; and the respect owed to the rights of others when political disobedience is carried out. Generally the council adjusted aspects of the Augustinian convergence to the more general lines of the Thomistic position: Within the natural law requirement to defend the self, individuals may seek alternative forms of defense with nonviolent methods. Augustine's requirement of individual, nonresistant love is qualified by the dictates of natural justice, leaving a residue of nonresistance as a judgment of proportionate reasoning.

Justice, broadly construed, provides the direction taken by subsequent Catholic teaching about the liberty of conscience, at least in the United States. In two pastoral letters (1968, 1976), the U.S. Catholic hierarchy generally left the notion of pacifism untouched, or undeveloped. Instead, they supplemented the official embrace of pacifism by appealing for selective conscientious objection, a position derived not from pacifist principles, but just-war criteria. In their first, fuller treatment—developed with conscription for the Vietnam War in the backdrop—the bishops note that the liberty of conscientious objection exists "only for those whose reasons of conscience are grounded in a total rejection of the use of military force." They then urge "that similar consideration be given those whose reasons of conscience are more personal and specific" through an amendment of the Selective Service Act. The goal is to make it possible "for so-called selective conscientious objectors to refuse—without fear of imprisonment or loss of citizenship—to serve in wars which they consider to be unjust or in branches of service (e.g., the strategic nuclear forces) which would subject them to the performance of actions contrary to deeply held moral convictions about indiscriminate killing." In keeping with the logic of *The Pastoral Constitution,* they add that "some other form of service to the human community should be required of those so exempted."[12]

For those whose consciences are guided by just-war criteria, some form of dissent and alternative service is commended when war or plans for war violate those criteria. In this respect the bishops reversed prior papal teaching which forbade selective conscientious objection.[13] But this reversal was hardly a triumph for Catholic pacifists hoping for a further radicalization of the Catholic hierarchy. Pacifism excludes selective conscientious objection as an option because such objection implies that some uses of violence are legitimate, at least in principle. Indeed, unconditional conscientious objection and selective conscientious objection result from two distinct patterns of moral reasoning: The latter presumes just-war principles, not a pacifist ethic.[14] The development of doctrine drew back somewhat from the teachings of the 1960s by developing the implications of just-war tenets rather than pacifist beliefs. In fact, neither the 1960s nor the 1970s occasioned theological, ethical, ecclesiological, or political reflection about pacifism by the Catholic hierarchy. Such reflection would have to wait until *The Challenge of Peace,* in 1983.

One chief objective of *The Challenge of Peace* is to place the nascent postconciliar tradition about war and peace within a wider theological perspective, a "theology of peace." Accordingly, the bishops turn to biblical sources to uncover a range of relevant terms for war and peace; postbiblical examples of nonviolence in the second, third, and fourth centuries; Christological and eschatological themes about the nature of peace for a community beckoned by the demands of the kingdom of God; and recent ethical theory to shore up the conceptual relation between pacifism and just-war tenets. But the details of a pacifist ethic, drawn from prior teachings, remain virtually unchanged. Nonviolence is embraced not absolutely, but only as a means of legitimate self-defense. War as a duty of self-defense is incumbent on those responsible for the common good.[15] Hence, it is only about means, not ends, that pacifists and nonpacifists may disagree, and disagreement is confined to the level of individual morality.[16] Moreover, although dissent from military participation is permissible for both pacifists and those who embrace just-war criteria, in either case some form of alternative service is required, "not related to military needs."[17] In all of these instances the bishops draw directly on the teachings set forth in *The Pastoral Constitution.* However well the bishops develop a theology of peace, their pacifist ethic remains hedged in by a theory of rights and justice, to the dissatisfaction of many Catholic pacifists hoping for a more radical position.[18]

The bishops contribute to the development of doctrine, without departing from prior teachings, in the area of social vision. The bishops make clear that a theology of peace, especially in its eschatological dimension, requires a transformationist rather than a sectarian ideal. Peace, the bishops say, "will be achieved fully only in the kingdom of God." Aspiring to the ideals of the kingdom, therefore, "is a continuing work, progressively accomplished, precariously maintained, and needing constant effort to preserve the peace achieved and expand its scope in personal and political life."[19] And, it must be added, the work of realizing peace occurs not only in the religious community, but in history at large. An eschatological notion of peace holds out an ideal of harmony and reconciliation, against which developments in human history should be judged, and toward which history ideally should tend. This means that the ideals of nonviolence can and should work their way into human history, as a leaven in individual and institutional affairs. As such, despite the bishops' affirmation of prior church teachings about the duty of self-defense, they add, "We believe work to develop nonviolent means of fending off aggression and resolving conflict best reflects the call of Jesus both to love and to justice."[20] They thus develop several suggestions for reducing the likelihood of conflict: bilateral, iterated disarmament; a nuclear freeze; a comprehensive test-ban treaty; and, most notably, nonviolent, organized popular defense as part of our government's contingency planning against aggression.[21] These are policy recommendations, not directed to believers only, seeking to lessen militaristic undercurrents in the social order.

Nonviolent civil defense, nonviolence *ad extra,* is not a new proposal in Catholic ethics, though for years its most important exponent found himself at the fringes of Catholic social thought. One of the few Catholic conscientious objectors in World War II, Gordon Zahn has argued for many of the views embraced by the Catholic bishops, operating out of a similar desire to transform a militaristic ethos. Although he avoids a systematic use of rights language to structure his views, Zahn nonetheless anchors his arguments to the same basic principle on which the bishops ground their position: the incomparable dignity and worth of the individual person. And for Zahn, no less than for the bishops, nonviolent means of resistance must be explored as an alternative method of conflict resolution and self-defense. Perhaps more than any other Catholic pacifist, Zahn has commended a wholesale restructuring of national defense, the goal of which is "a nation mobilized and trained in the use of civil disobedience and total noncooperation."[22] Hence, given the claim that defense is a legitimate end, Zahn excludes nonresistance as a deontic requirement. By his account the use of force in self-defense stops at the point at which harm will occur to an individual, a judgment cast in the general contours of proportionate reasoning.[23] In keeping with later Catholic teaching, Zahn's own pacifist witness in World War II led him to alternative service in the Civilian Public Service corps, defunct since 1946.[24]

Yet, for reasons I will examine in more detail, Zahn rejects just-war criteria. For Zahn, pacifism is not an option, but a duty incumbent on everyone. Hence, he departs from official teaching by extending the duty of pacifism, its range of obligation, to the entire national community. For Zahn this means that a radical vision must be forged to render the pacifist conviction more compelling. We need, he says, an alternative set of resources to fortify ourselves against the pressures of nationalistic loyalty, a new set of commitments to foster an "ascetic ideal."[25] To this end Zahn provides a more dramatic embrace of eschatological themes than found in the bishops, commending a "full commitment to the Spirit that breathes through the Gospels. A society composed of truly 'in-spirited' men and women, a network of interactors governed by dedication to love and non-violence even at the cost of humiliation and martyrdom, might yet convert the world."[26] We need loyalties that transcend nationalism, a universal vision to relativize the impulse toward survival. Zahn thus commends the vision of the Beatitudes and the Sermon on the Mount, which "combine to produce an 'otherworldly' perspective in which the practice of statecraft becomes at best a secondary consideration."[27]

Such "otherworldliness" has had (and continues to have) advocates more radical than Zahn in the Catholic community in the United States. Such pacifists have avoided the general structure of rights and their implications for the message of peace. Although the transformationism of the bishops may nudge Catholic discourse in the direction of nonviolent ideals, to a more otherworldly perspective official teaching still blunts the force of the gospel message and the duties of love. A more radical approach is less bound by the implications of justice and defense than by biblical stories and teachings. Moreover, those teachings call into question the desire, implicit in the official Catholic position, to save the social order from itself, expressing a more emphatic moral caution about resort to lethal force.

Eschatological Pacifism

Eschatological pacifism is distinguished by the general lack of desire to acquire political power or to control established social institutions. Rather, as Zahn says, there is the belief "grounded in the scriptural promises that God's power will be made perfect in our infirmity, that no matter how hopeless and threatening the situation may appear, the gates of hell will not prevail."[28] Nonviolence may not work, but it is aimed primarily at truth, not power. Given these commitments, eschatological pacifists find it easier to embrace the commandment to love one's enemies, furnishing the basis for nonviolence, in simple and absolute terms.[29] Zahn continues: "It does not say 'We shall overcome' so much as 'This is the day of the Lord,' and whatever may happen to *us, He* shall overcome."[30]

Doubtless the most notable Catholic representatives of eschatological pacifism in the United States have been associated with the Catholic Worker movement, founded by Dorothy Day and Peter Maurin in 1933. A decentralized anarchist movement, rather than an organization, the Worker originally committed itself to three ideals: "houses of hospitality" to carry out works of mercy, especially among the urban poor; roundtable discussions and the publication of a monthly newspaper for clarification of thought; and agronomic universities, self-sufficient utopian communities in which individuals taught, farmed, and lived together. Day never furnished a clear, definitive argument for the Worker's moral position against war, leading to certain ambiguities which seem endemic to eschatological ethics. Initially the pacifism of Day and Maurin was part of their anticapitalism and antistatism, a critique of imperialism drawing from socialist currents on the East Coast during the early 1930s.[31] The Worker's neutralist stand toward the Spanish civil war took such form, although it included some allusions to biblical themes and stories.[32] In the late thirties, disillusioned with socialist movements worldwide, Day cast her pacifism in theological terms. By the outbreak of World War II, Worker pacifism was framed in strict biblical language, reflecting the radical gospel perfectionism characteristic of many Protestant pacifists. Writing in 1942, Day delivered this message: "We are still pacifists. Our manifesto is the Sermon on the Mount, which means that we will try to be peacemakers." This means, Day added, that "we will not participate in armed warfare or in making munitions, or by buying government bonds to prosecute the war, or in urging others to these efforts."[33]

The position was unpopular, both in the Worker movement and without. During the early 1940s the *Catholic Worker,* the movement's penny-a-paper newspaper, lost one hundred thousand subscriptions.[34] Most Workers, moreover, enlisted in the war. Still, some Catholics refused to join the military, one hundred and thirty-five of whom entered the Civilian Public Service camps (of which Day never fully approved).[35] As Zahn's study of these men indicates, moveover, sixteen of them based their convictions "upon a literal interpretation of the Counsels of Perfection and the insistence that these Counsels must govern the life of the individual Christian."[36] As one camp member stated, "I believe it is my duty to follow the Counsels of Perfection as outlined by our Lord in His Sermon on the Mount."[37]

Yet at times Worker pacifism was derived from a wider personalistic philosophy developed by Maurin and Paul Hanly Furfey. Viewing each individual as endowed with inherent dignity and worth, these writers denounced militarism, bureaucracy, and coercion as various forms of impersonalism and manipulation. Day described her own formative stirrings in personalistic terms: "Disabled men, men without arms and legs, blind, consumptive, exhausted men with all the manhood drained from them by industrialism; farmers gaunt and harried with debt; mothers weighted down with children at their skirts, in their arms, in their wombs, and the children ailing, rickety, toothless—all this long procession of desperate people called to me."[38] Among personalists, war is seen as the nadir of dehumanization, the brutalization of human beings. In developing an argument for nonviolent defense, Zahn remarks, "Any course of action that involves the dehumanizing of the actor or his victim or both . . . may not be justified by the attainment or preservation of any material good or even of spiritual goods of a lesser order."[39]

Out of this ethical personalism, moreover, the Worker developed an anarchistic vision in opposition to commonplace forms of social organization. As an alternative to modern society, Maurin proposed a "green revolution" of "gentle personalism," a vision of small, preindustrial farm communes, not unlike decentralized Gandhian cooperatives.[40] Objecting to the contrived rhythms of the factory and the excessive division of labor, Maurin called for a return to an uncluttered agrarian way of life and nongovernmental, voluntary cooperation. Members would share work and ownership of the means of production and distribution, shifting responsibility for social and economic activities from the nation-state back to the individual. For Maurin such a vision was the only long-term solution to urban unemployment and class disaffection.[41]

This wedding of scriptural literalism and philosophical personalism means that often the basis for eschatological pacifism was both absolute and relative: absolute, by virtue of the love command; relative, as deriving from a more general account of the self and the duty to humanize the lives of others. Generally Day reconciled these justifications by joining what is called, in theological language, Christology and anthropology. The basic idea was to identify Jesus Christ with the sufferings of the least fortunate, to underscore the requirement to care for the downtrodden. Day remarks,

> Now it is with the voice of our contemporaries that He speaks, with the eyes of store clerks, factory workers, and children that He gazes; with the hands of office workers, slum dwellers, and suburban housewives that He gives. It is with the feet of soldiers and tramps that He walks, and with the heart of anyone in need that He longs for shelter. And giving shelter or food to anyone who asks for it, or needs it, is giving it to Christ.[42]

Enjoining fellow Workers to attend "to the least of these," Day insisted that humanizing the lives of others satisfies the radical Christian ideal, rendering Christ contemporaneous with the present age.[43] In so doing, she made it clear that the Worker places a premium on social action, suggesting a tight relation between gospel and law, religion and ethics.

During the 1940s, dissent in the Workers' ranks on the question of war created problems about the range of obligation of pacifism in the Worker movement. Was pacifism a duty incumbent upon all, or an individual option? Although Day's answer took the first course, she allowed nonconformity on the pacifist question. Yet her concession was accompanied by an ultimatum to other Catholic Worker houses to distribute only the New York version of the *Catholic Worker,* in which she published hard-line antiwar materials. Day's ultimatum precipitated a deep fissure between the New York and the Chicago, Seattle, and Los Angeles houses, leading to the painful departure of John Cogley from the Chicago Worker. After a meeting at the Maryfarm retreat, Day told Cogley that he and other non-pacifists were welcome in the movement.[44] And in 1942 Day acknowledged "great differences of opinion even among our own groups as to how much collaboration we can have with the government in times like these. . . . But we beg that there will be mutual charity and forbearance among us all."[45] At a theoretical level, the question remained ambiguous. A place was left for nonpacifism in the Worker, although the issue of ethical pluralism was never systematically developed. After Pearl Harbor the number of Worker houses declined rapidly, and after 1945 the issue of strict pacifism best represented the Worker's radicality.[46]

A similar vagueness has surrounded the moral vocabulary about methods proper to Worker pacifism. The relevant distinction between nonresistance and nonviolent resistance was all but absent from the moral lexicon during the Worker's formative period.[47] Day's pacifism was generally cast as a rejection of the social institution of war. In the event of an invasion, Day added, the Worker was "opposed to all but the use of nonviolent means to resist such an invader."[48] Yet Day's claim that the Sermon on the Mount serves as the Worker "manifesto" suggested a position of nonresistance at least on the level of individual morality.

Perhaps more appropriate to the Worker's methods are the notions of nonparticipation, cooperation, and scandal, terms drawn from Catholic moral theology. In an eschatological framework one of the most pressing problems concerns the way we maintain purity in a sinful world. Stated in traditional terms, the question turns on the problem of avoiding the occasion of sin (cooperation), or leading another to sin (scandal). As Paul Hanly Furfey writes in a book seeking to capture the spirit of radical Catholic social movements in the 1930s,[49] nonparticipation in the social order is the most feasible method of avoiding both of these problems. Accordingly, in the 1930s Furfey argued for a sectarian, rigorist ethic, one which removed the individual believer from worldly participation. Furfey offered instead a vision of separate, small Christian communities bearing witness to New Testament ideals.[50]

"Worldly action" in the form of nonviolent resistance came more easily to Day and the Worker as a method of civil disobedience, resistance *ad intra*. Civil disobedience differs from the kind of noncooperation espoused by Furfey: The latter seeks to reduce interaction with society, while the former seeks to heighten interaction, demanding a response to illegal acts.[51] The most dramatic Worker protest occurred in 1955, when all citizens of New York City were required to take shelter for at least ten minutes at the sound of an air-raid siren, to simulate action taken during a nuclear attack. Day and fellow Worker-anarchist Ammon Hennacy openly refused to cooperate, for which they were arrested and denounced as "murderers" by the ruling judge. Day returned annually to protest the drills until 1961 when the city discontinued them. By that point Day and

Hennacy had roused over a thousand people to join in their noncompliance.[52]

About her arrests Day remarks, "We were, frankly, hoping for jail."[53] And in jail, Day pondered the mystery of poverty and alienation, in solidarity with those prisoners about whom she had written for two decades. But as a form of political protest, Day's civil disobedience followed the lines of traditional nonviolence: direct action, following the dictates of conscience, against an unjust law, followed by submission to legal authorities upon arrest. That these protests may have changed policy was not her stated intent, but a serendipitous result of in-principled action. Rather, Day's goals were generally more persuasive than coercive. As Mel Piehl observes, "When they marched in picket lines, demonstrated at embassies, organized unions, or helped integrate all-white facilities in the South, the Workers insisted that they were not engaging in politics but performing one of the works of mercy—'enlightening the ignorant.'"[54]

The presence of Day and Worker members in acts of civil protest indicates that their social vision included a transformationist element, a goal of altering the path of history. Day remarks, "What we would like to do is change the world—make it a little simpler for people to feed, clothe, and shelter themselves as God intended them to do. . . . We can throw our pebble in the pond and be confident that its ever-widening circle will reach around the world."[55] To these ends Day and the Worker fought for social legislation for home relief, social security, labor unions, and farm workers. Yet this transformationism stands in tension with sectarian aspects that almost inevitably accompany political anarchism, the desire for moral purity, and an eschatological disregard for political effectiveness. Worker sectarianism, moreover, was symptomatic of Catholics' perception of themselves at the fringe of American culture until after the Second World War.[56] In contrast with the Social Gospel movement, members of the Worker did not take for granted the question of power and effectiveness, since they saw themselves as standing on the edge of Protestant cultural and religious hegemony.[57]

The Worker usually reconciled its transformationist and sectarian impulses according to the exigencies of the moment. Such reconciliation meant not a compromise of moral commitment, but an adjustment of social vision to the changing attitudes of the time. Worker transformationism gained strength when moorings connected them to social forces in the wider culture, while a sectarian sail would go up when the winds changed. Maurin, for example, never hoped that his vision of preindustrial communities would gain currency in the culture as a whole. Similarly, by the end of World War II, Workers assumed a sectarian self-understanding, recognizing that their aid to Catholic conscientious objectors ran against the grain of American society. A more transformationist vision was possible during the 1950s and 1960s, when the radical gospel ideals and nonconformism of the Worker resonated with the civil rights movement. But in its more difficult times, the Worker refused to revise its commitment to pacifism, voluntary poverty, solidarity with the poor, and social anarchism. As Piehl observes, "The contradictions between the movement's attempt to practice [gospel] ideals and its professed aims of altering society were consistently resolved in favor of the religious witness. The Catholic Worker did not seek isolation and political irrelevance, but it was willing to accept both as the price of its central vision."[58]

Yet this ambiguity about social vision typifies a more general deficiency of the Worker legacy, at least from a social-ethical point of view. The inability to clarify bases, means, limits, goals, social vision, and appropriate forms of political action means that the Worker platform remains nebulous. However important unconventional wisdom may be in an eschatological approach, without moral clarity there lies the danger of an ambiguous identity, an unclear banner to the masses, and confusion and turmoil when differences arise. Moreover, the absence of any clear argument on behalf of pacifism leaves the Worker open to the charge of anti-intellectualism.[59] Perhaps such is to be expected in an otherworldly ethic, one which relies on alternative modes of thought and action. Nevertheless, nagging questions remain about the type of pacifism most appropriate to the Worker legacy. Is loss of clarity about the moral grammar of pacifism also a price of the Worker's central vision?

Tensions between pacifist tenets and wider cultural expectations often haunt eschatological pacifists, who see truth as running contrary to the conventional wisdom of social life and politics. In this spirit Day once rejoiced in the "abundance of fools" in the Worker movement, of whom Maurin was perhaps an archetype.[60] But also operating in Catholic pacifism is an attempt to defuse the commonplace charge that nonviolence is wholly unconventional, operating apart from the canons of everyday knowledge and expectations. This latter current might be distinguished from the eschatological personalism of Day as "eschatological realism." Eschatological realism insists upon the practical veracity of nonviolence. Although traces of personalism can be found where eschatological realists criticize our technological ethos, such realists characteristically claim that the law of reality can be discovered through suffering love, that love can be used to change the moral fabric of human relations.

The most prominent exponent of eschatological realism, peace activist James Douglass, has devoted considerable energy over the past two decades to protesting the Vietnam War and the construction of the Trident submarine in Bangor, Washington.[61] The social sources of Douglass's dissidence owe less to the support of a sectarian enclave than to the mainstreaming of Catholics in postwar America. In this new context, quite different from the Worker's formative period, Catholics' general self-perception has changed, freeing them from demonstrating common ground between the Catholic tradition and the American ethos. Douglass's pacifism and civil disobedience must be seen against the backdrop in which Catholics are now more confident in questioning foreign policy without fearing cultural backlash.

Moreover, Douglass's eschatological ethic is both more literal and more contemporaneous than Day's use of scripture to support her pacifism. For Douglass, the distinctive feature of the present era, the nuclear age, is that we quite literally live on the brink of time. The power wrought by nuclear technology has brought our "quest for security through ever-greater destructive power to an absolute end." Nuclear weapons are "eschatological weapons" in that they are able to bring history to its termination. As such, we are in a peculiar historical and military bind: "The new threat of global suicide has redefined military power at its height as ultimately powerless, because its ultimate use would terminate the life of man."[62] We need, then, an ethic adjusted to the alarming facts of the day, for our present structures and institutions are radically incapable of meeting the needs of the globe.[63] For Douglass, such an ethic is found in the principles of "nonviolent liberation."[64]

Douglass also draws on a belief in what he calls Ultimate Reality, a structure of Being and Unity beneath the egocentric illusions of "the world." Reference to this underlying reality includes a belief in the unity of the human family, a unity that is distorted by worldly divisions and changing political factions. Efforts to establish our own interests curdle into particularistic perspectives and loyalties. Violence is both a symptom of and a catalyst for worldly particularisms that run contrary to the structure of Being itself.

We can discover the unity of reality by conforming to the truth of *agape,* understood as radical, self-emptying love. Such selflessness, says Douglass, is represented paradigmatically by the cross of Jesus Christ. Jesus' self-understanding was defined largely by the notion of *ebed Yahweh,* or suffering servant of the Lord, as described in Isaiah, chapters 42 and 53.[65] Other scriptural materials confirm and embellish the notion that Jesus' voluntary suffering and death are key to the work of his brief ministry. For Douglass, Jesus discloses the law of history, namely, that transformation is possible only by way of the cross. Moreover, Christians are called to make this truth present again by relinquishing their efforts to master themselves and others. At the heart of Douglass's ethic, then, is the imperative of "ego-crucifixion."[66]

In Douglass's mind the truth of suffering love is not exclusive to Christianity, for Gandhi discovered the same reality in the notion of *satyagraha* (truth force, soul force) independently of Christian revelation. In this respect Douglass reflects a characteristically Catholic approach to morality, in which basic ethical ideas are available in biblical and nonbiblical sources for those whose reason is uncorrupted. Both Jesus and Gandhi experienced the poverty of selfhood, a radical, kenotic self-emptying, opening themselves to an infinite reservoir of transformative power.[67]

That power, accessible to all persons, is found only by "reducing oneself to zero."[68] Drawing on Jungian categories, Douglass maintains that each ego has a "shadow," understood as "the sum of everything I refuse to acknowledge about myself." Elements of the repressed ego coalesce into a relatively autonomous psychic reality which, insofar as it remains repressed, invites destruction. One key to voluntary selflessness, then, is to open oneself up to the poverty and emptiness of the self, to acknowledge the "bottomless void" that opens us to the unity of all reality. By means of ego-crucifixion we can achieve a new vision, an epiphanic "flash of the profound unity of existence."[69]

In failing to relinquish our emptiness lie the roots of our quest for power and self-mastery.[70] One problem of the present age, Douglass alleges, is that we are fascinated with effectiveness and pragmatic efficiency. Contemporary society is dominated by a desire to control the world according to a "spirit of technique."[71] This spirit fails to acknowledge the "resistance of reality, which will not respond to my techniques by granting me my ends." Confronted with such resistance, "the philosophy of technique will always argue for more forceful means . . . whose recurring lack of results (toward a dimly remembered value) will deepen my bondage to self and ultimate futility."[72] Selflessness, in contrast, liberates us from the seduction of effectiveness. Rather than seek to create the way of truth, we should prepare for its arrival by removing the obstacles posed by egoistic assertiveness. Remarks Douglass, "The Way . . . is not effective. It is free."[73]

Within this framework a unique version of realism emerges. Douglass draws on quasi-factual metaphors to describe the practical veracity of suffering love. Love is the law of the cosmos, no less real than the physical laws of the natural world. Tremendous amounts of energy can be released from matter itself; an analogously powerful force lies at the heart of spiritual reality. Such spiritual energy, Douglass insists, is as objective and real as the physical laws of nature. Just as matter is transformed to energy as it is accelerated to the speed of light, so too can humanity be transformed by the power of suffering love. Successful "experiments" with these spiritual laws, especially by Jesus and Gandhi, corroborate the effectiveness of radical selflessness. A spiritual law of nature confirms its veracity to those in harmony with it, and nonviolent liberation must harness itself to such spiritual "facts." Douglass notes, "the imperative of our end-time is that we discover the spiritual equation corresponding to Einstein's physical equation, and that we then begin to experiment seriously in its world-transforming reality while there is still time."[74]

How, then, does this eschatological realism look as a pacifist ethic? Douglass holds together several of the distinctions within the elements I adduced above. His general justification for nonviolence, like Day's, is at once absolute and relative: absolute because the requirements of suffering love, following the teachings and example of Jesus, are simple, straightforward, and uncompromising; relative because voluntary suffering also derives from an account of the harmony of being and its resistance to human agency. Suffering love is both obedience to a command and a means to an end, the goal of metanoia, self-discovery, and an epiphany of Ultimate Reality.

Furthermore, Douglass's account of love joins self-sacrificial *agape* and harmonious relations in the belief that the former provides the necessary conditions for the latter. Harmony is part of the autonomous "resistance" of reality for which we can prepare by means of self-emptying. And, because Douglass's views are anchored to the end of metanoia, a radical transformation available to all persons, his social vision is transformationist rather than sectarian.

Like virtually all strict pacifists, moreover, Douglass extends the range of obligation to all. Although he admits that we can derive the position of nuclear pacifism and selective conscientious objection from just-war tenets, he insists that these tenets lack the conceptual and moral force to sustain a dissenting voice, to confront the machinations of nation-state politics in the nuclear era. The only solution to our eschatological age, Douglass insists, is to accept the cross of self-sacrificial love. At the level of policy this means nothing other than unilateral disarmament.[75] Given the evil of nuclear weapons and the eschatological nature of the day, the United States has no option but to explore nonviolent alternatives. However, unlike Zahn, Douglass leaves relatively short shrift to the possibility of nonviolent defense.[76]

Instead, Douglass confines the notion of nonviolent resistance to the realm of political action, resistance *ad intra*. In this respect he combines nonresistance and nonviolent resistance, usually distinct as methods of nonviolence, in a complex way. At the level of individual character, Douglass enjoins us to relinquish all claims, to deliver ourselves from the illusion of selfhood and agency. Yet at the level of action, Douglass adheres to the principle of nonviolent resistance. The biblical command, "Resist not evil," means, "'Do not resist violently in the manner of the Zealots.' That a *non-violent* resistance to evil is not only permissible but called for by the love on which Jesus based everything is evident in his own sharp responses to hypocrisy and injustice." Douglass concludes, "The Mennonite concept of 'non-resistance' is a little short of Jesus' meaning . . . [producing] today too passive an understanding of the ethic being laid down."[77] Nonresistance and "ego-crucifixion" denote terms of virtue, a spirituality of nonviolence, while nonviolent resistance governs an ethic of action, especially political disobedience.

In this vein Douglass recounts the Hickam action of 1972, when he and six others leafleted the Pacific Air Force Headquarters at Hickam Air Base in Hawaii. Douglass and another activist also poured blood on top-secret electronic warfare files, which can be seen as a form of direct action because the files themselves "could be shown to contain evidence of the U.S. Air Force's use of anti-personnel weapons, designed for civilians." Following traditional forms of civil disobedience, then, the Hickam action targeted what the activists perceived to be an unjust policy. Yet unlike traditional civil disobedience, Douglass's direct action had mixed goals, combining the goal of education with that of actually thwarting the war effort—"to draw attention to and hinder an enormous crime against life."[78] Eventually charges against the Hickam activists were dropped or reduced to misdemeanors. But those found guilty refused to submit to the penalty of a $500 fine.[79]

Douglass reconciles nonresistance as a virtue and nonviolent civil disobedience by interpreting the latter theologically. He did not actively seek pragmatic effectiveness in the Hickam action, he insists. On the contrary, truth "was realized gradually by holding on to that truth in spite of an apparently futile situation. . . . The members of our group only created conditions which allowed that force to surface in the Honolulu community." Nonpragmatic adherence to their beliefs, then, allowed Douglass and his compatriots to witness "the transformation of that truth into an objective reality which acted autonomously."[80] In this way Douglass seeks to avoid the charge that his civil disobedience is another instance of "technique," matching means to ends or manipulating outcomes. Rather, the course of events was directed providentially, in what Douglass calls "one of the most miraculous events I have experienced in a life which I can honestly understand as a series of miracles."[81]

Douglass's attempt to hold together selfless nonresistance with resistant political action reflects a tension between religion and ethics in his thought, about which I will speak more generally in chapter 5. In Douglass's case the religious deliverance of the self from the illusion of agency opens a space in which the power of Being may miraculously realize itself. The religion of the Way delivers the self from the burden of realizing consequences and the concomitant task of justifying those consequences. Stated in more traditional theological language, for Douglass repentance and the gospel provide freedom from the law. In this respect Douglass's approach differs significantly from the general approach of the Worker, for which religious beliefs are virtually interchangeable with ethical imperatives.

Several related features commonly recur in any religion of radical self-criticism and repentance. Often the religion frees the individual from having to sort out answers to specific ethical problems, leading to ethical quietism. In Douglass's case, radical self-emptying eliminates the possibility of positive "action-guides," because such guides presuppose the self as a locus of agency. More generally, freedom means freedom from ethical justification and ethical casuistry, the task of determining the right or the good according to shared canons of rationality. Moreover, any action subsequent to religious liberation is evacuated of ethical distinctions or judgments. Freed from such appraisal, that action takes on a self-evident righteousness of its own. God, or some suprapersonal, transhuman force, is the real agent in history, and the task of humanity is to prepare the way. The subsequent course of history may then be legitimated according to the grammar of belief.

Yet the freedom provided by self-emptying *agape* nonetheless raises several questions regarding religion, ethics, and their relation in Douglass's account. Is the Way evacuated of ethical content? Does harmony simply "occur" once we get our egos out of the way, or does it take more of our own doing? Is ethics as a guide for action reducible to "technique," pejoratively understood? If so, how then is civil disobedience *ethically* justified? Douglass's pacifism, distinctive as it may be in Catholic ethics, nonetheless raises an enduring question about the place of ethics in a religion with a radical self-critical dimension: Where is the place for justifications and commands for action after repentance, purification, and freedom?

For Douglass the absence of positive duties raises, at least in principle, the problem of ethical quietism following ego-crucifixion. In Douglass's case that problem is overcome in his political action. Yet this action is depicted as almost self-evidently right, needing no ethical justification. By construing direct-action raids theologically, as only "creating conditions" for the autonomous agency of truth, Douglass remains consistent in that he abstains from such justification. The absence of human volition removes the need for ethical justification and shared canons of rational inquiry. Entering the air base, entering the headquarters, and even receiving the directions to top-secret files from one of the sergeants, are all narrated in the grammar of belief, as events caused by transhuman forces rather than by human agency.[82] But in depicting the Hickam action as caused by Providence, rather than by humans matching means to ends in pursuit of effectiveness, Douglass's account reads like a *post facto* theological legitimation of the Honolulu resistance communities. At the very least, such a theological legitimation allows for a political praxis in which the ends justify the means.

The question of technique, effectiveness, and manipulation emerged as a vital issue for Catholic pacifists in the late 1960s and continues to haunt many today. The question usually accompanies anxiety about the degree to which civil disobedience includes elements of confrontation and subtle violence. For those more radical than eschatological pacifists, however, the question must be seen in light of the revolutionary, subversive goals of nonviolent belief and practice. Central to the revolutionary aspirations of many recent Catholic pacifists is the goal of tearing down the idols of militarism, the symbols of death and imperialism that form the sacred canopy of the nuclear age. With these goals in view, revolutionary pacifism includes a more robust account of the demands of agency in relation to belief, a tighter connection between religion and ethics, than one finds in many of Douglass's writings.

Iconoclastic Pacifism

The 1960s marked a turning point in Catholic pacifism, in which open displays of rebellion took on more dramatic and ceremonial elements than had previously been witnessed in the United States. The Vietnam War and the civil rights movement provided the backdrop, especially after 1965, when President Johnson announced the bombing of North Vietnam and Martin Luther King, Jr., led the march to Selma, Alabama. In October of that year, David Miller, a twenty-two-year-old Catholic Worker, burned his draft card at an antiwar rally. Miller's act was historic because he was the first individual to violate a law making the burning of draft cards a criminal offense, punishable by a $10,000 fine and/or five years in jail. A month later, Roger LaPorte, a Worker volunteer, poured gasoline on himself and immolated himself in front of the United Nations building. Before dying several hours later, LaPorte told the press, "I am a Catholic. . . . I am antiwar, all wars. I did this as a religious action."[83]

Soon Catholics were involved in a series of raids to protest the Vietnam War and the draft. In 1967 Philip Berrigan and three others poured blood on the draft records at the Baltimore Selective Service Board. Then followed perhaps the most notorious raid, when Philip and his brother Daniel, with seven others, poured homemade napalm on more than three hundred files from the Catonsville, Maryland, draft board, ignited the files, and prayed together while the police waited and the media watched. After the trial, Daniel went underground for four months, making numerous public appearances while eluding the FBI. Actions in Milwaukee, Delaware, Boston, Chicago, and Washington, D.C., soon followed, the last of which included an attack on the offices of Dow Chemical for its production of napalm.[84]

In 1971, eight persons including Philip Berrigan were indicted for plotting to blow up the heating systems of government buildings in Washington, D.C., and to kidnap Henry Kissinger. Thus began the trial of the Harrisburg Seven (one person chose to defend himself), one of the most troublesome chapters for what by then was called the "Catholic Left." Mutual incrimination and internal suspicions infected the defendants, weakening the movement from within. The defendants' principal counsel, Ramsey Clark, made a one-sentence statement, after which he rested his defense. The case ended with a hung jury, but the internal exhaustion wrought by the trial and the decline in conscription for the Vietnam War led to a significant hiatus in the Left's activities.

In the 1980s the Catholic Left resurfaced to protest the production of nuclear weapons. Taking literally the biblical prophecy, "They shall beat their swords into plowshares and their spears into pruning hooks" (Mic. 4:3), the Berrigans and several others embarked upon a series of "Plowshares Actions" on several military bases and in corporations across the country. In September 1980 eight persons entered the General Electric nuclear warhead plant in King of Prussia, Pennsylvania, and "disarmed" Mark 12A warheads. A series of similar Plowshares actions followed in Groton, Connecticut, and Wilmington, Delaware. On Thanksgiving Day, 1983, several individuals hammered and poured blood on a B-52 bomber armed with cruise missiles at Griffiss Air Force Base, and on Easter Sunday, 1984, members of Plowshares poured blood on and hammered Pershing II components at the Martin Marietta plant in Orlando, Florida. Similarly, Douglass has carried out a series of symbolic actions to protest the Trident missile in the Puget Sound. However, none of these actions received the media coverage that followed the draft-board raids of the 1960s and early 1970s.

Despite the changing membership of the Catholic Left, its internal troubles, and the decline in national interest, several strands have kept the movement conceptually distinctive from its inception. Generally the Catholic Left has justified its pacifism by placing the biblical command not to kill within a wider critique of the American ethos. Accordingly, Daniel Berrigan cites the Sermon on the Mount to support the claim, "Man is forbidden to kill." But he has emphasized more strongly the "system of idolatry," the "strange gods" of property and war.[85] During the Vietnam era, war was seen as symptomatic of a wider and more pernicious set of systemic forces, the "multiple idols . . . of racism, war-making, hatred, envy, neglect of the poor."[86] And almost two decades later, during the trial of the Griffiss Plowshares members, the defense spoke about the fiduciary dimension of American militarism, remarking, "We are compelled by this government into a stance of *false worship* of its weapons unless we act against them as we have sought to do."[87] Nonviolence, then, is not only a rejection of war; it is also an act of ritual purification, an attempt to deliver the nation from its supplication to "gods of death."[88]

The desire to purify the land means, among other things, that the Catholic Left has radicalized the problems surrounding cooperation and scandal, extending these ideas in a theological direction. Now the problem is not so much the "occasioning of sin" as a moral misdeed; rather, the problem concerns the fundamental object of loyalty. Purity is not moral purity, strictly speaking, but freedom from defilement, contagion, and the taint of association with the powers that be. After their imprisonment for the Catonsville raid, the Berrigans spoke of rejecting "complicity with a culture and a power structure which idolizes power and privilege."[89] Blood was used in several raids as a symbol of life and purification, juxtaposed with images of death.[90] As a theological imperative, purity requires an "apocalyptic sense," an acute consciousness of "the proximity of the end of things."[91] Hence the iconoclastic objective: to cleanse our culture of its graven images and its false consciousness about the meaning of peace.

Within an iconoclastic perspective, to call for a clarification of ethical thought—as I have with Day and Douglass—only begs more serious questions about the quality of our ethos and our poetry of self-description. "The history of ideas," remarks Daniel Berrigan, "is a sterile, effete hobby."[92] Real social change "has to do with new attitudes toward freedom, responsibility and love, which awaken neither as pure ideas nor as unrealized values."[93] What is necessary, then, is not "interminable intellectualism" but the capacity to put the truth in "shocking perspectives."[94] By juxtaposing images of life and death, e.g., blood and nuclear weapons, prayer and napalm, the ceremonial acts of the Catholic Left have been designed to disturb, to disorient, and to generate a crisis of self-understanding about the mechanisms of war and tools of rationalization.

Disturbing forms of action join both coercive and persuasive objectives, although the latter have assumed preeminence in the antinuclear protests of the Plowshares members. About the Catonsville action, Daniel Berrigan writes that the purpose was "to hinder the war in a literal way / an actual physical way." Burning the files was designed "to throw a roadblock into a system which [we] considered murderous."[95] Similarly, Philip Berrigan maintained that the burning of the draft files "will prevent a few aluminum coffins from coming home, and keep a few more innocent Vietnamese alive."[96] Yet such actions raised questions from more traditional pacifists who worried about the degree to which the Left's civil disobedience capitulated to the ethos of technique and manipulation, especially manipulation of the media.[97] Perhaps in response to these queries the Berrigans also alleged that nonviolence "cannot look to human outcomes for its justification."[98] The draft-board raids were "free speech acts," highly symbolic deeds "to raise a cry / an outcry at what was clearly a crime / an unnecessary suffering / a clear and wanton slaughter."[99] Even Daniel Berrigan's evasion of the law after the Catonsville action was legitimated in educative terms, "to draw attention to the continuing war."[100] Following this trajectory, moreover, the antinuclear action of Plowshares members has been cast almost exclusively as persuasive rather than coercive. The Griffiss action evoked a "spiritual epiphany," remarks Daniel Berrigan, a form of anticultural political action "putting to one side such considerations as efficiency, results, media snoop." The

Plowshares actions are cast as ends in themselves, as "good, and needful, and nonviolent, and thus joined to an immemorial tradition of conscience superceding [*sic*] law."[101]

Yet this embrace of educative rather than coercive goals by the Catholic Left ought not obscure its overriding revolutionary impulse. Running throughout the Berrigans' writings is the assertion that the American system as a whole is unjust. In this respect the Berrigans differ from previous Catholic pacifists, whose protests generally prescinded from judgments about revolutionary change. In 1967 Philip Berrigan remarked that American institutions were no longer reformable and that the chief order of business was "to confront the entrenched, massive, and complex injustice of our country."[102] Similarly, Daniel Berrigan on several occasions has compared the social ills in the United States to those facing Nazi Germany, likening the Vietnam War "in its genocidal character to Hitler's war and his near extinction of the German Jews."[103] So it is the legal system as a whole, not only particular laws, against which the Berrigans have directed their protest, premised on the complaint that "the American scene was no longer a good scene."[104] Against this backdrop they have been drawn by a transformationist impulse, although both Berrigans have recognized the fact that their views enjoy at best a minority following.[105]

The Berrigans' distrust of existing institutions means that the distinction between just and unjust laws, central to the distinction between direct and indirect action, is relatively unimportant. For if the system as a whole is unjust, then the laws within that system only typify a systemically corrupt regime. Consequently, we need not develop fine distinctions or protocols for resistance; the "establishment" in its entirety needs to be overhauled. Accordingly, the Berrigans have directed much of their action at the law and "beyond the law," translegally, "to embarrass and expose illegitimate power."[106]

Their general mandate for resistance does not mean, however, that the Berrigans have left casuistry and ethical distinctions entirely out of their account. The question for their casuistry concerns the place of violence in their raids against draft boards and corporations, especially where private property was destroyed. To what extent can we view such actions as nonviolent? Generally Philip Berrigan justifies the destruction of property along iconoclastic lines: "The Jews had their golden calf, Americans have their own property."[107] But more specifically he insists that the violence against draft boards was "spiritual rather than physical," a violence performed in the service of love.[108] By this account, violence is confined to physical violence against persons, distinct from psychological violence against persons or physical violence against property.

Yet even these distinctions are not meant to settle completely the morality of nonviolence, leaving unresolved the range of pacifist obligation. Writing about the ethics of violent revolution, Philip Berrigan has acknowledged that a Christian "may tolerate and approve—but not actively join—a violent revolution, having judged that political and social injustice had reached insufferable limits, without reasonable hope of redress." Berrigan embraces the idea that abandoning one's rights comes closest to the imitation of Christ, representing an ethic available to some but not all. Hence, "if the Christian refuses to vindicate his human rights for personal benefit, it is because the Lord refused such ambiguous human protection. . . . To possess enough faith to act in such a way is a singular and undeserved gift, which men less blessed can only partially comprehend." These less blessed "need their rights, their freedom to express them, and a visible response of justice." But they also need persons "of faith to take up their cause in conscience, even at the cost of freedom and life."[109]

Berrigan's definition of violence as physical harm and his prohibition of such harm both find their origin in the Augustinian convergence, as we have seen.[110] But for Philip Berrigan these notions raise one question about his pacifism as a social ethic. The distinction between persons and property seems overly sharp, and is incongruous with many of Berrigan's statements about the Vietnam War. It is doubtful, for example, that he would consider the American bombing of Vietnam property to be nonviolent. Moreover, the distinction between property and persons is incompatible with Berrigan's statements about the evils of contemporary America. Not only war but poverty at home and economic involvement with third world countries are denounced as forms of injustice. According to these latter claims, persons and property are not absolutely different. Recognizing the material conditions of human destitution would seem incompatible with the sharp distinction between property and persons in Philip Berrigan's casuistry of violence. Indeed, the close relation between persons and property explains why Christians have always viewed munificence as charity toward persons, and theft as violence against persons.[111]

Perhaps more problematic for the Berrigans, however, is the fact that they scarcely developed arguments on behalf of a positive vision to replace the America they denounced in quasi-revolutionary terms. Daniel Berrigan writes, for example, "'It is not a time for building justice,' wrote my brother from prison, 'it is a time for confronting injustice.' Say no! The 'No' makes the hero."[112] Yet this "saying no" of iconoclastic pacifism possesses the danger of an ethical vacuum, leaving us without guidelines for the future. What alternative ought to replace the present order? Iconoclastic pacifism departs from its Worker forebears, retaining the problem of Douglass's pacifism in an enlarged form: Can there be positive guides for action in a postapocalyptic situation? To what extent can conventional moral vocabulary like *justice* be carried over into a new constructive vision? What ethical imperatives are possible or even intelligible after radical critique, in this case sociocultural critique?

The Problem of Tradition

The question of positive injunctions following in the wake of radical personal or sociocultural criticism is not unique to Catholic pacifists. As H. Richard Niebuhr discovered in his study of American Protestantism, the place of constructive goals in a religion premised on protesting the status quo is no small problem.[113] As Niebuhr argued, one of the key difficulties accompanying a religion of protest—pertinent to Douglass and the Berrigans no less than to mainline Protestantism—is the future of tradition, the handing on of beliefs and practices. Assuming that the evils against which we protest are removed by repentance or purification, what then is to follow? How do we create a religious and social order that does not fall prey to the criticisms of the prior generation, those drawn together by the impulse to reform? How does a religion of protest institutionalize itself once it acquires the space to develop its own views without interference? How can such institutionalization maintain a dynamic, critical energy across time?

For Catholic pacifism, the problem of tradition possesses three specific permutations: continuity, coherence, and comprehensiveness. *Continuity* refers to the future of a tradition, *coherence* refers to the internal connections within a tradition, and *comprehensiveness* refers to the extent to which a tradition has developed its views in light of relevant critical questions. Continuity pertains to tradition as *tradere* (to hand on), the task of transmitting beliefs across time; coherence and comprehensiveness pertain to tradition as *tradita,* that which is handed on. In each case, Catholic pacifism as a tradition faces difficulties.

Continuity, the handing on of pacifist beliefs, is a problem in the official Catholic teaching given the range of obligation permitted to pacifist ideas. By *permitting* but not *requiring* pacifism, official teaching refuses to underwrite birthright pacifism, that is, pacifism that is passed on generationally as a fixed tenet or practice. If pacifism is to continue from the point of view of official teaching, it must rely on ongoing inspiration but not the weight of institutional obligation. In this respect Catholic pacifism will always differ from that of historic peace churches, e.g., the Mennonites. According to the logic of official teaching, then, the future of Catholic pacifism lies in the hands of those charismatic individuals who will carry the torch. If the torch goes out temporarily, there is nothing in the official position to mandate its relighting. Consequently, by leaving pacifism as a matter of individual choice, official Catholic teaching may be taking away with its right hand what it granted with its left.

Continuity is a problem for Douglass and iconoclastic pacifists, as I suggested above, given the tensions between radical critique and positive guides for action. In Niebuhr's terms, questions arise about "constructive Protestantism." What vision takes us beyond the present, providing continuity between the current protest and the future order? In what terms would pacifism commend itself in a new regime? On what foundation would a subsequent generation of iconoclastic pacifists build?

Coherence is a problem given the phenomenon of pluralism within and among Catholic pacifists. The apparent tolerance of different points of view creates problems for the future. In the Catholic Worker movement, for example, the nature of Worker pacifism remains unclear to prospective members called to a life of radical social work. The actions of the Catholic Worker may indeed speak louder than words, but those actions nonetheless require interpretation and a moral vocabulary for deciphering the meaning of Worker praxis.

The question of pluralism is even more nagging for official Catholic teaching. Despite the fact that official pronouncements praise those who practice nonviolence, many of those who are ostensibly praised fail to abide by the framework of a rights-based approach. With the exception of Zahn, eschatological pacifists and iconoclastic pacifists eschew one of the fundamental tenets of a rights-based approach, namely, the duty of nonviolent defense. Rather, these pacifists view nonviolent resistance chiefly as a form of civil disobedience *ad intra,* not as a mode of defense against an opponent, *ad extra.* Nor do Catholic pacifists speak much about repaying debts to the social order as a duty incumbent upon those with the liberty of conscientious objection during conscription. Justice qualifies a pacifist ethic in a rights-based approach, but these qualifications all but disappear for eschatological and iconoclastic types. Reconciling this plurality of views with official teaching may be impossible for the future of Catholic pacifism.

Comprehensiveness is problematic for Catholic pacifism as a tradition insofar as several of the elements of a pacifist ethic remain undeveloped in each of the three types. A few lacunae deserve mention. As I indicated above, pacifism as a social ethic for the Catholic Worker has drawn loosely on the elements adduced at the outset of this chapter, leaving the impression that Worker pacifism is both radical and ambiguous. On specific policy issues, e.g., conscription, eschatological and iconoclastic pacifists who protested the draft during the Vietnam War all but ignored the ethics of exemption (conditional or unconditional). And, although the official teaching answered that question in favor of conditional exemption "not related to military needs," it is still unclear how much, or in what sense, the pacifist is obligated to serve in war. (The Civilian Public Service in the Second World War was not related to military needs, but it often entailed busywork, leaving a mixed precedent for future wars.) Moreover, within the Berrigans' general mandate to resist the established order, little argument is given to support the judgment that the social order is relatively unjust. Nor do the Berrigans provide criteria by which we can gauge the relative justice or injustice of a political regime. Pacifist ideas have been put forward in different ways by Zahn, Day, Douglass, the Berrigans, and the Catholic magisterium, but for the future generation of Catholic pacifists—those looking for a nascent tradition to receive and carry forward—no comprehensive pacifist position has emerged from the United States.

One way to advance the discussion surrounding continuity, coherence, and comprehensiveness in Catholic pacifism is to draw on a facsimile of just-war tenets as an ethic of pacifist protest. One overall benefit would be to cast the morality of civil disobedience in a mold that has stood the test of time in Catholic social ethics, and which is designed as a general guide for political obligation and decision-making.[114] Extending the logic of just-war ideas developed in chapter 1 would begin with a prima facie duty to respect the law, leaving the burden of proof on those who disobey it. Those who override this duty could do so only on behalf of another duty, in a situation of arguable moral conflict. Moreover, overriding the prima facie duty to obey the law would nonetheless leave moral traces, requiring a respect for law and political institutions as part of the civil action (e.g., submission upon arrest). And, for those who maintain that the legal system as a whole is unjust, the burden of proof would require a supporting account, with clear criteria of political legitimacy, open to public scrutiny. Specific reference to just-war criteria as a framework for civil disobedience would take this form:

Just cause: This condition requires a defense of values either excluded or violated in public policy.

Competent authority: The just-war account of competent authority requires a representative of the community to declare war and marshal a defense, which is difficult for pacifists to replicate as dissidents. Nonetheless, the burden of proof implied by Childress's reconstruction of just-war tenets would require those involved in civil disobedience either to provide a public account of their actions, putting their views to public scrutiny, or to assent to others who speak on their behalf. Those critical of reigning authorities, adopting revolutionary rhetoric, ought to specify criteria of political legitimacy.

Right intention: This condition would require pacifists to order their aims toward peace and fairness, and to stabilize the conditions of justice by correcting its abuse.

Last resort: All legal alternatives within reasonable reach of the dissident must be exhausted.[115]

Reasonable hope for success: The achievement of persuasive or coercive goals should be probable. However, as in the case of war, it may be necessary for pacifists to testify to certain values even in a "losing cause." The general effect of this principle would thus be to prohibit rash or irrational recourse to civil disobedience.

Relative justice: Neither side has a monopoly on absolute justice in defense of its claims.

Proportionality: The foreseen risks of a concerted, ongoing movement of dissidence must not outweigh the prospective benefits.

Discrimination and *proportionality* as criteria for specific actions would require the actors to distinguish between legitimate and illegitimate "targets" of conscientious protest and to allow foreseen, unintended risks only if they are commensurate with the goods that justify the action in the first place.

Pacifists' use of a facsimile of just-war criteria would amplify the common ground between both moral vocabularies.[116] It would furnish a basis for pacifist casuistry about nonviolent resistance *ad intra* and a skeletal framework for assessing acts which are often coercive, even when the coercion is foreseen but unintended. And, equally important, this use of some facsimile of just-war tenets would help shape moral assessments by those who disagree with pacifist protest. With a common framework and a shared moral idiom, those on both sides of the question of war and political obligation might be able to identify the issues that divide them. They might also develop more fully the ethics of expressing publicly the nature of their disagreement, sharing a grammar for social criticism in a world of common moral interpretations. Doubtless a facsimile of just-war criteria hardly exhausts the pluralism and complexity of pacifism as a social ethic. But without a shared vocabulary and skeletal framework, Catholic pacifists may be left without the minimal benefits of an ethical tradition. And without these benefits, they may find themselves without a future and without a public with whom to converse. Such would be a large price to pay for those committed to the ideals of nonviolence, social criticism, and reform.

F O U R

Pacifism and Just-War Tenets:
How Do They Diverge?

The Point of Convergence

I concluded the last chapter by suggesting that moral grammar about war and peace might be clarified by honing the critical edge of pacifism against the stone of just-war ideas, the latter furnishing a structure for developing an ethic of civil obligation and disobedience. In so doing, I indicated a set of concerns around which pacifism and just-war tenets might be joined. In this chapter I will examine in more detail the promise of, and the limits to, such commonality.

The notion that pacifism and just-war tenets enjoy a close relation has become conventional wisdom in ethics subsequent to Childress's argument on behalf of a point of convergence, the bias against violence, and the logic of prima facie duties. In addition to those I mentioned in chapter 1, James Turner Johnson argues that just-war thinking and pacifism "have something profoundly in common: a searching distrust of violence."[1] James Finn likewise observes, "Both positions start with generally pacifist presumptions: Peace is an attainment and an aspiration of a high order; war is an evil and is to be avoided; the fraternal order in which humankind participates argues against the use of violence to resolve conflicts."[2] Interpreting the Catholic tradition, J. Bryan Hehir writes, "This presumption against war is reflected in the way Aquinas poses his *quaestio* regarding war: 'Is fighting in war always a sin?' In the pacifist tradition this 'strong presumption' becomes in effect an absolute rule admitting of no exceptions. The just-war ethic retains the presumption, but acknowledges exceptions to the rule."[3] Charles Curran also speaks of the "common ground" shared by pacifists and nonpacifists in the Christian community, saying, "All are called to work for peace." Drawing an analogy between religious vocations and the witness of pacifism, Curran argues that there should be "vocations in the Christian community through the gift of the Spirit for people to bear witness to the value of peace."[4] And among Protestant ecclesial pronouncements, the U.S. Methodist bishops invite "pacifists and nonpacifists . . . to recapture their common ground, such as their moral presumption against all war and violence."[5]

Nevertheless, significant differences can be obscured if we confine our attention to this point of contact without also recognizing the divergence that follows, conventional wisdom notwithstanding. For, however much pacifists might accept my suggestion to adopt the formal skeleton of just-war tenets for an ethics of civil disobedience, these approaches depart from each other when it comes to the morality of war itself. Usually, however, accounts of this divergence have proceeded with reference to nonpacifist criticisms of pacifism. Reinhold Niebuhr, to take the most famous example, argues that nonresistant pacifism stresses love at the expense of justice and order, while nonviolent resistant pacifism, seeking to reform others through nonviolent acts, reflects "the belief that man is essentially good at some level of his being."[6] From Niebuhr's point of view, neither nonresistant nor nonviolent resistant pacifists reckon adequately with the reality of self-interest and the will-to-power in human history, leaving the just or the innocent to suffer at the hands of an aggressor. Consequently, Niebuhr alleges, pacifists remain blind to the ambiguities, the stark realities, and the moral duties involved in resistance to aggression.

Ironically, however, a hasty appeal to Niebuhrian realism may obscure further differences between pacifists and nonpacifists because it ignores the criticisms that pacifists have placed at the doorstep of the just-war theorist. As even Niebuhr acknowledged, pacifists remind nonpacifists "that the relative norms of social justice, which justify both coercion and resistance to coercion, are not final norms." We need the idealism and perfectionism of pacifism, Niebuhr concluded, "lest we accept the warfare of the world as normative, lest we become callous to the horror of war, and lest we forget the ambiguity of our own actions and motives and the risk we run of achieving no permanent good from this momentary anarchy in which we are involved."[7]

In the years following Niebuhr's critique of pacifism, the divisions between pacifists and just-war theorists have become more complex, owing to the development of each tradition and an ongoing dialogue between them. In this chapter I wish to pursue the Niebuhrian notion that pacifism prevents nonpacifists from becoming inured to the phenomenon of war. But rather than let Niebuhr's emphasis on pacifist idealism set our agenda, I will allow pacifist voices to speak for themselves. To that end I will survey the contributions made to discussions of war and peace by those pacifists who criticize the stated or unstated premises of just-war ideas. My purpose is not to resolve the differences; rather, I wish to show that a study of such divergences may reveal yet more profound points of *convergence* than those adduced by either Niebuhr or contemporary ethical theory.

As I suggested in the last chapter, pacifism has assumed various expressions over the course of its rich and checkered history.[8] Yet even my topography of Catholic pacifism provides only a glimpse of pacifist claims. Religious and secular principles authorize pacifist arguments; within religious pacifism, Christian and non-Christian convictions obtain. For the purposes of this chapter I shall attend primarily (but not exclusively) to the vocabularies of contemporary Christian pacifists, for it is among them that a dialectical conversation with just-war ideas has been most pronounced. Representing broad theological and ethical currents in Protestant and Roman Catholic thought, Christian pacifists examine the stated and unstated axioms of just-war tenets. A close study of their critiques of just-war ideas indicates that the point of convergence between pacifism and just-war tenets is both more vexing and more suggestive than ethicists have heretofore maintained.

Theological Criticisms of Just-War Tenets

For many pacifists the problem of war is a crucible, perhaps a "limit question," in which the classical issues of religious faith are tested under intense heat and pressure. The meaning and ethical implications of several religious notions—creation, theology of history, anthropology, and theological method, to name a few—all undergo special trials when the morality of war is broached. Yet one problem that most pacifists face is the fact that just-war theorists in the Christian community rarely invoke theological authorizations to support their views. Generally, then, pacifists' criticisms of just-war tenets must proceed indirectly. Since just-war theorists seldom make appeals to theological warrants, pacifists must uncover the unstated premises and the final assumptions on which just-war ideas seem to depend.

Christian pacifists characteristically begin their theological critiques by objecting to the authoritative sources of just-war thought. Just-war theorists argue speciously, from a specifically Christian standpoint, insofar as they draw on extrabiblical sources, e.g., natural law morality, to derive a principle of justice. Yet natural law morality, John Howard Yoder argues, uses a "competitive revelation claim" as an authority for ethics. Relying on nonbiblical sources, just-war theorists have us place "our faith in some other channel of ethical insight . . . than that which is offered us through Jesus as attested in the New Testament."[9] At stake in this first objection, then, are methodological considerations about the proper authorities for any distinctively Christian treatment of war.

Yoder's argument has little relevance for those unconcerned about a distinctively Christian approach to war, but Stanley Hauerwas has sought to broaden the implications of Yoder's views by placing them within recent debates about foundationalism in contemporary ethics. Foundationalist philosophy attempts to ground moral reflection on an ahistorical Archimedean point, seeking a neutral basis on which to build ethical rules in a pluralistic society. Yet efforts to establish universality and neutral objectivity from an ahistorical vantage point, Hauerwas alleges, distort the true nature of moral experience. Our moral reflection, he insists, cannot be divorced from the relativity of its phenomenal, affective, historic, and communal aspects.[10] In his mind, attempts to authorize moral claims according to ostensibly universal criteria in fact require coercion, especially for dissidents. Ignoring the truth of historicity and context in moral reflection leads almost inevitably to confusion, social fragmentation, and violence in our moral grammar and corresponding social practices. A return to biblical authority and biblical narratives, in contrast, eschews such efforts to secure public approbation and, in turn, mitigates the kind of violence that accompanies the pretenses of public theology and ethical discourse today.[11]

Insofar as just-war theorists pursue foundational efforts, Hauerwas's critique issues in an ironic judgment: Reference to an Archimedean point will contribute to the social and intellectual fragmentation conducive to violence itself. The link between just-war ideas and foundational principles would lead, then, to the deconstruction of moral discourse designed to mitigate the use of violence. Although Hauerwas does not directly address those who embrace a point of contact between pacifism and just-war tenets, one inference seems clear: If the presumption against harm is meant to serve as a foundational principle for the just-war tradition, the convergence of pacifist and just-war tenets may actually be the place where the divisions between them are the greatest.

A concern for proper theological authorization and/or emphasis on scriptural narrativity in ethics lead many Christian pacifists to develop their case according to biblical insights. As is well known, the Sermon on the Mount enjoys a pride of place in pacifists' use of Scripture, and pacifists consistently refuse to weaken the "hard sayings" of Jesus by restricting them to individual relations, interior dispositions, private authority, or higher duties, those qualifications made famous by Augustine.[12] Jesus actively renounced the use of force and rejected all power by means of the sword; as such, his paradigmatic teaching and voluntary suffering lie at the heart of imitation and discipleship.[13] The cross is the summary of Jesus' ministry, defining the true pattern of social relations in history. The example of nonresistant love has radical social implications, which cannot be compromised or overridden by conflicting duties.[14]

Christian pacifists usually develop their use of biblical materials by constructing a theology of history. Most Christian pacifists believe that God is the sovereign agent who is directing history according to providential designs.[15] Efforts to control temporal affairs through human politics are bereft of trust in God's providential care. Insofar as just-war theorists place their faith in statecraft to steer the direction of history, pacifists allege, they lack patience and confidence in God's saving, sovereign purposes.

Hauerwas has devoted considerable attention to a theology of history and Christian eschatology to accentuate the differences between pacifism and recent just-war theories.[16] He addresses his criticisms to Hollenbach and the U.S. Catholic bishops, who frame their approaches in light of the interim between Jesus' first and second coming. Hauerwas insists that the theology of Hollenbach and the bishops is incompatible with the chief tenets of New Testament eschatology. A more adequate eschatology rests "not on the conviction the kingdom has not fully come, but that it has."[17] Jesus has inaugurated a new aeon which points forward to the kingdom, of which the present is a foretaste. Hence, our loyalties to the passing aeon must give way to the requirements of life in a new age. Peace is not only an eschatological ideal, Hauerwas argues; it is now present in Christian community. In the church, not the world, Christians learn the true meaning of history, namely, that "war is not a part of [God's] providential care of the world."[18] As members of a distinctive community, Christians must be confident that their historical destiny is not carried by the nation-state.

Christian pacifists also appeal to various theologies of creation to back their views. Martin Luther King, Jr.'s authorization of nonviolent resistance, for example, drew heavily on an inchoate theology of creation, a view premised on the organic mutuality and interdependence of all life. According to King, everyone is "caught in an inescapable network of mutuality, tied in a single garment of destiny. Whatever affects one directly affects all indirectly. I can never be what I ought to be until you are what you ought to be, and you can never be what you ought to be until I am what I ought to be."[19] King often referred to the "world house" and the "beloved community" to poeticize his sense of organic belongingness and unity. He saw the multiracial character of the civil rights movement as a microcosm of his vision of the beloved community, races coexisting in cooperation and mutual support.[20] For King, such cooperation was part of "the interrelated structure of reality."[21]

King's understanding of human relatedness also served as an important warrant for the practice of noncooperation and nonviolent resistance. On several occasions he insisted that to injure another was to injure oneself, implying that no one profits from the use of lethal force. His claim, "Whatever affects one directly affects all indirectly," can be translated, "Whoever injures some directly injures all indirectly." To harm others is to poison the entire community, black and white, innocent and guilty. By King's account there is no such thing as the individual in any unqualified sense. Rather, all persons are parts of a larger organic whole, a "single garment of destiny," and to damage any part of the garment is to injure the whole. For this reason King eschewed violence to advance what he considered to be just causes.

Seeking alternatives to the use of force, King appealed to the principle of noncooperation with evil as a religious and moral duty. Since all reality is interrelated, one can clearly and effectively frustrate another's unjust designs by refusing to cooperate. In this way King joined noncooperation and resistance, usually distinct as modes of protest.[22] Moreover, noncooperation would insure the moral purity of those who follow its course; noncooperation removes the self from the contagion of evil, the defilement of association.[23]

Other expressions of Christian pacifism invoke a theology of creation to criticize the implied theory of statecraft in just-war thought. As we saw in chapter 3, eschatological personalists and iconoclastic pacifists in Catholic ethics hold that just-war ideas can be co-opted by the militaristic hubris of nation-states. The state creates a theological problem insofar as it represents the order of creation, which is present but is passing away. While there is a tendency among pacifists, especially iconoclastic pacifists in Catholicism, to consider the state as inherently violent, some Christian pacifists nevertheless grant qualified legitimacy to the state. As part of the passing aeon, the state may be used by God for limited goals, e.g., maintaining peaceful order.[24] However, any exercise of politics and statecraft must be limited to legitimate means, which exclude the use of violence to secure otherwise legitimate ends.

But having granted some legitimacy to the state, Christian pacifists remain acutely suspicious of the imperial claims that states can make for themselves.[25] While this suspicion is not unique to pacifists, they are manifestly uneasy about ascribing much value to the exercise of politics. These authors underscore the frequency with which states presume uncompromising loyalties. Too often the orders of creation supplant the orders of redemption in Christian faith so that the state, not Christ, becomes the object of religious trust.

Suspicions about the state lead most Christian pacifists to place a premium on the distinctiveness of the Christian community. For Yoder and Hauerwas, the church is the social manifestation of the new aeon which has been inaugurated by Jesus.[26] The church is a countercultural social body which nurtures unique loyalties, universal or transcultural loyalties to supplant the narrower loyalties of nationalism. Relative to secular institutions, the church is a deviant institution and offers a distinctive cultural ethos.[27] Catholic pacifists, e.g., Zahn, invoke the traditional image of the church as the mystical body to develop similar ideas.[28] These authors define Christian community as a locus of universal loyalty in which alternative values and relations are nurtured. The church may be a source of cultural and political dissent; it must avoid all temptation to accommodate itself to the state. Virtually all of these authors criticize the "Constantinianism" of the church, which dulls its prophetic and critical edge.

Yet none of these authors adopts a radically sectarian ecclesiology whereby the church wholly eschews political and social responsibility. The task of the church is neither to convert the world according to a Constantinian self-understanding nor to ignore social problems. Rather, the church is to "witness" to its distinctive heritage, grammar, and ethos.[29] Although the meaning of *witness* is often unclear, two distinct currents run through pacifist literature. *Witness* may denote unswerving fidelity to the will of God, regardless of the consequences. In this sense the term denotes exemplary adherence to religious and ethical values. Yet *witnessing* may also refer to the contrary relation between church and world. As a sign of contradiction, the church unmasks the false pretenses of the secular order by posing a radically different social option.[30] Moreover, these two senses of *witnessing* may be woven together: The church unmasks the false pretenses of secular life by adhering to religious and ethical values. In this way the church remains socially responsible without accommodating itself to worldly compromises or Constantinian designs. However, when the church attempts to affect public policy by appealing to ostensibly secular terms like those found in just-war ideas, it compromises itself with the grammar and practices of the public realm.

A pacifist theology of history, theology of creation, and ecclesiology can be developed with reference to either the history of God's activity or the nature of God's being. Protestant pacifists characteristically appeal to historical revelation. As self-sacrificial *agape,* divine love is universal and nonpreferential. The ethics that derive from this theology, as we shall see, must correspond to the requirements of undiscriminating love. As G. H. C. Macgregor remarks, the ethics of pacifism is "based upon belief in a . . . God who loves all men impartially and sets an infinite value on every individual human soul."[31]

Using philosophical vocabulary, Douglass constructs a similar argument based on God's nature. As I indicated in chapter 3, Douglass defines the nature of Ultimate Reality and develops an ontology of nonviolence.[32] Beneath all the illusions of the world is the ultimate unity of the human family. We can unmask the obstacles and illusions of the world by conforming to the truth of the cross, the way of suffering love, to discover this fundamental truth about human unity. Ethical implications proceed from this theology: Authorizations for lethal force are contrary to the very structure of being itself, since violence is premised on particularism, worldly divisions, or human disunity.[33]

Christian pacifists' views of God, Jesus' message, the church, and history are often linked to a theological anthropology to further support the rejection of nonpacifist ethics. King, for example, drew his views from the tenets of Boston Personalism, the theological and philosophical outlook entrenched at Boston University, where he studied for his doctorate in theology. Boston Personalism emphasized the sacredness of the human personality and the personal nature of the sacred. King believed that human consciousness was a special mark of human nature and a trace of God's image. Violence against one's opponent is a religious problem because it defaces that image with suffering and pain. King believed that all people retained this sacred image, even whites who were irrepressibly racist. For this reason he commanded his followers to hate the deed but not the doer, to hate the sin but not the sinner.[34]

Theological anthropology is also relevant to the belief, widespread among pacifists, that one's enemy is not incorrigible. Pacifists generally insist that enemies may be converted and social relations may be improved by means of trust, patience, and love.[35] For Zahn, this means that one's enemy has a conscience that may be awakened by nonviolent witnessing, understood in both senses above.[36] Moreover, anthropology is linked to eschatology: A trust in the neighbor entails hope for what God can do in the neighbor. In the minds of many Christian pacifists, the resort to force—even as a last resort—signals a lack of patience and a corresponding lack of hope. Confident in God's providential designs, pacifists generally refuse to resign themselves to cynicism about the possibility of human transformation. As Thomas Merton remarks, pacifist convictions "are inseparable from an eschatological Christian hope which is completely open to the presence of God in the world and therefore to the presence of our brother who is always seen, no matter who he may be, in the perspectives of the Kingdom."[37] Acting out of this confidence in a hopeful destiny for others, many pacifists are willing to undergo great risks to effect personal conversion and social change.[38]

Taken together, the points adduced above indicate that Christian pacifists consistently underscore theological dimensions of the justification of lethal force. War is the crucible in which fundamental religious convictions either emerge or collapse under the pressure of political expedience. Whatever else is said about ultimate concerns during everyday life, one cannot eschew such concerns when war transpires. Hauerwas asks, "What is war but the desire to be rid of God, to claim for ourselves the power to determine our meaning and destiny?" In his mind, "our desire to protect ourselves from our enemies, to eliminate our enemies in the name of protecting the common history we share with our friends, is but the manifestation of our hatred of God."[39]

Christian pacifists seek to keep just-war theorists honest about their final vocabulary—those postethical assumptions on which just-war tenets rest. This means that one important task of pacifist theology is to press nonpacifists to come to terms with the background considerations on which their justification of war depends. The point is to show that war is a theory-dependent notion, an idea whose intelligibility is linked to a wider, often unnoticed, constellation of ideas. Those who justify some uses of violence may not be theological in any strict sense, but their view of war is unintelligible apart from basic views about human nature, history, and the ultimate concerns of human beings. Christian pacifists do not reduce the problem of war to theology, but their appeals to theological ideas are designed to unmask the assumptions on which just-war theorists rely.

Ethical Criticisms of Just-War Tenets

Christian pacifists amplify their criticisms of just-war tenets with several ethical arguments. While many of these claims depend on theological convictions, some proceed independently of religious belief, providing a bridge with nonreligious pacifism.

A recurring ethical criticism of just-war tenets draws on pragmatic considerations of the sort that might alarm advocates of Niebuhrian realism. Christian pacifists frequently claim that the just-war tradition is obsolete in the era of total war.[40] They insist that the idea of "limited" modern war is delusory and belies the general facts about how war has been waged in the twentieth century. Douglass, for example, argues that the danger of escalation in modern war is such that "any war today is necessarily an exercise in automated mass destruction." Hence, pacifist conclusions are more important today than the just-war premises from which one may begin.[41] In his terms, nuclear weapons are "eschatological weapons" because their use could end human history.[42] Just-war theorists operate in a different historical horizon than these facts permit, believing that military power may be used to *protect* one's history. Because the destructive power of nuclear weapons has ushered forth the end-time, we are unable to retain just-war assumptions about the utility of force in temporal affairs.

Pacifists frequently go beyond the exigencies of today to develop what might be called a "failure motif." The general allegation is that just-war thinking has always been ineffective in limiting the use of force, contrary to one of the chief pillars of just-war tenets.[43] Accordingly, the "history of effects" of the just-war tradition indicates that it has been ignored, compromised, or distorted by authorities who wish to cloak their decisions with moral language in times of conflict. Rarely, if ever, have just-war tenets been sufficiently operational in moments of international crisis.[44]

Authors who develop this failure motif argue on two fronts. One approach examines the historical factors that compromised the just-war tradition over the centuries. Yoder, for example, isolates a variety of complex and interrelated elements that have weakened just-war restraints. He begins by examining the social context of the church during the Reformation and the church's relation to the state in mainline Protestant confessions. The institutional collusion between church and state weakened the theologian's ability to criticize the decisions made by secular authorities. When theologians differed from their political protectors, Yoder avers, they were likely to recommend a greater amount of force to effect political goals.[45]

Philosophical and political currents during the Enlightenment likewise attenuated just-war restraints. With the rise of popular democracies and independent sovereign states, greater value was ascribed to the interests of nations, to the exclusion of transnational concerns.[46] Nations cultivated popular loyalties by waging war against rival nations. As social contract theories emerged, moreover, the idea of intrinsic, universal rights subsided.[47] Yoder thus echoes Hauerwas's critique of foundationalism, but from a more historical perspective. According to Yoder, Enlightenment efforts to anchor morality to a neutral foundation ironically generated strong preferential rather than universal duties. Such efforts were doomed to fail because attempts to place morality on a neutral foundation only secured protection for those envisaged within the social contract, especially when contractarian theory was wedded to nationalism. With this wedding, Yoder asserts, immunities once ascribed to "foreigners" were easily set aside.

By Yoder's account, the development of modern weapons furthered the weakening of just-war tenets. Nations now have unprecedented technological capabilities and the ability to mobilize entire populations on behalf of a war. Taken together, widespread mobilization and unparalleled material capabilities now strengthen the temptation to override just-war restraints in light of the demands of military necessity. Yet even in the face of these pressures, Yoder notes, certain wars may be unjust according to just-war criteria, and the only recourse may be to surrender.[48] Our failure to address this question and to make appropriate institutional preparations for defeat, Yoder argues, is but another symptom of the ineffectiveness of just-war ideas in political and moral discourse.

A second approach to the failure motif examines recent failures of just-war advocates to press their views effectively. Zahn develops such an account in his historical and sociological analysis of Catholic church leadership in Germany during the rise of Nazism.[49] Church leaders were unwilling to use moral principles to condemn Nazism, although the social injustices were morally unambiguous. Prelates sought to avoid rash judgment, persecution of the church, and placing individuals in a conflict of conscience. The fact that Catholic leaders set aside just-war principles for purposes of expedience should indicate that the tradition is "a patently useless and socially meaningless intellectual exercise."[50]

Zahn supplements his historical study of the German Catholic hierarchy by examining the assumptions that weaken the force of just-war tenets. During the thirties and forties, those adopting just-war criteria presumed the justice of political leaders, the effect of which was to restrict the scope of individual competence in moral judgment. German Catholic leaders explicitly removed the responsibility of moral judgment from individual believers by appealing to the prima facie legitimacy of secular power.[51] The subtle pressures of nationalism made it more difficult for individuals to dissent from political authority.[52] In order for the church to reverse its tendency to baptize political authority, it must detach itself from nationalist interests and accept suffering in the event that it must express prophetic criticism. The implication is that the just-war tradition will continue to fail so long as the church assumes a Constantinian or accommodationist stance vis-à-vis the state.[53]

Above and beyond this failure motif, Christian pacifists see themselves as members of a religious community with a distinctive ethos, which clearly departs from the ethos of violence in the secular state. Often these authors argue that "the modern state is essentially an engine of violence and tends to infuse its ethos throughout all life."[54] They view the state theologically as a vestige of fallen creation. Further, these authors allege, the ethos of militarism is conducive to habits inimical to trust in God's providential care.[55] Critical of the prevailing values in societies that continually prepare for war, Christian pacifists discern an erosion of moral sensibility in social attitudes and practices. Modern societies with elaborate defense capabilities breed competition, violence, and particularism. As Paul Deats remarks, "The ethos of war-making is conducive to cheapening the value of life in every area and to extending the range and severity of coercive measures."[56]

Although he has not systematically developed a pacifist position, Gibson Winter provides some helpful parameters for assessing militarism in the age of nuclear technology. At the heart of our present ethos is "nuclearism," which is "the knowledge and technical management of nuclear weaponry, a politics that takes their possible use for granted and a 'religious' sense that possession of nuclear weapons is foundational to national security."[57] Nuclearism is not an aberration of beneficent Western technology. Rather, it is the historical and logical consequence of Western thought and culture, which has deeply pathological elements.[58] The proliferation of nuclear weapons, Winter contends, is but one symptom of technical rationality divorced from basic human ends. As a result, we are alienated from the ontological harmonies that connect us with others and with the wider rhythms of the cosmos.

For Winter, moreover, nuclearism leads to a "numbing of consciousness," a deadening of moral sensitivity, which enables political authorities blithely to consider widespread death and destruction. Given the centralization of political and military authority, significant decision-making processes have been removed from popular control. Technical reason, divorced from its sources in creation, has produced conditions in which humanity will destroy, not serve, the wider interests of the cosmos. Indeed, the broader implications of militarism and nuclearism include widening circles of poverty and economic hardship throughout the globe. In Winter's mind, the connective tissues of nuclearism touch many dimensions of social life: "The search for security leads to deepening states of insecurity. To this extent, the religious refusal of finitude generates a politics of annihilation, oblivious to those ties that make life human and enjoyable, ties to children and parents, forests and rivers, familiar streets and corner stores."[59]

Similarly, Douglass questions burgeoning militarism and technical reason as a panacea for social ills.[60] Technology denotes not only a "huge power complex," but also a "state of mind" permeating the ethos of society. Contemporary society now trades in the currency of quantitative calculations, domination, power, and the standardization of lifestyles, all of which typify our dehumanized rationality. Alienated from the very purposes it is meant to serve, reason has created the conditions of self-destruction. We remain victims, in the words of Merton, of a "fetishism of immediate visible results."[61]

Several Christian pacifists amplify one difficulty that follows from these judgments about militarism in the social ethos. For such pacifists, war implies a view of the enemy as an objectified, impersonal "thing."[62] Preparations for war are the quintessence of impersonalism in modern culture, where the enemy is often depicted as evil incarnate.[63] Pacifists, in contrast, often insist upon the indisputable value of every person. Macgregor, for example, argues that "personality is the watchword of Christian theology," and that "there can be few actions more un-Christlike than . . . to de-personalize one's attitude to one's brother man."[64] Members of the Catholic Worker movement, as we have seen, invoke the personalist philosophy of Peter Maurin to ground similar convictions. In a personalist perspective, ideologies which justify war draw from a cult of the enemy and reduce the worth of others to that of "cannon fodder."

In moral philosophy Cheyney Ryan has developed an argument on behalf of ethical personalism that is designed to blunt commonplace criticisms by nonpacifists. Ryan begins by identifying the "pacifist impulse," the conviction that all persons share in a "fellow-creaturehood." This means that the pacifist cannot create, or does not wish to create, "the necessary distance between himself and another to make the act of killing possible." Sensitivity to the "deeper bonds" that all persons share proscribes the distancing of others required by killing, "regardless of the actions they might take toward you."[65]

Yet this position is problematic, Ryan observes, because violence may be a way of *bridging* the distance between oneself and another person, especially if violence is used to protect that person from attack by a third party. As Ramsey has argued, violence as a means of protecting others can be seen as an expression of care for innocent victims of aggression. Similarly, Ryan argues that there are legitimate concerns about what a refusal to protect would express about our relationships and ourselves, "for one of the ways we acknowledge the importance of a relationship is through our willingness to take such actions." The pacifist is left with a genuine dilemma: The personalist impulse may require that the pacifist "commit violence and that he not commit violence."[66]

But if this is a dilemma for pacifists, it is no less problematic for nonpacifists who accept the notion of fellow-creaturehood. The problem of violence pertains to both camps because in either case to ally oneself to one set of fellow-creatures means that others will suffer as a foreseen but unintended outcome of one's choice: The nonpacifist's decision to act means that the aggressor must suffer, while the pacifist's choice not to act means that the victim will suffer. In both cases violence is dilemmatic because it means accepting some persons as persons and regarding other persons as things. Ryan concludes, "If the pacifist's error arises from the desire to smooth this all over by hewing to one side of the dilemma, he is no worse than his opponent, whose 'refutation' serves to dismiss those very intractable problems of violence of which pacifism is the anxious expression." If we hasten the demise of pacifism, it may mean "that the dilemmas of violence have simply been forgotten."[67] Moreover, those who embrace either pacifism or nonpacifism continue to delude themselves so long as their grammar suggests that the use of lethal force is morally unambiguous. For Ryan, violence presents both vocabularies with an ethical choice, one which is structured by a situation of moral complexity.

Pacifists also criticize war and authorizations for war on the basis of their understanding of Christian discipleship. Virtually all of our authors identify the way of Christ in terms of voluntary suffering and universal *agape*.[68] Central to a life patterned on Christ's teaching and example is the duty of nonpreferential, nonresistant love of neighbor and unswerving loyalty to God. In the church, Christians are empowered to love the enemy and to discover, as Hauerwas remarks, that Christian "particularity is not destroyed but is enhanced by the coming of the stranger."[69] The ethos of the state, in contrast, is only able to empower its members to embrace preferential duties, duties to the proximate but not the remote neighbor. Yet to authorize war as a duty to our proximate neighbors runs contrary to the distinctive elements of Christian discipleship and the ethos of the church.

In response to these charges about preferential duties, just-war theorists often justify the use of force by drawing upon some notion of moral tragedy. Tragedy implies a dissonance between ideal goals and the realities of everyday experience. In Niebuhr's terms the recurrence of human will-to-power means that there will always be an element of friction and conflict in human affairs, that no human achievement can fully satisfy the law of indiscriminate love.[70] More recently, the U.S. Catholic bishops justify war as an unfortunate necessity in political life. Although they do not use the term *tragedy,* they frame their discussion of war and peace in terms of the tensions between the kingdom (ideal goals) and history. Prior to the fullness of the eschaton, we must settle conflict and recognize that, given the many conflicts of moral duties, at times we have no alternative but to use force to defend ourselves or others, to prefer the good of some over that of others.

Pacifists have recognized that this appeal to tragedy allows for certain concessions which they are unwilling to make. Rather than jettison an understanding of tragedy, however, they attempt to redefine it according to their own theological or ethical views. As Ryan suggests, violence ought to force pacifists and nonpacifists alike to acknowledge the tragic limits of protection and care. In a different vein, Hauerwas defines tragedy in terms of the tensions between peace and the fabric of secular society. Peace threatens the internal order of secular institutions because such institutions rely upon violent methods. (Violence, as Hauerwas uses the term, denotes not physical harm but the exclusion of strangers from human fellowship.) Indeed, violence is woven into the very structure of social life; it is "the warp on which the fabric of our existence is threaded."[71] Peace introduces an element of tragedy in secular life because it disturbs the subtle violence that cements social relations. Specifically, such relations require preferentiality and intimate friendship. Christian peace, in contrast, requires a commitment to the stranger in his or her strangeness. Such love unsettles the stability of our everyday relations; *agape* destabilizes *philia.* Insofar as peace threatens the order that derives from exclusive human friendships, it may be anarchic.

Operating at cross-purposes with the idea of peace as anarchic is a justification of nonviolence in the name of social stability and civil order. King, for example, constantly warned against the use of force, especially violence by African-Americans in retaliation against whites, fearing that violence would assume its own momentum and take an uncontrollable course. By King's reckoning, violence breeds retaliation and retaliation only leads to more violence, generating a cycle of recrimination that feeds on itself. Nonviolence, in contrast, serves the interests of all because it puts a stop to self-perpetuating patterns of harm and reciprocal injury. Against consequentialist critics of nonviolence, King argued that nonviolence has beneficial outcomes because it saves society from sowing the seeds of its own destruction.[72]

Whether pacifists look to nonviolence as anarchic or stabilizing, they generally understand their views as running against the grain of conventional political ideas about the utility of force in the international order. Such conventional wisdom, pacifists often allege, is socially and politically conservative, unimaginative, perhaps anachronistic. Several just-war theorists, for example, grant the "givenness" of the international system of sovereign states and attempt to introduce moral rules to govern the conduct of war.[73] Pacifists refuse to grant that war is a necessary feature of human behavior, arguing that such an assumption frequently becomes a self-fulfilling prophecy. Moreover, many insist that the present system of nation-states is obsolete for regulating global relations.[74] Insofar as just-war thought continues to operate within the framework of conventional statecraft, it will continue to beg the more important questions facing the globe today, including questions of how to reduce hostility and how to cultivate trust between people. For global relations to be improved, we need an alternative vision of social relations, one that encourages novelty and risk-taking. Drawing on the language of loyalty, virtually all of our authors insist that constructive visions must begin by assuming the importance of global loyalty as a religious and ethical imperative.[75] So long as just-war thought continues to flow from the reservoir of nationalism, these pacifists often allege, it will lack the prophetic vision necessary to advance the state of global affairs.

From Divergence to Convergence

The theological and ethical criticisms adduced above may lend the false impression that pacifism is a seamless garment, weaving together methodological criteria, biblical materials, ecclesiology, sociology, theological symbols, and ethical terms. However, the pragmatic and particularist character of pacifist thought often defies easy systematization. But even in this patchwork, these criticisms produce a common agenda for pacifists and just-war theorists. Indeed, three general inferences, suggesting three points of convergence with just-war tenets, can be drawn from the survey above.

First, pacifist theology and ethics suggest that the duty of nonmaleficence, as I developed its ethical and postethical meanings in chapter 1, captures only part of a wide constellation of Christian pacifist ideas. Christian pacifists develop their views by appealing not only to negative duties (e.g., nonmaleficence) but also to positive duties, theories of virtue, social ethos, the nature of violence, and the beneficial outcomes of nonviolence. Peace for Christian pacifists is a theory-dependent concept, a value whose full meaning cannot be reduced without remainder to the duty of nonmaleficence, the bias against suffering, the right not to be harmed.

This account of peace as theory-dependent also suggests that the wider implications of war may be concealed if we restrict our moral grammar about war to the logic of prima facie duties. The theological and ethical critiques developed above complicate the clarity and seeming simplicity by which just-war tenets might be structured. War and authorizations of war have social, religious, and ethical implications that go far beyond the logic of prima facie duties, and much of the project of pacifism is to unmask the wider implications of killing and war for our moral discourse. For this reason, pacifists attend with uncanny diligence to the many implications of war. Such diligence is a function of the claim, implicit throughout the criticisms above, that war is a limit situation, an extraordinarily complex and brutal affair, relatively unique on the terrain of our moral problems and deserving special attention if not grave suspicion.

Although the exceptional nature of war in moral discourse may be recognizable only after we sharpen the differences between pacifism and just-war tenets, it actually intimates an essential point of contact between pacifism and Childress's reconstruction of just-war ideas. As Barth recognized and as Childress's use of prima facie duties suggests, the use of force is an exceptional act, requiring special moral justification under grave circumstances.[76] Such claims override the basic duties that govern our ordinary commerce with each other. By this account, the use of force requires special permissions and grave limitations, however just its apparent cause might be. The fact that appeals to justice require such caution is only intelligible if the act itself—war—is perceived as an extraordinary affair, lying on the limits of our moral experience, disanalogous with other acts in which justice might be invoked without caution or qualification.

We might sharpen this first point by contrasting Childress's reconstruction of just-war ideas with Ramsey's understanding of the morality of war in light of the principle of *agape*. For Ramsey, the use of force to protect innocent persons requires no special permission or exceptional authorization. Engaging in war to protect the innocent is an expression, not a compromise, of *agape;* no duties are overridden, no qualifications are necessary so long as force is used to help innocent victims of aggression. The effect of Ramsey's argument is to render war analogous with other moral acts, to domesticate war, by suggesting that war is like other expressions of duty or virtue in which the needs of the innocent are special objects of care.[77]

Childress's argument, in contrast, suggests a greater dissonance between war and the fabric of ordinary moral experience. War immerses its participants and victims in an unusual realm of affairs—a realm of carnage, suffering, and waste that has few parallels with other moral acts in which we appeal simply or directly to love or justice as principles of authorization. Childress's construction of just-war tenets suggests a greater sense of moral tension than does Ramsey's; for Childress, a conflict of duties lies at the heart of moral discourse about the use of force.

And to the extent that war is perceived as an exceptional affair—a limit situation for its participants and victims—pacifist convictions and certain just-war tenets retain an important point of contact.

Second, granting that war is an extraordinary affair, standing on the limits of our moral experience, it follows that much of our fascination with war and the dilemmas of war ought to be removed from the center and placed at the periphery of our moral imaginations. If just-war ideas are designed to address the exceptional case of national or international conflict, then it seems that in the normal (rather than the exceptional) course of human commerce we should work more assiduously to make the requirements of peace central to moral discourse and practice. Indeed, assuming that just-war ideas pose duties for the exceptional case of war, it seems entirely coherent for the just-war theorist, no less than for the pacifist, to develop positive requirements of peace for the ordinary course of human affairs. Placing just-war ideas at the edge of our moral imaginations ought to create a clearing in which the requirements of peace can be pursued with a wider range of conceptual and practical strategies than those available in an ethos dominated by a fascination with war.[78] Relocating just-war tenets to the edge of our moral discourse may entail a dramatic change in research priorities, especially for those just-war theorists who persistently restrict their agenda to the dilemmas of war. If my second observation is correct, such exclusive attention to the dilemmas of war represents a myopic focus, one which misperceives the place of just-war ideas and eclipses considerations of the positive requirements of peace. More important, one can make such a charge either as a pacifist or as a just-war theorist who grants the exceptional nature of just-war tenets. Reservations about commonplace fascinations with war can be yet another point of contact between pacifists and those just-war theorists who recognize the "limits" of just-war ideas.[79]

This second point might be sharpened with reference to *The Challenge of Peace*. As I have indicated, the U.S. Catholic bishops affirm a point of contact between pacifism and just-war theory, claiming that both approaches share a moral presumption against war and in favor of peace.[80] Equally important, the bishops develop several constructive suggestions for building peace, including iterated, bilateral disarmament and a greater recognition of the practical requirements of global interdependence. To the bishops' credit, developing such positive suggestions constitutes an exception rather than the rule among just-war theorizing today. The bishops' ability to resist an exclusive fascination with the dilemmas of war seems to proceed from the clearing that is created once just-war ideas, cast in the language of presumptive duties, are relegated to the boundary of moral discourse.

Third, the notion that war is a limit situation suggests that, for pacifists at least, war has a profound religious dimension. War raises limit questions insofar as it forces us to consider ultimate concerns about the meaning of history, the human condition, the value of statecraft, and the proper objects of human loyalty. Thus, it is only natural that many pacifists turn to the symbols of their religious tradition to frame their discussion of war. Along these lines, Christian pacifists suggest that just-war theorists persistently fail to address the ultimate questions posed by war, especially when just-war theorists confine their terms to the language of duty.

Specifically, Christian pacifists suggest that such terms obscure a fundamental religious issue, namely, the nature and limits of loyalty to the state. Attention to the issue of loyalty should remind nonpacifists that even well-intentioned states can appeal to their own special necessities in the limit situation of war, and that such appeals easily curdle into tribalism, xenophobia, or neo-fascism. The point of pacifists' criticisms is to test the force of just-war tenets, to see whether just-war ideas have resources to resist the imperial claims that nations often make in the name of necessity during war. By broaching the issue of religious loyalty, then, Christian pacifists suggest a crucial difference between their broader agenda and that of nonpacifists.

Yet the effect of this criticism is to force yet another point of convergence into view. Although just-war theorists may not explicitly raise the issue of loyalty, just-war tenets are structured to restrict the kinds of claims that states may make in the name of necessity. The structure of just-war ideas according to the logic of prima facie duties places a presumptive weight in favor of nonviolence, shifting the burden of proof from the dissenter to those who justify the resort to lethal force.

While shifting this burden of proof may seem to lack any practical consequence, it actually distills the ethical agenda of many who dissented from the Vietnam War. According to Peter Brock, some selective conscientious objectors during the war used semantic games with the Selective Service Board to avoid the draft. These objectors sought exemption by overtly objecting to war in any form while holding, as a mental reservation, that participation in a future war might be possible. The general justification for this equivocation, Brock remarks, grew out of the objectors' belief that "the burden of proving that a war was 'just' lay . . . with the government."[81]

Shifting the burden of proving the justice of war likewise implies a basic suspicion at the heart of just-war tenets, allowing just-war theorists, no less than pacifists, to distance themselves from the regal claims of political authorities during times of conflict. The suspicion imposed by the prima facie duty of nonmaleficence suggests that neither the just-war theorist nor the pacifist may endorse uncritically the impulses of nationalistic fervor or patriotic zeal. Once its implications are recognized, moreover, such suspicion enables the just-war theorist to mitigate the charge that just-war ideas are incurably conservative.

These three inferences concern the exceptional nature of war, the place of just-war ideas in our moral discourse, and the constructive role that suspicion plays when we must assess the fiduciary dimension of war and statecraft. If the presumption against harm is taken seriously, then war appears to be an exceptional problem from the vantage point of both the just-war theorist and the pacifist. In addition, if just-war ideas are structured so that war is treated as an exceptional phenomenon, then a clearing is created in which we may pursue the positive requirements of peace during the normal course of human affairs, requirements that ought to bind the agendas of pacifists and nonpacifists alike. Finally, if just-war tenets establish a presumptive burden of proof against the use of violence, then pacifism and just-war ideas are bound together by a common suspicion about the kinds of claims that states often make to justify the use of force.

Points of contact between pacifism and just-war tenets may be most evident, oddly enough, when sharp differences between these rival vocabularies are first brought into focus. Yet these differences leave us with a mixed and complex conclusion. On the one hand, they indicate that pluralism in the ranks of Christians—pacifists and just-war theorists together—will inevitably include notable divisions in theology and ethics. On the other hand, these differences do not completely undermine the points of convergence between pacifism and just-war thought. Rather, these differences show, ironically enough, that the points of contact may be just the place where the pressures between pacifism and just-war tenets are the greatest.

Yet to assert that pacifism and just-war tenets converge in these ways may nonetheless delude us about the extent to which our moral vocabulary about war and peace masks deeper problems. For what is lacking in the dialectical conversation between just-war and pacifist tenets thus far is an account of their convergent deficits, their common conceits about the capacity of our moral vocabularies to interpret war and render a clear, disinterested verdict. Is the Niebuhrian notion underlying this chapter— that pacifism furnishes a solvent for nonpacifist convictions—not blind to the ambiguities of antiwarism? Are semantic games and mental reservations by conscientious objectors not morally problematic, a throwback to scholastic casuistry? Are the traditions of pacifism and just-war tenets invulnerable to common shortcomings? Ought we not turn protest and radical suspicion in on the idea that pacifism and just-war tenets converge?

To a self-critical moment from within the ethics of war we must now turn.

F I V E

A Protestant Protest and Transvaluation

... the awful ruin of the rebellious country is itself a punishment on the grandest scale and
ought to be sufficient; for the misery of [war]
is, that it falls on the innocent and not on the
leaders and projectors, who are the chief crimi-
nals.

Horace Bushnell, 1865

The Protestant Principle

"The Protestant principle," Paul Tillich writes, "contains the divine and human protest against any absolute claim made for a relative reality, even if this claim is made by a Protestant church. The Protestant principle is the judge of every religious and cultural reality, including the religion and culture which calls itself 'Protestant.'"[1] This means that the Protestant principle may express itself outside the religious traditions of the Refor-mation. Jewish prophets, proletarian social movements, and even radical Catholics are capable of protesting against absolute claims about relative values, so long as such protests are premised on a critical, transcendent principle. Even among philosophers, such protests are available to those who worry about self-righteousness and moral exceptionalism, be they Kantians, utilitarians, or those who embrace nothing more complex than the Golden Rule. Yet Tillich also suggests that the Protestant principle is self-reflexive, capable of turning inward on those who espouse Protestant beliefs. Protestantism in its purest form, according to Tillich, possesses the capacity to relativize itself.

In matters of war and peace, the Protestant principle usually conjures up the name of Reinhold Niebuhr, for whom the inexhaustible require-ments of love relativize and judge all human accomplishments in history. Love for Niebuhr is an "impossible possibility," an ideal to be pursued but never reached, the absolute standard for measuring relative embodiments of justice in temporal affairs. Yet about the morality of war Niebuhr never systematically developed the implications of the Protestant principle, probably because he was less concerned with theology in relation to ethics than with the social issues of his day. Rather, the gauntlet of theology and its relation to ethics was picked up by Niebuhr's younger brother, H. Richard, in what are now called the "war articles," a series of provocative essays published in the *Christian Century* during the 1930s and 1940s.[2]

These war articles have eluded analysis in recent studies of war and peace because Niebuhr's references to pacifism and nonpacifism seem either obscure or inconsistent.[3] In "The Grace of Doing Nothing" (1932), his first treatment of war, Niebuhr argued for nonintervention by the United States in the Sino-Japanese conflict. Niebuhr called his recommendation a peculiar kind of inactivity, "full of hope," thus implicitly allying himself with Christian pacifists.[4] Yet in the 1940s his claim that our "duty involves . . . resistance to those who are abusing our neighbors" allied Niebuhr with those nonpacifists who justified the use of force during World War II.[5]

Niebuhr's argument is puzzling not only because he apparently shifted his position, but because he distanced himself from those positions to which he seemed allied. In "The Grace of Doing Nothing" Niebuhr chided those pacifists whose renunciation of violence masked a righteous indignation, leaving them with a dangerous emotion, "the source of sudden explosions or the ground of long, bitter and ugly hatreds."[6] When his brother criticized the article and, during a temporary embrace of pacifism, called for the use of nonviolent coercion against Japan, H. Richard retorted, "To import pacifism of any sort into this struggle is only to weaken the weaker self-asserters."[7] The nonviolent coercion of "pragmatic pacifists," the younger Niebuhr soon argued, was a hopeless contradiction, a "utilitarian idealism" whose differences from nonpacifism were more apparent than real.[8]

In the 1940s, moreover, despite justifying the use of force, H. Richard Niebuhr rebuked those nonpacifists who distinguish "between unjust war—the act of transgression—and just war—the act of retribution and of defense of order."[9] Although he exhibited no familiarity with the details of just-war tenets during this time, he was clearly dissatisfied with references to justice and injustice in nonpacifist thinking. Such distinctions obscure the fact that the burdens of war fall on the innocent, not on those who are guilty of injustice. Consequently, those who hold to some semblance of just-war theory are unable to follow it in practice: "If they declare a present war to be just they must participate in inflicting suffering and death on the 'just' with the 'unjust'; if they regard a present war as unjust they must stand idly by while the 'just' are being made to suffer with the 'unjust.'"[10]

Niebuhr's dissatisfaction with Christian discourse about war in the 1930s and 1940s led him to chart an alternative course, one in which repentance to divine judgment, not moral action, is axiomatic. From the first to the last of the war articles he maintains that the suffering in war "is a call to repentance, to a total revolution of our minds and hearts."[11] The problem with conventional approaches of pacifism and nonpacifism, Niebuhr suggests, is that they focus attention on the wrong agents, or the wrong problems, because *we* are agents whose actions are problematic.

Further, Niebuhr insists that repentance is a response not merely to the events of war; it is also a response to a more dramatic series of events behind and within war. Conventional approaches "are inadequate and misleading, for [they] fail to account for all the relevant phenomena."[12] Something *more* than war is going on in these conflicts, Niebuhr argues, and conventional approaches lack the resources to disclose the true pattern in the particularities of current affairs.

But perhaps most perplexing about Niebuhr's bid for repentance is the suggestion that we are misled not only by conventional canons of morality, but by *morality itself*. Repentance requires all individuals, regardless of their position on war, to recognize the hubris behind every moral endeavor; repentance focuses our gaze in the direction of the divine—the eternal—rather than on the moral demands of the passing moment. A tension between religion and ethics underlies this puzzlement, for Niebuhr's call for repentance threatens to undermine any ethical approach to war, leaving Christians in the limbo of quietism: religiously contrite, but without ethical moorings to secure their judgments and decisions. For Niebuhr, "when we are in the wrong before God we are absolutely in the wrong and no kind of relative rightness can be made the foundation of an appeal to a higher court."[13]

However, Niebuhr's overall purpose in the war articles is not to undermine ethical discourse about war and peace but to *repoeticize* war, to provide an alternative metaphor for interpreting and evaluating war.[14] The goal, then, is not to address directly the ethics of war, but to outflank prior approaches by providing an alternative image. And in the process, Niebuhr's argument in the war articles transforms ethical discourse by developing a Protestant protest against ethical casuistry. Out of this protest he then develops some elementary benchmarks for thinking about the socioethical problem of war. Contrary to a common assumption about Niebuhr's ethics—that his approach is limited to dispositionalism, an exclusive concern for the moral constitution of individual agents[15]—the war articles display a constructive effort by Niebuhr to provide guidelines for social ethics.

Here I will examine Niebuhr's argument by addressing, in order, the puzzlements mentioned above: Niebuhr's critique of the substance of conventional approaches; his understanding of the real events to which they are blind; and the *necessary* tension between theology and ethics that follows from his critiques. These war articles are the only place where Niebuhr ever addresses a moral problem directly, and they include virtually all of the main currents of his thought, currents that are either presaged in earlier works or amplified in subsequent writings. By charting the course he sets in the war articles, then, we gain insight into the problem of ethics and war as well as into the distinctive stamp of Niebuhr's entire theological ethics.

Repentance and Conventional Discourse about War

Although Niebuhr's attempt to distance himself from pacifism and nonpacifism seems to place his entire argument on a theological axis, in fact his views are sustained by important nontheological considerations. Such considerations are guided by theories of action, metaphor and symbol, and social faith. These theories possess a relative autonomy in Niebuhr's overall method; they are distinct from his more explicit theological concerns and provide a distinctive angle of vision. But they are never irrelevant to Niebuhr's theological ideas as defined by his notion of radical monotheism.

Niebuhr's discussion draws, first, from ideas which fall under the rubric of "action theory." Although these ideas are, at best, inchoate in the war articles, Niebuhr suggests that pacifism and nonpacifism are dominated by models that, in *The Responsible Self,* he will call "man-the-maker" and "man-the-citizen."[16] In either model, Christians approach war prescriptively by constructing goals or duties for action, providing guidelines according to which individual agents may confidently assert themselves. As an alternative to such approaches, throughout the war articles Niebuhr places human action within an extensive field of interactive processes, not all of which are functions of our volition. His action theory, in short, is founded on the notion that history is not entirely under our control. We must therefore anchor morality to a theory of human agency as responsive, not assertive, because we are "thrown" into a web of influences on which our actions depend.

Niebuhr's theory of agency as responsive leads him to argue in 1932 that pacifists enjoin the wrong course of action because their views are tied to a naive confidence in the value of self-assertion. His refusal to accept his brother's call for nonviolent coercion in 1932, for example, is premised on the notion that such coercion is a form of assertiveness, which "will always involve us in the same one ceaseless cycle of assertion and counter-assertion."[17] For the younger Niebuhr, the key is to accept the Kingdom of God as an "emergent" within history—an unrealized potentiality—and to prepare for it by means of repentance. Indeed, he insists, the emergence of God's redemptive action will remain unrealized "so long as we try to impose our pattern, our wishes upon the divine creative process."[18]

Niebuhr thus spotted in 1932 the religious liberalism inherent in his brother's call for nonviolent coercion against the Japanese. However much the older Niebuhr would insist on the limited options in history, he nonetheless felt confident that human agency held the power to redirect the course of temporal affairs. Against the complaints of his increasingly influential brother, H. Richard prefers a more determinist outlook, noting, "Man's task is not that of building Utopias but that of eliminating the weeds and tilling the soil so that the kingdom of God can grow. His method is not one of striving for perfection or of acting perfectly, but of clearing the road by repentance and forgiveness."[19]

Further, as he would emphasize in the 1940s, typical approaches to war fail to apprehend the recurring fact of war, namely, widespread suffering of the innocent. "It is not the mighty, the guides and leaders of nations and churches, who suffer most in [wars]," Niebuhr observes, "but the humble, little people who have had little to do with the framing of great policies."[20] And, as he would later maintain in *The Responsible Self,* this fact of suffering ought to have a direct bearing on theories of moral agency. Suffering, Niebuhr observes, "is the exhibition of the presence in our existence of that which is not under our control, or of the intrusion into our self-legislating existence of an activity operating under another law than ours." Seen in this way, suffering "cannot be brought adequately within the spheres of teleological and deontological ethics, the ethics of man-the-maker, or man-the-citizen."[21] To gain access to the brute fact of human suffering we need an alternative approach to moral agency, one that places—and limits—human action within a complex network of personal and impersonal forces.

It follows for Niebuhr that moral theory premised on the fact of suffering and human limits must be initially descriptive rather than prescriptive. A prescriptive approach assumes that we are in control of historical affairs, that we can dictate the future course of events. A more descriptive method, in contrast, assumes that we are dependent on a wider set of interactive processes, about which we must be clear before prescribing action. Moreover, Niebuhr's approach attends to the special needs of other patients—especially those who are victims of historical forces—as essential to defining the proper course for human agents. Emphasis on description rather than prescription means that Niebuhr cannot begin his treatment of war with a set of established principles that he can then apply to the concrete particularities of the moment. Moreover, Niebuhr never flatly defines the single, proper course of action for Christians to follow, be it participation or nonparticipation in the wars. Rather, he begins with the particularities themselves by asking the question now familiar to students of his work, "What is going on?"[22] This method requires him to identify and organize a host of morally relevant features of a situation before developing an appropriate response. For this reason he is able to suggest different courses of action; the two situations of the 1930s and 1940s vary considerably and call for altogether different kinds of action (or inaction). Niebuhr's action theory yields an ethical method that allows for a large measure of flexibility and openness; it demands attention to the peculiarities of the situation and necessarily postpones ethical judgment to a second stage of deliberation.

The need to interpret the particularities of war is aided by a second set of resources, which fall under the rubric of "symbol theory." We are more symbolic than rational animals, Niebuhr later maintains; as image-using creatures, we organize our perceptions with signs and symbols, signs "that come to us in our dialogue with the circumambient world."[23] As he argues in *The Meaning of Revelation,* in the war articles Niebuhr maintains that the meaning of events is not self-evident, that reality is not transparently clear to the untutored eye.[24] Rather, meaning is conditioned by preunderstandings, which enable us to discern a basic pattern from within a complex array of events. In the war articles Niebuhr draws on the master trope of the Christian tradition—the cross—to define the whole within which human action ought to be a "fitting part." In 1932, for example, he insists that "China is being crucified (though the term is very inaccurate) by our sins and those of the whole world."[25] And, a decade later, he will devote an entire article to the notion of war as crucifixion, "a strange intermixture of justice and injustice on the side alike of those who regard themselves as the upholders of the right and on the side of the vanquished."[26] Niebuhr's symbol theory enables him to repoeticize war, to rearrange our vision of conflict and the various stakes involved. The problem with conventional approaches to war lies in assuming that the meaning of events is clear, that there can be some easy consensus about war's problems and its moral dimensions.

Niebuhr uses the metaphor of the cross to show that such epistemological self-confidence is deceptive, that our conventional wisdom fails to discern the whole because it obscures the fact that the burden of war falls on the innocent.[27] Pacifists and nonpacifists fail to detect this pattern in war because they are caught within the conventional categories of justice and injustice, purity and wickedness. They are led to these quick judgments, moreover, because they underestimate the importance of symbolic interpretation in moral evaluation. Niebuhr asks us to begin elsewhere, with the indicative preceding the imperative, however strange that may appear from conventional points of view.[28]

Finally, Niebuhr draws upon various currents in social theory to criticize the relativization of Christian values as these have been enshrined in conventional grammar about war and peace. His point is that conventional ideas typically reflect a narrow, provincial form of faith, furnishing a mask behind which nationalistic self-justification hides its face. Doubtless this concern about Christian factionalism and parochialism lies behind the statement, made in 1932, in which Niebuhr speaks approvingly of "cells of those within each nation who, divorcing themselves from the program of nationalism and capitalism, unite in a higher loyalty which transcends national and class lines of division."[29] Reference to social faiths in ethics is made even more trenchantly in "Man the Sinner" (1935), in which Niebuhr asserts a strong tie between the object of one's loyalty and the prospect for successful social action. Loyalty to self, nation, or class shapes the way we try to rescue ourselves from social ills. The consequence of parochial loyalties is that we become more deeply involved in our disloyalty to God while intensifying our parochial commitments. Niebuhr goes on to remark, "The situation is similar to the effort to bring about international peace through international war, which results only in the increase of national loyalties and the increase of war; it is similar also to the effort to bring about social justice through inter-class conflict which results in the increase of class loyalties and of social injustice."[30]

Attention to loyalty in social ethics runs throughout Niebuhr's corpus. In *Radical Monotheism and Western Culture* he develops in more theoretical terms the relation between loyalty and religious, political, and scientific activity. Specifically, Niebuhr distinguishes between monotheism, henotheism, and polytheism as these structure the ethos of various social practices.[31] The former refers to faith and loyalty to "the One beyond the many," faith in the "universal commonwealth of Being." Radical monotheism makes reference "to no one reality among the many but to One beyond all the many, whence all the many derive their being, and by participation in which they exist." Radical monotheism is one version of the Protestant principle, an all-inclusive, unconditional acceptance of the relativities of this world, which neither absolutizes the finite features of life nor denies their relative value. All finite realities have value not in themselves, but in "relation to the One to whom all being is related."[32]

Henotheism and polytheism, in contrast, are particularistic, not universal; they elevate some finite element within the many to the status of absolute value, thus sustaining a religious and ethical provincialism. Moreover, the chief rival to radical monotheism in Niebuhr's judgment is henotheism, a value system that elevates the social community to the status of absolute or ultimate concern. And, as he suggested in 1935, in *Radical Monotheism* Niebuhr insists that the most pervasive and troubling form of henotheism is nationalism. As a species of henotheism, nationalism "shows its character . . . whenever national welfare or survival is regarded as the supreme end of life; whenever right and wrong are made dependent on the sovereign will of the nation . . . ; whenever religion and science, education and art, are valued by the measure of their contribution to national existence." In Niebuhr's judgment nationalism pervades modernity, exhibiting its presence "every day in schools and churches no less than in political utterances and policies."[33]

The key point in Niebuhr's use of these categories in *Radical Monotheism* is that *all* of these forms of theism can coexist in the various practices of Western culture. Democracy, for example, can tend toward *either* a universal or a provincial form, as can scientific inquiry and traditional religious practices.[34] The contrast is *not* between monotheistic Christianity and henotheistic cultural practices, but between universalism and parochialism *within religious and cultural practices themselves.* In keeping with the self-reflexive nature of Protestant protest, Niebuhr invokes the notion of radical monotheism as a device for judging the practice of religion itself. He suggests that some versions of secular faith may be more monotheistic in their orientation than traditional religious beliefs, because the latter often curdle into self-defensiveness and divisiveness.[35] Niebuhr also suggests that Christian ethics can serve parochial interests, for Christian ethics may simply enshrine the subtle self-interests to which it is tied. With reference to the war articles, no doubt this concern—to deliver conventional discourse about war from provincialism, especially nationalism—lies at the heart of Niebuhr's critique of pacifism and non-pacifist ideas. In whatever moral language it is disguised, "Self-interest acts destructively in this world: it calls forth counter assertion; nationalism breeds nationalism, class assertion summons up counter-assertion on the part of exploited classes."[36]

Niebuhr makes much the same point about the role of secular faiths in *Social Sources of Denominationalism.* There he draws lessons from Weber and Troeltsch to expose the way religious traditions tend to rationalize their practices and petrify what was, at an earlier time, a more charismatic and vibrant set of beliefs. As a matter of social fact, Christianity exhibits the tendencies of all religious movements, that is, to justify an ethos and ethics according to the parochial interests of tribe, nation, class, or race.[37]

Hence, the problem of Christianity, although it is by no means peculiar to Christianity, is that its message has a history of losing its radical force, its summons to universal community, and its loyalty to a transcendent center of value. According to Niebuhr, "The church which began its career with the promise of peace and brotherhood for a distracted world has accepted the divisions it had hoped to transform and has championed the conflicts it had thought to transcend."[38] Christianity has slowly lost its force as it has accommodated itself to the protean exigencies of relative times and cultures; thus, the early unity of Christianity has given way to a Babel of voices, values, and practices. Within his own branch of Christianity, Niebuhr would later observe, such accommodationism produced "Culture Protestantism."[39] But regardless of the specific form, the accommodation and fragmentation of Christianity is a "moral failure," a "fatal division."[40] And, as the war articles suggest, the dangers of fragmentation become even more acute during times of international conflict. For, until the social sources (including nationalism) of Christian fragmentation are evident, Christian moral discourse will continue to reinforce the relativities "it had hoped to transcend." As members of a movement divided along national lines, moreover, the Christian churches will be unable to speak with one voice; rather, they will simply mimic the national conflicts already under way. To mitigate the social law of rationalization and petrification, Christians must put the practices of Christianity to ongoing criticism, through repentance, lest they take the shape of those self-interests they are designed to reform.

The social faiths of monotheism, henotheism, and polytheism likewise affect the interpretation of historical events. As Niebuhr remarks in *The Meaning of Revelation*, one's "inner history"—the events by which one understands the meaning of life—is conditioned by social theisms. "It is the gods," Niebuhr insists, "that give unity to the events of personal life." As such, "to have a god is to have history, that is, events connected in a meaningful pattern." Nations have internal histories insofar as they provide a common value, "some good for which [their members] live together, whether that be an abstract value, such as equality or democracy . . . or whether it be the personalized community itself, such as Athena, or Britannia or Columbia."[41]

Niebuhr's point is that our social faiths, the "theisms" of modern culture, will condition the way we interpret and organize the facts of history into an intelligible framework. And, because ethical judgments are shaped in part by prior descriptions, the theisms of social faith directly affect our moral evaluations. In the context of war, our interpretation of historical data and our subsequent moral judgments will be conditioned by our objects of loyalty. One implication of Niebuhr's views is that our interpretations and evaluations of history will be more self-serving than self-critical unless we purge them, by means of contrition, of henotheistic undercurrents.

In summary, Niebuhr seeks to underscore the importance of repentance and its implications in our accounts of war. At the level of agency, interpretation, and social analysis, contrition provides the path to self-criticism and social criticism. By leading us to a response rather than to a recipe for moral action, repentance deters us from acting hastily, from leaping into or out of war with moral certitude. By focusing attention on the problem of human suffering, repentance corrects our tendency—as pacifists or nonpacifists—to interpret war according to moralistic categories of guilt and culpability. And by focusing attention on our own present faults, repentance corrects the tendency of religious and moral traditions to confuse themselves with the earthen vessels in which they find expression. Contrition serves as a solvent, disciplining individuals and groups, lest they exacerbate rather than lessen the cruelties of war.

The Objectivity of God's Sovereign, Immanent Activity

Yet if we were to focus exclusively on the importance of repentance we would be examining only one side of the Niebuhrian coin. Repentance is the subjective aspect of the Protestant principle in the war articles, a response to a real, objective series of events. Throughout the war articles, Niebuhr's approach correlates the subjectivity of the responder with the objectivity of divinely ordained events; the two are inseparable, as Calvin insists in the opening page of the *Institutes*. And, with his Protestant forebear, Niebuhr is equally insistent that God is present in the secondary causes of nature and history, that Providence, in Calvin's terms, "is the determinative principle of all things in such a way that sometimes it works through an intermediary, sometimes without an intermediary, sometimes contrary to every intermediary."[42] For Niebuhr this means, in general, "God is acting in all actions upon you," and, in the war articles, "God rather than the self or the enemy is seen to be the central figure in the great tragedy of war."[43]

Central to Niebuhr's effort to distinguish his approach to war from other theological approaches is his notion of radical monotheism. Familiar religious approaches—be they pacifist or nonpacifist—may recognize the presence of divine purposes in historical affairs, but they tend to separate the finite from the infinite, or the particular from the universal. They thus construct a twofold set of actions for the individual: repentance toward the infinite, and self-confidence in the realm of finite, concrete action. As Niebuhr argues in his later writings, such an approach is "ditheistic," defining two actions and two corresponding responses.[44] Such a dualism, not uncommon to a religious ethic premised on two realms, is fundamentally at odds with the outlook of radical monotheism. The latter presses "for consistency in man's ethical response to his environment,"[45] eschews the division of labor between religion and morality, and approaches history as "one inclusive process," in which God is the central figure.[46] According to Niebuhr, "God is always in history; he is the structure in things, the source of all meaning, the 'I am that I am,' that which is that it is."[47] The task of radical monotheism is to discover the universal in every particular, "to affirm . . . that there is no person, no situation, no event in which the opportunity to serve God is not present." For Niebuhr this means that Christians ought to resist the bifurcation of reality and the dualism of action that accompanies traditional supernaturalism.[48]

Niebuhr's radical monotheism in the war articles also displays an effort to discern the real meaning of history, to uncover the intention of the divine as the active principle in every particular. The question, "What must I do?" must be preceded by the question, "What is God doing?"[49] In a typically apt phrase, Niebuhr will later describe such discernment as reading events as signs—signs "as words in a divine sentence."[50] Using the cross as his master image, Niebuhr argues that the divine is acting in war to carry out corrective justice through the suffering of innocent victims. The burdens of war fall on the innocent, and if history is to have any meaning, we must make sense out of this apparent travesty of justice by discerning some divine movement in and through the present state of affairs.[51]

To uncover such movement, Niebuhr poeticizes war as an exercise of divine judgment, meted out against just and unjust alike. Echoing a Calvinist view of Providence, Niebuhr in 1932 remarks that the "structure of the universe, that will of God, does bring war and depression upon us when we bring it upon ourselves, for we live in the kind of world which visits our iniquities upon us and our children, no matter how much we pray and desire that it be otherwise."[52] War has visited humanity because the forces of divine judgment are immanent in the personal and impersonal forces of history itself. Consequently, the question is not how to confront social problems with moral correctives, but how to respond to a total reality in which *we are already implicated.*

In 1932 Niebuhr speaks only obliquely about those factors that implicated the United States in the evils of war, referring to the "surprising discoveries as to the amount of renunciation of self-interest necessary on the part of this country and of individual Christians."[53] Not until 1942 is he more explicit about those factors according to which the apparently disinterested are being judged: "Our nation . . . has demonstrated its profound preoccupation with its own prosperity, safety and righteousness, so that in its withdrawal from international responsibilities, in its tariff, monetary and neutrality legislation, it has acted always with a single eye to its own interests rather than to those of its neighbors in the commonwealth of nations."[54] As an expression of judgment, both the Sino-Japanese War and the Second World War are arenas in which American iniquity is being placed "on the backs of the innocent."[55] In all events, there can be no removal of the self from implication, for there can be "no excusing of self because one has fallen less short of the glory of God than others."[56] Only after we give up the pretense of justice and self-righteousness, recognizing war as the product of complex expressions of human fault, can we construe accurately the meaning of current affairs.

Niebuhr's theological objectivism also leads to an understanding of war as, oddly enough, the place of redemption. The war as a whole is an imitation of Christ, a potentially transformative event in which the innocent are suffering vicariously for the welfare of a universal cause. Niebuhr remarks:

> Interpreted through the cross of Jesus Christ the suffering of
> the innocent is seen not as the suffering of temporal men but
> of the eternal victim "slain from the foundations of the world."
> If the Son of God is being crucified in this war along with the
> malefactors—and he is being crucified on many an obscure
> hill—then the graciousness of God, the self-giving love, is
> more manifest here than in all the years of peace.[57]

Thus, Christians are to respond to the events of history with patient hope and trust in divine redemptive purposes. Niebuhr points to Isaiah and Jesus, whose responses to divine action "built new community in the midst of tragedy, cleaned selves and society of egoism, fear and hatred, and opened up a productive future in which the tragedy was made the foundation of a new life."[58] For Niebuhr, the notion of divine corrective action suggests that a universal cause, not a particular cause, lies at the heart of war, a cause in which "the suffering of innocence is used for the remaking of the guilty."[59]

Conventional approaches to war typically misdescribe the situation at hand by suggesting that a particular cause is to be defined and defended in war. Pacifists make this error by construing war as a brute exercise of power, in the face of which they righteously refuse to cooperate. Non-pacifists make the same mistake by poeticizing war as the occasion for retributive justice or as the exercise of righteous defense against those who are morally guilty of aggression.[60] Against these notions Niebuhr appeals to the belief in the sovereignty of divine action, a belief which deflates the pretensions of moralistic judgments. If God is the chief agent in war, and if suffering and redemption are the meaning of the events, then it becomes impossible, indeed idolatrous, to ascribe "righteousness" to human action.

Implicit in Niebuhr's use of the cross in the war articles is his notion, developed most systematically in *The Meaning of Revelation,* of progressive revelation. Revelation, he claims, is subject to ongoing validation in the lives of believers, generation after generation. By this Niebuhr does not mean that new events can be substituted for the initial divine revelation. Rather, he means that the meaning of the revelation "is progressively validated . . . as ever new occasions are brought under its light, as sufferings and sins, as mercies and joys are understood by its aid."[61] Revelation is a "moving thing," because "its meaning is realized only by being brought to bear upon the interpretation and reconstruction of ever new human situations in an enduring movement, a single drama of divine and human action."[62] The wars of the 1930s and 1940s, understood as crucifixions, are but profound instances of the progressive validation of revelation. War both illuminates and is illuminated by the meaning of revelation insofar as war is brought under the light of the cross and is thus understood. As Niebuhr states, the notion of war as crucifixion "directs Christians to wrestle with the problem of the cross in new ways so that new light from it may fall upon the scenes of their present social life as well as upon their personal problems and tragedies."[63]

One apparent consequence of Niebuhr's theological objectivism is to relegate conventional wisdom about war and peace to the realm of deceptive appearances. Not unlike Socrates in the *Republic,* Niebuhr claims that our untutored senses deceive us; without the Form of the Good to illuminate our perception of the particulars, we live in the realm of the shadows. The Form for Niebuhr, as I indicated above, is the cross; it provides the paradigm that illuminates the real patterns within the particulars of history and society. And, like Socrates' depiction of the ideal philosopher, Niebuhr's views sound alien when juxtaposed to the opinions of the public, opinions that are dominated by Thrasymachean pursuits of either power or self-justification (or both). Such an alien status is almost inevitable, we might suspect, for a position premised upon a leap of illumination, a leap that Socrates' philosophy and Niebuhr's theology both make.[64]

Yet in *The Meaning of Revelation* Niebuhr's closing comments qualify in important ways the idea that he reduces the common opinions of humanity, like those codified in conventional approaches to war and peace, to the realm of deception. Of special importance are his claims about the relation between revelation and "natural religion." For Niebuhr, revelation is not initially nihilistic; it does not destroy the values of humanity only to supplant them with new supernatural verities. Niebuhr's understanding of revelation, in short, is not that of the early Barth. For Niebuhr, revelation inaugurates a revolution of continuous conversion; "it is the fulfillment and the radical reconstruction of our natural knowledge about [the] deity."[65] With revelation "all religious truths are painfully transformed and all religious behavior transfigured by repentance and new faith."[66]

The revolutionary consequences of revelation for conventional morality are also developed in *The Meaning of Revelation.* The effect of divine self-disclosure is to extend and intensify the moral law of humanity—to universalize it—so that it pertains to the broadest reaches of the natural order. Such universalizing eclipses any henotheistic restriction of the law's application. For, with revelation, all of reality "belong[s] within the network of moral relations"; consequently, "every death is a sacrifice," marking a loss to the total matrix of being. Because all reality now stands within the network of moral relations, moreover, "there is no possibility now of restricting moral obedience to the circle of the good, so that we love those who love us or who share our principles and do no harm to our values."[67] Rather, we are obligated to embrace the soul of the enemy as well as that of the friend, to "republish" the moral law not as the dictate of justice but as the imperative of universal loyalty.[68] In such a republication we learn in general what Niebuhr suggests about conventional approaches to war, namely, that without a transvaluation, even the highest law is a vehicle for sin, a lieutenant of self-righteousness and parochialism. Accordingly, we must do to pacifism and nonpacifism what must be done to all morality: purify them of the dross of human conceit. In that way we can elevate our moral conventions from the realm of deception to the realm of truthful guidance.

Further, Niebuhr's theological objectivism in the war articles—his understanding of secondary causes, progressive revelation, and corrective justice—briefly and poignantly compresses the main lines of his threefold understanding of divine activity. As immanent within the single drama of history, God is present as a creative force; as the sovereign judge of (and within) human history, God is present as the governing, ruling force; and as the agent of historical correction and purification, God is present as the power of redemption. The war is indeed a theological event for Niebuhr, an event in which, as Calvin averred, creation and Providence are one.[69]

Niebuhr's notions of God and history thus reverse the direction his analysis of war took along nontheological lines. From a nontheological perspective, the problem of conventional morality lies in the danger of relativization, the tendency of religious traditions or ethical principles to confuse themselves with the practices of particular times and places. Now, in a more explicitly theological domain, the problem lies not in the danger of relativization, but in its *necessity*. For, unless the moralistic pretenses of pacifists and nonpacifists are relativized in light of the sovereign, universal cause of divine action, they will assume a stature of theistic proportions. They will lead us to act in haste, confident that our cause is the right one, without any understanding of the true events of history and their actual meaning. Against such haste, the relativization wrought by Niebuhr's theological objectivism entails an essential delay, a religious detour that excises the subtle pretenses from our moral conventions.

The Transformative Tension between Theology and Ethics

Niebuhr's use of nontheological and theological sources to develop his argument on behalf of repentance follows a double movement, proceeding along the vectors of Christ and culture. On the one hand, he develops a cultural critique of Christianity by using nontheological sources to assess the relativization of religious values. The movement here exposes the petrification of radical values as they find a place in earthen vessels. On the other hand, Niebuhr develops a Christian critique of cultural values by drawing on theological sources to relativize the conceit of conventional ethical discourse. This second movement exposes the tendency of human beings to elevate their relative perspectives to the level of absolute truth. Moreover, while these movements seem to move in opposite directions, they actually reinforce each other. For Niebuhr goes to great lengths, in either case, to clarify the relation of the absolute with the particular and to insist on the self-critical reflection that repentance requires. The movement of Niebuhr's thought in the war articles along nontheological and theological lines is, in a Tillichian vein, a critical correlation of religion and culture, reinforcing from both ends the self-critical requirements of the Protestant principle.

Yet the fact that Niebuhr's argument for repentance is doubly reinforced still leaves him with a serious difficulty. That difficulty concerns the relation between religion and morality, for Niebuhr's insistence on contrition is not followed by a clear set of directives. We return, then, to the problem found in Douglass's and the Berrigans' pacifism, this time in a religious ethic critical of all moral canons of war.[70] Such a problem is especially acute for Niebuhr, for if we lack any clear directives, then we are left in one trap from which he sought to deliver us. That is, without moral guidance we are left with another ditheism, one that differs from the ditheisms he has mentioned. Most forms of ditheism identify two actions and two sets of responses: humility toward the divine and self-confidence in concrete action. In Niebuhr's ditheism, knowledge about and consent to the universal cause is coupled with uncertainty about particular action; a peculiar form of activity, repentance, seems to lead to nothing more than a religiously proper form of quietistic vagueness. Does repentance finally leave Christians morally paralyzed, unable to translate their beliefs into principles of action? Are Christians left unable to act, anxious that any action, however noble, will carry the seeds of moral conceit? Is it true, as John Barbour remarks, that in the war articles, "the only meaningful role for the Christian . . . seems to be inner reflection and repentance"? Barbour fears passivity and an undue attention to the dispositions in Niebuhr's ethics of war: "These internal processes are not seen as leading to overt action in the world. Such an understanding could lead the Christian to believe that there is 'nothing to be done' directly in historical situations when in fact creative action could decisively affect the outcome of events."[71]

Yet in fact Niebuhr has a response to this charge of dispositionalism and quietism, a response which falls into two categories. At the level of individual action, repentance enables one to galvanize the disparate roles of the self into an integral unity. The consequence of repentance is the subjective correlate of radical monotheism: Repentance enables one to act as a single, integrated agent, one who holds together a plurality of roles and perspectives in a coherent unity. As Niebuhr argues in *The Responsible Self*, response to the single ultimate action of God in the particulars of history "means to be one responding self amidst all the responses of the roles being played, because there is present to the self the One other beyond all the finite systems of nature and society."[72] Similarly, in 1943 he states that the cross "requires men to take their moral decisions with greater rather than less seriousness," because it reveals "the intense moral earnestness of a God who will not abandon mankind to self-destruction."[73] Response to a single, absolute value enables one to act as a single self, as an I. The alternative is to act as a fragmented self that is attracted now and then to a variety of competing idols. As such, repentance requires a crucial delay in moral action, the outcome of which is not quietism, but an accentuation of individual integrity and moral seriousness.

For Niebuhr, repentance also has important implications for ethical discourse and practical reasoning. In the war articles the self-criticism wrought by repentance is designed to purge moral action of self-interest and conceit. One implication is that Niebuhr's theology, especially his suspicion about self-justification, provides strong warrants for criticizing casuistical methods commonly associated with the ethics of war. There can be no entirely pure motives from Niebuhr's perspective; Christians must act with a "bad conscience" because war is an arena in which all participants fall short of divine righteousness.[74] The problem with casuistry is that it leads to self-confidence in moral reflection, allowing the self to define itself as the center of value. One effect of repentance is to excise the self and its moralistic conceits from discourse about war and peace, placing it under the universal judgment and corrective action of God's will. The outcome of Niebuhr's argument (to paraphrase him slightly) is not to demonstrate that we have the wrong standards of judgment, which we must correct or for which we must substitute a right standard of judgment, but to show that the whole effort to assess and judge goodness and evil, and to reward or punish accordingly, is mistaken.[75] Accordingly, for theological reasons Niebuhr is unable to approach war with general moral principles that he may then apply to the "case" of war. Moreover, given Niebuhr's insistence that God, not humanity, is the chief agent in history, and given the fact that history is necessarily open to change, it is impossible to strive for the conceptual precision and moral security often associated with casuistical procedures.

Yet this caution about moral discourse is not devoid of constructive content for social ethics. Instead, Niebuhr develops a series of benchmarks for thinking about war, benchmarks that move beyond a concern for self-criticism to a broader concern for social criticism. Indeed, the effect of Niebuhr's critique of pacifist and nonpacifist tenets leads to a transvaluation of conventional discourse about war and peace in at least four ways.

Chapter Five

First, by placing moral discourse under the form of the cross, Niebuhr extends, or universalizes, the moral law, the effect of which generates a theory of nonpreferential duty. *Nonpreferential duty* in Niebuhr's agenda denotes an ethic of universal responsibility, an ethic which prohibits preferential treatment of some on the basis of familiarity or friendship. Yet from underneath the umbrella of nonpreferentialism and universalism emerges a qualified preferentialism, for the innocent victims of war have a preferred status. It is on *their* behalf that we are to act, Niebuhr insists, whether we act as pacifists or as nonpacifists, because their suffering distinguishes them from the rest within the matrix of being. The effect of repentance, then, is to deliver us from the rationale of self-defense or self-righteousness as a basis for responding to the problem of war, binding us instead to "concentrate on the deliverance of [our] neighbors."[76]

In other words, once Niebuhr has secured a rationale for repentance, he returns Christians to an Augustinian basis for thinking about moral action in war: We are to act not in self-defense, but out of care for the needs of others. As Niebuhr states, "If we accept God's judgment on our self-centeredness we cannot respond to it by persisting in actions of self-defense and by fighting the war for the sake of our selves or our values instead of for the sake of the innocent who must be delivered from the hands of the aggressor."[77] Accordingly, Niebuhr's argument places moral grammar about war under the rubric of protection rather than self-preservation. The point of his critique is to eliminate self-regard and, simultaneously, to secure a strong basis for other-regard in the recourse to lethal force. This means that we may "wage war as those who will not withdraw when their own interests are no longer apparently imperiled while their weaker neighbors remain in danger."[78]

Other-regard, especially for innocent victims of harm, likewise holds for Niebuhr's reconstructed affirmation of pacifism. In keeping with his view about the duty to participate in some wars, Niebuhr insists that the self must be displaced from the center of pacifistic nonparticipation. Pacifistic nonparticipation is tenable, in other words, "only if it be part of a total action in which concern for others has been given preeminence over concern for self and its values."[79] In Niebuhr's judgment, self-centered nonparticipation is no less destructive than self-centered participation, because in either case the self remains blind to the real, objective needs of other persons and other causes in the course of history.

Second, Niebuhr's call for repentance mitigates the prospect of exceptionalism in moral discourse about war. Exceptionalism is the idea that a nation, or an alliance, may make special claims for itself by appealing to the moral fabric of its own political order, especially when juxtaposed to the relative evil of an opponent. Thus, in his own distinctive way, Niebuhr articulates a commonplace in contemporary just-war thought, the principle of relative justice. That principle, as Paul Ramsey recognizes and as the U.S. Catholic bishops underscore, holds that no nation has a monopoly on justice or moral rectitude in the course of war. Relative justice also forbids nations from making reference to the exceptional nature of their history or political philosophies to justify morally ambiguous acts, acts that would be condemned if the opponent were to carry them out instead.[80] In short, Niebuhr's critique of self-centeredness in war removes the possibility of a double standard in a nation's behavior. Both repentance and relative justice are structured to eliminate the language of saints and sinners in moral discourse about war. For Niebuhr there are strong theological reasons for subjecting such beliefs to social criticism.

Third, repentance is designed to secure the principle of other-regard in the course of war itself. That is, Niebuhr provides an important foundation for thinking morally about the methods of war, even if he devotes scant attention to those controverted terms. Repentance and care for the innocent ought to fortify moral action against slipping into extreme measures under the circumstances of a supreme emergency. Niebuhr's method "does not accept the counsel of despair in the midst of fighting, allowing vindictive measures because by 'fair fighting' our cause might be lost."[81] Consent to God's judgment displaces the self from the center of concern, precluding the notion of a supreme emergency altogether. The result is to secure fairness and care as grounds for moral action within the heat of battle.

Finally, Niebuhr's treatment of nonpacifism and pacifism suggests that neither approach is to monopolize our attitudes about the morality of war. Instead, Niebuhr affirms (with the qualifiers stated above) both approaches as legitimate options for individual consciences. Clearly, Niebuhr is reticent about moral specifics, leaving us with general reflections "which do not presume to say to anyone what his particular duty in response to God's judgment must be."[82] The affirmation of pacifist and nonpacifist tenets finds its way into the report of the Calhoun Commission (1944), a document that clearly and indelibly bears Niebuhr's signature.[83] It is also embraced, as I pointed out earlier, in recent pronouncements from Roman Catholic and Protestant churches.[84] Niebuhr's point is that both pacifism and nonpacifism may be legitimate, depending not on their conceptual merits, but on the extent to which the self has been displaced from the center of their respective systems of value.

A Repoeticization of War

Niebuhr's call for national repentance, his belief in corrective punishment under the providential direction of God, and his chiliastic confidence in the efficacy of future grace are but tropes of the American jeremiad—without, of course, the ideology of national election, progressive history, or Puritan errand.[85] But Niebuhr's use of religious symbolism resembles the jeremiad in that both were born in an effort to impose metaphor upon reality.[86] And in using religious tropes, Niebuhr traded on a moral vision deeply rooted in American theology and ethics, the belief that history proceeds under the imperiousness of Providence. In this respect, Niebuhr addressed war in the manner of a public theologian, developing social criticism by using a religious vocabulary with wide cultural currency.

Yet Niebuhr's attempt at a public theology of war should not obscure the fact that he was chiefly committed to a historicist project: the attempt to interpret and respond to reality from a particular point of view, relativistically. Niebuhr wrote when many presumed that historicism and public theology could be easily joined, especially in a Protestant culture. The assumption of cultural Protestantism makes it easier to speak to a public in the language of Christian faith; remove that assumption and such language sounds imperialistic or parochial (or both).

The cross furnishes the master trope in Niebuhr's grammar of faith, an image for repoeticizing the reality of war. This image requires us to reread the particularities of the moment, to establish a pattern in the array of historical facts, and to criticize the conceit of conventional ethical approaches to war. We certainly have little specificity for moral direction; at best, the central values of pacifism and nonpacifism have been criticized and reformulated under the sovereignty of the Protestant principle. But the brunt of Niebuhr's argument is that specificity will misguide us until our basic values have been properly ordered; specificity, in and of itself, is at best a delusory goal. His transvaluation of value in the moral discourse about war, in which repentance is axiomatic, secures the place of the other as an object of care, not judgment, and it unmasks the common pretenses of the self to invoke moral language for less than moral purposes. Such an exercise leaves us with little precision in the end, but doubtless Niebuhr neither would nor could have it any other way.

Niebuhr never developed the positive dimensions of his ethics of war after the early 1940s, returning instead to more general philosophical and theological interests. But his concern for the innocent, his principle of other-regard, and his suspicion about those who appeal to justice to distinguish the righteousness of participants in war were developed by his student, Paul Ramsey. Ramsey's work is driven by the conviction that the seemingly esoteric tropes in his mentor's work are directly relevant to problems surrounding modern statecraft and nuclear technology. To an analysis and critique of this Niebuhrian trajectory in nuclear ethics we shall now turn.

PART THREE

THE PROBLEM
OF NUCLEAR
DETERRENCE

Love, Intention, and Proportion: Paul Ramsey on the Morality of Nuclear Deterrence

Deterrence, Pacifism, and the Just War

Over the decades since Niebuhr wrote the war articles, plans for military defense and protection have been complicated by the advent of nuclear technology. The capacity of nuclear weapons to wreak massive destruction in a brief period of time is unique in human history, raising political and ethical questions that are vertiginous if not intractable. With the proliferation of nuclear weapons the chief goal of military and political policy is not to use lethal force, but to deter its use. To this end nations make conditional threats of nuclear attack, the putative effects of which are designed to raise the costs of war. The prospect of disproportionate damage is intended to reduce an enemy's incentives to initiate conflict, strengthening the threshold that separates crisis from lethal force. As the attempt to prevent nuclear war (and perhaps some conventional wars) by threatening to raise the costs of war to an opponent, nuclear deterrence is fundamentally paradoxical. Nations threaten to wage war in order to prevent war from being waged. Perhaps more than ever before, international relations are now ruled by the classical adage, *Si vis pacem, para bellum*.

Nuclear deterrence is, or ought to be, of common concern for pacifists and just-war theorists for complex reasons. Insofar as deterrence is designed to prevent war, it is germane to pacifism, since prevention ought to have at least prima facie attractiveness to those who wish to ban war. Yet insofar as deterrence includes the preparation to wage a certain kind of war, its morality is open to scrutiny according to just-war criteria. Without such preparations, it would seem that deterrence would lack credibility.

Recent efforts to assess the morality of nuclear deterrence have taken several forms and have produced diverse verdicts. But despite this diversity, the basic parameters of recent discussions have been set for over two decades. That fact is due in no small part to the work of Paul Ramsey, whose contribution to the debate about deterrence continues to serve as the point of departure for subsequent discussions. For example, the U.S. Catholic bishops, David Hollenbach, and John Finnis et al. take as their point of departure the issues surrounding deterrent intentions;[1] William O'Brien and James Turner Johnson call for a limited war-fighting strategy as essential to deterrence credibility;[2] J. Bryan Hehir and Hollenbach bid us to distinguish clearly between the ends of deterrence and the ends of fighting a war when assessing deterrent policy[3]—and in each instance these figures draw on or amplify a characteristic theme of Ramsey's contribution. But, unlike recent authors, Ramsey attempts to hold together these several issues, and in this respect his work constitutes the *Ursprung* from which subsequent efforts have explicitly or implicitly taken their cues. Indeed, the main currents of Ramsey's contribution have remained uncommonly topical, despite rapid changes in weapons technology and political climate during the past two decades. In order to grasp the issues surrounding deterrence, it is doubtless instructive to begin with Ramsey's work and to learn from the strengths and weaknesses of his prodigious attempt to conceive a possible moral deterrent.

In this chapter I will place Ramsey's discussion of nuclear deterrence in the wider context of his ethical theory, focusing on the deontic requirements of *agape,* or disinterested care, as his basis for an ethics of war. I will then show how Ramsey sought to reconcile his account of just-war ideas, especially his strict rendition of noncombatant immunity, with some forms of nuclear strategy. I hope to show that Ramsey's argument about the morality of nuclear deterrence falters, and that his errors can be traced to the fact that the implications of *agape* as disinterested care are attenuated by a subtheme in his argument, namely, the respect for order and its preservation.

Agape, War, and Moral Discourse

Central to Ramsey's effort is his attempt to bring the principle of *agape* to bear on issues of war and deterrence. Drawing upon New Testament materials, Kierkegaard, and the Kantianism of Anders Nygren, Ramsey defines *agape* as disinterested love, care that is unmotivated by the worth or merits of one's neighbor, concretely tailored to the neighbor's special needs.[4] *Agape* is selfless love, seeking no reciprocity or return. Such love disentangles self-love from radical other-regard, "attributing worth to the neighbor's needs infinitely superior to the claims of self."[5] Christian love, moreover, is a duty, not a good, defining obligations to others irrespective of the benefits that might accrue to oneself.[6] *Agape,* then, establishes "faithfulness claims," a set of obligations to which the Christian must remain steadfastly obedient. Modeled upon God's unconditional love for humanity, Christian love is equivalent to unsolicited, spontaneous care. Hence, for Ramsey, Christian morality is fiduciary and deontic, centered on canons of loyalty and modeled on the divine paradigm of absolute righteousness and covenant fidelity.[7]

Agape is crucial to Ramsey's treatment of nuclear issues because it lies at the heart of his construction of just-war ideas, and just-war ideas provide the prism through which he evaluates war, statecraft, and nuclear deterrence. For Ramsey, just-war criteria are grounded and ordered according to the requirements of *agape* or covenant faithfulness, "not primarily from considerations of abstract or 'natural' justice."[8] To support this claim, Ramsey looks to Augustine as the chief authority about the justification and limitation of force.[9] The crux of Ramsey's influential retrieval of Augustine is what David H. Smith calls a "protection paradigm."[10] In the context of war, this paradigm authorizes the use of force only when that force is designed to protect innocent victims from aggression. Lethal force can be justified, Ramsey argues, only as an exercise of other-regard or care for others, *not* as an expression of self-regard and "self-defensive self-protection."[11]

Ramsey develops these claims in light of his understanding of *agape,* and the brunt of his argument is to refine the complex relation between neighbor-love and violence. Whether love and violence are antithetical depends on the kind of social relation under consideration. On the one hand, love and violence are mutually exclusive in individual, or one-to-one, relations. Like Augustine, Ramsey insists that the use of force to protect oneself violates the requirements of disinterested neighbor-love, derived from the Sermon on the Mount. For Ramsey the aggressor must never be denied the love that Christ teaches; the enemy, however nefarious, remains one's neighbor—"for whom Christ died."[12] When conflicts arise in individual relations, with no reference to others' needs, *agape* binds Christians to an ethic of nonresistant pacifism.

On the other hand, Ramsey insists, against other pacifistic applications of *agape,* that love and violence are not always mutually exclusive. The key lies again in the kind of social relation in question. Violence can be an expression of love in "multilateral relations"—relations in which one set of neighbors harms another. In such circumstances a conflict of duties arises, forcing us to rank the duties placed on us by neighbor-love. *Agape* requires us to rank the claims of the innocent above those of the aggressors because love must be directed first to those whose concrete needs are neglected or under duress.[13] In multilateral relations, then, *agape* provides reasons for a qualified preferentialism: we are to prefer the claims of the needy—the innocent—over those of all the rest.[14] Indeed, love requires us to protect the needy, even if force is necessary to insure their protection. Ramsey thus reconstructs the *jus ad bellum* by combining his view of *agape* with an understanding of the multiple demands of social relations. Christian morality must be an expression of care, and when violence protects innocent people it can be an exercise of Christian care.

Because he requires nonresistant pacifism at the level of individual relations and just wars in multilateral relations, Ramsey is often held up as a modern exemplar of the Augustinian convergence. Doubtless his notion of *agape* is stripped of the metaphysical aspects of Augustine's *caritas* and the idea of peace-as-order. But this rendition of *agape* and the protection paradigm are sufficiently close to Augustine's formula to support the widespread perception that, under Ramsey's authority, medieval ethics remains useful in the modern age.

As if to lend further credence to this perception, Ramsey has sharpened his retrieval of Augustine's views by distinguishing it from alternative attempts to build a bridge between pacifism and just-war tenets. Central to Ramsey's claims is his insistence that *agape* is a positive, unalloyed duty, not an exception to the presumption against violence. He thus rebukes those who argue on behalf of a point of convergence between pacifism and just-war tenets, and the logic of prima facie duties in just-war reasoning. Ramsey remarks, "Pacifism's presumption is in favor of peace. . . . Just war's presumption favors the defense of an ordered *justice*. . . . Just cause* is overarching in just-war theory; *within that,* last resort comes into play. If and only if there is found in justice a possible cause of war is there a presumption against resorting to violence to be taken into account. Thus a presumption against *injustice* is a lexically *prior* presumption to the 'presumption against going to war' under 'last resort.'"[15] As Ramsey has constructed just-war tenets, the use of force in multilateral relations is an unambiguous, unqualified duty, absent conflict with other duties. The duty to use force must be seen as analogous to other forms of care, in which those in need are given assistance.

According to Ramsey's agenda, moreover, there is no special reason to commend pacifists for their integrity. Rather, the implied critique of pacifists is that, failing to recognize the requirements of *agape* for those in need, *they* compromise the extensive requirements of care. The effect of Ramsey's appeal to *agape* is to render war less unusual than it often appears in moral discourse. By his logic, war is not a "boundary" case for morality, standing on the precipice of our moral experience; rather, it is yet another sphere in which care is obligatory. As Ramsey remarks, the use of force "for love's sake" is "not really an 'exception' but a determinate expression of justice and mercy."[16]

Agape also lies at the heart of Ramsey's understanding of *jus in bello* considerations. As a principle that limits the use of force, *agape* protects any innocent party—friend or foe—from direct attack. From the notion of *agape* as care for the innocent Ramsey thus derives the principle of noncombatant immunity as an inviolable, nonpreferential duty. Directly to attack innocent people, regardless of one's cause, is to violate both the spirit and the letter of neighbor-love.[17]

It is a common assumption in popular discourse about war that non-combatant immunity prohibits any and all killing of innocent parties in war, but such an interpretation of *in bello* criteria is wrong and Ramsey has endeavored to correct this misunderstanding.[18] According to *in bello* criteria, some innocent life may be lost as a result of the foreseeable, indirect consequences of battle. The loss of such innocent life is not necessarily prohibited by just-war tenets.

Moral judgments about such losses in war must be assisted by the rule of double effect, a commonplace in traditional Catholic moral theology and a device Ramsey uses to refine his application of *agape*.[19] According to the traditional interpretation of this rule, one must distinguish evils that are directly intended from the unfortunate evils that may result from the unintended, but foreseen, effects of one's actions. The distinction between direct evils and indirect evils, for example, allows one to distinguish between mugging and surgery.[20] In both cases harm occurs, but in the former it is direct while in the latter it is foreseen and indirect. The same basic point holds with evils in war. The distinction between the direct killing of innocent civilians and the indirect loss of life is not unlike the difference between mugging and surgery; the former is always impermissible while the latter is not. More specifically, the direct taking of innocent life is categorically proscribed by the principle of discrimination, while the indirect taking of innocent life is subject to judgments guided by the principle of proportionality. *In bello* criteria thus place a twofold restriction on the use of force in war. Military acts must not be indiscriminate, and even if they are discriminate, they may be morally reprehensible if the unintended evils outweigh the goods that are pursued. Indeed, the course of war may become disproportionate well before it becomes indiscriminate.[21]

Especially important in Ramsey's reconstruction of *in bello* tenets is his insistence that discrimination and proportionality must be lexically ordered. Following his overall insistence upon a deontic method of moral reasoning, Ramsey argues that consequentialist calculations are appropriate only after our duties have been met. Within our discourse about war, judgments about moral means (i.e., noncombatant immunity) must precede judgments about whether consequences can be "prudentially balanced." Anything less would weaken the strict demands of noncombatant immunity, placing the morality of means on a slippery slope.[22]

As one surveys Ramsey's discussion of the morality of force and the relation between love and violence, it becomes readily apparent that he has devoted most of his attention to the importance of noncombatant immunity, deontically construed, rather than *ad bellum* considerations of "just cause" or the *in bello* principle of proportionality. At least two reasons account for this emphasis, both of which shed light on his general ethical agenda and his treatment of nuclear deterrence. First, Ramsey exhibits an Augustinian and Niebuhrian reluctance to determine "absolute justice" in times of war, a reluctance that prevents him from entering into debates about whether a "just cause" exists to authorize the use of force. Following Augustine, Ramsey argues that states are bound together not by principles of justice, but by common loves.[23] The common love that unites a group tends to be absolutized by that group, thus distorting its perception of "objective" or "absolute" justice. Given the dangers of collective pride and self-interest, it is notoriously difficult for one side to claim justice as the basis of its cause. Ramsey thus exhorts us to confine our judgments to the morality of means instead of attending to the intractable problems of determining who is just. As he remarks, "Since at least everyone seeks peace and desires justice, the *ends* for which wars may legitimately be fought are not nearly so important in the theory of the just war as is the moral and political wisdom contained in its reflection upon the *conduct* or means of warfare."[24]

Ramsey insists, moreover, that judgments about a "just cause" stand within the domain of political prudence, about which Christian ethics has no privileged perspective. The same holds for *in bello* estimations of proportionality because in both cases one must "prudentially balance" the foreseen goods and evils in an act.[25] Prudential balancing entails consequentialist judgments and, although he does not wish to jettison consequentialist concerns altogether, Ramsey subordinates such judgments to the deontological requirements of *agape* throughout virtually all of his ethical reflections. Christian ethics, Ramsey tirelessly insists, must begin with a deontic understanding of *agape*. If prudential concerns are relevant, they must depend on or derive from a prior ethical principle.[26] Without such principles to anchor moral reasoning, ethical reflection reduces to a vague and ultimately incalculable estimation of ends—a "wasteland of utility."[27] As such, discourse about "just causes" and proportionality falls under Ramsey's general disparagement of consequentialist ethics: Consequentialism "produces some version of the opinion that the end justifies the means."[28] To avoid this "wasteland," we must revive a concern for the morality of the means themselves, a concern that is advanced by a deontic application of *agape,* and a focus on the means of war.

One implication of Ramsey's doubts about "just causes" and prudential calculations, although he does not draw it, strengthens a basic suspicion about the kinds of self-justifying claims that collectivities often make on their own behalf. The subtle distance he places between *agape* and justice, reinforced by his emphasis on restriction of means rather than the authorization of ends, fortifies his position against the intellectual vagaries and potential duplicity of political discourse. As a nonpreferential term, *agape* relativizes the kinds of self-exalting claims that political leaders make, claims that often appear in language like *justice*. Echoing a powerful refrain from H. Richard Niebuhr—that monotheistic loyalty transcends and relativizes all finite allegiances, especially nationalism— Ramsey states that "covenant obedience holds firmly onto the conviction that man's ultimate loyalty transcends every earthly system or center of human power. This gives man whereon to stand in opposing the present shape of the world; it provides at least some indication of how big tyrants ought not to be and places an ultimate limit on the totalitarian demands of the state."[29]

Yet an important undercurrent moves within Ramsey's agenda, a sub-theme in his grand concerto—quite distinct from his Augustinian suspicion of self-interest, his emphasis upon disinterested love, and his caution about prudential matters. That theme, subtle but audible throughout, is the qualified respect for self-preservation and the preservation of order, especially political order. In *Basic Christian Ethics,* for example, Ramsey constructs a *derivative* basis for self-defense. As a requirement of love, it may be a duty for the Christian to protect herself insofar as her own existence is a condition for relieving the burdens of others. As Ramsey remarks,

> Whenever sacrificing himself, or in any degree failing to protect himself and his own, actually would involve greater burdens or injury to others, surely then a Christian should stick to his post whether he wants to or not. . . . Making use of this distinction between "self-defensive self-protection" and "neighbor-regarding self-protection," self-defense may be but an extreme instance of those "duties to the self" which are a part of Christian vocational obligation.[30]

And, concerning collective self-preservation, Ramsey intimates much the same point in a comment in *War and the Christian Conscience,* developed against those who cast our future in terms of two prospective options, "dead or Red." Ramsey remarks that

> there has never been *justitia* imprinted in social institutions and social relationships except in the context of some *pax-ordo* preserved by clothed or naked force. On their way to the Heavenly City the children of God make use of the *pax-ordo* of the earthly city and acknowledge their share in responsibility for its preservation. Not to repel injury and uphold and improve *pax-ordo* means not simply to accept the misshapen order and injustice that challenges it at the moment, but also to start down the steep slope along which justice can find no place whereon to stand.[31]

While not an absolute value, political order is nonetheless an important value for Ramsey—a "proximate" value, he might say[32]—and its preservation is a genuine duty. Indeed, the duty to preserve the *ordo pacis* is analogous with Ramsey's understanding of "neighbor-regarding self-protection." In both cases we are to protect ourselves as a condition for other-regard. As Ramsey states in his discussion of political affairs, order is not a higher value than justice, but "order is for the sake of justice since the only real political justice is an ordered justice."[33]

Ramsey's attention to the relative value of order and self-preservation constitutes what I shall call a "preservation motif." The duty of self-preservation goes beyond the protection paradigm because the justification for coercion may include qualified reference to self-defense and prudential concerns, which otherwise would be eclipsed by the dominant refrain of the protection paradigm. Thus, in the final analysis, Ramsey does *not* adhere without qualification to the substance of the Augustinian convergence, since self-preservation at the level of private, individual relations is not entirely ruled out. In Ramsey's moral universe, the victim of attack is left with more than a phone call to the police; those who defend themselves are no moral vigilantes.

This difference between Ramsey and Augustine does not mean, however, that Ramsey discerns the duty of individual or collective self-preservation as a crude utilitarian principle, sneaked in under some other guise. Rather, the preservation motif derives from the duty to protect the innocent. Like the duty of individual self-preservation, the protection of the *ordo pacis* is a prudential concern that has been transformed by *agape*.

I suspect that Ramsey's reference to prudential ideas can be explained in large part by his desire to craft a "responsible" political ethic, one that is practically feasible. Reference to prudential ideas, even as a subordinate refrain, allows Ramsey to consider the concrete implications of his views. Should prudential calculations lead to the same conclusions as those derived from prior deontic considerations, then Ramsey can commend his position as "realistic." Concurrence from deontic and prudential points of view is a desideratum for Ramsey because it fortifies his position against the charge that an in-principled ethical agenda is winsomely idealistic, removed from the concrete, finite exigencies of practical decision-making and political responsibility.[34] Indeed, Ramsey adamantly insists that "ethics are not logically, externally related to politics. . . . Our quest should be for the clarification of political ethics in its *specific* nature, for the ethical ingredient inherent in foreign policy formation, for the wisdom peculiar to taking counsel amid a world of encountering powers."[35]

Further, insofar as Ramsey endeavors to join care with prudence, he likewise seeks to join the right and the good, while keeping the latter subordinate to the former. Such a wedding is but a corollary of the fact that realistic benefits are linked to an ethics of care. More to the point, in joining the right and the good as he does, Ramsey is able to address the question of moral motivation. By Ramsey's account, we have every reason to be motivated to do the "right thing" if he can show that such a path will lead to outcomes that are politically or prudentially attractive.

Unfortunately, however, Ramsey's brand of political realism and its corresponding attention to moral motivation imperils his argument about the morality of nuclear deterrence. As we shall see, the subordinate, prudential concern for preservation finally prevails in his attempt to conceive of a morally justifiable nuclear deterrent, overriding the implications wrought from *agape,* deontically construed.

Morality and Nuclear Deterrence

Ramsey's retrieval of *agape* to structure his just-war tenets is important for nuclear issues because it forms the backdrop for his treatment of war and deterrence. Central to Ramsey's discussion is the issue of intention—specifically, whether it is possible to construct a morally viable nuclear strategy, one that does not entail a murderous intention. Although this emphasis on intention might seem irrelevant to the principal term—*agape*—in Ramsey's ethical agenda, just the contrary is true. For Ramsey, *agape* is essentially an expression of intention, and by intention Ramsey means the direction or orientation of the will.[36] In other words, Ramsey's effort to think about the morality of nuclear issues is controlled by the query, Can nuclear war and deterrence be *agapistic?* His detailed attention to intention—and this cannot be emphasized enough—is merely a refinement of the dictates of *agape.*

Axiomatic in his analysis of nuclear deterrence, moreover, is the moral equivalence between action and intention, that is, the claim that whatever is immoral to do is immoral to intend to do. It follows that murderous acts may never be morally intended, even if such intentions are effective in preventing the outbreak of nuclear war.[37] It also follows that, as a first step in an analysis of deterrence, it is necessary to determine what sorts of acts are morally acceptable within the compass of just-war ideas.

Ramsey proceeds through this first step by applying just-war criteria to possible uses of nuclear weaponry. He arrives at a conclusion about which he argued tirelessly over the course of the past three decades: Modern war must be limited to counterforce targets—combatants, military installations, and supporting industries. Strategies premised on the theory of total war, or massive retaliation, are tantamount to murder, contrary to the fundamental dictates of Western thinking about morality and war.[38]

Ramsey's argument on behalf of limited war, moreover, closely follows his general desire to show the convergence of deontic and prudential considerations. The "moral premise" from which he begins draws on *in bello* criteria, leading Ramsey to insist that preparations for total war entail a murderous intention to kill innocent victims. The "strategic premise" draws upon calculations of credibility in deterrent strategy. According to Ramsey and other limited-war strategists, the credibility of deterrence depends upon a nation's perceived ability to fight a war. Massive retaliation strategies are incredible to an opponent because they lack any rational, political utility. Consequently, the policy of limited war commends itself according to Ramsey's realist desideratum, for it meets the requirements of both the protection paradigm and the preservation motif.[39]

In his most comprehensive treatment of counterforce war and counterforce nuclear war, *The Just War,* Ramsey weaves the gist of his limited-war position into an elaborate nuclear strategy. Two basic features of this refinement stand out. First, Ramsey argues that, as a matter of policy, the United States should renounce the first use of all nuclear weapons, except tactical weapons used in defense against invasion. That is, the United States should renounce the first use of any and all nuclear weapons against an enemy's homeland, even against counterforce targets like military installations.[40] The first use, then, should be confined to Western territory and would be designed to supplement conventional forces.

The basic objective of this strategy is to establish, or reestablish, the recognition of territorial boundaries, boundaries that have been trespassed by invading forces. Drawing on the strategic theory of Thornton Read, Ramsey avers, "The objective in this use of tactical nuclears will not be 'victory' but defense strictly understood as sealing the border." Because this use of tactical nuclear weapons is confined to defensive purposes, moreover, it stands within the compass of just-war ideas. And from the standpoint of political prudence it is a credible plan as well, because the use of tactical weapons has clear, practical utility.[41]

Second, nuclear capability must also be maintained for counterforce strikes—strategic strikes—over an enemy's homeland. Such strikes have the dual purpose of defense (destruction of an enemy's military capability) and punishment (in response to an enemy's prior violations).[42] Such strikes would be retaliatory in nature, to be carried out after the opponent has attacked the United States with either a counterforce or counterpopulation strike. The retaliation must be confined to counterforce measures, never to be conflated with countercity strategic targeting. The objective of such counterforce, strategic targeting is to eliminate, or at least reduce, an enemy's military strength, or to induce the enemy to withdraw from one's territory.

Ramsey's proposals for a counterforce nuclear war thus entail a graduated targeting system, which progressively raises the risk of strategic counterforce warfare. The second step in the process—strategic counterforce strikes—is the upper limit, beyond which it is immoral and imprudent to proceed. Countercity retaliation, Ramsey maintains, is simply incoherent: If it is immoral for one society to destroy another, then it is unjust for either side, regardless of who initiates the first countercity volley. For Christians, moreover, such reprisals are acts of revenge, contrary to the dictates of charity. And, to those for whom justice or charity are not plausible reasons, Ramsey insists that countercity targeting lacks any identifiable goal. Trading cities is nothing more than a "spiritualization of warfare," a matter of resolve in which force loses its political purpose. Violence becomes an end in itself, contrary to moral wisdom, political reason, and self-interest.[43] As such, countercity targeting is untenable according to judgments that again reflect Ramsey's realist desideratum: The strategy is untenable, for both deontic and prudential reasons.

When Ramsey proceeds from the issue of use to the morality of deterrence he advances his views yet another step.[44] Although he does not change his counterforce position as a war-fighting policy, he argues that an acceptable deter-the-war policy may reside in "more than" a fight-the-war policy. The exact nature of this "more than" involves a lengthy and often gymnastic application of the rule of double effect, as well as an analysis of the ambiguity that inheres in nuclear weapons themselves. Ramsey authorizes a graduated deterrent, the effectiveness of which rests on the dangers of widespread, unintended collateral damage to combatants and noncombatants, and on the ambiguity of nuclear weapons as devices of potential countercity destruction. Specifically, an effective deterrent can derive from (1) the prospect of disproportionate combatant damage; (2) the prospect of extensive disproportionate noncombatant casualties; and (3) the "dual nature" of the weapons themselves.[45]

The first two of these possible deterrents turn on the effectiveness of unacceptable, indirect consequences of nuclear damage. Together they should be seen as relying on the same logic. The legitimate targeting of nuclear weapons—counterforce targeting—would include foreseeable, unavoidable, unintended damage. This widespread collateral damage strengthens the deterrent "cash value" of a counterforce policy. In Ramsey's words, the deterrent effect would be a "direct effect" of the "foreseeable indirect effects of legitimate military conduct."[46] The shared dangers of nuclear damage, *anticipated in advance,* would rest not on counterpopulation targeting, but on the use of nuclear weapons "which would be licit or permitted by the traditional rules of civilized conduct in war."[47] The impact, "when future, hypothetical, and merely in prospect," of such damage should generate fears sufficient to deter an enemy from initiating war, escalating war, or intimidating nonnuclear states.[48] Although the prospective damage within war might be disproportionate, such damage is proportionate to the wider ends of deterrence, namely, preventing the outbreak of war. Thus, it is possible to construct a sound deterrent, *one that does not rely on a murderous intention.*

Central to Ramsey's argument on behalf of his first two deterrents is the claim, "The threat of something disproportionate is not necessarily a disproportionate threat."[49] His point rests on a carefully nuanced distinction between two kinds of proportionality—proportionality relative to the ends of war and proportionality relative to the ends of deterrence. Disproportionate acts in war, says Ramsey, are not identical to disproportionate threats; the former can fall within wider purposes or ends to which deterrence may be ordered. To anticipate such disproportionate damage and to anchor one's deterrent policy to the likelihood of such damage is not intrinsically wrong, since such anticipations do not necessarily entail a murderous intention.

Elaborating on the claim that "the threat of something disproportionate is not necessarily a disproportionate threat," Ramsey insists that we be clear about this vital distinction between two determinations of what is proportionate. Judgments about proportion in war rest on a prudential balancing of prospective goods and foreseen, indirect evils. Judgments of proportion in deterrence depend

> on the gravity of the evil (general war) and the greatness of the good (the peace of the world) toward which the threat is proportioned. Or, during war, whether a deterrent threat is proportionate depends on the gravity of the evil (escalation) and the greatness of the good (keeping war limited) to which the threat is oriented.[50]

Or again:

> If a deterrent threat here and now genuinely terminates in the doing of a disproportionate act of war, that would be a disproportionate threat. And if the "threat" always and inalterably depends on real intention, that would be a disproportionately immoral (not, however, a "murderous") intention. But the analysis of deterrence has to be fundamentally altered when we take into account the fact that deterrent intention terminates rather in the prevention of the grave evil of general war and in the enforcement of limits upon any actual outbreak of hostilities. These are the great goods toward which deterrent threats are oriented.[51]

Acts which are disproportionate may have proportionate deterrent utility,

> so long as they are unemployed, and are intended to be unemployed, or so long as they are employed for deterrent effect, to enforce shared limits upon actual fighting, and to keep war itself proportionate to political purposes.[52]

It is vital, in other words, to distinguish between the ends of war and the ends of deterrence. It is equally important to discern the relation of these ends to the issue of intention. The ends of war-fighting are to prevail according to the requirements of morality and prudence. The conduct of war ought to be discriminate and proportionate, although it might become disproportionate for unintended reasons. The menace of prospective disproportionate damage may be measured by a second set of ends, namely, preventing war or nuclear blackmail (i.e., the goals of deterrence).[53] It is realistic to think that counterforce targeting will raise the costs of war, and this prospect is entirely proportionate to the preventive aims toward which deterrence is ordered.

Ramsey's comment that certain weapons should be "intended to be unemployed" is clearly unhelpful, for he is not developing a full-blown bluff posture in either of his first two possible deterrents, nor is he moving toward nuclear pacifism. Indeed, he is quite emphatic that his notion of a *just* "fight-the-war" policy may include some nuclear weapons. However, he wishes to consider the deterrent effects of the foreseen, unintended effects of use. Even without the threat of counterpopulation strikes, the prospective use of nuclear weapons according to counterforce planning clearly generates fears sufficient to deter their actual use.

To advance his argument Ramsey draws from an interesting medical analogy, citing an instance in which research is carried out on embryos that are procured from pregnant women who must undergo hysterectomies. The hysterectomies are medically indicated, prescribed as necessary for the health of the women. The research on the "aborted" embryos is a "direct effect" of the operation, although the abortions themselves are indirect. The research is morally legitimate, even for those who object to elective abortion, because the embryos are collected as by-products of a legitimate surgical procedure. Hence the analogy: The indirect effects of counterforce war are proportionate to the ends of deterrence just as the indirect abortions are proportionate to the wider ends of genetic research. Like the unintended but beneficial outcomes of the prospective collateral damage for deterrence, the knowledge gained from this genetic research "may be described as arising *immediately and directly* from grave indirect or collateral consequences of properly targeted surgical action."[54] And, according to the analogy, murder is neither committed nor intended as a means to the beneficial outcomes of deterrence or genetic research. If the analogy holds, both nuclear deterrence and this genetic research can be justified as beneficial outcomes of legitimate intentions.

Ramsey's authorization of the first two possible deterrents enumerated above draws on considerations of proportionality in ways that are unusual for such a strident opponent of consequentialism. His usual method is to move to estimations of proportionality as a second consideration after making deontic judgments. He justifies this departure from his usual practice by appealing to an important factual supposition: War tends to become disproportionate before it becomes indiscriminate.[55] Accordingly, Ramsey's evaluations of deterrence proceed within the constraints of his realist desideratum: He begins with considerations of proportionality so that his method can suit the practical exigencies of war and deterrence. Ramsey thus proceeds from the "bottom up" of *in bello* criteria, as he has lexically ordered them, to construct a morally viable deterrent strategy.

The last of the possible deterrents conceived by Ramsey, as stated above, rests on the "dual nature" of nuclear weapons. "Dual nature" denotes the fact that nuclear weapons can be used against either strategic forces or population centers. The danger that such weapons *might* be used against a city constitutes a menace regardless of a nation's declared intentions to use nuclear weapons discriminately, and may well create fears sufficient to curb an enemy's adventurism or aggression. As with Ramsey's first two deterrents, this means that nuclear weapons have the capacity to deter *apart from the intention to use them discriminately;* all three theories rest on deterrent effects that can be derived apart from the intention to use nuclear weapons according to restrictions derived from the principle of noncombatant immunity. Here the point is that nuclear weapons may deter as a "subjectively unintended" consequence of their existence.[56] Regardless of one's declared intention, the enemy may never be sure in the course of war that its cities will not be destroyed. This uncertainty, generated by the nature of nuclear weapons themselves, may be a sufficient source of fear to deter aggression.

Ramsey refines this third theory by considering the deterrent effectiveness of nuclear weapons used *in* war. In this respect his position resembles the theory of graduated deterrence or assured destruction, especially as it was developed by Thomas Schelling in the 1960s.[57] With both Ramsey and Schelling, the deterrent effect of nuclear weapons resides in their capacity to raise the risks associated with war.[58] Schelling's theory, based on the "risk that leaves something to chance," is designed to raise the costs of general war and may include counterpopulation bombing as a last resort. The theory is premised on the prospective dangers of unintended escalation in nuclear war, escalation which may take both sides over the brink of destruction. Ramsey's third possible deterrent, when construed in light of the exigencies of battle, can also fit within a theory of graduated deterrence, but without the counterpopulation factor. For Ramsey, the use of nuclear weapons is designed to raise the costs of *counterforce strategic war,* not general war. While Schelling, like Ramsey, sought to construct a theory of limited war as an alternative to strategies of massive retaliation, Ramsey places further limits on Schelling's theory, limits that likewise affect the issue of intention. We must not be *resolved* to lose control in the course of war, Ramsey insists; a sufficient deterrent resides in the possibility, the *unintended* contingency, of escalation.[59] Dangerous risks inhere in the nature of the weapons, and such risks can be exploited for deterrent purposes apart from any explicit intention to use them murderously.

In sum, Ramsey constructs a theory of an effective deterrent, one that is not linked to intentional civilian targeting. Over and against both nuclear pacifists and counterpopulation strategists, he argues that there is an effective deterrent that lies in counterforce targeting. We might borrow Kantian terminology to say that a just and effective deterrent relies not on the noumenal will of the agents of war, but on the accidents, the predictable tragedies, that appear in war. Fears sufficient to deter an adversary may be located in the unintended events of war, or in the unintended but perceived (i.e., phenomenal) features of the weapons themselves.

Intention: Thin or Thick?

The power and precision of Ramsey's argument are virtually without parallel in the work of Christian ethicists today, and are rivaled only by the U.S. Catholic bishops' pastoral letter in its articulation of the complex factual and strategic dimensions of nuclear strategy. And, like the bishops, Ramsey seeks to weigh the moral issues surrounding nuclear war and deterrence without departing from an understanding of moral principles, especially the *in bello* principle of discrimination, as disinterested and universal. Unfortunately, however, Ramsey's endeavor is flawed at the level of moral theory and application, leaving us to wonder whether his version of a counterforce nuclear deterrent is reconcilable with just-war tenets, deontically construed.

At the level of ethical theory, Ramsey's criticisms of the presumption against harm and the logic of prima facie duties in just-war reasoning are premised on a faulty understanding of the relation between negative and positive duties. As I argued in chapter 1, negative duties (e.g., the duty not to harm) are more extensive than positive duties (e.g., *agape*)—although this does not mean that positive duties are trivial or subject to capricious application. Were positive duties as extensive as negative duties, we would be guilty of culpable neglect for failing to assist all persons in need within our reach. Moreover, the fact that negative duties are more extensive than positive duties means that we may not do just anything in order to satisfy the requirements of care, like harvest kidneys from healthy persons without their consent while seeking to assist others with renal failure. Casting the ethics of war in the idiom of (prior) negative duties serves to capture the important relation, and moral conflict, between the requirements of nonmaleficence and the subsequent justification of the use of force to protect victims of aggression.

Hence, Ramsey has it wrong when it comes to interpreting the logic of prima facie duties in just-war reasoning, especially when he contends that "the original just-war 'assumption' is that 'social charity' comes to the aid of the oppressed, and yet, secondarily, the *burden of proof* should be placed on resort to violent means."[60] Of course there is an assumption against injustice implied by the criterion of just cause. But the logic of prima facie duties is meant to underwrite a logically prior presumption *against* violence in response to injustice, a presumption premised on the priority of negative over positive duties.

Further, the presumption against violence is not expressed simply in the criterion of "last resort," as Ramsey alleges; rather, it shapes the entire morphology of just-war reasoning. This presumption articulates the prior (negative) duty not to harm, a fundamental duty of our common life. The duty of nonmaleficence may be *overridden* when the conflicting (positive) duty provides sufficient reason, occasioned by another's maleficence (just cause). The emergency wrought by another's maleficence allows one to exercise maleficence as a form of defensive protection. Once the prior duty is overridden, however, it nonetheless leaves moral traces, requiring caution and restraint in the subsequent course of action. The logic of prima facie duties, then, is designed to give the ethics of war an idiom that expresses more fully than *agape* the context, and the moral tensions, occasioned by the phenomenon of violence.

Ramsey's complaint against using the presumption against violence to structure just-war criteria is, in part, theological. Reference to a point of convergence, he alleges, "tells us quite clearly that pacifism and just war have little or nothing in common—if the question was their theological and moral *sources* or points of departure in moral reasoning."[61] Indeed, to hold that there is a principled presumption against violence suggests a dualistic, Manichean outlook. Rather, Ramsey adds, "*in a fallen world . . . the presumption is to restrain evil and protect the innocent..*"[62] Cast in the language of positive duties, Ramsey suggests, just-war criteria more adequately reflect the exigencies of history to which they are addressed—the inevitability of human egoism in the form of unjust aggression and tyranny.

Yet, as I have endeavored to show throughout this book, the notion that pacifism and just-war tenets share a point of contact has deep roots in Western theology. Attention to, and refinement of, the convergence between pacifism and just-war tenets is doubtless recent on the map of ethics. But the apparent novelty of this point of contact should not obscure the fact that these ideas have traditional sources in Western thought and religious belief. Indeed, a proper interpretation of Augustine, as I pointed out in chapter 1, shows that Augustine's ethics of war is not structured exclusively in terms of charity as a positive duty, but also in terms of the tensions between nonmaleficence and protection of others, in which the latter duty relativizes the force of the former.

Moreover, the tensions suggested by Childress's formulation of just-war criteria are entirely compatible with the kinds of theological beliefs about the problem of human fault and egoism found in Ramsey's theory. Cast as a conflict of duties, the structure of just-war criteria coheres with the Augustinian and Niebuhrian conviction that moral action in the limits of history is not morally pure, that *we ourselves* make moral trade-offs once we make recourse to lethal force in response to egoism, injustice, and tyranny. This sense of moral conflict is entirely congruent with theological beliefs about the limits of human action in history, the finite options at our disposal. Ramsey overlooks this element of conflict in just-war criteria structured in terms of prima facie duties. This oversight leads him to dismiss too hastily insights about the limits of human action in history implied by Childress's theory, insights that are entirely compatible with Augustinian ethics.

At the level of application, Ramsey's formulation of a possible nuclear deterrent, resting on the proportionate threat of disproportionate civilian damage, is inconsistent with his emphasis on a limited counterforce war-fighting strategy. In his first two formulations, Ramsey labors to establish a possible deterrent that presupposes the just, legitimate use of nuclear weapons. The deterrent effect derives from prospective, unintended effects of such use. Ramsey suggests that not to intend such effects is sufficient to establish a just fight-the-war policy. The problem for Ramsey is that, insofar as his theory *permits* foreseen, disproportionate use against noncombatants, it violates the limits imposed by just-war criteria. Regardless of the fact that such effects are "future, hypothetical, and in prospect," they nonetheless fall outside the compass of what Ramsey calls the "traditional rules of civilized conduct in war."[63] Even a strategy premised on hypothetical outcomes can corrupt our moral character, and Ramsey's appeal to such outcomes requires public officials to implicate themselves in morally corrosive planning.

Interestingly, Ramsey's medical analogy exposes this flaw in his position. He argues that his first two authorizations of nuclear deterrence are not unlike authorizations of genetic research carried out on embryos that are indirectly aborted from women who must undergo medically indicated hysterectomies. The weakness of the analogy lies in the fact that Ramsey fails to identify the disproportion in the medical operation that becomes proportionate given the prospective goods of the medical research. In fact, the operation is proportionate relative to the ends of genetic research *and* relative to the medical needs of the women. Thus, the research is disanalogous with nuclear deterrence in that the research is *not* a proportionate measure that relies upon other disproportionate means.

More than a logical snag, this disanalogy between deterrence and genetic research bears directly upon Ramsey's effort to justify some forms of deterrence without compromising his rendition of just-war ideas. Ramsey argues that *the beneficial outcomes of deterrence do not rest on evil means.* However, insofar as his proportionate deterrent relies upon prospective disproportionate use against civilians or combatants, his argument clearly falters.[64]

Second, Ramsey's theory of intention presents special difficulties. Intention, as he construes it in his discussion of war and deterrence, is restricted to what might be called a "thin theory" of intention, in which the requirements of a good intention are narrowly defined. A thin theory sharply distinguishes intended harms from foreseen, unintended harms. A thick theory, in contrast, would also distinguish such harms, but would include the duty to *reduce* the unintended but foreseen harms that accompany an act.

The point can be illustrated with yet another medical analogy. Given Ramsey's notion of intention as he uses it in his discussions of war and deterrence, it is legitimate for a doctor to perform an operation without due concern for the foreseen but unintended harms that a patient will experience. All that is necessary is that the doctor confine her goals to the medical indications of the case, narrowly construed. A thicker theory of intention, in contrast, would hold the doctor responsible for reducing those harms as much as possible. Accordingly, the doctor would be responsible for limiting the pain and cost that accompany an operation as foreseen but unintended harms. Failure to limit such harms would be construed as a failure to care for the well-being of the patient.

The distinction between thin and thick renditions of intention has important implications for Ramsey's attempt to derive deterrent cash value from a discriminate, counterforce nuclear strategy. A thicker theory of intention would require military planners to limit the unintended harms that occur in the course of war, including the collateral damage that can be foreseen in a discriminate, limited war-fighting strategy. Applying just-war criteria with a thicker theory of intention ought to attenuate those foreseen, collateral factors on which Ramsey's theory of deterrence rests.[65] This would mean that military planners at the very least would be required to dissociate themselves from strategies premised on disproportionate destruction.

The implication of a thicker theory of intention, especially as it bears on the possibility of foreseen, collateral damage in nuclear targeting, is drawn out by the U.S. Catholic bishops, whose discussion of these issues presents a helpful contrast to Ramsey's views. According to the bishops, an exclusive adherence to the principle of discrimination as a moral criterion for evaluating nuclear deterrence is insufficient, "for it ignores some evil and unacceptable consequences" that are likely to occur in a limited, counterforce strike.[66] The problem, the bishops emphasize several times, is that industrial or militarily significant targets are located within heavily populated areas, or in areas where the effects of radioactive fallout from a counterforce strike "could well involve such massive civilian casualties that, in our judgment, such a strike would be deemed morally disproportionate, even though not intentionally indiscriminate."[67] It is imperative, the bishops insist, to be thorough and consistent in the application of just-war criteria to prospective effects of counterforce nuclear war. Although they never address Ramsey directly, the bishops clearly reject an approach confined to the issue of intention, without due attention to prospective consequences, as incomplete. In their words, "It would be a perverted political policy or moral casuistry which tried to justify using a weapon which 'indirectly' or 'unintentionally' killed a million innocent people because they happened to live near a 'militarily significant target.'"[68] The bishops suggest that restrictions on a morally acceptable policy ought to be tighter than Ramsey allows. Indeed, such restrictions must refer not only to the principle of discrimination, but also to the principle of proportionality.[69] A genuinely moral targeting policy, for purposes of either use *or deterrence,* must be governed by both terms in the *jus in bello.*

The key to Ramsey's problem in his treatment of deterrence is that he fails to join deontic and prudential considerations; his realist desideratum eludes him. The fact that he permits foreseen, disproportionate casualties in counterforce targeting, compounded by the fact that he fails to consider reducing those dangers as part of a moral fight-the-war policy, indicates that the disinterestedness of *agape* is weakened, not fortified, by other, more practical, considerations. And the clue to Ramsey's problem lies in his addressing considerations of proportionality prior to those of discrimination. As I indicated above, Ramsey departs from his usual method in order to adjust his procedures to the concrete exigencies of war, deterrence, and responsible statecraft. Ramsey's use of *in bello* criteria "starts from the bottom and moves upward in the scale." Such a method, he continues, "seems . . . to follow from an attempt to take seriously the just war theory as an ethics intrinsic to the nature of politics and to a purposeful use of force, and not as an ethics externally imposed on a neutral and alien realm of behavior."[70] Yet it is just this ranking of prudential ideas above deontic principles, seeking not to impose ethics externally, that plagues his treatment of deterrence. If he were to remain consistent with his overall method, his willingness to countenance the prospect of disproportionate damage to civilians for the sake of deterrence would entail a failure to care. As it stands, Ramsey's theory countenances an evil means, anticipated in advance, for a positive outcome.

Integrally related to Ramsey's ranking of prudential ideas over deontic principles in his discussion of deterrence is the subtheme in his grand concerto, the preservation motif. Ramsey takes great pains not only to create a possible deterrent absent a murderous intention, but also to conceive a means of protecting the *ordo pacis*. The "peace of the world" is the goal toward which deterrence is ordered, beckoning Ramsey to weigh matters according to prudence and proportionality.[71] This means that Ramsey must conceive a means of preserving political order—in this case, international order—without intending to commit an evil deed. By narrowly defining his understanding of intention, and by ranking prudential concerns over deontic principles, he seems able to hold together moral ideals with the exigencies of political responsibility, his realist desideratum. Self-preservation and conserving the political order of the present age are no trivial values, either within Ramsey's agenda or without. But within Ramsey's agenda, the interests that surround self-preservation ought to remain subordinate to the radical disinterestedness of *agape*. As this comparison with the bishops' argument indicates, however, Ramsey's attention to prudence, proportionality, and preservation emerges as an irrepressible subtheme in his treatment of the morality of nuclear deterrence, at the expense of the full ramifications of disinterestedness implied by his protection paradigm.[72] An understanding of *agape* as disinterested protection should not countenance the prospect of disproportionate damage as a means to the prudential goal of "the peace of the world"; moreover, a "thick" understanding of *agape* would require us to reduce (or to intend to reduce) indirect evils as part of a fully moral act.[73]

Ramsey's problems at the levels of ethical theory and application are not unrelated. Perhaps if he had cast his logic of just-war criteria according to the presumption against harming others, his account of *agape* would have been sufficiently sturdy to resist the pressures of prudence and realism. The shadow cast or the moral traces left by nonmaleficence as a prima facie duty, shaping the morphology of just-war tenets, would purify disinterested positive duties of the dross of political interest. Using a chastened principle of *agape,* then, Ramsey might have carried out a treatment of deterrence congruent with his own best intentions. But if he had, his morally tenable deterrent would have been shaped by a robust intention, ruled by the discriminate and proportionate uses of nuclear weapons.

Conclusion

Those who follow Ramsey's lead are left with three related issues to consider when assessing the morality of nuclear deterrence: the meaning and range of intention, especially the relation of intention to foreseen outcomes in an act; the place of putative consequences in the moral calculus of war-fighting plans and corresponding deterrent strategies; and the role of political self-preservation in the application of moral principles, especially when the duty of self-preservation derives from the prin-

Chapter Six

ciple of disinterested care. Even if Ramsey's approach to these issues is finally unsatisfactory, his contribution defines the parameters within which these topics have been subsequently debated. As we shall see, recent efforts to justify nuclear deterrence continue to wrestle with the tensions in Ramsey's work. To a discussion of those efforts we shall now turn.

S E V E N

The Morality of Nuclear Deterrence: Obstacles on the Road to Coherence

Conventional Approaches to the Morality of Deterrence

As I suggested in the last chapter, Ramsey's attempt to reconcile his rendition of just-war tenets with a conceivable nuclear deterrent provides a fountain from which other developments in moral casuistry have sprung forth. Several trajectories can be traced out of Ramsey's argument. Those who emphasize utility rather than intention tend to call attention to the beneficial outcomes of deterrence, furnishing a consequentialist approval of the deterrent status quo.[1] In such arguments, the subtext of Ramsey's position—the preservation motif—becomes more explicit, if not the ruling paradigm. A second group insists that a morally acceptable deterrent must be linked to a discriminate *and* proportionate war-fighting strategy, proceeding within the general framework of Ramsey's argument, but refusing to underwrite foreseeable disproportionate damage as the means of deterrence. A third group argues that the ends of deterrence are wholly different from the ends of war, requiring a different moral logic for evaluating deterrence. This approach intensifies Ramsey's distinction between the ends of war-fighting and the ends of deterrence. A fourth approach arrives at a realist desideratum of a different sort than Ramsey's, arguing that deterrence is not necessary now but may be in the future. By this account, we are justified in retaining nuclear weapons in anticipation of a different political climate. A fifth effort maintains that Ramsey's account of deterrent intentions is deceptive, that we must admit both the political necessity and the murderousness of deterrent intentions. A sixth argument prescinds from Ramsey's Augustinian reluctance to compare the relative differences between warring parties and insists that comparative justice is crucial to any realistic ethics of war and deterrence.

In these efforts, all of which I shall examine more thoroughly below, those who debate the morality of nuclear deterrence have been arguing in various ways with or against Ramsey. Moreover, as plans proceed in public policy to enhance deterrence,[2] questions surrounding the morality of deterrence assume new gravity: What are the bases for, and the limits of, deterrent threats? What is the logical and moral structure of deterrent intentions? What is the relation between the morality of using nuclear weapons and the morality of deterrence? To what extent can the facts of history be used to commend or critique deterrence?

Efforts to answer these questions take several forms, employ different methods, and invoke a variety of moral principles. Within this variety, however, five arguments presently constitute the conventional wisdom about nuclear deterrence, providing cautious and attractive justifications for the continuation of deterrent threats: the success thesis, the just-war thesis, the anticipatory thesis, the argument from "supreme emergency," and the exceptionalist thesis. The attraction of the success thesis lies in its appeal to the beneficial consequences of nuclear deterrence, namely, the prevention of nuclear war during the past forty years. The just-war thesis draws upon a well-known body of ethical wisdom to assess deterrence, appealing to what James Turner Johnson calls the "consensual tradition in Western culture" about the morality of war and peace.[3] The anticipatory thesis uses recent history to critique deterrence, but also observes that history may change, that we should not tie our hands by assuming that superpower relations will remain relatively peaceful. The argument from "supreme emergency" focuses on the intractable problems posed by nuclear technology, leaving room for the limit situation of survival where we may have to override traditional canons of morality. And the exceptionalist thesis grants philosophical validity to the intuition, especially attractive to the defenders of democracy against antidemocratic regimes, that we must assess the relative morality of opposing polities during times of conflict.

Despite these apparent attractions, however, this conventional wisdom about nuclear deterrence is gravely and dramatically ill-conceived. In this chapter I will argue, in critical dialogue with representatives of the arguments mentioned above, that the claims on behalf of deterrence are variously infected by inconsistencies, disanalogies, historical inaccuracies, practical difficulties, and logical fallacies. These obstacles to coherent reasoning exist at a variety of levels in moral and political discourse about nuclear policies, yet they remain hidden in the current debate about the justification and continuation of deterrent threats. As debates about deterrence go forward, it is imperative to take stock of these problems facing deterrence, to uncover the errors concealed within the conventional wisdom, and to face soberly and critically the difficulties that beset a coherent and moral deterrent strategy.

The Success Thesis

Doubtless one of the most frequent claims about deterrence appeals to the apparent truth of deterrent success. Nuclear deterrence, it is held, has prevented a major conflict between the superpowers over the past four decades, and this success provides sufficient justification for the continued possession and improvement of the nuclear arsenal. The argument is, in essence, consequentialist: The positive benefit of nuclear deterrence—the fact that nuclear deterrence has worked—justifies the means necessary to render credible the threat of nuclear war in some form. As Caspar Weinberger remarks,

> [The policy of the United States] to prevent war since the age
> of nuclear weapons began has been one of deterrence. . . . The
> idea on which this is based is quite simple: it is to make the
> cost of starting a nuclear war much higher than any possible
> benefit to an aggressor. This policy has been approved,
> through the political processes of the democratic nations it pro-
> tects, since at least 1950. Most important, it works. It has
> worked in the face of major international tensions involving
> the great powers, and it has worked in the face of war itself.[4]

Although Weinberger's claim that deterrence has been approved through fully democratic processes is surely arguable, the confidence that deterrence has worked is now widespread in the scholarly debate. As Richard Wasserstrom observes in a double volume of *Ethics* devoted to the problem of nuclear deterrence, "Our ideas about nuclear deterrence are all fixed within a context in which successful and effective threats are in one way or the other unreflectively presupposed."[5] Yet in the conventional wisdom the presupposition of success is more explicit than unreflective. Among noted international lawyers, for example, William V. O'Brien states emphatically, "MAD [mutual assured destruction] . . . has in fact deterred superpower confrontations and nuclear war itself."[6] Johnson similarly asserts, "Thus far strategic nuclear deterrence has been remarkably effective—ironically, a much better barrier to war than the Kellogg-Briand Treaty of 1927, the 'agreement to abolish war,' whose effect endured with manifest fragility for only a decade."[7] Indeed, the success thesis has been so much a part of accepted dogma within strategic circles that, as Solly Zuckerman states, "if a presumed intention of the U.S.S.R. which was, or is, contrary to the West's political interests does not materialise, we conclude that it did not do so because the U.S.S.R. feared a nuclear onslaught."[8] Among political essayists, Leon Wieseltier comes close to doubting the merits of the success thesis, but it proves irresistible. Wieseltier remarks,

> Deterrence is often said to have "worked," and if anything has
> "worked," it has; but we cannot be sure. . . . To be a little more
> precise, deterrence is a proposition that may be known to be
> false, but not to be true. When it fails, we will know that it

was false, or a few of us will. Until then we will persist in believing that it is true, and not entirely without reason. Deterrence is probably more than a necessary fiction and probably less than a law of history.[9]

Within religious ethics the success thesis has likewise made its mark. As I pointed out in chapter 2, the U.S. Catholic bishops refrain from condemning deterrence in part because they believe it has been instrumental to a "peace of a sort." Indeed, according to Robert McKim's careful analysis of the subtle shifts in the bishops' treatment of deterrence in the last three versions of their pastoral letter, the bishops were initially skeptical of the success thesis, "but not *so* skeptical that they are prepared to dismiss it."[10] The fact that the bishops grew progressively more reluctant to condemn nuclear deterrence, McKim argues, suggests that the success thesis became increasingly attractive as they developed their position. Reference to the success thesis is even more prominent, as we shall see, in David Hollenbach's attempt to provide guidelines for nuclear deterrence and future nuclear strategy.[11] Hollenbach's position finds resonances in the pastoral letter of the French Catholic bishops, who insist that nuclear deterrence "has staved off direct suicidal confrontation between the superpowers."[12] Even the U.S. Methodist bishops, who condemn nuclear deterrence unequivocally, provide a muted acknowledgment of the success thesis when they say, "Whatever the objective truth about the effects of deterrence, faith in that doctrine will not die quickly."[13]

Despite its widespread popularity, however, the argument from success rests on an improper form of inductive reasoning. In the grammar of informal logic, to argue that the absence of war proves the success of deterrence is to embrace the *post hoc, ergo propter hoc* fallacy. The success of nuclear deterrence is assumed because certain facts exist, facts which would have to exist if the induction were to be true. Doubtless much respectable inductive reasoning may involve post hoc argumentation, as J. L. Mackie instructively argues. But the problem with the success thesis is that a simple concurrence of the threat of nuclear war and the lack of nuclear war is not sufficient to establish a causal relation between them.[14] As is typical of fallacious post hoc arguments, the success thesis fails to eliminate rival hypotheses for the nonoccurrence of nuclear war, e.g., the absence of any strong motive of aggression on the part of the Soviets.[15]

One way we might salvage the success thesis against the allegation of post hoc reasoning is by appealing to specific historical data, e.g., the Cuban missile crisis of 1962. In that instance the Soviets yielded to American superiority and bellicose threats, and lacking such threats the United States would have been unable to deter undesirable Soviet behavior. Here, then, a positive correlation between deterrent threats and the absence of war seems relatively strong, lending credence to Weinberger's claim, "It has worked in the face of major international tensions involving the great powers, and it has worked in the face of war itself."

Unfortunately, however, this use of history conceals at least one problem that proponents of the success thesis have failed to address. The problem can be stated rhetorically: If deterrence and nuclear strength are so effective, then what allowed the Soviets to act in the first place? What failed to deter them from building nuclear weapons on Cuban soil? The Cuban missile crisis is a case in which deterrence almost failed to prevent the outbreak of war, and certainly failed to deter the Soviets from taking initial steps of an adventurist sort. These events suggest that success presupposes a *deterioration* of nuclear deterrence as a prior condition of championing deterrent effectiveness. For without a prior erosion of deterrence—the event of "the crisis"—there would be no context for citing the deterrent effectiveness of nuclear threats. The success thesis lacks the resources to account for this prior deterioration, even though it relies on the context of crisis, in this case, for its intelligibility.

The use of history to support the success thesis is further complicated by the problem of predictability. Even if it were logically plausible to assert the success thesis, the past success of nuclear deterrence provides no guarantee of its future effectiveness. In the words of Sissela Bok, to conclude that nuclear weapons will not be used in the foreseeable future, based on the evidence of past nonuse, "requires a vast leap of inductive faith."[16] And if the deterioration of nuclear deterrence serves as a prelude to at least some forms of deterrent success, then we clearly have more to fear than the success thesis would lead us to believe, for there is no necessary reason to think that future crises would be followed by successful deterrent threats.

A final problem with the success thesis emerges when one considers its implications for the use of nuclear weapons in the event of unsuccessful deterrence, that is, if deterrence fails. According to the success thesis, the possession of nuclear weapons is justified according to beneficial outcomes, namely, the prevention of nuclear war. It is also true that representatives of the success thesis insist that deterrence can succeed only if deterrent threats are backed by strategies to use nuclear weapons in some fashion.[17] Yet the implications of the success thesis are incoherent with strategies for use, because success presupposes that the "use" that is planned should never occur. As Wasserstrom remarks, "If using nuclear weapons, should deterrence fail, is required in order to promote successful deterrence, the two contexts of successful and unsuccessful deterrence are introduced within the same overall account, but only incoherently so."[18] For, once deterrence fails, the raison d'être for nuclear weapons (prevention of use) evanesces. Thus, using nuclear weapons would make little sense; indeed, such use would contradict the reason for their existence in the first place.

Those who wish to follow the success thesis, then, are left with at least four obstacles on their road to coherence. First, if the beneficial consequences (prevention of use) justify the possession of nuclear weapons, then it would hardly make sense, in order to promote successful deterrence, to plan genuinely to use them, because such plans must presuppose a context in which nuclear deterrence has already failed. Indeed, using such weapons would subvert the very rationale for justifying their existence (again: nonuse). Second, efforts to cite prior specific instances of successful deterrence entail a prior erosion of deterrence to establish the context necessary for championing deterrent effectiveness. Moreover, such past successes, whatever sense can be made of them, furnish no guarantee of future deterrent effectiveness. Finally, these difficulties emerge only if one opts to ignore the most tenacious obstacle, namely, that appeals to success entail the fallacy of *post hoc, ergo propter hoc* reasoning.

The Just-War Thesis

Representatives of the just-war thesis begin their arguments with a moral assessment of the use of nuclear weapons as a first step in evaluating nuclear deterrence. The general premise, in contrast to versions of the success thesis, is not that using nuclear weapons, should deterrence fail, is required to promote successful deterrence.[19] Rather, the structure of the argument follows Ramsey: If deterrence fails, the response to aggression should conform to the requirements of a just war. It is therefore necessary to determine the moral limits of a nuclear war as a condition for a morally acceptable nuclear strategy. By making reference to the requirements of justice rather than effectiveness, moreover, representatives of the just-war thesis are not necessarily thwarted by the obstacle of post hoc reasoning should they conclude by supporting deterrent threats.

One of the most celebrated efforts to consider nuclear deterrence within the strictures of the just-war tradition is found in the pastoral letter of the U.S. Catholic bishops. The bishops begin their discussion of nuclear war and deterrence by affirming a fundamental tenet of the just-war tradition, namely, the imperative that war must be discriminate and proportionate. Turning to the details of U.S. nuclear strategy, they identify three possible contingencies in which nuclear weapons might be used: countercity targeting, first-strike counterforce targeting, and second-strike counterforce targeting.

The gist of their analysis of the morality of using nuclear weapons is to apply *in bello* criteria to these prospective uses, leading to three conclusions.

First, the bishops argue that countercity strikes are immoral since they would violate the strict requirements of discrimination. In this respéct the bishops follow Ramsey's relentless condemnation of counterpopulation targeting.

The bishops then turn to first-strike counterforce nuclear warfare. Contrary to Ramsey's permission of first-strike counterforce warfare over one's own territory, the bishops argue that any use of nuclear weapons in any counterforce first-strike attack stands outside the compass of just-war restraints, given the fact that counterforce nuclear war is likely to escalate beyond the control of its engineers. Even if the United States could cross the threshold from conventional to nuclear war according to discriminate methods, the bishops aver, the likelihood of escalation is such that the foreseen, unintended harms would far outweigh the putative values that are defended, contrary to the principle of proportionality. Blending "moral principles with empirical assessments of the chances of escalation,"[20] then, the bishops rule out any first use of nuclear weapons, even in defense against overwhelming conventional aggression.

Third, about the morality of using nuclear weapons for second-strike counterforce purposes (that is, in response to the first use of nuclear weapons by an opponent), the bishops proceed cautiously. Despite the many statements in the document suggesting an endorsement of nuclear pacifism, the bishops do *not* close the door on all uses of nuclear weapons. Choosing not to adjudicate the technical debate about the possibility of fighting a limited nuclear war, they instead pose a series of questions "which challenge the real meaning of 'limited.'" Would leaders have sufficient information about what is happening? Would precise decisions be possible? Could computer errors be avoided? "Unless these questions can be answered satisfactorily," they remark, "we will continue to be highly skeptical about the real meaning of 'limited.'" Backing off from a categorical judgment, the bishops place the burden of proof "on those who assert that meaningful limitation is possible."[21] This burden of proof leaves a "narrow margin where use has been considered, not condemned but hardly commended."[22]

That the bishops leave open the possibility of second-strike counterforce war is, as I shall show below, incoherent, given their arguments against first-strike counterforce nuclear warfare. Their position does have the merit, however, of apparently avoiding the position of nuclear bluffing. Leaving the door slightly open to some form of nuclear warfare, the bishops are able to endorse some forms of deterrence that can be backed with credible, and morally acceptable, uses of nuclear weapons. As they remark, the "narrow margin" about use is a function of "the quest for a coherent connection between deterrence and use policies."[23]

When the bishops turn directly to the morality of nuclear deterrence, they structure their position according to the moral equivalence of action and intention, again following Ramsey. As they state in the summary, "No *use* of nuclear weapons which would violate the principles of discrimination or proportionality may be *intended* in a strategy of deterrence. The moral demands of Catholic teaching require resolute willingness not to intend or do moral evil even to save our own lives or the lives of those we love."[24] In keeping with their discussion of using nuclear weapons, then, the bishops are logically bound by this axiom of moral equivalence to proscribe countercity targeting or initiating a counterforce nuclear war as integral to a policy of nuclear deterrence, since their prior discussion of nuclear war concluded with such proscriptions. And, at least to some extent, this is how they argue. About countercity targeting, the bishops maintain that "it is not morally acceptable to intend to kill the innocent as part of a strategy of deterring nuclear war." Strategies of massive retaliation are thus condemned, however much they might contribute to the prevention of nuclear war. About counterforce targeting, the bishops repeat their skepticism about the tenability of fighting and winning a nuclear war, noting the destabilizing effect of counterforce targeting on deterrent relations between the superpowers. They then conclude their analysis of deterrence by providing a "strictly conditioned moral acceptance" of nuclear deterrence, adding, "We cannot consider it adequate as a long-term basis for peace."[25]

The bishops articulate three conditions for accepting nuclear deterrence. They are:

> 1. If nuclear deterrence exists only to prevent the *use* of nuclear weapons by others, then proposals to go beyond this to planning for prolonged periods of repeated nuclear strikes and counterstrikes, or "prevailing" in nuclear war, are not acceptable. They encourage notions that nuclear war can be engaged in with tolerable human and moral consequences. Rather, we must continually say "no" to the idea of nuclear war.
> 2. If nuclear deterrence is our goal, "sufficiency" to deter is an adequate strategy; the quest for nuclear superiority must be rejected.
> 3. Nuclear deterrence should be used as a step on the way toward disarmament. Each proposed addition to our strategic system or change in strategic doctrine must be assessed precisely in light of whether it will render steps toward "progressive disarmament" more or less likely.[26]

Barring these conditions, nuclear deterrence is unacceptable given the strictures of just-war tenets applied to deterrent intentions in light of the axiom of moral equivalence.

The critical question that emerges, however, is whether these three conditions are compatible with the bishops' judgments about fighting a nuclear war within the compass of just-war tenets. That question must be answered negatively for each of the three conditions, leaving the bishops with an incoherent position on nuclear war and deterrence.

Consider the bishops' discussion of using nuclear weapons in relation to the first condition they impose on an acceptable nuclear deterrent. In their analysis of different uses of nuclear weapons, the only form of nuclear war they do not completely condemn is that in response to an initial nuclear strike, that is, a counterstrike. And it would be highly imprudent to launch such a counterstrike unless one were cognizant of the likelihood that such a counterstrike would signal a willingness and ability to fight a limited nuclear war, creating a context for strikes and counterstrikes. The bishops *might* have in mind the hope that a counterstrike would generate sufficient fears on both sides to produce an immediate stalemate, without either side prevailing or continuing in battle. But as their proscription of initiating a nuclear war indicates, they hold to the notion that nuclear war cannot be kept limited, that stalemates are not conceivable once the nuclear threshold has been crossed. Thus, their muted acceptance of the possibility of second-strike counterforce war is bound by their prior argument that limited war-fighting scenarios, not stalemates, are virtually inevitable when resort to nuclear force occurs. However, if the bishops hold that using nuclear weapons in a second-strike counterforce manner commits one or both sides to a limited war-fighting situation, where the goal of prevailing is exigent, then their position on use and deterrence is incoherent. Recall that one of the conditions for accepting deterrence is that it *cannot* be linked to a war-fighting strategy, that is, plans for "prevailing" in a nuclear war of "repeated nuclear strikes and counterstrikes." Unfortunately for the bishops, it is not possible to hold together their rejection of first-strike counterforce war, their muted acceptance of second-strike counterforce war, and the first condition they impose upon an acceptable nuclear deterrent.

One wonders, then, what sorts of uses would be acceptable to the bishops for a policy of nuclear deterrence, since the two other types of use—countercity and first-strike counterforce—have also been excluded according to their application of just-war criteria. The bishops' proscription of these two forms of nuclear warfare according to just-war criteria, together with their proscription of any nuclear war-fighting strategy as a condition for accepting nuclear deterrence, leaves them with no real uses of nuclear weapons to support, or render credible, deterrent threats. And without credible threats, the bishops have argued themselves into the corner of nuclear bluffing, despite their efforts to avoid such a conclusion.

Further, the second condition—that "'sufficiency' to deter is an adequate strategy; the quest for nuclear superiority must be rejected"—is incompatible with the material requirements for maintaining a second-strike counterforce capability. The reason here turns on the complex logic

Chapter Seven

of deterrent strategy and incentives for arms competition in a counter-force world. To grasp this complex logic, assume for the moment two parties involved in a deterrent relation, A and B. Following the bishops' moral stance on the use of nuclear weapons, A adopts a deterrent strategy whereby it threatens to carry out retaliatory counterforce strikes against B's second-strike force (since, by definition, A's retaliatory strikes would be carried out after B launches an attack against A; hence, A's retaliation must be targeted against B's second-strike force). The problem for the bishops is that the deployment of counterforce weapons by A generates incentives for B to develop its own counterforce capabilities to neutralize the threat to its retaliatory forces posed by A. Without its retaliatory forces relatively secure, B's deterrent strength diminishes. And, once B develops weapons to neutralize A's threat, A must develop weapons to neutralize B's new weapons; otherwise, the threat posed by A's original counterforce arsenal has been nullified by B's newly developed weapons. The outcome is a cycle of competition whereby each gives the other incentives to build weapons, and where neither can feel secure absent a position of superiority.[27] But if, as the bishops argue, deterrence is unacceptable once it is linked to a "quest for superiority," then the material requirements for a second-strike counterforce arsenal cannot be satisfied.

The third condition posited by the bishops—that nuclear deterrence should be used as a step toward disarmament—is equally problematic. For, in a counterforce world fueled by arms competition, it is difficult to imagine how disarmament would be possible. In a competitive counterforce world the incentives are to build up one's reserve of nuclear weapons, not to disarm. How the bishops can reconcile their call for progressive, bilateral disarmament with the material requirements of a second-strike counterforce strategy remains unclear.

Finally, as I suggested above, it should be noted that *within* the bishops' analysis of counterforce nuclear war an inconsistency mars their discussion of first and second use. One possible use of nuclear weapons—to *initiate* a counterforce nuclear war—is deemed unacceptable according to a mixture of moral principles and empirical assessments. Yet when they turn to the possible use of nuclear weapons in a *second*-strike situation, they shift their ground. The earlier conclusion—that the dangers of escalation are so great as to render the initiation of nuclear war unjustifiable—now has a different conceptual force: Doubts about limiting a nuclear war lead them to a grave skepticism, but not a categorical judgment. Yet if the danger of escalation rules out the first use of nuclear weapons, then that same danger should rule out *all* uses, since the danger of escalation is no less under the conditions of second use than under the conditions of first use. The trajectory of their argument against initiating a nuclear war, carried to its logical conclusion, ought to lead the bishops to the position of nuclear pacifism.[28]

A second representative of the just-war thesis, David Hollenbach, attempts to get beyond this last obstacle to the bishops' position by embracing the position of nuclear pacifism. Like the bishops and Ramsey, Hollenbach readily concludes that countercity strikes would be categorically immoral because they would be indiscriminate, violating the principle of noncombatant immunity. Yet Hollenbach goes beyond the bishops and Ramsey by concluding that, in all probability, *any* form of counterforce nuclear war would escalate beyond the control of its engineers, leading to disproportionate damage as a first step on the way to wanton mass destruction. Subsequent nuclear escalation, Hollenbach argues, would violate the *in bello* criteria of discrimination and proportionality, as well as the *ad bellum* criterion of reasonable hope of success.[29]

Given the axiom that immoral acts may never be morally intended, it would seem that the intention to use nuclear weapons in either a counterforce or countercity strike is immoral. And if the intention to use nuclear weapons is necessary to sustain a nuclear deterrent, then nuclear deterrence itself must be condemned. Yet in Hollenbach's view we must separate our assessment of deterrence from the issue of use. Such a separation rests on an understanding of deterrent intentions as distinct, both logically and morally, from intentions to use nuclear weapons. The intention of nuclear deterrence is not the exercise of war, but the prevention of war. Assessments of nuclear deterrence, and the intentions of deterrence, must first come to terms with a fundamental paradox, namely, that "intention (nuclear war prevention) and action (the preparation and threat to unleash nuclear war) move in opposite directions."[30] Conceived in this way, deterrent intentions are (in the words of Douglas Maclean) "self-stultifying": They are structured so that, ideally, what is threatened will *not* be carried out.[31]

Commonplace discussions of the morality of nuclear deterrence often fail to develop the implications of this paradox. Such discussions thus conclude that the morality of use is equivalent to the morality of deterrence. If this were the case, then Hollenbach's condemnation of use would entail a condemnation of nuclear deterrence. But if intentions to use and intentions to deter are logically separate, then the argument of moral equivalence does not hold. It therefore becomes possible for Hollenbach to proscribe the use of nuclear weapons and still leave open the possibility of a morally acceptable deterrent, since deterrent intentions have now been wrenched free of considerations of use.

Yet Hollenbach does not wish to suggest that *all* deterrent intentions are equally tenable from either a moral or a strategic point of view. His own effort to establish moral guidelines for deterrent intentions is couched in terms of revisionist proportionalism, a method of moral reasoning used in more liberal currents of contemporary Catholic moral theology. Hollenbach remarks, "One cannot determine what an agent intends to do without considering the consequences which the agent foresees will follow from the contemplated action. If an agent chooses to perform an action whose good consequences are reasonably judged to be greater than are its evil consequences, this . . . school would judge that the intention is a morally upright one."[32] Intention, within this framework, is determined not simply in terms of the objective, or goal, of one's choice, but also in terms of the *foreseen consequences* of that choice. Determining what is actually intended in a deterrent threat should first include a reasonable prediction about what will result from making such a threat. Moral evaluations of deterrent intentions are thus contingent upon additional judgments about the prospective outcomes of any specific deterrent strategy. In Hollenbach's terms, the "moral judgment on the intention embodied in the deterrent policy is . . . inseparable from an evaluation of the reasonably predictable outcomes of diverse policy choices."[33]

Hollenbach is less interested in defending deterrence in principle than in providing criteria for assessing the moral wisdom of any shift in deterrent policies. To this end he refines his considerations of "reasonably predictable outcomes," specifying two goals toward which deterrent strategies should be ordered: (1) policies must make war less likely than do policies presently in effect, and (2) policy proposals must increase the possibility of arms reduction.[34] Any change in deterrent policy is acceptable to Hollenbach only if it can promise, in light of these criteria, to improve the status quo.

This argument on behalf of possessing nuclear weapons for purposes of deterrence, coupled with a condemnation of use, is tantamount to nuclear bluffing. And while Hollenbach may be the most rigorous exponent of this position, he is certainly not alone in holding it. The French Catholic bishops argue, for example, that "threat is not use," that the immorality of use does not automatically nullify the moral tenability of deterrent threats.[35] The West German Catholic bishops embrace a more muddled but perhaps widespread trust in a nuclear bluff. They argue on behalf of deterrent threats while adhering to the hope "that a situation will never occur in which somebody is confronted with such decision-making" about resorting to nuclear force if deterrence fails.[36]

The difficulty in all these cases turns on the issue of credibility in public policy: No one will believe such threats if they are tied to a condemnation of use.[37] Hollenbach acknowledges this difficulty, but he defends his argument for "threats without use" by appealing to the success thesis. We must note, Hollenbach states, "a single, massive historical fact: large numbers of nuclear weapons are already deployed and ready for use by both superpowers. Though incompatible on the level of ideas and logic, deterrence and non-use are concretely and existentially interlocked in our present world."[38] For Hollenbach, then, the problem of credibility for the "threat without use" is pertinent in the realm of abstract logic, but credibility becomes a nonproblem once we recognize the *historical success* of nuclear deterrence—the concrete interlocking of "deterrence and non-use."

One clear strength of Hollenbach's contribution to the debate about deterrence is that his criteria require us to think about the future direction of deterrent policy. The effect of his argument is to shift moral analysis from looking backward to looking ahead, moving us beyond moral judgments that lament the dawn of the nuclear age. Hollenbach thus places the onus of responsibility on those who have inherited the task of managing nuclear policies but who were in no way directly involved in their creation.

Despite this strength, however, four distinct problems plague Hollenbach's challenging contribution to the debate about the morality of deterrence. First, there is a problem surrounding his reference to history to support his case for the credibility of a "threat without use" nuclear deterrent. Even if, as Hollenbach argues, "deterrence and non-use are concretely and existentially interlocked in our present world," this "interlocking" cannot be attributed historically to a policy of "threat without use." As Lawrence Freedman's magisterial study of the history of nuclear strategy indicates, deterrent strategy in the United States has been consistently premised on threats that have been backed by a readiness and willingness to use nuclear weapons under specified conditions.[39] And, according to Paul Bracken's study, present command and control systems are now mechanized so that the release of nuclear weapons under the situation of attack would be virtually automatic.[40] As such, if we place nuclear strategy within its actual historical context, it becomes clear that deterrence must be "interlocked" with threats that are backed by a genuine readiness to use nuclear weapons, *not threats that are linked to a policy of nuclear pacifism.* History, then, cannot come to the aid of nuclear pacifism when it is criticized, in light of the requirements of deterrence, as incredible.

Second, the material requirements of Hollenbach's "threat without use" theory are morally unfeasible. By this I do not mean that his position is not credible, but that there are *moral* problems that surround making it credible *as an institution.* Even if it were possible to institutionalize a "threat without use" policy at the highest levels of military command, the consent to use nuclear weapons must be institutionalized in the *praxis* of lower-level officials who consent to carry out commands, or assume command, in a crisis. Unless one is willing to argue that *everyone* involved in the chain of command should know that nuclear weapons would *never* be used (hardly a credible policy), then one must grant that even a bluffing policy entails the cooperation to use nuclear weapons by lower-level individuals who would authorize, or who intend to carry out, the release of nuclear weapons.[41] Essential to such cooperation are human intentions which remain open to acts that Hollenbach has proscribed according to just-war criteria. In the language of traditional moral theology, an *institutionalized* bluff position entails the occasion of sin at lower levels of command.

Third, Hollenbach's attention to the moral problems of unsuccessful deterrence, coupled with his reference to the success thesis to ward off the problems of incredibility, places him in a curious bind. If deterrence is successful, then the moral issues surrounding unsuccessful deterrence (i.e., whether any uses of nuclear weapons would be acceptable) are moot. Yet if unsuccessful deterrence is a genuine problem, a real possibility calling for moral analysis aided by just-war criteria, then the success of deterrence cannot be a secure anchor for thinking about nuclear policies. And if the success of deterrence is not secure, neither is the basis on which Hollenbach solves the problem of credibility as it pertains to his theory of "threat without use." To paraphrase Wasserstrom, if not using nuclear weapons, should deterrence fail, is required by just-war tenets, and if deterrence and nonuse are "concretely and existentially interlocked in our present world," the two contexts of unsuccessful and successful deterrence are introduced into the same overall account, but only incoherently so.

Finally, it is not clear that Hollenbach's argument for "threats without use" can pass his own test for assessing the moral tenability of specific policy choices. If, as he maintains, the "moral judgment of the intention embodied in the deterrent policy is . . . inseparable from an evaluation of the reasonably predictable outcomes of diverse policy choices," then it remains unclear whether Hollenbach's position, *taken as a whole,* has been sufficiently established. For, given this definition of intention, it would seem necessary to show that proscribing the use of nuclear weapons and maintaining possession for deterrent purposes will yield, in all likelihood, a positive outcome. Unfortunately, his appeal to the success thesis to establish a positive outcome is logically and historically untenable, as I have argued above.

The Anticipatory Thesis

The anticipatory thesis alleges that nuclear deterrence under present conditions is unwarranted, for current history fails to support the idea that the Soviets need to be constrained by intimidating threats. James Sterba, who developed this view, interprets the data of the past forty years quite differently from those who adopt some version of the success thesis. Given the relevant history of superpower relations, Sterba argues, "it is difficult to discern grounds for thinking that the Soviet Union's intentions with regard to strategic arms are radically different from those of the United States."[42] The absence of nuclear war, the relative parity of military spending between the superpowers, and the fact that the Soviets modernized their weapons in response to destabilizing deployments by the United States underwrite the belief that neither nation intends to use nuclear weapons unless reasonably provoked by the other, and that arms competition has occurred largely through reactive rather than belligerent designs. Hence, Sterba concludes, it is false to argue that nuclear deterrence is morally justified, since there is no real and present danger from which we must protect ourselves.

But this verdict does not lead Sterba to conclude that either nation is morally obligated to disarm unilaterally. There remains the possibility, Sterba contends, that political relations can change for the worse, requiring some form of nuclear protection or intimidation. Anticipating a crisis, "a nation could legitimately maintain a survivable force so that it could quickly threaten nuclear retaliation should conditions change for the worse. For as long as nations remain armed with nuclear weapons, such a change can occur simply with a change of leadership, bringing to power leaders who intend to carry out a nuclear first strike."[43] Under such conditions it may be morally justified to threaten some form of limited nuclear retaliation, and to carry out that threat "against tactical and strategic targets . . . in order to restore deterrence." Moreover, under grave conditions it may be justifiable to "bluff but not threaten massive nuclear retaliation."[44]

Sterba thus reverses the terms of the bishops' conditional acceptance of deterrence: Deterrence is not morally tenable now, but may be under future conditions. To communicate this posture to one's opponents, moreover, it is imperative for public officials to renounce under present conditions the use of nuclear weapons. And by carrying out this public renunciation, our nation would arrive at one goal to which Ramsey directed his attention, namely, the moral integrity of those working in the deterrent regime. According to Sterba, by renouncing the threat of nuclear retaliation now, public officials deliver those involved in building and maintaining a nuclear arsenal from implication in evil intentions, or the occasion of sin.[45]

Yet the chief problem with the anticipatory thesis is that Sterba may expect too much from the imperative to renounce nuclear retaliation under present circumstances. Public renunciation hardly exempts those at the lower levels of the deterrent regime from immoral intentions in the event of a bluff, as I have argued against Hollenbach. Moreover, by requiring public renunciation of retaliatory threats, Sterba suggests that possession combined with renunciation is sufficient to maintain a relatively benign international context, that superpower relations are not poisoned by the possession of retaliatory capabilities absent public threats. Though admittedly arguable, this idea remains dubious. Sterba seems to separate superpower relations from the possession of nuclear weapons as a substance is separated from its accidents. It seems more accurate to see the possession of nuclear weapons as constitutive of, rather than accidental to, superpower relations, and as corrosive rather than benign. Renouncing the threat to retaliate while retaining a nuclear arsenal is hardly ameliorative, given the nature of the weapons in question. By this I do not mean to suggest that the possession of nuclear weapons is sufficient for deterrence absent the organizational will to use them. Rather I mean that possession is sufficient to justify feelings of intimidation, fear, anxiety, and suspicion on the other side. To prepare for deterioration, in short, is to enter an interactive relation in which one's preparations are a constitutive part, sending messages to one's opponent. Even absent any explicit threat, the possession of nuclear weapons scarcely mollifies the terms of the game, and may very well contribute to the deterioration for which one is preparing. Surely those who equip their homes with massive armaments during peaceful times, anticipating a deteriorating neighborhood, already contribute to its demise.

The anticipatory thesis, then, must face several questions about the relation between possession, renunciation of use, and the tenor of superpower relations: Can we construe the possession of nuclear weapons in anticipation of deteriorating relations as something other than a self-fulfilling prophecy? (Surely there are lessons to be learned from the First World War in this respect.)[46] More specifically, can we expect the renunciation of retaliation to be credible to a suspicious opponent? Can we be confident that suspicions are placated by renunciation when it is coupled with the possession of massively destructive weapons?

The Argument from "Supreme Emergency"

A fourth attempt to justify nuclear deterrence, by Michael Walzer, begins by assessing nuclear war within the compass of just-war restraints, but emphasizes the qualitatively unique dangers of the nuclear era and the virtually intractable moral situation in which we find ourselves. The objective is to leave some room for the requirements of necessity, at least in extreme cases of unmitigated disaster.[47] Walzer's position is not entirely bound by the demands of justice, and the obstacles therein, characteristic of the just-war thesis. Nor does it construe the present state of affairs along the lines of the anticipatory thesis, maintaining instead that history has changed irrevocably with the advent of nuclear technology.

Interestingly, Walzer's argument anticipates by several years the chief currents in the bishops' and Hollenbach's arguments. Like the bishops, Walzer begins by embracing the axiom of equivalence between intention and action. Yet, like Hollenbach, Walzer insists that no uses of nuclear weapons, under the ordinary circumstances of war, could pass the test of just-war criteria. In Walzer's terms, nuclear weapons "explode the theory of the just war." As the case of Hiroshima illustrates, nuclear destruction wreaks "indiscriminate slaughter, the killing of the innocent . . . on a massive scale."[48] Accordingly, if the use of nuclear weapons is murder, then the intention to use such weapons is a commitment to murder. Consequently, Walzer notes, nuclear deterrence must be condemned insofar as it relies on such an intention.

Yet having arrived at this judgment, Walzer proceeds to embrace arguments that are more sympathetic to nuclear deterrence. Generally such arguments make some reference to the success thesis, pointing to the putative beneficial consequences of nuclear deterrence. Historically, nuclear deterrence has been fashioned under the banner "Better dead than Red," and has furnished the best safeguard against the twofold danger of nuclear blackmail and nuclear destruction.[49]

Moreover, Walzer argues, the dangers surrounding nuclear war are qualitatively different from the dangers of conventional war. It is therefore simplistic to draw on moral criteria that derive from conventional, rather than nuclear, contexts. Moral analysis must adjust its sights to the different stakes of the nuclear age:

> The case . . . is very different from that which arises commonly in war, where *our* adherence to the war convention puts us, or would put us, at a disadvantage vis-à-vis *them*. For disadvantages of that sort are partial and relative; various countermeasures and compensating steps are always available. But in the nuclear case, the disadvantage is absolute. Against an enemy actually willing to use the bomb, self-defense is impossible, and it makes sense to say that the only compensating step is the (immoral) threat to respond in kind.[50]

Walzer draws briefly on his notion of the "supreme emergency" to buttress his argument. Such an emergency, in Walzer's sense, "is defined by two criteria . . . : the first has to do with the imminence of the danger and the second with its nature."[51] Under the circumstances of dire and imminent danger, when conventional methods of resistance are hopeless, "anything goes," that is, anything necessary to win.[52] A supreme emergency allows one to override strict moral principle (e.g., noncombatant immunity) in the limit situation of survival, the situation in which "our history will be nullified and our future condemned unless I accept the burdens of criminality here and now."[53]

Supreme emergency is particularly relevant to nuclear issues, in Walzer's mind, because nuclear weapons now pose an imminent and irreversible danger to the international order. Indeed, Walzer claims that supreme emergency is now a *permanent fixture* of international relations, in which nuclear deterrence is the only available means for stabilizing relations in a world of sovereign states.[54] In this respect Walzer adumbrates my critique of Sterba, arguing that we cannot separate the moral fabric of superpower relations from the existence of nuclear capabilities. Moreover, given the stakes involved in the nuclear age, nuclear deterrence should not be judged solely in terms of murderousness; instead, we must make some concessions to necessity. As such, Walzer contends, nuclear deterrence may be the least evil strategy at our disposal: "We threaten evil in order not to do it, and the doing of it would be so terrible that the threat seems in comparison to be morally defensible."[55]

Walzer formulates a position, then, uniquely suited to deal with special problems in war, like those in which one is forced to confront an enemy who systematically violates moral codes. His theory of the supreme emergency, for example, allows for considerations of necessity against the perils of Nazism.[56] With their "backs to the wall" against such an enemy, the Allies were on the edge of moral experience, proceeding along the precipice of desperation and disaster. And it is this kind of limit situation that constitutes our present condition. Like the early Allied bombing of German cities, Walzer avers, nuclear deterrence is an act of necessity, placing us in the moral paradox where "we move uneasily beyond the limits of justice for the sake of justice (and of peace)."[57]

Unfortunately, however, Walzer equivocates about the meaning and ethical implications of a supreme emergency. On the one hand, *supreme emergency* denotes a discrete, extraordinary event, one that requires unique moral decisions on the boundary of ordinary human experience. At such a precipice, we may violate the requirements of justice so that the conditions of justice might be restored. On the other hand, however, Walzer calls the supreme emergency a *permanent condition* in the nuclear age; it is not an extreme case on the edge of an otherwise ordinary set of conditions, but an extreme set of conditions now defining the context of international relations, and the problems therein.

Coordinating the ethical implications of the first and second senses of *supreme emergency* generates two problems for Walzer's argument. First, if *supreme emergency* in the first sense establishes conditions for violating moral laws in the name of necessity, what can we say about moral laws under conditions in which the supreme emergency is *permanent?* It appears that, for Walzer, nuclear deterrence can be justified because *anything* can be justified between the superpowers in the name of necessity now that the emergency has been construed in permanent terms. The effect of Walzer's argument is not to provide a principled justification for nuclear deterrence, but to define a set of conditions in which moral principles lose their force. Walzer's construal of the present state of affairs may prove too much: Because the emergency is permanent, so is the eclipse of moral principle.

A second difficulty follows. The outcome of Walzer's position is to commit him to a view of superpower relations in which expectations of morality are now permanently effaced. As a result, it is now impossible to hold others accountable to moral principles, since in the permanent condition of the supreme emergency, necessity and not moral principle is the law of the land. The effect of Walzer's argument leaves him in a difficult bind: It may be possible to justify one's own deterrent threats, but it is impossible to condemn as irrevocably evil the threats expressed by one's opponents.

For those who follow Walzer's lead, then, two stubborn obstacles remain. First, there appear to be no moral limits between the superpowers in the nuclear era, now that supreme emergency has become a permanent condition; second, Walzer is unable to discriminate morally between the necessities of one superpower polity and another in a supreme emergency.

The Exceptionalist Thesis

Arguing that Walzer's difficulties stem from his liberal political philosophy, Gerald Mara turns to Aristotelian sources to salvage the notion of supreme emergency from the problem of moral limits and the problem of discriminating between the necessities of different polities in a supreme emergency, construed as permanent.[58] Mara argues that the task of political order is to create virtuous citizens and to create an ethos that simultaneously mirrors and reinforces virtuous behavior. Accordingly, Mara notes, different political regimes can "be evaluated in terms of how well *their* particular values match the life that is most desirable for members of the human species."[59] It thus becomes possible to discriminate morally between regimes, and to criticize various regimes for failing to create the conditions for human well-being and moral action.

The effect of Mara's argument is to furnish grounds for distinguishing between different kinds of necessity in war, corresponding to the relative goodness of political regimes. Necessity, within this perspective, takes on varying moral force, depending on "the dominant community values that are in jeopardy."[60] There are notable differences between the morality of one regime and that of another, and such differences can make all the difference when it comes to justifying acts in the name of necessity. Mara remarks,

> A well-ordered, just society appeals to a different type of necessity in defense of *its* ultimate values than does a rapacious and tyrannical one. When evil regimes are placed (or place themselves) in situations where additional crimes are *truly* necessary to preserve their collective identities, they appeal to a kind of necessity that is nearly subhuman in nature. There is a difference between an appeal to necessity in the name of survival alone and an appeal in the name of survival and justice.[61]

Yet there are also resources in an Aristotelian perspective, Mara observes, to restrict a good regime's recourse to the rationale of necessity. Resort to necessity must be judged in terms of its effects on the quality of life in a regime: "Within Aristotle's perspective, means are not related to ends merely instrumentally. Rather, practical actions taken in pursuit of some good materially affect the actor's capacity to achieve or enjoy that good."[62] And, Mara contends, this truth about the dynamic relation between moral action and individual character likewise pertains to the character, or ethos, of communities. Reference to necessity, over the long haul, will affect the character or ethos of a community, cheapening the value of life. This is especially the case with communities which commit themselves, as a strategy of deterrence, to threats of massively destructive acts; such threats will poison the character of life within the community making those threats. And if the goodness of a community is determined by the extent to which it conduces to virtue and *eudaimonia* among its citizens, then there are strong moral reasons to be critical of nuclear deterrence as one symptom of a permanent condition.

In essence, then, Mara seems to chart a way over the obstacles to Walzer's notion of the supreme emergency, without capitulating to the current regime of nuclear weapons and superpowerism: Reference to the moral differences between opposing polities allows one to retain moral conventions in international relations, furnishing a way to distinguish between one version of emergency and another in times of conflict.

Nevertheless, Mara's attempt to salvage Walzer's theory is not without three grave difficulties, of which the first two are ethical and the third is historical. The first problem is that of exceptionalism in moral judgments about necessity and duress. Mara's position allows a nation, or an alliance, to make special claims for itself by referring to the superior morality of its own political order when juxtaposed to the relative evil of an opponent. Accordingly, in a time of duress, one party may commit acts that would be condemned if the opponent were to carry them out instead. The effect of the argument is to open the door to a double standard in judgments about war and necessity, allowing one polity to exempt itself from the standards by which it judges another polity's wartime acts. And if the supreme emergency is a permanent condition, as Walzer maintains, it seems doubtful that there can be resources within Mara's position to curb the ongoing possibility of self-justifying abuse.

Second, Mara's position is problematic for most Christian ethicists insofar as it ascribes final or supreme value to human community, especially the nation-state. Christian ethicists, in general, would be averse to assigning ultimate value to the survival of the nation-state, given the fact that human communities are, at most, relative rather than absolute values.[63] In Christian ethics it is more difficult to cite the moral goodness of the community as a warrant for overriding moral duties, like that of noncombatant immunity, unless one is willing to relate the survival of the nation-state to divine purposes.[64]

Third, the gravest question for Mara is whether the modern nation-state bears sufficient similarity to the Aristotelian polis to justify his attempt to think about the modern situation along Aristotelian lines. As MacIntyre has trenchantly argued in retrieving Aristotelian ideas for post-Enlightenment philosophy, modern government owes more to the instrumental practices of post-Weberian rationalism than to Aristotle's idea of an authentic political and moral community. In "advanced societies," MacIntyre argues, "government does not express or represent the moral community of the citizens, but is instead a set of institutional arrangements for imposing a bureaucratized unity on a society which lacks genuine moral consensus." In contrast, the polis fosters an authentic sense of community and political representation, where patriotism is "founded on attachment primarily to a political and moral community and only secondarily to the government of that community."[65] Juxtaposed to MacIntyre's Aristotelian critique of the modern nation-state, Mara's position seems anachronistic, one which fails to distinguish the conditions for an authentic community from the "bureaucratized unity" of large, industrial, institutional societies.

Mara anticipates this criticism, arguing that "the hostility of modern society to virtuous practice—noted by MacIntyre, for example—appears to be a conclusion to be firmly established rather than preemptively stated." Mara adds, "It is as encouraging as it is intimidating to realize that adopting the classical perspective is a commitment to developing and asking certain questions rather than the process of applying principles that are foregone conclusions."[66] But Mara fails to indicate how modern society can possess the moral consensus, and the corresponding sense of authentic political representation that renders intelligible Aristotle's notion of community, and the argument on behalf of moral differences between communities. For without these Aristotelian presuppositions, there would seem to be no basis for Mara to judge the relative ability of a community to foster virtuous practices and the realization of *eudaimonia*. MacIntyre's critique of modernity points to a grave disanalogy between the modern nation-state and the Aristotelian polis. This disanalogy has philosophical, political, and sociological dimensions. It also undermines Mara's effort to salvage the supreme emergency along classical lines in the present age.[67]

Conclusion

Each of the arguments cited above—the success thesis, the just-war thesis, the anticipatory thesis, the argument from supreme emergency, and the exceptionalist thesis—attempts to furnish, if not a moral rationale, at least a framework in which to salvage nuclear deterrence as a plausible moral institution. There is no doubt that a massive bureaucratic institution in the United States military has been fashioned out of deterrent policies, that individuals and groups have committed themselves to the maintenance and improvement of the nuclear arsenal, and that the institution is likely to continue—however complex may be the ethical debate. But if these arguments provide a clue, then nuclear deterrence remains an institution, with a corresponding set of financial and practical commitments, in dire need of a clear and consistent argument. For those of all stripes—pacifists and just-war theorists—it is clear that such a state of affairs affords little comfort. As the current debate about the morality of nuclear deterrence goes forward, it is now timely that we take cognizance of the many obstacles along the way, logical and practical obstacles that we continue to overlook only at our collective peril.

PART FOUR

PRACTICAL REASONING AND PUBLIC DISCOURSE

E I G H T

History, Moral Discourse, and the Problem of Ideology

History: Didactic or Ideological?

Mara's exceptionalism is scarcely one more problem alongside the success thesis, the anticipatory thesis, the argument from supreme emergency, etc. Rather, the problem of exceptionalism is a function of ideology, deeply rooted in American civil religion. And insofar as exceptionalism is ideological, it shapes the moral arguments, interpretations, and moral visions of just-war theorists and pacifists alike—or so I want to argue in this chapter.

By *ideology* I mean, following Raymond Geuss, "such things as the beliefs the members of the group hold, the concepts they use, the attitudes and psychological dispositions they exhibit, their motives, desires, values, predilections, works of art, religious rituals, gestures, etc."[1] As I am using it here, ideology can be both a neutral category and the pejorative notion of "false consciousness." In a neutral sense ideology includes generally shared beliefs which have a wide and deep influence on our behavior, those attitudes about the world that are not easily given up. And, as Geuss observes, ideologies usually come in bundles. That is, they hold together with some coherence a variety of attitudes, goals, and beliefs, providing a "characteristic structure which is often discernible even to an outside observer."[2] Ideologies thus provide the grammar for our rituals of socialization, those cultural practices by which we foster personal identity and communal solidarity. But perhaps most important, ideologies serve an interpretive function. They provide the means by which we clothe history with myth, enabling us to single out and ascribe significance to the events of human experience. An ideology, then, is rarely an object of thought, about which we reflect; rather, it constitutes the background of our ideas, with which we ponder our experience and its moral dimensions. For this reason ideological approaches to deterrence differ from the other approaches, more directly accessible to criticism, that I discussed in the last chapter. More encompassing than objects of thought, ideologies (including exceptionalism) carry the danger of illusion. When they do, we stand in need of a self-reflexive critique, one with subversive, therapeutic power.

Reference to the relation between history and moral arguments, of course, points us in the direction of historicism in ethics. Historicists hold that ethical ideas are in some sense the product of historical forces. They also contend that ethical ideas are not debilitated simply because they are implicated in such forces. Historicists hold out the hope that we can morally evaluate *other* products of history, like our religious beliefs or social policies—even when these, too, are implicated in a shared history. According to historicism, we need not seek some ahistorical vantage point, one that transcends human experience, to gain some critical leverage on that experience.

Yet the idea of ideology—the notion that history is clothed with myth—raises difficult questions about the role of history in ethics. How reliable are the historical sources on which an ethicist depends? The fact that ideologies themselves are products of history means that the relation between ideology and history is profoundly complex. If history shapes the culture that shapes our interpretation of the historical record, then we seem locked into a vicious circle of knowledge, experience, and belief. Can we break out of this circle, thus gaining some critical distance on our beliefs? Is there a vantage point above the taint of cultural bias from which we can adjudicate conflicting beliefs? If, instead, we remain locked in our circles of belief and experience, how might we judge our beliefs as inadequate or call our experience into question? Those who defend historicism are thus confronted with the question of distance: How much distance on our experience can we acquire in order to judge its adequacy? Without sufficient distance we may be unable to engage in social criticism, owing to a lack of objectivity. How much distance is necessary?

To date we have been furnished with scant resources to address these questions in ethics. Generally "the use of history in ethics" has meant that history serves some didactic function, that there are important moral lessons from the past. James Turner Johnson, for example, speaks often of "the wisdom of historical moral traditions," like that of the just-war tradition.[3] The use of history in Johnson's hands means drawing on prior ideas, arguments, customs, and technological developments as reference points for applied ethics in the present. For nonpacifists in Western culture, the just-war tradition provides such a legacy, about which Johnson has written at length. And in his surveys of the just-war tradition, Johnson makes it clear that we must refer to ideas *and* events, arguments *and* customs, in our fidelity to that tradition. But the main point for Johnson, as I have suggested, is that history is a source of moral information, a deposit of teaching to be recalled and transmitted. Essentially we look back to the past for ideas that have stood the test of time. Lest we forfeit the lessons of history, the ethicist must serve as a curator of the past, reminding us how "moral values are perceived by individuals and cultures in the encounter with history."[4]

Yet there remains a zone mediating between our ideas and historical experiences that has remained relatively unexamined by Johnson and, for that matter, virtually everyone who has broached the topic of history in ethics.[5] That zone, as I have suggested above, is filled by ideology. The path between idea and experience (and back again) is not uncluttered, but is filled with a complex matrix of beliefs, relatively unknown to the agent. These beliefs shape the way we extract ideas from custom, form codes for behavior, or fashion arguments to justify our claims against our critics. Likewise, ideological beliefs condition the manner in which our practices shape our ideas and our perception of the significant facts of history. Doubtless the avenue between ideas and practice is heavily trafficked, allowing for a dialectical interchange. And in understanding that interchange, we must pay heed to the role of ideologies and their mediating influence.[6]

In this chapter I hope to show how ideologies function in moral discourse about war and peace by focusing once again on the American scene. Canvassing numerous sources of oratory and literature, I will first explore several tropes of what I consider to be American ideology par excellence, namely, the belief in American exceptionalism. I will then turn to the nonpacifist arguments of William V. O'Brien and the pacifist ethics of Martin Luther King, Jr. My goal is to show how American ideology has served, respectively, as an obstacle to and a resource for moral vocabularies about war and peace. Indeed, exceptionalism has had such a tenacious influence on the American moral imagination that even attempts to question the American dream nonetheless trade, intertextually, on the beliefs according to which that dream is commonly understood. But first: What, more precisely, is meant by exceptionalism? What are its predominant motifs? What bundle of beliefs mediates American self-understanding? What resources might exceptionalism provide for social criticism in a historicist vein?

The Grammar of American Exceptionalism

The idea that throughout their history Americans have been possessed by a sense of uniqueness and election has been widely recognized.[7] Here I wish to survey the grammar of exceptionalist ideology as it has shaped rhetoric and debate at different points in American history. As a piece of political oratory, religious metaphor, poetic image, and philosophical conviction, exceptionalism has enjoyed wide currency as a figural outlook for Americans during times of national crisis and patriotic ceremony. Exceptionalism provides, among other things, the poetry of American self-understanding.

Four distinct but related features comprise exceptionalist ideology: the belief in providential direction; the belief in exemplary status; the belief that the suffering of Americans is instrumental to a wider redemptive process; and the belief that Americans are called to obey a higher law, inaccessible to outsiders or critics. Like dominant and recessive genes these beliefs are not active all at once, but come to the fore when conditions dictate. But together they comprise an ideological bundle with which Americans continually interpret themselves and their ongoing history.

* * *

Doubtless the most pronounced feature of exceptionalism is the belief in providential election, the secular equivalent for which is "destiny." *Providence* designates the belief in God as the stage manager and set designer of history, the divine impetus behind the human drama. During the colonial period, for example, Virginians were told by Alexander Whitaker that "the finger of God hath been the onely true worker heere; . . . God first shewed us the place, God first called us hither, and here God by his speciall providence hath maintained us."[8] Puritan settlers were apt to encounter something like Edmund Johnson's assertion that New England was the place "where the Lord will create a new heaven and a new earth . . . new churches and a new commonwealth together," since these colonists saw themselves as carrying out the Protestant Reformation. Viewed providentially by early Americans, history was symbolic, revealing a wider divine design. And, as Robert Handy has observed about the early colonial period, this was true up and down the eastern seaboard. Handy remarks, "Anglicans and Puritans both exhibited the sense of destiny, of being the chosen people, of special mission," however much they may have disagreed about issues of theology or civil order.[9]

Drawing on providential beliefs inherited from Puritanism, Jonathan Edwards interpreted the Great Awakening through a lens provided by the Bible. The frontier revival of 1734–35 was, for Edwards, "an Extraordinary dispensation of Providence."[10] Drawing inferences from the prophet Ezekiel, Edwards predicted that "the very uncommon and wonderful circumstances and events" in the settlement of New England "seem . . . strongly to argue that God intends it as the beginning or forerunner of something vastly great."[11] For Edwards and others like him, American history operated under the typology of promise and fulfillment, for which the Bible provided images and clues. Stoking the fires of millennial fervor, he thus remarked, "What is now seen in America, and especially in New England, may prove the dawn of that glorious day."[12]

Indeed, virtually any event, especially those which seemed epochal in American history, would serve as grist for the providential mill. The Revolution was especially revelatory in the eighteenth century. In the mind of Samuel McClintock, for example, the entire victory came from the "government of Providence."[13] For Ezra Stiles, the Revolution was but an allegory, where events pointed to something hidden and supernatural. Washington's victory at Princeton, the discovery of Arnold's conspiracy, the arrival of the French fleet, and the victory at Yorktown all testified to "the indubitable interposition and energetick influence of Divine Providence."[14]

Westward expansion in the early nineteenth century likewise proved divinely directed. Citing Edwards's opinion "that the millennium would commence in America," in 1835 Lyman Beecher wrote, "America is, in the providence of God, destined to lead the way in the moral and political emancipation of the world."[15] Beecher's *Plea for the West* is a thinly veiled apologia for seminary education in general and for Lane Theological Seminary, over which he presided, in particular. If, indeed, "the religious and political destiny of our nation is to be decided in the West," as Beecher wrote, it was necessary to have "a pious and educated clergy, educated in the West."[16] Taking the notion of Western civilization and destiny even further, John O'Sullivan put the notion of "manifest destiny" into wide currency to justify the annexation of Texas. In 1845 O'Sullivan decried European attempts to "check the fulfillment of our manifest destiny to overspread the continent allotted by Providence for the free development of our yearly multiplying millions."[17]

Even national schism and civil war were divinely ordained. Most notable was Abraham Lincoln's description of war as a judgment of God, anticipating the repoeticization of war by H. Richard Niebuhr almost a century later. Declaring March 30, 1863, a national fast day, Lincoln set forth the idea that the war between the states was "but a punishment inflicted upon us for our presumptuous sins" so that the entire nation might be redeemed.[18] Lincoln felt that his views would not be immediately popular, since people "are not flattered by being shown that there has been a difference of purpose between the Almighty and them." But to deny this difference, he added, "is to deny that there is a God governing the world."[19]

At the close of his second inaugural address in 1865, Lincoln embellished upon these views. He observed that both sides in the Civil War "read the same Bible, and pray to the same God; and each invokes His aid against the other. . . . the prayers of both could not be answered; that of neither has been answered fully." Lincoln then remarked,

> The Almighty has His Own purposes. . . . If we shall suppose that American Slavery is one of those offences which, in the providence of God, must needs come, but which, having continued through His appointed time, He now wills to remove, and that He gives to both North and South, this terrible war, as the woe to those by whom the offence came, shall we discern

therein any departure from those divine attributes which the believers in a Living God always ascribe to Him?[20]

Yet if some Americans believed that the Civil War was the divine corrective judgment for the institution of slavery, from another point of view the national schism was rightly foreordained. In this vein Benjamin Palmer wrote that the separation of North and South "was surely decreed of God, and has as certainly been accomplished by the outworking of great moral causes, as was the separation of the Colonies from their English mother." For Palmer and like-minded southerners, states' rights—"the last hope of self-government upon this Continent"—were divinely sanctioned. The North's materialism, its indifference to law, its atheism, and its "idolatry of history" have led to a series of events in which the South has "rather been sinned against than sinning." According to this providential vision, northerners "have sowed the wind, they must reap the whirlwind."[21]

Often these providential beliefs were adorned in racial dress, as if to say that Anglo-Saxons were singled out for superiority by divine decree. During the eighteenth century the native American was one object of racial scorn. Cotton Mather, for example, guessed "that probably the *Devil* decoyed those miserable savages hither, in hopes that the gospel . . . would never come here to destroy or disturb his absolute empire over them."[22] In Mather's opinion "the best thing we can do for our Indians is to Anglicise them."[23] In 1782 Hugh Henry Brackenridge, a jurist from Pennsylvania, called for the "extermination" of "the animals vulgarly called Indians."[24] A decade earlier a student on the Harvard debating team justified slavery on the grounds that an African-American was "a conglomerate of child, idiot, and madman," expressing attitudes that would retain currency for two more centuries, often with the aid of biblical authority.[25]

Providential and racial ideology found new objects by the mid- and late nineteenth century, when Americans faced new waves of immigration, conflicts with their neighbors, and difficult questions about territorial expansion. Despite the fact that Catholics from immigrant stock would soon be the largest denomination in the United States and that African-Americans numbered almost five hundred thousand in the South, Robert Baird claimed in 1844 that "our national character is that of the Anglo-Saxon race." Baird, one of America's first major church historians, added that those who are "essentially Germanic or Teutonic" are "the chief supports of the ideas and institutions of evangelical Christianity," for which America was the base of operation.[26] Soon thereafter, in debates about the Mexican war, Walt Whitman advocated sending thirty thousand troops into Mexico and thirty thousand more along the border, describing Mexicans as "ignorant, prejudiced and perfectly faithless people."[27] Even Albert Gallatin, a critic of racial comparisons during this debate, admitted "with respect to Mexico, the superiority of race."[28] Speaking in 1870, Samuel Harris of Yale would summarize these racial beliefs: "God has always acted by chosen peoples," he observed. "To the English-speaking people more than to any other the world is now indebted for the propagation of Christian ideas and Christian civilization."[29]

During the Spanish-American War these racial and providential claims reached a new pitch. Surveying recent events, the editor of the *Methodist Review* said, "We shall be much disappointed if the final outcome of the war does not show that it was one of God's most efficient agencies for the advancement of true Christian civilization and the ushering in of brighter times for the human race."[30] In 1908 Albert Beveridge argued that the "logic of civilization" required that the Philippines be annexed "by those in whose blood resides the genius of administration."[31] (The idea was sufficiently appealing to be used in the Republican party's National Campaign Document.) During the same time Washington Gladden wrote that "the great mass of these inhabitants of the New World belong to that Aryan race, whose teeming millions have been hurrying westward since the dawn of time."[32] With the acquisition of new territories in the 1890s (the Hawaiian Islands, Puerto Rico, the Philippines), Americans were prone to see themselves on the brink of a world victory for "Christian civilization" and Anglo-Saxon cultural preferences. Summarizing the crusading spirit of this time, Lyman Abbott wrote, "It is the function of the Anglo-Saxon race to confer these gifts of civilization, through law, commerce, and education, on the uncivilized people of the world."[33]

Economic growth was likewise interpreted providentially and racially in the American gospel of self-help. Advocating the belief that "Godliness is in league with riches," William Lawrence described in 1901 how European immigrants "evolve" under economic prosperity. Poles and Italians, he said, have a "lifeless expression, [a] hangdog look, . . . [an] almost cowering posture." Give them five years of work in the United States, and "note the gradual straightening of the body, the kindling of the eye, and the alertness of the whole person as the men, women, and children begin to realize their opportunities, bring in their wages, and move on to better quarters."[34]

In a more explicitly secular century, providential beliefs would be pruned of some, but not all, of their religious elements. To be sure, optimism about election and confidence about the United States on the stage of history have hardly waned. In this vein Woodrow Wilson would say that America's global responsibilities came "by no plan of our conceiving, but by the hand of God who led us in this way." For Wilson "America had the infinite privilege of fulfilling her destiny and saving the world."[35]

Reference to atomic weapons at the close of the Second World War was likewise dressed in providential garb. As Paul Boyer shows in his study of mass culture at the dawn of the nuclear era, politicians, ecclesial figures, and ordinary citizens alike raced to biblical sources to interpret their recent history in mythical terms. The Manhattan Project, one reader of *Life* magazine remarked, was "a direct intervention of the Almighty in human affairs." Evangelist Carl McIntyre assured his audience that "God has given us these weapons." So, he added, "let us use them." Jews turned to Providence to explain how Americans rather than Germans discovered the secret of the atom. According to the *Jewish Record,* "God did not want the Germans to find the secret of the bomb so he caused the Jewish scientists to shake the dust of Germany off their feet."[36] In a similar spirit, Arthur Compton, a Protestant layman, queried rhetorically in 1946, "Atomic power is ours, and who can deny that it was God's will that we should have it?"[37] With the development of thermonuclear weapons in the early 1950s, one writer for *Reader's Digest* opined, "We want *permanent* peace. Let us follow the light that can lead us to it. . . . There has to be an ultimate beckoning concept. We call it human brotherhood. Or, since the stars gave us the hydrogen bomb, we can call it the saving Star of Bethlehem."[38]

Even in the wake of two world wars, Bernard Brody would muse about his faith in American destiny and the future. Writing in 1954, the same year that "under God" was added to the Pledge of Allegiance, Brody remarked that after the "thunder of war, the stench of concentration camps, the mushroom cloud of the atomic bomb, my faith in the future, though somewhat shaken, is not destroyed. . . . If I sometimes doubt that man *will* achieve his moral potentialities, I never doubt that he can. I still believe that with courage and intelligence we can make the future bright with fulfillment."[39] During the same decade, Eisenhower asserted, "America is the mightiest power which God has yet seen fit to put upon his footstool." Echoing an optimism virtually unscathed by the prior two decades, Eisenhower added, "America is great because she is good."[40]

A decade later such optimism would find its way into modern, liberal theology. At the time of the publication of Harvey Cox's book *The Secular City* in 1965, Americans were profanizing the sacred, embracing the notion that the urban landscape, the modern technopolis, was the product of biblical belief. According to Cox, growing secularization, urbanization, accelerated mobility, and anonymity in contemporary culture "do not represent sinister curses to be escaped, but epochal opportunities to be embraced."[41] This is because modern trends are all traceable to biblical images and theological motifs. Most notable for Cox was the modern disenchantment with nature, which provides the precondition for natural science, the technical city, and modern urbanization. This disenchantment lies, Cox argued, not in the rejection of biblical religion, not in criticisms of religion, but in the essence of biblical theology itself. According to Cox, the doctrine of creation set the terms for a postmagical approach to religion, delivering biblical religion from beliefs about nature as an "enchanted forest." Because creation posits Yahweh as outside the natural process, we can "perceive nature itself in a matter-of-fact way."[42] Similarly, the desacralization of politics, so important to modernity, can be traced to biblical beliefs about Exodus. Exodus symbolizes "deliverance . . . out of a sacral-political order and into history and social change, out of religiously legitimated monarchs and into a world where political leadership would be based on power gained by the capacity to accomplish specific social objectives." Cox argued for a happy marriage between biblical theology and modernity, interpreting the city, especially the American city, as the theater of religious meaning. Even modern relativism derives from the Bible, because relativism "stems in part from the biblical opposition to idolatry."[43] Cox's theological interpretation of modernity seemed to reverse the terms of providential grammar by collapsing the sacred into the profane. But this reversal nonetheless required a figural outlook, allegorizing recent events with images furnished by biblical religion. Cox's reading of culture suggested that history continues its procession from biblical beliefs into the present, as if by some consistent, inexorable law. He too found no exit from the grammar of providential conviction.

Whether they sacralize the profane or profanize the sacred, Americans have refused to give up the notion that they have a unique status, legitimated in a recognizable religious idiom. Its theological grammar steeped in the Puritan past, belief in providential direction remains a decisive element in the civil religion of Americans, underwriting their ongoing chiliasm, their self-interpretations, their optimism about the future. Believing in Providence, or destiny, or the promise of the future, Americans hold to the notion that history is proceeding by its own plan. History becomes a set of signifiers, inviting us to discern a divine order behind and beneath the appearances of events. Americans remain under the imperiousness of history, understood as a wider, transcendent set of sovereign forces.[44]

* * *

When in 1630 John Winthrop remarked on the *Arabella,* "Wee must Consider that wee shall be as a Citty upon a Hill, the eies of all people are uppon us,"[45] he set in motion what was to become the second major feature of exceptionalist mythology, namely, the belief that Americans by their example can lead the world toward virtue, especially during times of crisis or change. In the words of Uriam Oakes, "our Common-wealth seems to exhibit a little model of the Kingdom of Christ upon Earth."[46] Stated in secular terms, Americans believe they might "allure the world to freedom by the beauty of its illustration."[47]

Like other exceptionalist beliefs, this one has been brought out as a device for sacralizing profane events. A century after the Puritan settlement, Stiles noted that the American Revolution "would be attended to and contemplated by all nations."[48] About the discovery of America, David Humphreys, a protégé of General Washington, asserted that "America . . . was probably discovered, in the maturity of time, to become the theater for displaying the illustrious designs of Providence, in its dispensations to the human race."[49] And the idea that America's westward movement was *manifest* destiny was meant to point up the contrast between the United States and the "prior" Israel. Traditional Christianity explained Israel's election in terms of God's mysterious, hidden will. But unlike the apparently undeserved election of Israel, the election of the United States was explicable in terms of American virtue, location, or freedom—visible rather than invisible traits.[50]

Americans have found it easy to distinguish themselves from other nations, "which are shut out from the life-giving light of truth," as O'Sullivan said, seeking to separate the United States from treaties in disputes over western territories.[51] But more frequently this idea has inclined Americans to welcome events abroad which seemed to mirror their own history, especially during the nineteenth century. It was widely hoped, George Bancroft wrote, that within twenty years not a monarch would be left in Europe. For John Quincy Adams, writing in 1821, the American Revolution stood as a paradigm for others, as "a beacon . . . on the summit of the mountains, to which all the inhabitants of the earth may turn their eyes."[52] About the framing of the Constitution, Rabbi Isaac Wise noted in 1869 that the "people of the United States . . . had formally and solemnly chosen its destiny, to be now and forever the palladium of liberty and its divinely appointed banner bearer, for the progress and redemption of mankind."[53]

Being the standard for others could, of course, cut both ways, leading to self-criticism as well as self-congratulation. Sounding a critical voice, Gallatin argued against the notion of manifest destiny and westward expansion by asserting that the United States was to be a "Model Republic," a standard for other people to emulate.[54] Placed "by Providence in a position never before enjoyed by any other nation," American government represents "the first large-scale experiment in representative democracy." So, to others who may have feared the power of the people, Gallatin observed, "the answer ever was, 'Look to America.'" In these terms he argued in 1847 against sending troops to Mexico, contrary to the goals of the Polk administration. America's mission, Gallatin added, was "to be a model for all other governments and for all other less favored nations, to adhere to the most elevated principles of political morality, . . . and, by [its] example, to exert a moral influence most beneficial to mankind at large." Instead, the war with Mexico appealed "to [America's] worst passions; to cupidity, to the thirst of unjust aggrandizement by brutal force; to the love of military fame and of false glory."[55]

Serving as a "city on a hill" became even more pronounced by the turn of the century once Americans became more conscious about their global relations. But even then the terms of this trope hardly changed. In 1909 Gladden remarked, "What has caught the world's attention is the illustration in the life of a Christian nation of the Christian virtues." Caught up in the fervor of nationalism and Christian missionary voluntarism, he continued, "God has commissioned this nation . . . to show the non-Christian nations what Christianity means."[56] A decade later, on the eve of World War I, Rev. C. F. Thomas of St. Patrick's Church in Washington, D.C., remarked, "The whole world looks to us to carry to the future what will save the future from disorder, confusion, anarchy, perhaps dissolution."[57] Echoing this same confidence at the end of the war, Wilson intoned, "America in truth shall show the way. The light streams upon the path ahead, and nowhere else."[58]

While the Second World War may have chastened this self-image, Harry Truman nonetheless proclaimed that the United States stood in "a conspicuous place" before the judgments of history for its role in the war.[59] Similarly, Arthur Schlesinger's *Political and Social Growth of the American Peoples,* published during the war years, begins by noting that "the record as a whole sums up a people who, despite the ills to which mankind is prey, managed to fashion a way of life and a system of government which at every period of American history served as a beacon light for struggling humanity everywhere."[60] Even during the cold-war years, belief in America's example provided one strategy for dealing with the Soviets. Writing in 1951, George Kennan thus sought to put relations with the Soviet Union on a measured, realistic foundation: "The most important influence that the United States can bring to bear upon internal developments in Russia will continue to be the influence of example: the influence of what it is, and not only what it is to others but what it is to itself."[61]

Whatever the circumstances, belief in the United States as a model to others remains durable. The idea is that moral leadership proceeds by way of shining example, that American history beckons others to emulate. And after the civil rights movement, Vietnam, Watergate, and the decline of American influence abroad, Americans still believe that they might "allure the world to freedom by the beauty of its illustration." In this vein Ronald Reagan traded on these beliefs in his rhetoric of nostalgia, telling a "watching world" in 1981 that Americans "will be again the exemplar of freedom and a beacon of hope for those who do not now have freedom."[62] This claim suggests that American history provides hope to others with similar aspirations. It also suggests that Americans are morally superior, that others deficient in liberty have a standard for measuring their growth in democracy.

* * *

In 1958 Jacques Maritain called attention to "a certain hidden disposition" among Americans, namely, the tendency to view themselves "as bruised souls." For citizens of the United States, Maritain added, the "tears and sufferings of the persecuted and unfortunate are transmuted into a perpetual effort to improve human destiny and to make life bearable; they are transfigured into optimism and creativity."[63] Maritain's remarks point to the third feature of exceptionalist ideology, the belief that Americans can bring about progress, perhaps redemption, often by way of innocent suffering. Reflecting a strong millennial strain in American piety, this belief defines America as an instrument of historical improvement. It thus includes the non-Augustinian notion that the Kingdom of God can be realized in the finitude of time, that the conspiratorial powers of Babylon will recede, that the United States will become the seat of the New Jerusalem. By this account, the United States plays a soteriological role in human history.

The mission of redemption was one of the key objectives of colonial America. In 1610 the Virginia Company mandated: "The principal and main ends are first to preach and baptize into the Christian religion and . . . to recover out of the arms of the Devil a number of poor and miserable souls."[64] Seventeenth-century New England likewise embraced the commitment to reform and redeem. As Perry Miller has observed, the Puritans saw themselves as "a society despatched upon an errand that was its own reward."[65] Not without ties to the past, the Puritan errand was the last stop on the road of the Reformation, the final stage in the purification of Christian religion and society.

For Edwards, the Great Awakening continued this errand: "Our nation," he said, is "principal nation of the Reformation."[66] By divine plan America was discovered "but little before" the Reformation so that "the new and most glorious state of God's church on earth might commence there; that God might in it begin a new world in a spiritual respect, when he creates the *new heavens and the new earth.*" Because Christ was slain in the Old World, God "probably reserved the honour of building the glorious temple to the daughter that has not shed so much blood, when those times of the peace, prosperity and glory of the church . . . shall commence." Stirring the hopes that would be so important to his revivals, Edwards concluded that the work of redemption in New England "must be near."[67]

Soon the narrow attention to the colonies would broaden into more robust millennial visions about the role of Americans on the stage of history. Accordingly, Ezra Stiles asserted, "It may have been of the Lord that Christianity . . . in its purest body should be evidently advancing forward, by an augmented natural increase and spiritual edification, into a singular superiority—with the ultimate subserviency to the glory of God, in converting the world."[68] Similarly, John Adams noted, "I always consider the settlement of America with reverence and wonder, as the opening of a grand scene and design in Providence for the illumination of the ignorant, and the emancipation of the slavish part of mankind all over the earth."[69] Coordinating these views with the march of time, Americans suggested that the last days were prefigured in American history. So Nathaniel Emmons, president of the Massachusetts Missionary Society, wrote in 1800 about his belief "that God is about to transfer the empire of the world from Europe to America, where he has planted this peculiar people." Consequently, Emmons surmised, "this is probably the last peculiar people which he means to form, the last great empire which he means to erect, before the kingdoms of this world are absorbed into the kingdom of Christ."[70]

Soon Americans would begin excising religious references from this belief while preserving its meaning. So Thomas Yarrow of New York declared that "from their birth," the American states were "designed to be the political redeemers of mankind!"[71] The goal of converting the world to Protestant Christianity was replaced by the more general, secularized notion that the nation, with free institutions and rational discourse, would lure others by a self-evident, intrinsic force. Appealing to the virtues of Enlightenment reason, historian Marcius Willson expressed his confidence that the American example was "destined yet to regenerate the world upon the principles of universal intelligence."[72] According to many Americans, the liberative aspects of American institutions reflected the wisdom not of revelation but of natural reason. In this vein Emerson wrote in 1867, "The office of America is to liberate, to abolish kingcraft, priestcraft, caste, monopoly, to pull down the gallows, to burn up the bloody statute-book, to take in the immigrant, to open the doors of the sea and the fields of the earth."[73]

Reference to human rationality rather than revelation opened the door for religious outsiders to draw on this trope of redemption. Writing in 1856 on the "Mission of America," Catholic convert Orestes Brownson wrote that God "has chosen us to work out for the world a higher order of civilization than has hitherto obtained." Americans have indeed a manifest destiny, wrote Brownson, "the realization . . . of the Christian Ideal of Society for both the Old World and the New."[74] But Brownson was less interested in familiar versions of this belief than in turning it on its head, undermining the Protestant basis from which it derived. As if to provide an apology for the infusion of Catholic immigrants, Brownson added that America's mission could be accomplished only in terms of Catholic tradition and through the labors of "foreign-born as well as native-born Catholics."[75] Although the United States was founded by Protestants fleeing the absolutism of Europe, American civil institutions in fact rely on a theory of the natural law, a tenet which Protestants must deny. It was as if, through the providential cunning of history, Americanism was founded in terms compatible with Catholicism. The founders of America adopted the "natural law, natural reason, and justice." But these rational notions are incompatible with Protestantism, Brownson insists, because Protestantism "asserts the total depravity of human nature, declares all acts done in a state of nature to be sin, and denies nature to make way for grace, and reason to make way for faith."[76] Thus, Brownson concludes, Roman Catholicism is the "Church of the Future. . . . and it is through Catholicity bringing the supernatural to the aid of the natural, that the present evils which afflict us are to be removed, and the country is to be enabled to perform its civilizing mission for the world."[77]

During the late nineteenth and early twentieth centuries, an additional gloss on this redemptive trope took shape. Rather than understand their history as allegorical of wider redemptive forces, Americans substituted the notion that salvation, especially Christian salvation, could be exported. In debates about the Mexican war, Commodore Robert Stockton talked of "redeeming Mexico from misrule and civil strife." Such redemption was part of an overall "duty to fulfill the great mission of liberty committed to our hands." It was imperative to invade Mexico, Stockton added, in order to defend religious toleration there![78] In a more general vein, William Seward dreamt of spreading Christian principles in political matters, making "a new and further development of the Christian system of the introduction of the golden rule of benevolence in the science of human government."[79] Belief in historical redemption thus led Americans to conclude, not disinterestedly, that what was good for Americans was good for the world.

Swept up in a wave of missionary enthusiasm during the late nineteenth century, Americans embraced wholeheartedly the belief that salvation by Protestant faith alone could be exported. So Royal Wilder in 1861 expressed his confidence that "the Church of Christ is able to evangelize the heathen world in one short generation."[80] Exporting Christianity to non-Christian lands meant that others would now have reason to interpret their history in allegorical terms, that the United States would be instrumental in sanctifying the history of foreign peoples. Ministers of salvation bring allegorical grammar, the rhetoric with which an alien history might be repoeticized. Perhaps this is the most subtle form of imperialism: requiring others to redescribe their history, imposing a figural imagination shaped by a foreign idiom. In this spirit Samuel Worcester described the aim of Indian missions in 1816 as that of making "the whole tribe English in their language, civilized in their habits, and Christian in their religion."[81] Similarly, Arthur Pierson, missionary to Japan in the late nineteenth century, spoke of rapid conversions to Christianity and "the rapid elimination of the Asiatic features from the government."[82]

At the turn of the twentieth century, when Christian missions reached their high-water mark, there were more than fifty mission boards in the United States and fifty auxiliary societies, all committed to spreading Protestant Christianity abroad. By 1910 North American missionaries made up about one-third of the total Protestant world missionary staff of twenty-one thousand and one-half of the financial support came from the United States and Canada.[83] Speaking of these trends, in 1909 Gladden asked whether we have "clearly before our minds the fact that the nation is to be an important agency in bringing in the kingdom? Has not the time come when we must learn to look for the employment of the nations by the divine Power, in the evangelization of the world?"[84] As if to answer this question, Theodore Roosevelt remarked that the mission of the United States was to extend "the ideas of civilization and Christianity" over the globe as needed.[85]

Well before Americans began to export the ideals of Christian civilization, however, they began to refashion their notion of redemptive mission. Starting with the Civil War, beliefs about redemption provided grammar for the cult of the dead. In Lincoln's mind, "We hoped for a happy termination of this terrible war long before this; but God knows best, and has ruled otherwise. . . . Surely He intends some great good to follow this mighty convulsion, which no mortal could make, and no mortal could stay."[86] In 1865 Horace Bushnell eulogized the war dead, proclaiming that "in this blood our unity is cemented and forever sanctified." As a result of the war, "we are not the same people that we were, and never can be again." Bushnell added, "In these rivers of blood we have now bathed our institutions and they are henceforth to be hallowed in our sight. Government is now become Providential,—no more a mere creature of human will, but a grandly moral affair. . . . The stamp of God's sovereignty is also upon it; for he has beheld their blood upon its gate-posts and made it the sign of his passover."[87] Only with the tragedy of the war do we now have a nation, Bushnell averred, for "nations can sufficiently live only as they find how to energetically die."[88]

With this belief in historical redemption Americans could perceive the rebirth of their nation through the sacrifices of their national martyrs, the war dead. By the turn of this century they would add the notion that a service was performed, a mission was advanced beyond American shores, when Americans put their lives on the line on behalf of a cause. Writing at the end of the Spanish-American War Albert Beveridge would join the cult of the dead with imperialism, parading itself in disinterested terms. "God," Beveridge averred in 1900, "has made us the master organizers of the world to establish system where chaos reigns. . . . He has marked the American people as his chosen nation to finally lead in this regeneration of the world."[89] Theodore Roosevelt opted for less direct language a year later, but insisted nonetheless that American law and civilization and the American flag were "agencies of God" intended to make "shores hitherto bloody and benighted . . . henceforth beautiful and bright."[90] For Roosevelt, this meant that the United States had "the privilege of playing a leading role in the century that has just opened," a leadership which "has been determined for us by fate, by the march of events."[91] At the end of World War I, Wilson sought support for the League of Nations by linking it to the war dead, enjoining the Senate "to see the thing through, to see it through to the end and make good their redemption of the world."[92]

By the middle of the twentieth century, references to redemptive suffering would be a permanent, almost predictable, fixture in politicians' rhetoric, especially when they sought support for the use of force. Seeking to fan the flames of national zeal during the Second World War, Franklin D. Roosevelt returned to this trope. Roosevelt proclaimed an "all out war" against the Axis powers, saying once more that American lives are risked for the benefit of all. In 1942, he remarked, "We are fighting today for security, for progress, and for peace, not only for ourselves, but for all men, not only for one generation, but for all generations." Adding a soteriological gloss, he noted, "We are fighting to cleanse the world of ancient evils, ancient ills."[93]

American religious authorities generally supported the war effort, although they sometimes tried to introduce a note of moral ambiguity, as in the Calhoun Commission report.[94] The Calhoun report resisted the belief in the United States as a redeemer nation, arguing instead for a mixture of good and evil even in a justified conflict. Yet in 1942 that sense of ambiguity was nonexistent, at least for the moment. In a widely circulated "Statement of Guiding Principles," the Federal Council of Churches emphasized that "a special relationship rests upon the people of the United States" in the war.[95] That same year Rev. Fulton J. Sheen allegorized the Allied effort in terms of the Passion narrative: "In the catalogue of Fascism, Nazism, and Communism you will find those who in their youth signed with the sign of the Cross, sealed with the seal of salvation, and then like Judas bargained away their Christian heritage for thirty pieces of silver from the coffers of a transitory political power."[96] Sheen continued, "Pilate too still lives. He lives in all those teachers and jurists who deny an absolute; . . . who, when they are brought face to face unequivocally with Divine Truth, ask the same question asked by Pilate: 'What is Truth' and then turn their back on it. Put the Creed therefore in the present tense: 'Christ is suffering under Pontius Pilate.'"[97] Sheen admonished his readers to "realize that in some mysterious way Christ is living, suffering, thirsting, starving, and being imprisoned and dying in us, and that this War is His Passion."[98] So that the soteriological idea would not be missed,

Sheen added, "The Son of God . . . has called each of us to be a redeemer with a small 'r' as He is the Redeemer with a capital 'R.'"[99]

From the mid-fifties through the seventies, in the wake of turbulent social change, the grammar of redemption would go underground. But once the door opened for neoconservatism in the early 1980s, the rhetoric of America's salutary role in history would recur. In this vein Richard John Neuhaus holds up as "a kind of litmus test" the following proposition: "On balance and considering the alternatives, the influence of the United States is a force for good in the world."[100] Failure to answer this question affirmatively, Neuhaus maintains, is an expression of disloyalty, barring the dissenter from any conversation about matters of social justice in America. Neuhaus provides no criteria for measuring what counts as "good for the world," suggesting instead that evidence of American benevolence is self-evident. Admission to conversation must begin with a testimony of civic faith about America's salutary role in history, for which criteria of "the good" are unnecessary.

Expressed in terms of religious reform, natural justice, territorial expansion, Christian colonialism, or global benefits, belief in the redemptive mission of Americans can take several forms. But regardless of the variety, faith in America's soteriological duties remains deeply ingrained in the American mind. At heart an evangelical refrain, this redemptive trope entails the notion that Americans can generalize from their own good to the good of the world. It is often acultural, blind to the integrity of cultural differences. When it is combined with the belief that American travail is instrumental to global redemption, this idea can be especially militant. It strengthens the mandate for others to change by joining that mandate with the cult of the dead, the pathos of human suffering. It thus allows Americans to elevate their suffering to a higher plane, the redemptive march of history.

* * *

Historically, the idea of America as exemplar and the idea of America as redeemer nation have led to contradictory impulses, the former supporting an isolationist stance, the latter supporting an interventionist, imperialist approach to foreign affairs. Doubtless historical circumstances have dictated when and why one impulse prevailed over the other. But when it comes to reconciling these impulses in theory, Americans may have recourse to the fourth feature of exceptionalist ideology. In this instance Americans see themselves as obeying a higher law, inaccessible to outsiders or critics. This belief allows, among other things, Americans to reconcile opposite tendencies, leaving the contradiction in the eyes of the "watching world." Since they are unique, Americans need not heed conventional expectations of outsiders. Outsiders may be left with a failure of understanding, frustrated by an American inability to conform. And, in its most extreme form, this belief separates the world into the powers of light and darkness. Insofar as Americans obey a higher law, they can look down on their moral inferiors as, at times, moral reprobates.

Reference to nonconformism typically begins by noting that an American respect for written law is qualified by a stronger respect for a transcendent, unwritten law. When the voice of conscience conflicts with the civil code, Americans have recourse to a more general account of justice or law of nature, some higher standard according to which written laws are to be measured. Appeals to an unwritten, transcendent moral ideal have thus provided the backbone of American civil disobedience, for which Thoreau's night in jail in the 1840s continues to serve as a model for political dissidents today. Thoreau refused to pay the poll tax for the Mexican war, arguing that his money would support the injustice of southern slavery. His nonconformity found justification in the discrepancy between civil law and the voice of conscience, guided by a transcendent norm.

Yet American grammar for nonconformity is more nuanced and complex than this example of civil disobedience suggests. Reference to a higher law trades on the belief in American uniqueness, where uniqueness connotes faith in the United States as immune from the forces which shape (or ought to shape) the lives of other nations. So Thomas Jefferson would describe the United States as "kindly separated by nature and a wide ocean from the exterminating havoc of one quarter of the globe."[101] Those more inclined than Jefferson to see American history in apocalyptic terms nonetheless sought to drive home the same basic belief. In 1822, Samuel Miller pondered the drama of Armageddon, Satan's last stand before the return of Christ. According to Miller, the final conflagration would cause more misery in "the old Latin Earth" than where true Christianity had triumphed. He prayed "that our beloved Country, which has so little of *the blood of the saints* in its skirts, may be in a great measure exempted from the horrors of that awful scene!"[102] For Miller, Americans' separation was cast in an idiom traceable to Puritan forebears, as righteous and pure. Not long thereafter Whitman would state these beliefs in more secular terms, saying, "I hold it to be the glory and pride of America not to be like other lands, but different, after its own different spirit."[103]

To be distinctive in ethical terms has meant that Americans are bound by unconventional canons of morality, duties that cut against the grain of (especially) European practice. So, for example, regarding disputes with Britain about its claim to the Oregon Territory south of the forty-ninth parallel, Frederick Stanton wrote in 1846, "It does not follow that we are to be bound by these conventional arrangements. Our relations to this continent are widely different. We have arisen here, a mighty nation, fast approaching, and destined soon to surpass, the greatness of any European power."[104] In a similar vein, John O'Sullivan sought to exempt the United States from conventional terms of agreement in debates over the Oregon Territory: "Away, away with all these cobweb tissues of rights of discovery, exploration, settlement, continuity, etc." The United States is led to Oregon "by the finger of God himself." The true title lies not in conventions based on the past, but "in our future."[105]

American expansionism likewise found justification in the grammar of uniqueness and the duties of a higher law at the turn of the twentieth century. Mixing beliefs in election and American virtue, Beveridge asserted that "the astronomy of Destiny, American Opportunity, American Duty and American Preparedness are in conjunction." So he defended annexing the Philippines according to "the high ordinances of universal and racial morality," in contrast with "the misapplied individual moralities that would give Australia back to its Bushmen, the United States to its Indians, Ceylon to its natives, and the whole world back to barbarism and night." For Beveridge, the higher law of Americans was the inexorable march of destiny. History, not the law of nature, set the standard. Thus, Beveridge noted, Americans must not resist "the onward forces which were making of the American people the master Nation of the world." According to a "destiny neither vague nor undesirable," but "definite, splendid and holy," Americans have a duty to "give the Philippines such a civil government as the situation demands, under the Stars and Stripes." Those who opposed this plan, Beveridge suggested, failed to recognize the course of events. Understood as the "Gulf Stream's mighty current," history has assigned a special role for Americans, providing a law to which they must dutifully conform.[106]

In its most radical form, this belief provides the basis for Americans to hold their views above critical scrutiny. Especially during times of war, this belief has shown great usefulness. Promising to keep the United States out of the Great War, Wilson said in 1916, "There is such a thing as a nation being so right that it does not need to convince others by force that it is right."[107] Wilson suggested not only that the United States was in accord with the highest principles of morality, but also that Americans were exempt from having to conform to standard ways of defending their beliefs.

Doubtless this belief found some of its greatest use at the close of the Second World War, after atomic bombs were dropped on Hiroshima and Nagasaki. During this time, the grammar of uniqueness and the corresponding exemption from standard moral canons found several spokespersons. Writing in December 1945, the National Catholic Welfare Conference eschewed the topic of atomic weapons, but nonetheless traded on the idiom for authorizing their use: "The heart and hand of America are called upon in a way that is unique, not only in the history of our country, but even in the annals of mankind." The NCWC looked ahead to the portending clash of political ideologies between the United States and the Soviet Union, reminding its readers that the specter of totalitarianism had not disappeared with the defeat of Germany. So the authors added, "We must be true to ourselves. We must hold fast to our own free institutions. . . . On bended knees let us ask God in his Blessed Providence to help us to be the vigorous champion of democratic freedom and the generous friend of the needy and oppressed throughout the world." Uniqueness and integrity, not responsibility for the past, were crucial virtues in a world characterized by "profound differences of thought and policy between Russia and the western democracies."[108]

Those who commented on the use of atomic weapons in the grammar of a higher law did so unabashedly. About the bomb Truman remarked, "We thank God that it has come to us, instead of our enemies; and we pray that He may guide us to use it in His ways and for His purposes." The Hearst press took a more certain stance. Readers of the *New York Journal American* were assured that "Divine Providence has made the United States the custodian of the secret of atomic energy as a weapon of war." Glossing these beliefs with the claim that a higher law pits Americans against the powers of evil, Edgar Guest put to rhyme these exceptionalist ideas:

> The power to blow all things to dust
> Was kept for people God could trust,
> And granted unto them alone
> That evil might be overthrown.[109]

These last three examples indicate that this fourth trope is sewn together with the first, from which it derives its theological justification: The meaning of America's higher law, and the unconventional duties therein, is finally to be found in the providential will of God. Such legitimation, as Reinhold Niebuhr observed, leads easily to the "sense of superior virtue over the alleged evils of European civilization,"[110] and over the alleged barbarism of non-European people. Americans often separate themselves from their neighbors, confident that their nonconformity is in accord with cosmic principles which only they can ascertain. Consequently, they are able to exempt themselves from convention, from traditional notions of morality.

The language of nonconformism and uniqueness likewise reflects an American disdain for imitation. Americans frequently champion beliefs in self-reliance and self-creation, beliefs which run from Emerson through Dale Carnegie to Harold Bloom and Richard Rorty.[111] "Whoso would be a man," Emerson wrote, "must be a nonconformist." Those who break from custom to create themselves are able to say, "Be it known unto you that . . . I obey no law less than the eternal law." Against those who recommend custom and tradition, Emerson adds, "Your own gift you can present every moment with the cumulative force of a whole life's cultivation; but of the adopted talent of another you have only an extemporaneous half-possession." Thus the highest truth for Emerson: "The way, the thought, the good, shall be wholly strange and new. It shall exclude example and experience."[112]

Perhaps for this reason the image of the American legal eccentric has retained its grip on the American popular imagination. Whether he is Shane, Maverick, the citizen-vigilante (*Mr. Smith Goes to Washington*), the police-vigilante (*Dirty Harry*), or the war-vigilante (*Rambo*), the legal eccentric violates conventional expectations in his pursuit of right action, often to the consternation of the community. Naturally, peace and justice are eventually restored, corruption is exposed, and the conventional way of life is redeemed, albeit by methods that stand outside the normal moral order. Americans are thus provided with the grammar of ethical exceptionalism and its double standards, premised on the moral asymmetry between the American hero and everyone else. Belief in their own uniqueness and transcendent duties allows Americans to be beckoned by an alternative morality. But this does not always mean that morality ought to be absent in the lives of non-Americans. At times the belief in American nonconformity means that Americans can hold others to ethical expectations that they need not heed themselves.

* * *

The grammar of exceptionalism has scarcely been conspicuous in moral discourse about war and peace. Nevertheless, it is not entirely absent. In many respects this grammar cries out for a theory, or at least some rational, structured account. Theories often rationalize myths, carving ideological beliefs into stone for the popular imagination. And in the ethics of war, such rationalization is not difficult to carry out. Among recent accounts of the just-war tradition, a theoretical structure for exceptionalism has been provided by the Catholic scholar of international law, William V. O'Brien.

Comparative Justice and the Law of Nature

The grammar of exceptionalism finds one route into the ethics of war by way of O'Brien's rendition of just-war criteria. For O'Brien it is essential to frame such criteria according to natural law morality interpreted through the lens of political science and international law. In the process, O'Brien produces a version of just-war tenets that privileges the protection of Western democracy, turning a cultural preference into a law of nature. In O'Brien's work we do not find explicit reference to Providence, example, redemption, or higher laws. Rather, O'Brien gives us a theory which codifies these beliefs, providing a structure according to which such beliefs can find rational expression and legitimacy.

Taking his bearings from Aquinas, O'Brien begins his reconstruction of just-war criteria by emphasizing the three components of the *jus ad bellum* from the *Summa Theologiae:* competent authority, right intention, and just cause. Of special importance—where O'Brien departs from Aquinas—is the last of these terms. For Thomas, a cause is just when those who are attacked "deserve it on account of some fault." Following Augustine, Aquinas describes a just cause as "one that avenges wrongs." This may include punishing an enemy that refuses "to make amends from wrongs inflicted by its subjects, or to restore what has been seized unjustly."[113] Modifying Aquinas's account, O'Brien restricts the meaning of just cause to defensive wars against an unjust foe. (The original sense would allow also for offensive wars to punish unjust foes, e.g., to menace an unjust polity.) Moreover, and more important, O'Brien argues that the meaning of just cause must now include a *comparison of the polities that oppose each other.* Just cause refers not only to the problem of unjust aggression, but also to the kind of aggressor one is resisting. Applying just cause to the ethics of war, then, we must weigh the difference of comparative justice, the justice of the opposing regimes.

This notion of comparative justice in the *jus ad bellum* turns on a unique interpretation of the principle of proportionality, the relative balancing of risks and benefits when considering the use of force. According to O'Brien, the justice of war is relative not merely to the immediate goal of self-defense, but also to the putative long-range consequences of defeat by an evil opponent. In a conflict "between a just or tolerable polity and an unjust or intolerable polity, a victory of the unjust will probably result in a forceful imposition of an unjust social order on the defeated polity."[114] With O'Brien's modifications, the criterion of just cause would now require Western leaders to consider both the threat of unjust aggression and the kind of political transformation that would occur in the wake of defeat.

Implicit in O'Brien's concern for measuring comparative justice are some natural law assumptions about the moral value of community as well as some political judgments about the differences between the Warsaw bloc and NATO. According to natural law morality, the polis is a natural institution, essential to the end of human development. Thus, there is a natural right of self-governance and a correlative right of communal self-defense.[115] Supplementing these moral ideas are claims about the moral standing of states. Given the political differences between the superpowers, O'Brien avers, we cannot ignore the dangers of totalitarian rule.[116] O'Brien's interpretation of the *jus ad bellum,* then, consists largely in an understanding of radical difference, contrary to the direction of Catholic just-war theory as I recounted it in chapter 2.

When he turns to a discussion of *in bello* criteria, O'Brien rightly observes that the standard account of noncombatant immunity prohibits the direct attack of noncombatants. But contrary to this account, he proceeds to qualify the principle of discrimination in light of his interpretation of the *jus ad bellum*. Specifically, O'Brien prefers to "balance" noncombatant immunity against considerations of military effectiveness. In contrast to Ramsey and the U.S. Catholic bishops, O'Brien insists that a strict application of the principle of discrimination would undermine military efficiency, leaving moral nations at a disadvantage against an implacable foe. The most we can say, then, is that discrimination is "a relative principle enjoining the maximization of noncombatant protection."[117]

Perhaps most notable about O'Brien's reconstruction of these just-war tenets is his account of the relation between, or the ranking of, *ad bellum* and *in bello* criteria. O'Brien holds that the *ad bellum* authorization of war has clear priority over the limitations imposed by the *jus in bello*. As he says, it "is pointless to concede and condone a continued right to recourse to armed force without authorizing the means which will render such a right meaningful."[118] This means, among other things, that we must relax our interpretation and application of discrimination. Otherwise we tie our hands in defense of a just cause, denying ourselves the means necessary for self-defense.

O'Brien defends this overall account by insisting that an absolutist application of discrimination has never been seriously advanced in Christianity. Indeed, he notes, the origins of noncombatant immunity can be traced to the medieval chivalric code, which reflects the cultural values and material limits of earlier Western society. During this time the duty to protect innocent life against direct attack was not designed to answer questions posed by the advent of strategic bombing and nuclear technology; to extract a strict rule from medieval ethics is, at the very least, anachronistic. Rather, it is more pertinent to weigh the consequences of defeat given the differences between the warring parties today. Once a just cause has been established, O'Brien insists, there are strong reasons for maintaining resistance if the adversary represents a totalitarian regime with a will to dominate. Thus, in the limit situation of survival, the requirements of necessity may outweigh the immunities provided by *in bello* limitations.

The problem with this kind of account, as I indicated in the last chapter, is that it invites a double standard, allowing one side to commit the kind of practices that would be condemned if the other side committed them instead. But perhaps more troublesome is the fact that O'Brien fails to provide any criteria with which comparative judgments are intelligible. Without some principle that can avoid a quick sanctification of Western democracy and its survival, how could we relativize the self-justifying claims that are likely to appear in the heat and passion of war? As it stands, O'Brien's account allows us to privilege the moral prerogatives of Western democracies, drawing sharp differences between "us" and "them." The idea of radical difference may well be readily apparent to O'Brien, but it lacks any resources to prevent it from becoming a banner of collective egoism and national self-righteousness.

This latter problem is especially acute because O'Brien seeks to inscribe the notion of radical political difference on just-war criteria themselves. As a matter of historical fact, however, just-war theorists have generally prescinded from comparing the relative differences between warring parties, adopting a position of political neutrality toward the agents in question. Indeed, in most recent accounts of just-war criteria, the trend has moved in a direction opposite to O'Brien's theory, emphasizing relative justice in the list of *ad bellum* criteria. This means that neither side may imagine itself as having a monopoly of righteousness or justice in defense of its claims. The trend, in short, has been to retrieve Augustine's suspicion about the kinds of claims that nations often make on their own behalf. Only in O'Brien's hands has the criterion of relative justice been replaced by comparative justice.

The difference is no small one. Comparative justice allows us to ideologize *ad bellum* criteria, in which cultural and political preferences—the Western democratic way of life—can assume a privileged status within the law of nature. And by cloaking such cultural and political preferences with the language of universal natural law, O'Brien elevates the relative and the particular to a language of universal ends. In this respect he goes beyond the exceptionalism of Mara by furnishing an account of "the way things are"—the natural law—to justify a special status for nontotalitarian regimes in the ethics of war.

O'Brien thus produces something akin to what Marx saw as the attempt by the ruling class to cast its preferences in the guise of impartial, universal needs, parading its interests in ethical language meant to govern all. In O'Brien's case, just-war criteria structured in light of comparative justice provide a theoretical justification of exceptionalism, allowing us to draw distinctions to our advantage on a permanent basis. In this way he furnishes rational discourse for legitimating the mythic grammar of American ideology. But if just-war criteria are to maintain any critical force today, if they are to remain free of political manipulation, they must be structured in ways to resist ideological pressures and other forms of accommodationism. Otherwise they are doomed to collapse into yet another banner for the providential errand, devoid of possibilities for genuine social criticism.

In making this complaint, I do not mean to suggest that exceptionalism is always and everywhere a form of false consciousness or a banner of self-righteousness. Such a general dismissal would not only be hasty and moralistic, it would also circumvent the kind of careful attention to moral vocabularies that I have sought to provide throughout this book. Without such attention, the jury on exceptionalism is still out. The exceptionalism that invites double standards is an easy target, and any quick dismissal may lead us to overlook its more subtle uses as a tool for social criticism.

There are good historical reasons for this caution. As I suggested earlier, exceptionalism has had such a pervasive hold on American imaginations that even attempts to call it into question have traded on the terms it provides for American self-understanding. Exceptionalism provides the idiom not only of ideology, but also of counterideology. To see how this is so, we must examine the strategies of one of America's great rhetoricians, a pacifist who understood the requirements of moral discourse in the public realm.

Intertextualism and Nonsectarian Pacifism

Martin Luther King, Jr.'s leadership in the civil rights movement was directed against racial exceptionalism, the belief that white Americans were separate from and superior to slaves from Africa and their descendants. Yet in his narratives, sermons, and speeches, King clothed his justification of civil disobedience and nonviolent resistance with the mythology of American exceptionalism, interpreting history under the allegory of destiny. Poeticizing history as a providential drama, King sought to render his strategy for social change alluring to a wide audience. He dipped into the well of American ideology freely, mixing biblical and civic images to convey the "best in the American dream and . . . the most sacred values in our Judaeo-Christian heritage."[119]

From the outset of the civil rights movement, King spoke about the intertwining of civil rights and biblical religion. In his first major public address, during the initial stages of the Montgomery bus boycott, King told a rally at Holt Street Baptist Church, "We are not wrong in what we are doing. If we are wrong, the Supreme Court of this nation is wrong. If we are wrong, the Constitution of the United States is wrong. If we are wrong, God Almighty is wrong!"[120] Those inaugural words led to a mass protest that lasted over a year and involved over fifty thousand participants. Later, after violent white backlash in Birmingham in 1963, King invoked ideological grammar to assure his readers, "Abused and scorned though we may be, our destiny is tied up with America's destiny." Adding a more explicit providential reference, King added, "We will win our freedom because the sacred heritage of our nation and the eternal will of God are embodied in our echoing demands."[121]

Providential tropes were rarely far from King's glossary. He was fond of quoting the line from the abolitionist preacher Theodore Parker, "The arc of the moral universe is long, but it bends toward justice," to remind his audiences that nonviolent protest required patience, that taking the long view was necessary during periods of white rage.[122] Faith in providential justice also authorized the notion that whites were not incorrigible, that there was hope for reform on the other side of social conflict. In *Strength to Love*, published during the heat of the Birmingham protest, King reiterated his providential beliefs, saying, "I am convinced that the universe is under control of a loving purpose, and that in the struggle for righteousness man has a cosmic companionship."[123] For King this meant that "history does not pose problems without eventually producing solutions."[124] And the solution for the civil rights movement, King insisted, lay in the "miracle of nonviolence."[125]

That nonviolent confrontation was providentially decreed meant that a light shined out to the watching world. In 1960, when students began sit-ins at lunch counters in Greensboro, King remarked that the protests were "destined to be one of the glowing epics of our time."[126] By commending the students, King sought gently to rebuke his peers who remained suspicious of the students' initiatives. And, once freedom rides, further sit-ins, and voting registration drives gathered momentum, King invoked the exemplary trope to commend the civil rights movement to Americans at large. Those African-Americans committed to nonviolence, King averred, "might . . . set an example to a whole world caught up in conflict."[127]

The movement's successes in 1963–64 led King to speak confidently of the exemplary nature of nonviolent resistance. After meeting with President Kennedy in 1963, King stated that "every dedicated American could be proud that a dynamic experience of democracy in his nation's capital had been made visible to the world."[128] Upon winning the Nobel Peace Prize a year later, King assured his audience that "the entire world now looks to the Negro in America for leadership in the whole task of building a world without want, without hate, and where all men live together in shared opportunity and brotherhood." King added, "There are billions of colored people who look to the United States and to her Negro population to demonstrate that color is no obstacle or burden in the modern world."[129] For King, African-Americans played a special, paradigmatic role in the movement to freedom, one which the world could admire. He thus traded on the notion that history could be guided by race, while turning the white supremacist version of that belief in on itself.

King drew even more fervently from the exceptionalist conviction that suffering, especially innocent suffering, was redemptive. In a letter from prison in Reidsville, Georgia, King sought to relieve his wife, then pregnant with their third child, by saying that "this is the cross that we must bear for the freedom of our people. . . . I have the faith to believe that this excessive suffering that is now coming to our family will in some little way serve to make Atlanta a better city, Georgia a better state, and America a better country."[130] In one of his later homilies, he noted that the Christian must "take up his cross, with all of its difficulties and agonizing and tragedy-packed content, and carry it until that very cross leaves its marks upon us and redeems us to that more excellent way which comes through suffering."[131] The key for those committed to civil rights, King claimed, was to "transform . . . suffering into a creative force."[132]

Yet the real arena for redemption, King often asserted, was the nation as a whole. He thus spoke of the civil rights movement as redeeming the redeemer nation from within. This conviction found its way into the motto of the Southern Christian Leadership Conference, for which King served as founding president at the age of twenty-eight: "To save the soul of America." Redeeming the redeemer nation took the edge off the race issue, rendering it more palatable to those who questioned King's patriotism. Only after segregation was removed, King insisted, would Americans "be able to bring into full realization the dream of our American democracy—a dream yet unfulfilled."[133] Speaking in opposition to separatist African-Americans, King claimed that the American dream was a noble one; the idea of civil rights was not to undermine that dream, only to increase its share. So, King wrote, "those who are working to implement the American dream are the true saviors of democracy."[134] King sought to show that the cause of civil rights was beneficial to Americans as a whole, that what was right was also good. The civil rights movement, King noted, "stimulated a broader social movement that elevated the moral level of the nation."[135]

King's last public address provided a classic mix of redemptive and civic images, echoing the Puritan confidence that the Kingdom of God was present in a special way on the American shores. In April 1968, King poeticized himself in such terms:

> We've got some difficult days ahead. But it doesn't matter with me now, because I've been to the mountain top. And I don't mind. Like anybody, I would like to live a long life; longevity has its place. But I'm not concerned about that now. I just want to do God's will. And He's allowed me to go up to the mountain. And I've looked over. And I've seen the promised land. I may not get there with you. But I want you to know tonight that we as a people will get to the promised land. And I'm happy tonight, I'm not worried about anything. I'm not fearing any man. Mine eyes have seen the glory of the coming of the Lord.[136]

This concluding line comes, of course, from a Civil War hymn, written by Julia Ward Howe in 1862. Howe drew on apocalyptic grammar to interpret the Civil War as a great cosmic battle between light and darkness. And, as Ernest Tuveson has argued, Howe's hymn "conveys a message about the precise place and point of the war in the pattern of salvation." About the first line of "The Battle Hymn of the Republic," Tuveson observes the great millennialist, redemptive belief "that 'the coming of the Lord' is an allegory of the victory of Christian principles." The "glory" denotes "the wonder and the terror of the beginning of the transition to the millennium."[137]

King's millennialism was less militant than that of the Puritans, their successors, or Howe. But he eschewed neither the idiom of expectation nor its rhythms. The title of his third book, for example, traded on an ambivalence, one side of which echoed millennialist ideas. *Why We Can't Wait* suggested an answer to those who called for gradual reform and, more important, sounded a note of anticipation, arousing hopes for imminent change. Linking the civil rights movement to revolutions going on elsewhere in the world, King observed how "continents erupted under the pressures of a billion people pressing in from the past to enter modern society."[138] After riots in Watts and on the eve of riots in Newark and Detroit, King adopted a more ambivalent title for his fourth work, *Where Do We Go from Here: Chaos or Community?* Holding to the millennialist belief that progress was possible, in these later years King was forced to admit that gains for the social gospel were incomplete and fragile, that history might slip back into the hands of darkness. King's rhythms thus echoed the poetry of the American jeremiad, mixing hope with trepidation. And like the jeremiad, King's oratory sought to stir his audience to repentance, renewal, and further action toward realizing social reform.

Reference to Providence, example, and redemption came together in what was perhaps the most pronounced feature of King's exceptionalist rhetoric, the belief that civil rights embodied an unconventional ethic, a higher law, a moral asymmetry. Suffering on behalf of desegregation meant calling the nation "to a higher destiny, a new plateau of compassion, to a more noble expression of humaneness." But this also meant marching to a different beat. "Giving our ultimate allegiance to the empire of justice," King stated, "we must be that colony of dissenters seeking to imbue our nation with the ideals of a higher and nobler order." To this he added a gloss about redemptive suffering: "We are superbly equipped to do this. We have been seared in the flames of suffering. We have known the agony of being the underdog. We have learned from our have-not status that it profits a nation little to gain the whole world of means and lose the end, its own soul."[139] King justified civil disobedience and dissent by arguing that respect for political rule must be based on the congruence between civil law and transcendent norms of justice. Only just laws ought to be obeyed, and a "just law is a man-made code that squares with the moral law or the law of God. . . . To put it in the terms of St. Thomas Aquinas: An unjust law is a human law that is not rooted in eternal law and natural law." Justice, for King, was cast in the grammar of personalistic philosophy: "Any law that uplifts human personality is just. Any law that degrades human personality is unjust. All segregation statutes are unjust because segregation distorts the soul and damages the personality."[140] Echoing a deep American respect for transcendent, unwritten law, King affirmed the right of conscience and a version of the law of nature, a higher standard by which to measure written laws.

To undermine laws of segregation, King sought to expose the asymmetry between justice and racial discrimination. The effect of this asymmetry was to separate the world into the powers of good and evil. Nonviolence, King noted, "made clear who was the evil doer and who was the undeserving victim."[141] Thus the incendiary cry to "fill up the jails" throughout the South, to refuse bail, and even to permit civil disobedience by children in Birmingham. Each of these events was meant to underscore the moral issues beyond the law, to sharpen the discrepancy between conscience and law. Echoing a related exceptionalist refrain, King added that success in civil disobedience lay in being a "transformed nonconformist," one who distinguishes between "the music of time" and the "soul-saving music of eternity."[142] Civil disobedience thus functioned translegally, to point to moral values in stark contrast with the social and legal realities of the day.

References to America's providential direction and its need for a chosen race, its exemplary status, its redemptive mission, and its nonconformist morality, all dipped from the well of American civil religion. King's attempt at social criticism borrowed widely and freely from this idiom, providing a language for speaking to a pluralistic public. Yet King's art lay in turning this mythology on its head, using it as a tool for counterideology, criticism from within. Indeed, of King we can say what Sacvan Bercovitch says of exponents of the American jeremiad in general: "The dream that inspired them to defy the false Americanism of their time compelled them to speak their defiance as keepers of the dream."[143] Poeticizing the civil rights movement as a providential drama, King sought to render his strategy for social change alluring to a wide audience. He was able to make nonviolence intelligible to a culture that is generally not a pacifist culture, justifying nonviolence and civil rights with a language that Americans understood.

King's use of exceptionalist grammar thus conveyed a deep commitment to public discourse. By drawing on a moral grammar with wide currency, he eschewed the sectarian path down which most Christian pacifists are walking today. For King the danger of sectarianism was posed by Black Muslims, who sought to instill racial pride through self-help groups, schools, and neighborhood associations in the inner cities. King generally resisted the rhetoric of African-American separatists, while sharing their commitment to increase racial self-esteem. Adopting the strategies of public discourse, King sought to make social criticism intelligible by casting it in an idiom with publicity, or wide currency. In the process, he was able to refer to the grammar with which Americans understood themselves, while changing that grammar from within.

King thus represents what Walzer calls "connected critics," those who oppose the present order without trying to detach themselves from it.[144] Such critics do so by using large, ambivalent ideas, like equality, or freedom, or rights. They do so, Walzer suggests, because ideologies create expectations that cannot be fulfilled to everyone's satisfaction. Ideologies take the preferences of some and parade those as the preferences for all. But when the preferences of the marginal classes remain unmet, or when the experience of oppression is flagrant and long-standing, those classes have a vocabulary for expressing their dissatisfaction, their alienation from ideological promises. Ideologies, by this account, are inherently ambivalent, providing an idiom of expectation, alienation, and subsequent social criticism.

As a connected critic, King demonstrates that distance from our beliefs may be less important than the ability to interpret them, that finding some external vantage point is no self-evident desideratum. Instead, a connected critic speaks intertextually, drawing out moral meanings from a language that is widely shared. King traded on the language of exceptionalism in order to attack exceptionalist practices, especially those having to do with race. In order to do so he joined the powers of interpretation with social criticism, rediscovering deeper meanings and charting alternative paths for a culture in crisis.

Rationalization and Counterideology

The use of history and its ambivalent grammar is itself an ambivalent task in ethics, yielding no simple formula or manifesto for historicism. Instead, the use of history in ethics requires us to scrutinize carefully the grammar of ideology: its vocabularies, its plasticity, its oppositional uses. As the cases of O'Brien and King show, the cultural effects of history can shape ethical discourse in widely different ways, providing the idiom of either rationalization or counterideology.

This means that history as a deposit of moral teaching about war and peace, as Johnson suggests, provides an incomplete paradigm for thinking in historicist terms. Ideology is too elusive and too malleable to yield confidence that there are "lessons of history," that we can directly turn to the past, as if our turning were not already guided by mythological forces and historical powers. If there is no escape from history—no "Esperanto" above the flux of time and place—then thinking that historical lessons are transparently clear can do us no good. Such a view suggests that we are *ahistorical viewers* looking back, that our vision and hearing are unaffected by rituals of socialization. But if, as social critics, we are to be curators of the past, we must recognize that our powers of perception are themselves shaped by the history whose ethical artifacts we seek to privilege. It is better in my judgment to draw lessons from ideology as I have examined it here: History shapes the culture that shapes our account of historical events. Those same cultural forces shape our moral grammar for evaluating those events. If, in this view, social criticism is to occur, it must trade on terms that we share, the language with which we describe ourselves. It must make the most of moral and interpretive ambiguity, connecting us to the past and to a future thus far unknown.

If this account of history in relation to ethics is correct, then we are left with at least one more question about public discourse: Assuming that just-war criteria provide the framework for public debate about the morality of particular wars, how can we protect such criteria from the pressures of ideological distortion? What measures can we adopt to provide a moral idiom for public debate about the events in war? Are there additional resources from within our moral discourse to which we may turn for assistance in these matters? If we cannot look ahistorically to our ethical vocabularies, what ambiguities can we exploit to prevent those vocabularies from becoming ideological rationalizations? To a discussion of such questions we must now turn.

N I N E

On Duty, Virtue, and the
Interpretation of Conflict

Plurality and Ambiguity

The idea that pacifism and just-war tenets share a moral presumption against war suggests that "pacifists and proponents of just-war theories really need each other." As Childress observes, just-war theorists need pacifism to remind them of the presumption against force and war, while pacifists need just-war criteria as a framework to assess the relative morality of particular wars, assuming that some wars can be more pernicious than others.[1] During the Vietnam War, for example, pacifists and nonpacifists drew on just-war criteria to evaluate morally the involvement of U.S. forces.[2]

Unfortunately, however, pacifists and just-war theorists have devoted scant attention to the order and weight of just-war criteria. Thus, the application of just-war criteria to particular wars or particular acts in war, the task of practical reasoning, may elude those seeking a framework for public debate. In classical just-war reasoning, the problem of practical reasoning emerged (at least implicitly) as soon as just-war ideas were organized systematically by Aquinas. After enumerating the three criteria of a just war (proper authority, just cause, and right intention) in the *Summa Theologiae,* he states, "It can happen that even given a legitimate authority and a just cause for declaring war, it may yet be wrong because of a perverse intention."[3] Although a wicked intention renders the war immoral, Aquinas does not say whether wars which satisfy only the criteria of intention and cause are morally better than wars which satisfy only the criteria of intention and authority. In Aquinas's thought, then, the relative weights of authority and cause in moral judgment remain unclear.

Among contemporary just-war theorists the problem of practical reasoning has become even more complex, either because additional criteria have become part of the just-war tradition subsequent to Aquinas, or because the meaning of traditional criteria has become subject to dispute. O'Brien, as we have seen, insists that the *in bello* principle of noncombatant immunity is to be applied flexibly in the ethics of war, preceded by considerations of proportionality.[4] In contrast, Ramsey and the U.S. Catholic bishops quite emphatically reverse this priority and insist that noncombatant immunity provides an exceptionless rule.[5] Those turning to the just-war tradition for guidance, then, are met by a plurality of interpretations among just-war theorists themselves. Moreover, there is the problem that in the course of war, nations may satisfy some just-war criteria and violate others. If a few criteria are violated, is the entire effort rendered immoral? How can we evaluate morally the behavior of nations at war?

Addressing such questions, Childress identifies a spectrum of possible solutions. These range from the idea that violating any one criterion renders an entire war unjust to the notion that just-war criteria could be arranged in lexical order so that some must be met before others can be considered. According to one end of the spectrum, then, if one criterion is violated, the justice of the war is vitiated, even if more important criteria have been satisfied. Those operating at the other end apply the criteria in the order of their importance. Thus, for example, if there is no just cause, "there is no reason to consider proportionality, for the war cannot be justified."[6]

Yet it remains unclear according to this latter suggestion how we are to judge the morality of war. If we arrange the criteria lexically, what happens to moral judgment once one criterion is violated? Is the violation of one criterion (e.g., last resort) morally negligible when measured against a cluster of other, weightier criteria that have been satisfied (e.g., just cause and competent authority)? Or would violating a criterion of lesser weight in the *jus ad bellum* nullify the justification provided by weightier criteria? Even more difficult is the problem of the relative weight of *ad bellum* criteria when measured against *in bello* criteria. If a nation has satisfied the *jus ad bellum* in its recourse to war, does that nation nullify the validity of its cause when it repeatedly violates the *jus in bello?* About these types of questions Childress rightly observes, "It is unfortunate that philosophers and theologians have not devoted more attention to the order, mode of application, and weight of the various criteria."[7]

One possible solution to this problem is advanced by Ramsey, who argues that just-war ideas only provide clear criteria for assessing the means of warfare, about which ethicists may speak unequivocally. Thus, Ramsey has spoken emphatically about the immorality of the bombings of Dresden, Tokyo, Hiroshima, and Nagasaki.[8] Whatever the justice of the American cause, these means violated the *in bello* canons of discrimination and proportionality. Yet about the larger ends of war and the relation of those ends to the evils of war, conscientious persons may legitimately disagree, for such judgments are matters of political prudence about which conflicting conclusions are possible. During the 1960s, about "the particular decision concerning the greater or lesser evil in the whole of Southeast Asia," Ramsey insisted that "no Christian can fault the conscience of another."[9]

Ramsey thus seeks to limit the application of just-war criteria to *in bello* considerations, believing that we can then eschew interminable debates about whether the cause of war is just. Such debates turn on calculations of political prudence, requiring us to determine whether recourse to force is, on balance, politically and morally feasible. Ramsey's Augustinian suspicions of prudential calculations require him to abstain from such judgments. Thus, he all but eclipses the moral parameters provided by *ad bellum* criteria. He hopes that by focusing on the methods of war we will achieve greater precision in our moral judgments.

Yet, as we have seen, Ramsey's desire to restrict our focus to *in bello* criteria provides no guarantee of moral precision. Proportionate calculations (and the vagaries therein) are scarcely absent when it comes to the question of the means of war, since proportionate reasoning still obtains: *In bello* considerations require us to balance foreseen evil and good effects. And, as we have seen, even in Ramsey's hands reference to *in bello* criteria is affected by prudential considerations, like the importance of order and what I called the preservation motif. Ramsey's recommendation to resist the pressures of proportionate reasoning is belied when he applies *in bello* criteria in his casuistry of nuclear war and deterrence. His own application of *in bello* criteria shows that a focus on the means of coercion is not immune from the kinds of political and pragmatic calculations from which he otherwise wishes to prescind.

Another, more skeptical, response to the problem of practical reasoning might argue that ethical judgments in modernity can never be precise because fragments of prior moral traditions have been wrenched free from the social forces from which they once derived intelligibility. As MacIntyre has argued, in the present age we must choose between competing and incommensurable goods, but we can never settle our differences in the court of reason.[10] According to this kind of diagnosis, the problems posed by practical reasoning in war are symptomatic of our modern situation, where rival moral judgments escape adjudication, leaving us in a culture and ethics of emotivism. Arriving at judgments about war, drawing on MacIntyre's argument, would require us not to rank and apply conflicting duties, but to retrieve an ethics of tradition, community, and virtue.

Yet, contrary to MacIntyre's description of contemporary moral debates, the task of practical reasoning in war does not constitute a modern moral dilemma, because the terms of debate are not structured by rival claims whose ancestry can be traced to heterogeneous origins and cultures. Thus it is not sufficient to call for a rehabilitation of tradition as an antidote to the endless moral debates of modernity, because just-war ideas themselves comprise a tradition, which has remained relatively stable over the past fifteen hundred years in Western culture. MacIntyre wants us to retrieve tradition to overcome the perils of pluralism. But what happens when traditions themselves are marked by moral plurality?

The real problem posed by the just-war tradition is that just-war criteria leave us with several duties to satisfy. In our moral interpretations of conflict, reference to the just-war tradition can produce a conflict of interpretations, since the variety of just-war criteria can lead to different moral assessments of historical wars, or acts of war. This means that, in the act of practical reasoning, we must contend with history itself as morally ambiguous. This ambiguity is not one in which we are forced to choose from competing rival goods within a relative clear historical moment, but one in which there may be a conflict of interpretations about the morality of historical events. The question of practical reasoning remains: Given the plurality of just-war criteria, how might we carry out moral casuistry in war, especially when both sides violate some just-war canons? If a few criteria are violated, is the entire effort rendered immoral? How do we interpret and evaluate the behavior of warriors as battles wear on?

If the solution to these questions does not depend on deliverance from our allegedly emotivist culture, such a solution is nonetheless close to MacIntyre's prescription for moral theory today. For, to solve the conflict of interpretations about war, we must have recourse to a theory of the virtues, a theory that usually rivals theories of duties. According to Aristotle, the term *virtue* designates an excellence of character, displayed in deliberative choice, and augmented in the performance of such choices. Virtues are honorable powers, which abide and strengthen over time. Duties, in contrast, furnish the grammar of obligation, defining imperatives at the level of action. Duties focus our moral attention on discrete deeds rather than on powers or moral traits. Hence, duties lack the resources for guiding moral judgment, since they do not tell us how to move from principles to application, the art of moral casuistry. As the problem of practical reasoning suggests, moral judgments reach an *aporia* when we are left with only just-war duties for evaluating the morality of war. Rather, we must supplement those duties with the virtue of discerning judgment, a power independent of the duties implied by *ad bellum* and *in bello* criteria. As Hans-Georg Gadamer observes, "For the application of rules there exists in turn no rule."[11]

This does not mean, however, that just-war duties cannot contribute at all to the task of practical reasoning, only that they are not sufficient. It is also the case, I hope to show, that practical reasoning in war can be aided by the more general values inherent in just-war criteria, like those I discussed in chapter 1. There I argued that just-war tenets begin with reference to a presumption against harm, enshrined in the duty of nonmaleficence. This presumption implies impartial fellow-feeling, an ethic of compassion for those who suffer, an intolerance of cruelty and wanton violence. These inferences were drawn out at the postethical level of moral discourse, defining the general beliefs on which moral and ethical interpretations of nonmaleficence depend. And, as we shall see, these inferences are relevant to the task of casuistry, for they can serve as a counterweight to possible deficiencies in practical reasoning itself. Without this bias against cruelty, practical reasoning can easily curdle into self-aggrandizement and xenophobia. Once the fellow-feeling implied by the duty of nonmaleficence recedes, practical reason can weaken, having lost its vision of anything but the self and its favored friends. In its weakened form, then, practical reason can easily underwrite self-justification in the heat of warfare, intensifying claims against the "other," the threat from without.

This relation between practical reasoning and nonmaleficence will produce a complex understanding of moral casuistry in war. It means not only that pacifists and just-war theorists need each other, as Childress observes; it also means that in the course of practical reasoning, duties and virtues about the morality of war correct each other, dialectically.[12]

Phronesis, Memory, and Nonmaleficence

Aristotle defines practical reasoning, or *phronesis,* as "a reasoned and true state of capacity to act with regard to human goods."[13] *Phronesis* is the virtue of deliberation, which terminates in right conduct: rightness with respect to "the end, the manner and the time" of an action.[14] Practical reasoning attends to the variables of a situation and apprehends the proper choice from an array of possibilities. Thus, *phronesis* is concerned not with the universal truths of science, but with the ultimate particular fact, that which is unique and unrepeatable, the punctual act demanded by the situation at hand.

This account constitutes the conventional notion of practical reasoning in much of Western ethics, leading many followers of Aristotle to concentrate on the important relation between *phronesis* and the qualities of specific acts, e.g., the excellences of timing and proportion, discipline and improvisation, feeling and thought, and the relation between these excellences and specific choices.[15] But there lies hidden in Aristotle's discussion of *phronesis* a broader and more subtle epistemological agenda, suggesting what Aquinas called virtues "annexed to prudence."[16] These more general powers consist in the skill of discernment, the ability to perceive the morally relevant features of an event.

Throughout book 6 of the *Nicomachean Ethics,* Aristotle draws several analogies between prudence and perception. Referring to "people of practical wisdom," Aristotle observes that "experience has given them an eye [with which] they see aright."[17] *Phronesis,* Aristotle adds, is like an "eye of the soul," a power of sight or insight.[18] Further, good judgment (*gnome*)—one skill that converges with *phronesis*—is a kind of intuitive reasoning, a form of perception. This does not mean that for Aristotle practical reasoning is entirely clairvoyant, for *phronesis* must draw on general rules. But together with the use of summary rules, practical reasoning requires us to apprehend configurations of parts and wholes in the phenomena of experience. Recognizing such configurations requires a skill more like sense perception than deductive scientific knowledge (*episteme*). The perception required by practical reasoning is akin to the intuition required by theoretical *nous*, since neither the universals of theoretical *nous* nor the particulars of practical reasoning admit of final, external justification. As we proceed to the extreme of either theoretical knowledge (i.e., universals) or practical reasoning (i.e., particulars), we reach a limit to what can be said. At that limit moral knowledge relies on intuitive apprehension rather than discursive argument.[19]

Aristotle likens this form of perception to the skill of discerning how a certain figure is composed of triangles.[20] Aquinas likewise calls such powers of discernment "an interior sense," contrasted with the "external senses" by which we encounter empirical data.[21] Aristotle suggests that *phronesis* enables us to discern parts, wholes, and their interrelation in practical affairs, allowing us to grasp the practical meaning of concrete particulars. Without this form of insight it would be difficult to integrate our actions into a larger whole, to see the configuration of particulars within which human action must situate itself. Thus, to choose prudently—to select the mean between a pair of extremes relative to the agent—requires what David Wiggins calls "situational appreciation" of an agent's social and historical context. What Aristotle provides, by Wiggins's account, is a notion of *phronesis* "which articulates the reciprocal relations of an agent's concerns and his perception of how things objectively are in the world."[22] Thus, according to Aristotle, there cannot be prudence without interpretation, for action gains its intelligibility relative to a larger context.

For Aristotle the skill of prudence is aided by experience—either our own experience, or that of others. At first we are to rely on "the sayings and opinions of experienced and older people," those individuals who have special skills in practical reasoning.[23] But eventually such wisdom is to be appropriated by the agent herself. So Aquinas characterizes the virtuous "inner sense" as that which is "seasoned by memory and experience, and so ready to meet the particular facts encountered."[24] *Phronesis* is the kind of skill acquired in the course of training for a practice, requiring not just intelligence but also moral character. Among the several fruits of moral training is the capacity for participatory knowledge, knowledge that is perfected in the performance of a practice. *Phronesis* thus cultivates not the skill of abstract, detached reasoning about the morality of acts or character, but an ability to apprehend the moral dimensions of a practice from within that practice itself. Developing virtue requires us to acquire excellences intrinsic to the performance of an act (strategic acumen in chess, eloquence in writing and speech, anticipation in sport, control and rhythm in dance) as distinct from benefits that may accrue to those excellences from without (e.g., financial gain). Hence, training in virtue, especially the virtue of practical reason, demands that we cultivate the skill to distinguish goods internal and external to our acts.[25] The intellectual virtue of practical reasoning exists in reciprocal relation with the moral virtues, the excellences of character, all of which are perfected over the years.

The experiences of others, especially those who are older and wiser, are also important for the interpretive dimension of *phronesis*. Reference to such experiences suggests that moral perceptions are informed by traditions, those practices and narratives whose truth possesses presumptive weight. Through the appropriation of received traditions, the meaning of past events—their development and interrelation, their relation to the present—becomes apparent to us. The political ideals of a culture are regularly rehearsed in those monuments, holidays, and memorials which testify to the formative events of a culture's past, providing rituals of socialization. Such rituals retrieve the essentials of what Robert Bellah et al. call "communities of memory":

> Communities . . . have a history—in an important sense they are constituted by their past—and for this reason we can speak of a real community as a "community of memory," one that does not forget its past. In order not to forget that past, a community is involved in retelling its story, its constitutive narrative, and in so doing, it offers examples of the men and women who have embodied and exemplified the meaning of the community. These stories of collective history and exemplary individuals are an important part of the tradition that is so central to a community of memory.[26]

Part of the training in the virtues, then, consists in receiving cultural narratives according to which the memories of history and its meaning are passed on. Narratives are retrieved, rethought, and rewritten, thus connecting the present generation with its forebears. *Phronesis* as dependent upon the reception of past traditions must "annex" the exercise of memory understood as the appropriation of custom and convention.[27] Without such conventions, we lack an idiom for making sense of ourselves in relation to history and society, the grammar of our self-interpretation.

Reference to memory and narrative in practical reasoning thus consists in framing present events within a larger descriptive apparatus, using what I called in the last chapter a culture's ideology. *Ideology* refers to the moral commitments of a culture, about which a public consensus, if not civil religion, generates widespread agreement. Ideologies shape self-interpretations and communal solidarity. Moreover, such beliefs illumine the meaning of historical events like war: Wars are construed as the defense of democracy, or the liberation of an oppressed people, or the protection of economic partners, or corrective punishment. In each of these construals the events of war are brought under one paradigm, or image, according to which those events are arranged and rendered meaningful. Ideologies dress history with myth, requiring a figural point of view. Practical reasoning as a hermeneutical skill in the context of war requires us to relate a community's narratives and traditions, the understanding of a culture's purposes, to the purposes risked in war. In the process we use the grammar of our culture to make sense of war, to give it some historical and cultural rationale, and to interpret ourselves in relation to war's mythic structure.

Important as memory and tradition are for *phronesis,* however, the intelligibility provided by tradition is scarcely unambiguous. The tendency of a culture to recount its history as a progressive narrative, a march toward civilization, is rarely resisted. Progressivists view history teleologically, as a march toward the goal of human fruition or civilization. But teleological accounts of history must excise narratives of defeat, or moral failure, or regression. As Bellah et al. remark,

> The stories that make up a tradition contain conceptions of character, of what a good person is like, and of the virtues that define such character. But the stories are not all exemplary, not all about successes and achievements. A genuine community of memory will also tell painful stories of shared suffering that sometimes creates deeper identities than success. . . . And if the community is completely honest, it will remember stories not only of suffering received but of suffering inflicted—dangerous memories, for they call the community to alter ancient evils.[28]

Bellah et al. suggest that under the banner of a nation's or culture's self-understanding we can discover conflicting and troubling accounts. Progressivists tend to view history as a narrative of improvement, culminating in the present. In their selective narrations, however, they eschew reference to those of less than exemplary character, or accounts of "suffering inflicted," or the dangerous memory. As we saw in the last chapter, it is not uncommon for Americans in particular to interpret their history as one of election, progressing under the direction of Providence. But American or not, teleological or progressive versions of history include, in the words of Howard Zinn, "the quiet acceptance of conquest and murder in the name of progress," premised on amnesia about conquered individuals or cultures.[29] Progressivist memory is well edited, providing the grammar of self-congratulation for those who have survived, or profited from, history's travails.

Equally problematic is the issue of provincialism in the use of narrative. Provincialists use narratives that elevate the excellences of the local group. Their views are focused not on time, but on place. Provincialists claim cultural superiority, perhaps by appealing to some higher, inscrutable law. Conversation with those from other provinces would require provincialists to respect, if only momentarily, narratives from without. But by drawing sharp boundaries between those within and those without, provincialists exonerate themselves from having to confront an other respectfully, from having to listen to an alternative voice. Instead provincialists take local pride to an ontological extreme, parading their parochial preferences as the absolute good.

As Hauerwas has posed the problem, provincialism is aided and abetted by the cult of war itself. War, Hauerwas contends, is the organizing feature of social histories. Through the narratives of war deeper identities are forged, the past is linked to the present, and suffering is given meaning and purpose. Thus, regardless of the attractions of peace, we need war because it furnishes the chief structural principle in our memory and historical self-understanding. Contrary to the notion that our interpretation of war is shaped by wider cultural narratives, wars themselves shape the interpretation of cultural identity. Wars provide us with a story, or constitute the "major characters" in our individual and collective stories. We are unable to exclude war from our narratives, Hauerwas argues, because "we fear we will lose the ability to locate ourselves in a worthy story or as participants in the ongoing life of a people."[30]

The problems of memory, then, raise ideological questions for *phronesis* as a narrative-dependent, hermeneutical endeavor. By drawing on the vocabulary of a culture, practical reasoning is historically implicated, rooted in time and place.[31] But in its implication, practical reasoning is vulnerable to self-aggrandizement, to distortion, turning cultural preferences into universal principles.

Several complex questions about practical reasoning thus emerge: Is it possible to withstand the pressures of ideology, to be effective social critics while reasoning practically about war? How might we resist the tendency of communal narratives to efface the ambiguities of history, to forget the victims of fear, error, and conceit, to proceed under the banner of progress? How do we measure the meaning of past events against beliefs about moral excellences that are not embraced within the culture? By what means can we sustain the notion that cultural pride may be structured independently of conflicts against outsiders? How is it possible, in Gadamer's terms, "to keep oneself open to what is other, to other, more universal points of view," to distance oneself from oneself and one's own cultural purposes, looking at things in the way that others might see them?[32] What resources enable us to include dangerous memories, the recollection of history's victims, those whose stories are lost or forgotten in the aftermath of social struggle?[33] What can be the criterion of ambiguity, the means by which moral interpretation can proceed as a dialectic of retrieval and suspicion?[34]

One way to answer these questions, as we have seen, is to draw on distinctively Christian imagery to repoeticize war in nonideological terms. So H. Richard Niebuhr uses the cross as a metaphor to interpret the events of war, focusing on the suffering of the innocent, the chief victims of international conflict. Without such a critical hermeneutical principle, Niebuhr suggests, we interpret wars in one of two ways: either with reference to justice and injustice, as conflicts between those who are deserving and undeserving of victory; or as exercises of brute power, in which all forms of morality have been jettisoned. In either case, Niebuhr contends, we lack sufficient resources for self-criticism and social criticism.

For Niebuhr, reference to the cross militates against interpreting history as the battleground of moral and immoral forces, requiring attention to the victims of war on either side of battle. The almost forgotten stories of the vanquished, those who are "crucified," haunt the dangerous memories of war. Recalling these victims requires us to interpret wars as morally ambiguous arenas of human action, since evils occur on both sides of battle. Such memories also rupture the stream of history, denying us the satisfaction of interpreting historical events as progress or triumph—even in those wars where triumphs occur.[35]

The cross, then, provides one way to integrate suspicion into *phronesis,* permitting neither progress nor parochialism, but an outlook of ambiguity toward the moral reality of war. Yet, however bold and helpful Niebuhr's repoeticization might be, its merits are clearly limited. For, contrary to Niebuhr's wishes, the cross itself is an ambiguous trope. It not only illumines the reality of innocent suffering in history, it also legitimates the manipulation of those adopting a stance of voluntary suffering and nonresistance in the name of the cross. Such dangers are particularly real given Niebuhr's Christian chiliastic hope that war would redeem the guilty and innocent alike. As Gutierrez has trenchantly argued, the promise of redemption instills passivity and complacency about the direction of historical events, contrary to requirements for social change implicit in the eschatological orientation of Christian faith.[36] As a symbol of docility in the face of power, then, the cross itself requires retrieval mediated by suspicion.

Perhaps it is for this reason—the ambiguity of "crucifixion"—that Tillich insisted on viewing the cross as a self-reflexive critical image, one with the capacity to criticize and revise itself in the interpretation of human experience.[37] Such a theology was key to Tillich's Protestant principle, turned reflexively toward Protestant religion itself. Used self-reflexively, Tillich hoped, the cross could enable Christians to resist parochial efforts to absolutize any particular cultural appropriation of the symbol in the interpretation of events. As a transcendent, critical principle, reference to the cross should illumine the ambiguity of all efforts to appropriate it by the cultural imagination. And, by exposing the ambiguity of human aspirations, the cross carries with it a set of resources to withstand any effort to domesticate it ideologically, as a figural outlook for construing human events.

Subsequent to Niebuhr and Tillich, Christian thinkers have insisted on the need for a critical practical hermeneutic, one which is both nonideological and self-reflexive. The goal of such a hermeneutic is to recall the vanquished of history in the retrievals of tradition and narrative without chilling the passions for social criticism and reform. Unfortunately, however, no one has accomplished this task within a decidedly public argument, one which can reach beyond the bounds of Christian symbols, faith, and practice. And unless some nonconfessional equivalent is found, those calling for a nonideological principle of criticism, a counterideological trope, will fall prey to the charge of "culture Christianity." They will be dismissed for expressing yet another form of provincialism in a culture of religious and ethical pluralism. Modern Christian ethics thus stands on the threshold of an *aporia,* stalled at that point where practical reasoning must integrate a criterion of ambiguity, a nonconfessional idiom to resist the ideology of memory.

The quest for a nonconfessional criterion of ambiguity, one which is compatible with but not exclusive to Christianity, can best be advanced by returning to the resources provided by the duty of nonmaleficence. As I argued in chapter 1, nonmaleficence must be understood not only as a duty; it also draws on postethical beliefs about our relations to others. At this more general level of discourse, nonmaleficence expresses the sentiments of empathy and other-regard, establishing moral obligations irrespective of those features that distinguish some persons as "other." Like Ramsey's and H. Richard Niebuhr's qualified preferentialism, nonmaleficence here expresses an intolerance of cruelty, a compassion for those who suffer. Nonmaleficence does not endorse ethical passivity, indifference, or lack of active resolve; rather, it entails an active intolerance of suffering. Interpreted in this way, the duty of nonmaleficence is the expression of nonpreferential compassion, a respect for others, a willingness to hear the voices of those from without. Unlike Ramsey's protection paradigm, however, nonmaleficence is first and foremost a negative obligation, establishing at least a prima facie duty not to harm. As a point of contact between pacifists and just-war theorists, the duty not to harm enshrines the notion that others deserve respect and moral attention, including those who are "remote" as well as "near neighbors."

Against provincialism in practical reasoning, nonmaleficence as nonpreferential compassion draws no ontological distinctions between those within and those without the community. It thus decries the use of narratives that exclude reference to the excellences of others, excellences that are not part of one's ideology or culture. Indeed, as I have interpreted it, nonmaleficence militates against the construction of radical "otherness" to stoke the fires of racial or cultural zeal, to inflame the passions of those who serve, or have served, the community. Nonpreferential notions, like the duty not to harm, are not designed to efface cultural differences, except when cultural differences become differences in value. Reference to nonmaleficence in practical reasoning, then, requires suspicion about narratives which can record only the heroes and excellences of those within the tribe, or kinship system, or community.

Against progressivism in practical reasoning, nonmaleficence militates against the notion that history is a grand march toward civilization. As an expression of nonpreferential compassion, the duty not to harm insists on an account of the suffering, losses, and agony as an ingredient in any honest, sober narration. In its most radical version, this empathetic approach contends that the ideology of a "march toward civilization" is an argument from silence, the silence of those victims of historical struggle whose anguish is either unrecorded or only partially transcribed. The tropes of nonmaleficence remind us that historical records are not only selective but forever incomplete, that not all the data can or will be in, that the quiet victims of history have only fragmentary accounts and occasional representatives to testify on their behalf. Thus, nonmaleficence as a postethical claim requires suspicion about those accounts in which suffering is omitted, or repressed, or neglected. Like Niebuhr's notion of repentance in historical interpretations about war, such postethical claims require relentless self-criticism in *phronesis* understood as a historical, hermeneutical skill.

It is often stated that the just-war tradition furnishes a theory of statecraft, a basis for responsible political leadership.[38] But according to the argument developed here, just-war ideas constitute a theory of *limited* statecraft, one which requires us to resist the ideologies of historical progressivism and communal provincialism. Further, by this account, just-war criteria provide a *limited theory* of statecraft, for the duties themselves require supplementation by a theory of practical reasoning. Here I suggest that we might resist the pressures of progressivism and provincialism by drawing upon counterideological beliefs, like those implied by the duty not to harm and compassion for those who suffer. Such beliefs might function like what David Tracy calls an "interruption" in our stories and narratives, requiring us to pause and think self-critically about how we are reasoning practically about the events of war.[39] Such interruptions would enable us to expand our field of vision to include those forgotten victims of social conflict, the silent and the innocent whose travails comprise the underside of history.

Against Realism and Confessionalism

The view of practical reasoning developed above—as interpretive, historical, and dialectically related to postethical aspects of nonmaleficence—constitutes a middle way between two reigning approaches to practical reasoning in ethics today.

At one extreme is the approach of "realism." Realism typically refers to necessities in human experience—those stubborn facts, in the words of Reinhold Niebuhr, "which offer resistance to universally valid ideals and norms."[40] Niebuhr's special brand of theological anthropology led him to conceive of human egoism as the chief necessity for realistic thinking. Yet other necessities can also be candidates for a realistic practical reasoning about war, e.g., the "unforgettability" of nuclear physics, the unique destructive capacities of nuclear weapons, the intractability of the current sovereign states system, and the recurrence of war in human history, to name a few. Reference to such necessities is meant to keep ethical inquiry "out of the clouds," introducing a set of moorings to which ethical discourse must be soberly, if reluctantly, tied.

Necessities, then, are both amoral and moral, at least as these terms are broadly understood. They are amoral in that they must be taken as self-evident "givens," forces over which we have little or no control. Necessities have a surdlike character; as nonmoral facts, they are not subject to change under the power of individual or collective agency. Thus, necessities are amoral in the sense that no one can now be praised or blamed for them; as recalcitrant to human agency, necessities often stand outside the conditions of moral accountability. Yet necessities are moral in the sense that, without reference to them, an ethical verdict seems unbalanced and impractical. Failure to account for relevant necessities seems to absent our moral verdicts from the domain of common human experience; as a result, we sound naive, or platitudinous, or irresponsible. From a realistic perspective, then, it is normative that our normative discourse be adjusted to the facts of human necessity. Realists insist that we establish, to paraphrase Niebuhr, the most tolerable form of peace and justice under conditions set by necessity.[41]

One problem with contemporary versions of realism—why they depart from the account of *phronesis* I developed above—is that they convey confidence that necessities are transparently obvious, that the facts of experience are hermeneutically bare. Ironically, when contemporary realists presume direct access to stubborn facts of experience, they actually depart from a fundamental tenet of Niebuhrian realism: Niebuhr insisted that reference to human egoism be mediated by symbols which illumine the data of experience. Hermeneutical transparency about necessities is beguiling, for it suggests that practical reasoning may proceed independently of narratives, or history, or moral assumptions which condition our perceptions and judgments about necessities.

The problems surrounding this realist theory of self-evident necessities can be illustrated by returning to the work of William O'Brien. As I pointed out in the last chapter, O'Brien has sought to wed Catholic natural law teaching, especially just-war tenets, to the exigencies of modern war and statecraft. One goal is to integrate realistic necessities into natural law morality. According to O'Brien's realism, there are two stubborn facts about statecraft today: The present international order of sovereign states is unlikely to change soon, and war will remain a recurrent feature of human experience.[42] Proposals for world government and plans to eliminate war from political affairs are irresponsibly optimistic, lacking a sober sense of the stubborn necessities of experience.

Such a concern for realism means that natural law morality, and just-war criteria in particular, must be adjusted to meet the cultural attitudes and material facts of the day.[43] As we have seen, O'Brien's notion of comparative justice, distinguishing the moral qualities of polities in the ethics of war, turns on some judgments about political differences between East and West. Given such differences between the superpowers, O'Brien holds, we cannot realistically ignore the dangers of totalitarian rule. Thus, for reasons of realism, it is imperative to integrate an account of comparative justice into the structure of the *jus ad bellum*.

Moreover, for reasons of realism O'Brien dismisses a strict application of the principle of discrimination, preferring to "balance" this principle with considerations about military effectiveness in war. A strict application of noncombatant immunity in military policy would prohibit virtually all forms of modern warfare, leaving moral nations helpless against implacable adversaries. If the principle of discrimination is to have any continuing relevance to responsible military and political commanders, it must be modified and reinterpreted according to the capabilities of warring parties today. Thus, O'Brien construes discrimination "as a relative principle," ranked beneath proportionality in *in bello* criteria.[44]

In both of these instances—the insistence upon comparative justice, and the ranking of *in bello* criteria—realism places restrictions on what might be expected in the ethics of war, setting boundaries for ethical judgment. To extend morality beyond the limits set by realism—to expect ideological adversaries to overcome their differences, to end war, or to adhere strictly to *in bello* restrictions in war—is, by this account, patently delusory. Necessities come first, putting up fences, defining the territory for moral expectations about human conduct.

But when O'Brien embarks upon some concrete recommendations of his own, he fails to abide by this account of the relation between necessity and morality. Discussing the ethics of war and deterrence, for example, he calls for a shift from massive retaliation to a counterforce strategy in United States military planning. He acknowledges that such a shift would entail some risky initiatives, since the present world order is premised on a series of countervalue threats, which have established some measure of international stability. Shifts from countervalue to counterforce planning may destabilize relations between the United States and the Soviet Union, thus jeopardizing the present but fragile peace between the superpowers.[45]

O'Brien seeks to deflect this problem by arguing that changes to counterforce procedures may actually be more stabilizing than they first appear, since they rest on a stronger "moral foundation" than that provided by massive retaliation. As O'Brien states, "We must have a morally acceptable deterrence posture in order to pursue arms control with confidence." A morally tenable nuclear deterrent will furnish some assurance for further arms control negotiations, in contrast to the present deterrent system, which "we increasingly agitate to have it condemned as immoral."[46] The implication, although O'Brien fails to notice it, is that policy planners are not bound by the necessities characteristic of the present international order. Morally tenable policies may provide the leverage necessary to move international relations to a stronger foundation. In his mind, shifts to counterforce planning provide that moral leverage, freeing us from the instabilities of the present fragile peace.

In order for O'Brien to make this claim, however, he must alter his account of the relation between necessity and morality. He is now arguing not that moral options are restricted according to the facts of recent history or realistic necessities, but that moral proposals—as moral—can furnish the bedrock for revising strategic planning and altering the relations between the superpowers. The parameters of realism, the fences established by necessity, have been lifted momentarily for a moral foundation to be laid for future policy. No historical precedents, no supporting facts, no stubborn realities appear to supplement the case for counterforce targeting. The idea that counterforce targeting might be dangerous and idealistic is answered with reference to further moral ideals, not necessities. But if it is possible to lift such realistic restrictions, even momentarily, one wonders if it is not possible to recommend even more radical moral ventures, since morality can proceed somewhat independently of realistic restrictions. With the relation between morality and necessity reversed, it becomes possible to consider alternatives to arms control, including some forms of disarmament, since they too may provide a moral foundation. O'Brien fails to pursue such a trajectory, even if he has opened the door by shifting the relation between moral principles and necessity, allowing the former to proceed without initial restrictions provided by the latter.

This apparent reversal in O'Brien's method is less of a shift than an instance of phronetic reasoning. O'Brien does not pursue other possibilities, e.g., disarmament, because he is advancing a judgment about the wisdom of counterforce targeting as both right and good. Whether that judgment is sound or unsound is not the concern here; rather, my point is that realism belies him, and in belying him it uncovers the role played by nonrealistic factors in practical judgment. The argument for counterforce targeting relies on the application of just-war criteria to the use of nuclear weapons, leading to a condemnation of countercity targeting. It also relies on some predictions about the putative benefits for arms negotiations that derive from morally viable policies. In neither his case for counterforce strategy nor his prediction about negotiations can facts or necessities be cited as supporting reasons. Rather, O'Brien's shift, or judgment, indicates that reference to necessities as transparent data is untrue to *phronesis;* lurking not far behind, or within, those facts are more subtle preunderstandings and beliefs about the meaning of necessities and their role in moral discourse about war. In other words, he is engaging in practical reasoning as hermeneutical, where necessities and their relation to ethical norms must be interpreted, weighted, and mixed in a complex exercise. Necessity itself is not self-evident, nor does it define wholly the limits within which moral expectations operate.

At the other extreme from O'Brien in contemporary ethics is confessionalism. Confessionalists approach practical reasoning by insisting on the radical particularity of all knowledge. They thus deny the existence of a neutral, universal vantage point from which we can adjudicate our different judgments. This position, whose recent theological roots lie in the writings of Karl Barth and the H. Richard Niebuhr of *The Meaning of Revelation,* is developed most recently by the Christian pacifist John Howard Yoder. Yoder develops a "radical Protestant" account of practical reasoning, one which relies upon the "scribal memory" provided especially by the Bible, mixed patterns of ethical reasoning (relying on rules, virtue, and consequences), and conversation guided by various leaders in the community of Christian faith.[47]

This "communal hermeneutic" draws on a conception of the church as a community of moral discourse and stresses tradition as a source of moral wisdom. Indeed, *all* practical reasoning—Christian and non-Christian—is limited in its perspective by community and tradition. Tradition or religious confession, not necessity, puts up fences within which perceptions are nourished, character is formed, and notions of realism are defined. Thus, the most we should hope for in practical reasoning and public debate, Yoder states, is "to translate and to work at a reciprocal adjudication of the varieties both of perception and of evaluation, where one provincial vision clashes and overlaps with another. . . . By 'overlap' I mean that two provincial visions are dealing with the same subject matter of bringing people into common enterprises."[48] We have, then, not a common language, but coinciding commitments from different starting points. Without sacrificing our identity, Yoder suggests, we might be able to chart out those areas where our visions overlap with those of others.

Excluded from this approach is the belief that there is a common substantive and epistemological basis for moral debate, like that found in a theory of the natural law. One error in natural law ethics, Yoder asserts, "is that the dominant moral views of any *known* world are oppressive, provincial, or (to say it theologically) 'fallen.' . . . There is no 'public' that is not just another particular province."[49] Moreover, according to Yoder, the traditional notion of natural law "was *not* the modern one of knowing how to talk with outsiders." Rather, "natural law was developed in a world where there were no non-Christians present in the neighborhood, and no non-theists in the known world needing to be convinced."[50] Rather, says Yoder, reference to the natural law served the purpose of distinguishing those elements of guidance in Scripture that everyone must obey from those elements which can be left to Jews. By this reading, then, "the appeal to 'nature' was an instrument of *less* rather than *more* commonality with non-Christians."[51]

With reference to my concern here, practical reasoning, it may be that Yoder's theological conviction that the public is fallen proves too much for his argument. For if the public is indeed fallen, then there seems to be little gained by conversing—in "overlap" and "conflict"—with members of other provinces. Indeed, given Yoder's notion of the public, it is difficult to imagine what "bringing people into common enterprises" might mean. It would rather make sense to eschew contact as much as possible, to reduce implication in the fallenness of another's enterprises, to move in Mara's and O'Brien's direction by distinguishing between relatively good and evil provinces.

Even more problematic for Yoder, however, is that his rejection of the public undermines the conditions for conversation itself. In order for conversation to occur, there must be some transprovincial agreements about how a conversation may proceed. There must be some means by which "the common" can be identified in those "common enterprises" held up by Yoder as the goal of moral discourse. Minimally, there must be a willingness to listen, a respect for otherness, a commitment to clarity and coherence, a loyalty to intelligibility, a vulnerability to criticism, an openness to revising our points of view. As Tracy has argued, conversation has generic rules: "Say only what you mean; say it as accurately as you can; listen to and respect what the other says, however different or other; be willing to correct or defend your opinions if challenged by the conversation partner; be willing to argue if necessary, to confront if demanded, to endure necessary conflict, to change your mind if the evidence suggests it."[52] These are indeed "public" criteria, not provincial ones, providing rules for the game of dialogue. But if, as Yoder alleges, these criteria—as *public* criteria—are "fallen," then the prospect of conversation may lie beyond his theological grasp. We would do better, from Yoder's theological judgment, not to overlap with others who are different, but to champion the beliefs that make us different. But once we do so, we have given up the idea that differences are to be translated and adjudicated, that there are judgments to contest, that ethics is anything more than confident testimony. We thus gainsay the requirements of *phronesis,* understood in terms of cultural memory chastened by the convictions that cruelty is full of horror and grief, that compassion is owed to those who suffer, and that conversation with an other might broaden our moral and cultural horizons.

Practical reasoning as I have described it seeks to avoid those realist approaches according to which access to facts proceeds in the absence of interpretive devices, and those confessional approaches which stress the importance of religious faith at the expense of any publicly accessible phenomena, open to conversation and debate. In contrast to realism, reference to narrative and memory presupposes that facts must be interpreted. However much the necessities of experience may limit moral expectations, reference to necessity depends on memory, narrative, and judgment to infuse such facts with meaning and moral import. In contrast to confessionalism, *phronesis* demands attention to the particulars of experience, the facts of the case, within an overall framework defined by the requirements of conversation. Even though memory and narrative provide limited, particular frameworks for interpretation, reliance on postethical implications of nonmaleficence protects our particular interpretations from the provincialism implied by confessionalism. It thus requires us to remain open to the notion that knowledge is gained in conversation with others, that through such conversation we can expand our moral horizons beyond the convenient boundaries of province and belief. Interpretation and memory, in dialectical relation with the tropes of nonmaleficence, may achieve the goal sought by Yoder (and others): practical reasoning within the tensions of commonality and differences. But it relies on terms more interpretive and more public than O'Brien and Yoder, respectively, permit.

Can Pacifists and Just-War Theorists Tell a Just War?

To approach the problem of practical reasoning in war, duties and virtues really need each other. The duty of nonmaleficence needs the virtue of *phronesis* to assist in the move from principle to judgment. In turn, practical reasoning needs the notion of nonmaleficence as nonpreferential compassion and respect for others. Seen in this way, nonmaleficence requires us to withstand the pressures of progressivism and provincialism in our historically implicated *phronesis*. We may confront the *aporias* posed by practical reason, then, where duty and virtue are brought together in a critical, dialectical relation.

Like Ramsey's use of *agape* in his ethics of war, here the notion of nonmaleficence forms the bedrock of moral grammar about war and peace. But nonmaleficence is both more and less ambitious as a basis for moral discourse about war than Ramsey's notion of *agape*. It is less ambitious because, unlike the notion of *agape,* nonmaleficence does not furnish the basis for either the *jus ad bellum* or the *jus in bello*. Ramsey develops his account of just-war ideas under the sovereign aegis of care and protection, viewing the use of force as an exercise, not a compromise, of disinterested love. By my account, a rationale for violence must *overcome* the presumptions established by the duty not to harm. Nonmaleficence is less ambitious than *agape* because the justification of war must hurdle over the obstacles presumed in the duty not to harm. Those hurdles are not general principles applied directly, in a downward linear fashion, to the case of war. Instead, just-war ideas developed along the lines of nonmaleficence presume a conflict of duties as structuring moral discourse about war, and the requirements implied by nonmaleficence place pressure on the subsequent course of action. According to the ideas presented in these pages, grammar about the morality of war must be structured conflictually, to capture, however fragmentarily, some notions about the phenomenon of violence itself.

Yet nonmaleficence in the discourse about war is more ambitious than Ramsey's notion of *agape,* because it carries within it resources for mediating from principle to judgment about the morality of wars, enabling us to withstand the forces which imperil his casuistry of war and deterrence. As I have argued above, that mediation requires us to supplement the duty of nonmaleficence with an account of *phronesis* as interpretive and historical. This supplementation in turn requires us self-critically to recall the implications of nonmaleficence as nonpreferential compassion, respect for others, and intolerance of cruelty. Out of this dialectical relation between duty and virtue, pacifists and just-war theorists can proceed in the common venture of interpreting and evaluating the conflicts of history.

This venture, as I have described it, requires moral inquiry to proceed not beyond ambiguity, but within it. The moral ambiguities of war are interpreted and assessed within an epistemological framework informed by narratives and memories; the ambiguities of those narratives and memories, in turn, are held in critical check by the "interruptions" implied by the postethical tropes of nonmaleficence. Such tropes, moreover, draw from within the idiom of Western ethics, not from without. To resist the pressures of ideology, then, the grammar of counterideology can be found intertextually, from within interpretations of our moral grammar about war. Interpretation and social criticism need not eschew the language, the history, or the place of their origin. Instead, we need to understand our moral vocabularies and their implications, drawing new wine from old wineskins. In so doing we might quench the thirst of those committed to *phronesis,* pacifists and just-war theorists alike.

Epilogue: Pluralism and Irony

Throughout this book I have sought to join two rival vocabularies about the ethics of war by developing a dialogue between them. That dialogue has ranged over a common set of values, problems, or interests: the duty of nonmaleficence, the relation of justice and order, the ethics of civil disobedience, the suggestive tensions between pacifism and just-war tenets, the problem of self-righteousness in moral discourse about war, the ethics of nuclear deterrence, and the problems surrounding ideology and public discourse. If the book has been successful, then worries about "overcoming pluralism"—like those expressed by Mannheim (in the Introduction), but felt more keenly by theologians, philosophers, and social critics today—ought to be of little interest unless we have some detailed information about the rival vocabularies in question.

That information, if we are to be properly informed, must include an analysis of levels of moral discourse. Distinguishing between such levels illumines those points at which moral convergence and disagreement are meaningful, furnishing tools for discerning how a conversation between traditions might proceed. We should also become aware of how religious and secular sources have informed our rival vocabularies, so that we understand how those vocabularies, along with their terms and assumptions, relate to those of the past. Further, we should be shown how other related issues "fan out" from the central problem under review, since few if any ethical problems stand wholly in isolation. Finally, we will need some technical knowledge about those issues under review: scientific, social-scientific, and historical information, for seldom do ethical questions remain in an ethical vacuum. If this analysis of pacifism and just-war tenets has shown us anything, it should be that addressing pluralism in detail requires a wide range of social-scientific, factual, theological, literary, and philosophical tools.

If I am correct about how a dialogue between rival moral vocabularies might proceed, anxiety about pluralism in the abstract is likely to become irrelevant, or at best "merely academic." As an alternative, proceeding down the low road in ethics may point us toward new meanings in our moral vocabularies, leading us out of pluralism as a reified problem back into the thicket of moral analysis and debate. Whether a path toward new meanings can be traced in other areas of ethics today—in, say, debates about abortion, or affirmative action, or conflicts of interest—lies beyond my vista. We will see only once we try. Only after we have engaged in the long and laborious task of examining topics along the low road of ethics will the time have come to ask what "pluralism" might actually be, what sort of questions and problems we ought to have in mind when theorizing about the problem of pluralism in religion and culture today.

As a study of moral pluralism, this has also been a book written in what Rorty has called an "ironist" style. Ironists, Rorty notes, have continuing doubts about their moral vocabularies because they are impressed by rival vocabularies provided by a culture of moral pluralism. But rather than whimsically running to the other side or building up the fortress walls, ironists "play off vocabularies against one another," using different self-descriptions and alternative idioms to clarify their own.[1] Ironists, Rorty suggests, are the dialecticians of postmodernity. They respect their close rivals because they see that neither they nor their rivals have a corner on the ethical market. Ironists recognize that moral ambiguity is synonymous with moral complexity, not lack of moral resolve. Perhaps we can learn more about our own grammar, refine our resolve, by sharpening our vocabularies in dialectical interchange. In any event, such an interchange between pacifism and the just-war tradition requires a measured dose of Rorty's ironism if conversation is to proceed, if each side is to be impressed by its alternative.

Ironism of the sort I have provided in these pages requires us to converse with an "other," an alternative idiom. The hope is that we might then be able to redescribe the meaning of and limits to the vocabulary we embrace in the ethics of war, that we might expand our conceptual horizons once we encounter an adversarial voice. Encountering a grammatical other, engaging in direct dialogue, is certainly not new, but it is the only recourse for those who eschew the temptation to find some point of view neutral to the rivals in question.

But more to the point, if we can respect others in the relatively tame confines of intellectual inquiry, perhaps we can respect them in person as well. Success in doing so, ironically enough, might mean fewer occasions in which conflicts and their interpretations—political or military conflicts, not just conceptual ones—would be necessary. I would like to think that such an irony would be welcome. For we should be concerned not only about pluralism, but also about overcoming otherness, in our ethical inquiry today. An ethical style suited to such problems lies before us, a step toward which I hope to have provided here.

Notes

Introduction

1. Karl Mannheim, *Ideology and Utopia: An Introduction to the Sociology of Knowledge,* trans. Louis Wirth and Edward Shils (New York: Harcourt Brace Jovanovich, 1936), p. 9.

2. Ibid., p. 6.

3. Thomas Aquinas, *Summa Theologiae,* I-II, Q. 94, A. 2.

4. See John Rawls, *A Theory of Justice* (Cambridge: Harvard University Press, 1971); Alan Gewirth, *Reason and Morality* (Chicago: University of Chicago Press, 1978); Ronald M. Green, *Religious Reason: The Rational and Moral Basis of Religious Belief* (New York: Oxford University Press, 1978). In continental philosophy this path is associated largely with the work of Jürgen Habermas. For an instructive study, see Raymond Geuss, *The Idea of a Critical Theory: Habermas and the Frankfurt School* (Cambridge: Cambridge University Press, 1981), esp. pp. 64–75. See also Karl-Otto Apel, "The Common Presuppositions of Hermeneutics and Ethics: Types of Rationality beyond Science and Technology," *Research in Phenomenology* 9 (1979): 35–53.

5. See, for example, Alasdair MacIntyre, *Whose Justice? Which Rationality?* (Notre Dame, Ind.: University of Notre Dame Press, 1988); Richard Bernstein, *Beyond Objectivism and Relativism: Science, Hermeneutics, and Praxis* (Philadelphia: University of Pennsylvania Press, 1983), pp. 16–20.

6. See, for example, Stanley Hauerwas, *The Peaceable Kingdom: A Primer in Christian Ethics* (Notre Dame, Ind.: University of Notre Dame Press, 1983); John Howard Yoder, *The Priestly Kingdom: Social Ethics as Gospel* (Notre Dame, Ind. University of Notre Dame Press, 1984).

7. David Burrell, "Theology and the Linguistic Turn," *Communio* 6 (Spring 1979): 98.

8. Michael Walzer, *Interpretation and Social Criticism* (Cambridge: Harvard University Press, 1987).

9. James F. Childress, "Just-War Criteria," in *War or Peace? The Search for New Answers,* ed. Thomas A. Shannon (Maryknoll, N.Y.: Orbis Books, 1980), pp. 40–58.

10. MacIntyre, *Whose Justice? Which Rationality?* p. 398 (see n. 5).

11. My treatment of just-war tenets and pacifism in terms of convergence-and-difference is friendly to more theoretical uses of analogy in recent discussions of language and theology. Yet proceeding along the low road of ethics requires greater attention to specific moral vocabularies than is characteristic of such theoretical inquiries. A more abstract approach than the one I develop in this book is provided by David Tracy in *The Analogical Imagination: Christian*

Theology and the Culture of Pluralism (New York: Seabury Press, 1981) and *Plurality and Ambiguity: Hermeneutics, Religion, Hope* (San Francisco: Harper & Row, 1987).

12. See Jenny Teichman, *Pacifism and the Just War: A Study in Applied Philosophy* (Oxford: Basil Blackwell, 1986), pp. 4–5.

13. See, for example, LeRoy Walters, "Five Classic Just-War Theories: A Study in the Thought of Thomas Aquinas, Vitoria, Suarez, Gentili, and Grotius" (Ph.D. diss., Yale University, 1971); Frederick H. Russell, *The Just War in the Middle Ages* (Cambridge: Cambridge University Press, 1975); James Turner Johnson, *Just War Tradition and the Restraint of War: A Moral and Historical Inquiry* (Princeton, N.J.: Princeton University Press, 1981); Lisa Sowle Cahill, "Nonresistance, Defense, Violence, and the Kingdom in Christian Tradition," *Interpretation* 38 (October 1984): 380–97.

14. In explicating these just-war criteria, I am indebted to the U.S. Catholic Bishops, *The Challenge of Peace: God's Promise and Our Response* (Washington, D.C.: United States Catholic Conference, 1983), pars. 85–110.

15. *The Pastoral Constitution on the Church in the Modern World,* in *Renewing the Earth: Catholic Documents on Peace, Justice and Liberation,* ed. David J. O'Brien and Thomas A. Shannon (Garden City, N.Y.: Image Books/Doubleday, 1977), par. 80.

Chapter 1

1. For an eloquent discussion of the relation between injury and war, see Elaine Scarry, *The Body in Pain: The Making and Unmaking of the World* (New York: Oxford University Press, 1985), pp. 60–81 and passim. As the forthcoming analysis will show, problems surrounding injury are morally relevant not only to war, but also to the ethics of individual self-defense and the defense of third parties by private individuals.

2. Childress, "Just-War Criteria," p. 42 (see Introduction, n. 9).

3. *The Westminster Dictionary of Christian Ethics,* 2d ed., s.v. "Conflict of Duties," by A. C. Ewing. For an extended account of presumptive duties in practical reasoning, see Albert R. Jonsen and Stephen Toulmin, *The Abuse of Casuistry: A History of Moral Reasoning* (Berkeley: University of California Press, 1988).

4. W. D. Ross, *Foundations of Ethics* (Oxford: Clarendon Press, 1939), p. 86. Elsewhere Childress amplifies the criteria, beyond nonmaleficence, in his ethical theory. See Thomas Beauchamp and James F. Childress, *Principles of Biomedical Ethics* (New York: Oxford University Press, 1983).

5. Childress, "Just-War Criteria," pp. 45–50.

6. I borrow this distinction from Rawls, *A Theory of Justice,* p. 388 (see Introduction, n. 4).

7. Childress, "Just-War Criteria," p. 40.

8. Augustine, "Letter 47, to Publicola," in *A Select Library of Nicene and Post-Nicene Fathers,* vol. 1, ed. Philip Schaff (Grand Rapids, Mich.: Eerdmans, 1956), p. 293. See also Augustine, *City of God,* trans. Henry Bettenson, with an introduction by David Knowles (New York: Penguin Books, 1972), bk. 1, pars. 21, 24.

9. Augustine, *City of God,* bk. 19, par. 14.

10. I will elaborate on this distinction between nonresistance and nonviolent resistance, along with other criteria for pacifism, in chapter 3.

11. Augustine, *On Christian Doctrine*, trans. and with an introduction by D. W. Robertson, Jr. (Indianapolis: Bobbs-Merrill, 1981), bk. 1, pars. 26–27.

12. Augustine, "De Libero Arbitrio," I, 5, in *Fathers of the Church*, vol. 39, trans. Robert P. Russell (Washington, D.C.: Catholic University of America Press, 1968), p. 82.

13. Ibid.

14. Augustine, "Reply to Faustus the Manichean," in *A Select Library of Nicene and Post-Nicene Fathers*, vol. 4, ed. Philip Schaff (Grand Rapids, Mich.: Eerdmans, 1956), p. 301.

15. Ibid.

16. Ibid.

17. Augustine, "De Libero Arbitrio," I, 5, p. 81; cf. *City of God*, bk. 1, par. 21. Augustine briefly and cryptically acknowledges a right to private self-defense in a letter written in 414, after he developed the main lines of his approach to "private" killing in his letter to Publicola and "De Libero Arbitrio." In a letter to the public official Macedonius, Augustine makes the following comment about killing in self-defense: "It makes a great difference when one man is killed by another, whether it happened through a desire of injuring him, or of carrying off something dishonestly, as it might be done by an enemy, a thief; or whether it happened in the course of inflicting punishment or carrying out an order, as by a judge, an executioner; or through self-defense or the rescue of another, as a thief is killed by a traveler or an enemy by a soldier."

Here Augustine seems to conceive of killing in private self-defense absent reference to the problem of inordinate attachment, contrary to his ethic of individual, nonresistant pacifism. Yet this exception points to other factors relevant to his reasoning about the ethics of killing, especially the importance of a well-ordered society in which offices exist for the protection of the innocent. Private self-defense is possible when public officials are not available, e.g., for a traveler attacked by a thief. Otherwise, private self-defense constitutes vigilantism. After the fall of Rome, Augustine may well have concluded that not all cases of private resistance can be considered with the assumption of public officials in the background. In any event, the exception to the duty of nonresistant pacifism—self-defense for those outside a hierarchically ordered society—actually proves the rule according to which Augustine approaches the ethics of killing. In the cases of private nonresistance and its exception, violence is considered in light of whether it will diminish a hierarchically established order. See Augustine, *Letters 131–164*, in *Fathers of the Church*, vol. 20, trans. Wilfrid Parsons (New York: Fathers of the Church, 1953), p. 294.

18. Augustine, "De Libero Arbitrio," I, 5, p. 81. As I shall argue more fully below, the presumption in favor of higher public authorities and the idea that those acting under their command are blameless seem strange in an age in which the scope of professional responsibility has broadened, especially because this presumption generates a strict duty of obedience. Would we not expect someone to break ranks from those who are commanded to carry out vicious acts? But given certain assumptions, Augustine's conviction that subordinates have a strict duty to obey their superiors might not seem so odd. For example, Augus-

tine could assume that if the duty to obey one's superiors is somehow left to individual discretion, we leave ourselves open to more danger than if we hold to a strict duty of obedience. Is it not likelier, he would ask, that unjust subordinates will break ranks and act on their own discretion when they view the duty of obedience as open to doubt rather than in strict, inflexible terms? And is this likelihood not greater than the prospect that unjust commanders will commission vicious acts? If so, then it is better, all things considered, to maintain a strict duty of obedience. Generally speaking, Augustine might say, we should worry less about maniacal leaders than about subordinates of lesser virtue, or vicious subordinates, who believe they know how and when to take justice into their own hands. The strict duty of obedience, then, is premised on the judgment that unjust leaders are less of a danger than the prospect of blind conviction or vigilantism at lower levels in the chain of command.

Those who quarrel with Augustine's notion of the strict duty to obey would thus have to do more than insist that he is a child of his age. Augustine's notion of the strict duty to obey can be seen as something other than an uncritical embrace of a presumption in favor of higher authority. Rather, one would have to argue that he is wrong in his judgment about what would happen if the duty to obey were somehow qualified. The argument would thus include the judgment that Augustine's fears are less likely to materialize in professional contexts in which individuals are granted a greater measure of autonomy. In other words, a rebuttal to Augustine would have to argue that granting greater autonomy to subordinates (in the context of very disciplined training) *decreases* the likelihood that they will have weak characters and become inclined to break ranks from a just commander according to their own individual discretion. Then it would be necessary to show that the balance of Augustine's position must shift, that we must view the dangers of unjust leaders as greater than the prospective dangers surrounding the acts of subordinates.

19. For a helpful discussion of these distinctions in early Christian discourse about war, see James F. Childress, "Moral Discourse about War in the Early Church," *Journal of Religious Ethics* 12 (Spring 1984): 2–18. Childress also notes the distinction between higher and lower, which led medieval theorists to prohibit members of religious vocations from committing acts of violence as part of a higher calling. Augustine holds that some biblical commands are meant for some vocations, leading to a prohibition of violence on the part of monks, religious clergy, and secular clergy. See Augustine, *On Christian Doctrine,* bk. 3, par. 17; cf. Thomas Aquinas, *Summa Theologiae,* Blackfriars edition (New York: McGraw-Hill, 1972), II-II, Q. 40, A. 2. (Unless otherwise noted, all references to the *Summa Theologiae* will be to the Blackfriars edition.) Useful discussions of Augustine and Aquinas include Roland Bainton, *Christian Attitudes toward War and Peace* (Nashville, Tenn.: Abingdon Press, 1960), pp. 91–98, 108; Cahill, "Nonresistance, Defense, Violence, and the Kingdom" (see Introduction, n. 13).

20. For a study of the medieval period, see Russell, *The Just War in the Middle Ages* (see Introduction, n. 13). Aquinas, as we shall see, draws on these three criteria to specify a just war. Following Augustine, Aquinas also bans the clergy from war. See Thomas Aquinas, *Summa Theologiae,* II-II, Q. 40, A. 2. Moreover, aspects of Augustine's influence are retained by Luther and Calvin.

Evidence in the former's works is found in *On Temporal Authority: To What Extent It Should Be Obeyed,* in *Luther's Works,* vol. 45, ed. Helmut T. Lehmann (Philadelphia: Fortress Press, 1962), and *Sermon on the Mount,* in *Luther's Works,* vol. 21, ed. Jaroslav Pelikan (St. Louis: Concordia Publishing House, 1967); evidence in the latter's works is found in *Institutes of the Christian Religion,* bk. 4, chap. 20.

21. Augustine, *City of God,* bk. 19, par. 13.

22. Ibid., par. 12.

23. Ibid., par. 13.

24. Ibid., par. 17.

25. Ibid., pars. 7, 12.

26. Augustine, "Reply to Faustus," p. 301 (see n. 14).

27. For a careful and accurate discussion of the punitive aspects of Augustine's notion of peace, see John Langan, "Elements of St. Augustine's Just War Theory," *Journal of Religious Ethics* 12 (Spring 1984): 19–39. It should be added, however, that punishment for Augustine is instrumental to the right ordering of relations.

28. Augustine, *City of God,* bk. 19, par. 7.

29. This interpretation of Augustine is meant to correct the view that he justifies war based on the requirements of love in third-party relations. According to such a view, Augustine's notion of charity requires the use of force to protect other individuals who may be victims of harm. Augustine thus seems to develop a paradigm from third-party relations for thinking about a just war as an exercise of charity. The problem with this view is that it suggests that Augustine seeks to authorize *private* individuals to jump to the defense of others. It thus overlooks Augustine's third set of distinctions for relativizing the force of nonmaleficence. James Turner Johnson seems to err in this direction, although in places he vacillates. Cf. James Turner Johnson, *Can Modern War Be Just?* (New Haven: Yale University Press, 1984), pp. 2–4, 19; *Just War Tradition and the Restraint of War,* p. 48 (see Introduction, n. 13).

30. Aquinas, *Summa Theologiae,* II-II, Q. 25, A. 1.

31. Ibid., Q. 26, A. 4.

32. Ibid., Q. 25, A. 8.

33. Ibid., Q. 64, A. 7, ad 1. Since grace does not destroy nature for Thomas, he can subsume the imperatives wrought from the natural law within his ordering of charity. For an excellent study of the way in which Aquinas incorporates the dictates of nature into his ordering of charity, see Stephen J. Pope, "The Moral Centrality of Natural Priorities: A Thomistic Alternative to 'Equal Regard,'" *Society of Christian Ethics Annual* (1990): 109–29.

34. Aquinas, *Summa Theologiae,* II-II, Q. 64, A. 7.

35. Ibid., Q. 40, A. 1.

36. Ibid., Q. 25, A. 6. Hence another, and perhaps more important, reason that Thomas prohibits intentional harm by private individuals: Such individuals are not authorized to pass judgments about the injustice of their opponents. And they lack authorization, Aquinas would add, because they cannot order their punitive responses to the common good. For the ethics of private self-defense, then, two implications of charity bear upon Aquinas's position: first, there is the commandment to love the neighbor, even the enemy; second, there is the duty to

order punitive judgments toward the common good, which is possible for public officials alone. For these reasons Aquinas is led to prohibit intentional harm in private self-defense.

I hasten to add that the difference between private killing and public killing should not be exaggerated. Although Aquinas proscribes intentional killing in the former case and allows (even requires) it in the latter case, he is worried that killing another individual, either privately or by public authority, will generate disordered passions. In this respect, despite the fact that he differs from Augustine on the issue of private self-defense, Thomas is similarly concerned about how one's character might be weakened or corrupted when one resorts to force. For Aquinas, the implications of charity are invoked to insure that justice does not curdle into a passion for vengeance.

Viewing Thomas's ethic in this way suggests that the implications of charity are invoked to guarantee that natural justice occurs. If the private individual or public official orders his actions along Thomas's lines, the belligerent will receive just desert. On the need for charity to restore us to our natural virtues, see Aquinas, *Summa Theologiae,* I-II, Q. 109, A. 2.

37. Few interpreters of Thomas have recognized the parallels between his account of self-defense and his restrictions on the intention of the competent authority in war. One exception to this trend is John Finnis, Joseph Boyle, and Germain Grisez, *Nuclear Deterrence, Morality and Realism* (New York: Oxford University Press, 1987), pp. 313–14. Yet as Finnis et al. observe, they argue more restrictively than Thomas by insisting that "military action must be directed toward stopping the enemy's unjust use of force, not toward killing those who are bringing that force to bear. By requiring that the death of an enemy soldier be brought about only as a side effect of a military act having a different appropriate object, our moral theory would limit warfare as stringently as possible to the pursuit of the good purposes which can justify it." See Finnis et al., *Nuclear Deterrence, Morality and Realism,* p. 315.

38. Paul Tillich, *The Protestant Era* (Chicago: University of Chicago Press, 1948), pp. 162–63.

39. Calhoun Commission, "The Relation of the Church to the War in the Light of the Christian Faith," *Social Action Magazine* 2 (December 1944): 3–79.

40. Ibid., p. 3.

41. Ibid., p. 8.

42. James M. Gustafson, *Protestant and Roman Catholic Ethics: Prospects for Rapprochement* (Chicago: University of Chicago Press, 1978), p. 40.

43. H. Richard Niebuhr, *The Meaning of Revelation* (New York: Macmillan, 1941), pp. 44–54.

44. Calhoun Commission, "The Relation of the Church to the War," p. 29.

45. Ibid., pp. 32, 36.

46. Ibid., p. 35.

47. Ibid., p. 34.

48. Ibid., p. 40.

49. Ibid., p. 39.

50. Ibid., pp. 38–39.

51. Ibid., pp. 13–14.

52. Ibid., p. 45.

53. Bainton, *Christian Attitudes toward War and Peace* (see n. 19).

54. Calhoun Commission, "The Relation of the Church to the War," p. 63.

55. Karl Barth, *Church Dogmatics*, III/4, trans. A. T. MacKay et al. (Edinburgh: T. & T. Clark, 1961), pp. 397–470.

56. Ibid., p. 430.

57. Ibid., p. 431.

58. Ibid., p. 432.

59. Ibid.

60. Ibid., p. 435.

61. Ibid., p. 454.

62. Ibid., p. 453.

63. Ibid., p. 451.

64. Ibid., pp. 454, 456.

65. Ibid., pp. 458–59.

66. See Michael Walzer, *Just and Unjust Wars: A Moral Argument with Historical Illustrations* (New York: Basic Books, 1977), pp. 251–68.

67. Barth, *Church Dogmatics*, III/4, p. 461.

68. Ibid.

69. Ibid., p. 462.

70. Ibid., p. 463.

71. Ibid.

72. U.S. Catholic Bishops, *The Challenge of Peace*, par. 74 (see Introduction, n. 14).

73. Ibid., par. 121.

74. Ibid., par. 70; see also pars. 80, 83, 93, 120–21.

75. Ibid., par. 83, emphasis in original.

76. Ibid., par. 222.

77. *Pastoral Constitution*, par. 78 (see Introduction, n. 15), cited in U.S. Catholic Bishops, *The Challenge of Peace*, par. 222.

78. U.S. Catholic Bishops, *The Challenge of Peace*, pars. 221–30.

79. I will develop some inferences about the rights and limits of pacifism in Catholic teaching about war in chapter 3.

80. David Hollenbach, *Nuclear Ethics: A Christian Moral Argument* (New York: Paulist Press, 1983), p. 37.

81. Ibid., p. 31.

82. Ibid., p. 33.

83. Ibid., p. 32.

84. Ibid., p. 38.

85. James Douglass, *The Non-Violent Cross: A Theology of Revolution and Peace* (New York: Macmillan, 1966), pp. 171–81; cf. Robert L. Holmes, *On War and Morality* (Princeton, N.J.: Princeton University Press, 1989).

86. Hollenbach, *Nuclear Ethics*, pp. 47–62.

87. United Methodist Council of Bishops, *In Defense of Creation: The Nuclear Crisis and a Just Peace* (Nashville, Tenn.: Graded Press, 1986), p. 13.

88. For a discussion of the Methodist letter, see J. Philip Wogaman and Paul Ramsey, "Two Reflections on *In Defense of Creation*," *Circuit Rider* 10 (September 1986): 8–10. Instructive responses to Wogaman and Ramsey are found in *Circuit Rider* 11 (January 1987): 19–22.

89. Henry David Aiken, *Reason and Conduct: New Bearings in Moral Philosophy* (New York: Alfred A. Knopf, 1962), chap. 4.

90. Ibid., p. 68.

91. Ibid., p. 70.

92. Ibid., p. 74.

93. Ibid., p. 80. Not only do ethicists tend to move back and forth between levels in the course of constructing an argument, they also tend to use *moral* and *ethical* interchangeably to designate ways of justifying or evaluating human behavior. This book will be no exception, although in this section I will adhere strictly to Aiken's distinction between moral and ethical levels of discourse to clarify how pacifism and just-war tenets overlap and diverge.

94. In theory at least, a pacifist may hold that nonmaleficence is a prima facie duty but that the duty to protect oneself or others with lethal force is an insufficient basis for overriding the presumptive duty not to harm. Such a view would prohibit us from "trumping" the duty not to harm with rival duties which allow the use of lethal force. This would produce a pacifism which is based (in theory) on nonmaleficence as a prima facie duty and (in fact) on nonmaleficence as an absolute duty.

95. Phillipa Foot, *Virtues and Vices and Other Essays in Moral Philosophy* (Berkeley: University of California Press, 1978), chap. 2.

96. *The Encyclopedia of Bioethics,* 1st ed., s.v. "Death and Dying: Euthanasia and Sustaining Life: Ethical Views," by Sissela Bok.

97. Aiken, *Reason and Conduct,* pp. 86–87.

98. For a discussion of "common sense" as that which founds a community, see Hans-Georg Gadamer, *Truth and Method* (New York: Seabury, 1975), pp. 19–29.

99. Childress, "Just-War Criteria," p. 43.

100. Alan Gewirth, *Human Rights: Essays on Justification and Applications* (Chicago: University of Chicago Press, 1982), p. 13.

101. Ibid., pp. 13–14.

102. Henry B. Veatch, *Human Rights: Fact or Fancy?* (Baton Rouge: Louisiana State University Press, 1985), pp. 163–64.

103. Ibid., p. 166.

104. Richard Rorty, *Contingency, Irony, and Solidarity* (Cambridge: Cambridge University Press, 1989), pp. 33–35.

105. Ibid., pp. 91, 146; emphasis in original.

106. Ibid., p. 177.

107. Ibid., p. 75.

108. David H. Smith, *Health and Medicine in the Anglican Tradition* (New York: Seabury Press, 1986), p. 6.

109. Rawls, *A Theory of Justice,* p. 18 (see Introduction, n. 4).

110. Søren Kierkegaard, *The Present Age,* trans. Alexander Dru with an introduction by Walter Kaufmann (New York: Harper & Row, 1962), pp. 51–59.

111. Determining whether the duty not to harm in a nonpreferential sense has resonances in other vocabularies lies beyond my objectives here. Doubtless my discussion of this bias against harm as a postethical value is confined to Western values and moral vocabularies. For this reason my account may suffer the charge of ethnocentrism. But as Rorty remarks, what takes the edge off this charge is

that intolerance toward cruelty is part of a culture committed to enlarging itself, "to creating an even larger and more variegated *ethnos*." An expansive, non-preferential horror toward cruelty, in short, is part of the legacy of "the people who have been brought up to distrust ethnocentrism," residing in a province seeking to resist provincialism. See Rorty, *Contingency, Irony, and Solidarity*, p. 198.

112. By "those who are innocent of aggression" I mean those who are not materially cooperating in the war effort.

113. For a helpful account of conscientious objection and law, see Peter Brock, *Twentieth Century Pacifism* (New York: Van Nostrand Reinhold, 1970), pp. 105–13, 171–205, 255–60. For a discussion of legislation in the United States, see Eileen P. Flynn, *My Country Right or Wrong? Selective Conscientious Objection in the Nuclear Age* (Chicago: Loyola University Press, 1985), chap. 2. As Flynn points out, until 1965 it was difficult for those who were not members of historic peace churches to acquire status as conscientious objectors in the United States. After "nonreligious" pacifists were deemed acceptable in 1965, they were nonetheless required to show a level of conviction comparable to belief in some Supreme Being.

Chapter 2

1. See, for example, Paul Ramsey, *War and the Christian Conscience* (Durham, N.C.: Duke University Press, 1961), pp. 39–45.

2. For a survey of medieval and postmedieval theories of tyrannicide, see Oscar Jaszi and John Lewis, *Against the Tyrant: The Tradition and Theory of Tyrannicide* (Glencoe, Ill.: Free Press, 1957). For a discussion of Aquinas and political science, see Walter Ullmann, *A History of Political Thought in the Middle Ages* (Middlesex, England: Penguin Books, 1965), pp. 174–84; R. W. Carlyle and A. J. Carlyle, *A History of Medieval Political Theory in the West*, vol. 5 (London: William Blackwood & Sons, 1928).

3. Aquinas, *Summa Theologiae*, I-II, Qq. 90–97. For Thomas on the best form of rule, compare *Summa Theologiae*, I-II, Q. 105, A. 1, with Thomas Aquinas, *On Princely Government*, chap. 2, in *Aquinas: Selected Political Writings*, trans. J. G. Dawson, ed. and with an introduction by A. P. D'Entreves (Oxford: Basil Blackwell, 1970). In the former, Thomas commends a mixed form of government, while in the latter he commends monarchy as the best form of rule. Since the former appears in the context of Thomas's discussion of the rule of the Israelites, it seems fair to conclude that this commendation of monarchy is his own position.

4. Aquinas, *On Princely Government*, chap. 1, in *Aquinas*, ed. D'Entreves, p. 3.

5. Aquinas, *Summa Theologiae*, I-II, Q. 90, A. 4.

6. Ibid., Q. 91, A. 3; Q. 94, A. 2.

7. Thomas Aquinas, *Summa Contra Gentiles*, III: 64, in *The Basic Writings of Thomas Aquinas*, vol. 2, ed. and with an introduction by Anton C. Pegis (New York: Random House, 1945); see also Aquinas, *Summa Theologiae*, I-II, Q. 103, A. 3.

8. Aquinas, *Summa Theologiae*, III, Q. 8, A. 3.

9. See Ernst H. Kantorowicz, *The King's Two Bodies: A Study in Mediaeval Political Theology* (Princeton, N.J.: Princeton University Press, 1957).

10. Aquinas, *Summa Theologiae*, I-II, Q. 96, A. 5.

11. Ibid., Q. 90, A. 1.

12. Charles Howard McIlwain, *The Growth of Political Thought in the West: From the Greeks to the End of the Middle Ages* (New York: Macmillan, 1932), pp. 330–31.

13. For a chronology and catalog of Aquinas's works, see James A. Weisheipl, *Friar Thomas D'Aquino: His Life, Thought, and Work* (Garden City, N.Y.: Doubleday, 1974), pp. 351–405.

14. Thomas Aquinas, *Commentary on the Sentences of Peter Lombard*, in *Aquinas*, ed. D'Entreves, p. 185.

15. Ibid., pp. 183–85.

16. Aquinas, *On Princely Government*, chap. 3, in *Aquinas*, ed. D'Entreves, p. 15.

17. Ibid., chap. 6, p. 29.

18. Ibid., p. 31.

19. Ibid., pp. 31–33.

20. See, for example, Bainton, *Christian Attitudes toward War and Peace*, pp. 108–9 (see chap. 1, n. 19); Jaszi and Lewis, *Against the Tyrant*, pp. 26–27; Wilfrid Parsons, "The Medieval Theory of the Tyrant," *Review of Politics* 4 (1942): 141; Dino Bigongiari, "Introduction," in *The Political Ideas of St. Thomas Aquinas*, ed. Bigongiari (New York: Hafner, 1953), pp. xxxi–xxxiii; Carlyle and Carlyle, *Medieval Political Theory in the West*, pp. 90–96.

21. These are the years during which Aquinas wrote the *secunda pars* of the *Summa Theologiae*. See Weisheipl, *Friar Thomas D'Aquino*, p. 361.

22. Aquinas, *Summa Theologiae*, II-II, Q. 42, A. 2.

23. Aquinas, *Summa Theologiae*, I-II, Q. 96, A. 4. The Latin reads, "Et huiusmodi magis sunt violentiae quam leges," which loses its force when translated, as it is in the Blackfriars edition, "These are outrages rather than laws." That Thomas construes unjust laws as acts of violence will become important when we turn to civil war in the modern paradigm.

24. Aquinas, *Summa Theologiae*, II-II, Q. 42, A. 2 (my translation); cf. *Summa Theologiae*, II-II, Q. 108, A. 1, ad 5. Thomas does not provide an exact formula for determining when one might be justified in charging a sovereign with sedition. Such a judgment would rely on the circumstances, interpreted in light of prudence, or practical reason.

25. Aquinas, *Summa Theologiae*, II-II, Q. 42, A. 1. Thomas's views were developed against the backdrop of thirteenth-century Italy, whose city-states were prone to fierce internal turmoil. For an overview, see J. R. Tanner, C. W. Previte, and Z. N. Brooke, eds., *The Cambridge Medieval History*, vol. 6 (Cambridge: Cambridge University Press, 1936), chaps. 6–7.

26. See, for example, Ewart Lewis, *Medieval Political Ideas*, vol. 1 (New York: Alfred A. Knopf, 1954), p. 249; Jaszi and Lewis, *Against the Tyrant*, p. 27.

27. Aquinas, *Summa Theologiae*, I-II, Q. 96, A. 4 (my translation). In perfect circumstances, of course, justice and order must coincide. But Thomas assumes that in the historical order political life is less than perfect, that life in the community is characterized by a set of moral trade-offs. A theological explanation would hold that the lack of harmony between justice and order is a fruit of sin. Sin vitiates neither the prospect of justice nor that of order; rather, it means

that one value might be more easily achievable than the other. It also means that there may be varying degrees of deficiency of each at different points in time. This theological explanation allows for a view of history as the arena of moral complexity and ambiguous moral options, although such a view is not exclusive to a theology of history.

Combined with my discussion of Aquinas in chap. 1, the idea that we must interpret Aquinas's ethic in light of the condition of fallenness is meant to underscore the importance of theology in his thinking about justice, war, and killing. Over and against neoscholastic interpretations of Thomas, which focus exclusively on the imperatives of justice and the natural law, my account is meant to show how the dictates of justice are qualified by the ordering of charity (chap. 1) and the condition of fallenness (chap. 2). Interpretations which focus on justice to the exclusion of these wider implications of grace and sin—viewing Aquinas as only a philosopher—extract his ideas from the wider fabric of his theological thought.

28. Aquinas, *Summa Theologiae*, II-II, Q. 40, A. 1.

29. For Aquinas on the structure of moral actions, see *Summa Theologiae*, I-II, Q. 18.

30. Aquinas, *Summa Theologiae*, II-II, Q. 42, A. 1.

31. Ibid.

32. Aristotle, *Nicomachean Ethics*, bks. 8, 9.

33. Aquinas, *Summa Theologiae*, II-II, Q. 101, A. 1.

34. Ibid., II-II, Q. 26, A. 7.

35. Alasdair MacIntyre, *After Virtue: A Study in Moral Theory*, 1st ed. (Notre Dame, Ind.: University of Notre Dame Press, 1981), p. 147.

36. Aquinas, *Summa Theologiae*, II-II, Q. 29, A. 2; see Augustine, *City of God*, bk. 19, pars. 12–14.

37. Aquinas, *Summa Theologiae*, II-II, Q. 37, A. 1.

38. For a more general reading of Aquinas on justice and the value of community, see Jean Porter, "Moral Rules and Moral Actions: A Comparison of Aquinas and Modern Moral Theology," *Journal of Religious Ethics* 17 (Spring 1989): 123–49.

39. Caution is not altogether lacking in the morality of the just war, as I argue in the previous chapter.

40. See, for example, Walters, "Five Classic Just-War Theories"; Johnson, *Just War Tradition and the Restraint of War* (see Introduction, n. 13).

41. J. Bryan Hehir, "The Just-War Ethic and Catholic Theology: Dynamics of Continuity and Change," in *War or Peace?* ed. Shannon, p. 17.

42. For relevant texts by Vitoria, see Arthur F. Holmes, ed., *War and Christian Ethics* (Grand Rapids, Mich.: Baker Book House, 1975).

43. Jaszi and Lewis, *Against the Tyrant*, pp. 68–70.

44. For a useful discussion of Pius XII, see Thomas A. Shannon, *What Are They Saying about Peace and War?* (New York: Paulist Press, 1983), pp. 22–26.

45. See Pius XII, Christmas addresses for 1941, 1951, 1952, 1953, and 1956, in *Major Addresses of Pius XII*, vol. 2, ed. V. Yzermans (St. Paul, Minn.: North Central, 1961).

46. Pius XII, "War and Peace," an address to delegates to the eighth congress of the World Medical Association, September 30, 1954, in *Pattern for Peace:*

Catholic Statements on International Order, ed. Harry W. Flannery (Westminster, Md.: Newman Press, 1962), p. 237.

47. Peace on Earth, par. 1, in Renewing the Earth, ed. O'Brien and Shannon (see Introduction, n. 15).

48. Ibid., pars. 8, 98, 132, 137, 138, 163.

49. Hehir, "The Just-War Ethic and Catholic Theology," p. 20.

50. Peace on Earth, par. 114.

51. Pastoral Constitution, par. 78.

52. Ibid., par. 79.

53. Ibid.

54. Ibid., par. 80.

55. U.S. Catholic Bishops, The Challenge of Peace (see Introduction, n. 14).

56. Ibid., par. 236.

57. Ibid., par. 242.

58. Ibid., par. 243.

59. Ibid., pars. 255, 258.

60. Ibid., par. 255.

61. Ibid., par. 268.

62. Ibid., par. 236.

63. See Childress, "Just-War Criteria," pp. 40–58 (see Introduction, n. 9).

64. U.S. Catholic Bishops, The Challenge of Peace, par. 83, emphasis in original.

65. Ibid., par. 93.

66. Ibid., par. 101.

67. Ibid., par. 152.

68. Ibid., par. 188.

69. Ibid., par. 186.

70. Ibid., par. 174.

71. Raymond Hunthausen, "In Support of Protestors," in For Swords into Plowshares, the Hammer Has to Fall, ed. Daniel Berrigan (Piscataway, N.J.: Plowshares Press, 1984), pp. 8–11.

72. For a study of civil conflict within the parameters of the traditional paradigm, see William V. O'Brien, The Conduct of Just and Limited War (New York: Praeger, 1981), chaps. 7–8.

73. Gustavo Gutierrez, A Theology of Liberation, trans. and ed. Caridad Inda and John Eagleson (Maryknoll, N.Y.: Orbis, 1971); 2d ed., 1988. It may well be, as John Langan has reminded me, that liberation theologians have become more cautious about recommending violence over the twenty years since Gutierrez first published A Theology of Liberation. And Gutierrez himself has modified his rhetoric in the second edition of this work. Yet in Gutierrez's case such changes are designed to remove misinterpretations rather than to revise the main lines of the liberation approach. Below I will rely on the first edition of Gutierrez's work and will note differences between the first and second editions where appropriate.

74. See Gutierrez, A Theology of Liberation, 2d ed., pp. 157–59, where he goes to great lengths to show continuity between his views and papal references to class differences and social conflict. For a study of Gutierrez emphasizing this issue of radical difference, see Rebecca S. Chopp, The Praxis of Suffering:

An Interpretation of Liberation and Political Theologies (Maryknoll, N.Y.: Orbis, 1986), pp. 46–63, at p. 47.

75. Gustavo Gutierrez, "Freedom and Salvation: A Political Problem," in Gutierrez and Richard Shaull, *Liberation and Change,* ed. with an introduction by Ronald H. Stone (Atlanta: John Knox Press, 1977), p. 76; cf. Gutierrez, *A Theology of Liberation,* 2d ed., p. xxi and passim.

76. Gutierrez, "Freedom and Salvation," p. 77.

77. Gutierrez, *A Theology of Liberation,* 1st ed., p. 273; cf. 2d ed., p. 159, where Gutierrez modifies his rhetoric but maintains the substance of this view: "The social realities to which I have been referring [e.g., class conflict] are difficult and much debated, but this does not dispense us from taking sides. It is not possible to remain neutral in the face of poverty and the resulting just claims of the poor; a posture of neutrality would, moreover, mean siding with the injustice and oppression in our midst."

78. See "The Medellin Conference Documents," in *Renewing the Earth,* ed. O'Brien and Shannon.

79. Gutierrez, *A Theology of Liberation,* 1st ed., pp. 289, 291; cf. 2d ed., pp. 164, 165.

80. Gutierrez, *A Theology of Liberation,* 1st ed., pp. 146, 171; cf. 2d ed., pp. 81, 100.

81. *A Call to Action,* pars. 3–4, in *Renewing the Earth,* ed. O'Brien and Shannon. Cf. Gutierrez, *A Theology of Liberation,* 1st and 2d eds., chap. 6.

82. Gutierrez, *A Theology of Liberation,* 1st ed., pp. 172–74; cf. 2d ed., p. xliv, where Gutierrez insists upon "the *continuity* that leads [liberation theology] to sink its roots deep in scripture, tradition, and the magisterium" (his emphasis).

83. Gustavo Gutierrez, "Liberation Praxis and Christian Faith," in *Frontiers of Theology in Latin America,* ed. Rosino Gibbelini (Maryknoll, N.Y.: Orbis, 1979), p. 22; cf. Gutierrez, *A Theology of Liberation,* 2d ed., p. xxxiii.

84. Gutierrez, "Liberation Praxis and Christian Faith," p. 23; cf. Gutierrez, "Freedom and Salvation," pp. 79–80.

85. Gutierrez, *A Theology of Liberation,* 1st ed., p. 276; cf. 2d ed., p. 159, where Gutierrez remarks, "Recognition of the fact of class struggle means taking a position, opposing certain groups of persons, rejecting certain activities, and facing hostilities."

86. Gutierrez, "Freedom and Salvation," p. 76.

87. Gutierrez, *A Theology of Liberation,* 1st ed., pp. 276, 308; 2d ed., pp. 160, 174.

88. Gutierrez, *A Theology of Liberation,* 1st ed., pp. 108–9; 2d ed., pp. 63–64. On institutional violence in Latin America, cf. "The Medellin Conference Documents," in *Renewing the Earth,* ed. O'Brien and Shannon, par. 16.

89. Gutierrez, *A Theology of Liberation,* 1st ed., p. 275; cf. 2d ed., p. 152, where Gutierrez again revises the rhetoric but maintains the substance: "Indeed, it is not a question of whether the Church should or should not use its influence in the Latin American revolutionary process. Rather, the question is in what direction and for what purpose is it going to use its influence: for or against the established order, to preserve the social prestige which comes with its ties to the groups in power or to free itself from that prestige with a break from these

groups and with genuine service to the oppressed?" (See also n. 77 above.)

90. Jon P. Gunnemann, *The Moral Meaning of Revolution* (New Haven: Yale University Press, 1979).

91. Ibid., p. 43.

92. Ibid.

93. Here, and throughout this chapter, I have been influenced by Michel Foucault, *The Archaeology of Knowledge*, trans. A. M. Sheridan Smith (New York: Pantheon, 1972), chap. 2.

94. Rawls, *A Theory of Justice*, pp. 3–4, 586 (see Introduction, n. 4). Yet even Rawls shows a concern for order as a rival value to justice in his discussion of political obligation and the justification of dissent; see his pp. 373–74.

95. In these concluding remarks I have been instructed by the work of Michael J. Sandel, *Liberalism and the Limits of Justice* (Cambridge: Cambridge University Press, 1982), pp. 31–35, 168–69.

Chapter 3

1. For an instructive use of types in this way, see James M. Gustafson, *Christ and the Moral Life* (Chicago: University of Chicago Press/Midway Reprint, 1976). As shall become apparent below, none of the pacifists considered in this chapter falls exclusively under one type.

2. This list of criteria is aided by, although it does not follow closely, three discussions of civil disobedience: James F. Childress, *Civil Disobedience and Political Obligation: A Study in Christian Social Ethics* (New Haven: Yale University Press, 1971); James F. Childress, "Nonviolent Resistance: Some Conceptual and Moral Considerations," *Journal of Religious Studies* 2 (Autumn 1970): 28–44; Peter Brock, *Pacifism in Europe to 1914* (Princeton, N.J.: Princeton University Press, 1972), pp. 471–76.

I should add that criteria pertaining to civil disobedience are applicable to nonpacifists who may object to a particular war after judging that such a war fails to meet just-war criteria. (I will discuss reasons why nonpacifists might selectively object to war below.) A nonpacifist who protests against a particular war may consider it appropriate to engage in some forms of civil disobedience. Such nonpacifists obviously touch upon terms in the fifth and sixth pairs I list here (i.e., nonviolent resistance *ad intra*). Nonpacifist objectors to war would then have to consider questions pertaining to the seventh, eighth, ninth, and tenth pairs of terms.

3. *Pastoral Constitution*, par. 78.

4. Ibid., par. 79.

5. Ibid., par. 16.

6. I am assuming in this sentence that it may be possible for a just law to lose its legitimacy outside a relatively just political arrangement. My inferences about the council's attitude toward indirect action are assuming a framework in which that action is occurring in a nonrevolutionary political environment. As we shall see, iconoclastic pacifism is distinguished by its belief in a relatively unjust political system.

7. *Pastoral Constitution*, par. 79.

8. For an instructive account of noncombatant military service of pacifists in

Great Britain during World War II, see Brock, *Twentieth Century Pacifism*, pp. 157–71 (see chap. 1, n. 113).

9. Again, I am assuming a context of national conscription. For a discussion of the relation between just-war morality and the pacifist prerogative to dissent, focusing on the writings of the U.S. Catholic bishops, see Norbert J. Rigali, "Just War and Pacifism," *America* 150 (March 31, 1984): 233–36.

10. For a constructive development of "fair play" as a metaphor of political obligation, see Childress, *Civil Disobedience*, pp. 123–49, 173–202 (see n. 2).

11. These observations are informed by the more general discussion of pacifism and rights in Cheyney C. Ryan, "Self-Defense, Pacifism, and the Possibility of Killing," *Ethics* 93 (April 1983): 508–24.

12. U.S. Catholic Bishops, "Human Life in Our Day," in *Renewing the Earth*, ed. O'Brien and Shannon, pars. 151–52.

13. For a useful discussion of this reversal in official Catholic teaching, see Shannon, *What Are They Saying about Peace and War?* pp. 25, 37 (see chap. 2, n. 44).

14. For a discussion of the methodological problems this pluralism creates for Catholic social teaching, see Hehir, "The Just-War Ethic and Catholic Theology," p. 25 (see chap. 2, n. 41). See also Kenneth R. Himes, "Pacifism in the Catholic Church," *Ecumenist* 25 (March–April 1987): 44–48.

15. U.S. Catholic Bishops, *The Challenge of Peace*, pars. 81–83.

16. Ibid., pars. 73–75.

17. Ibid., par. 233.

18. See, e.g., Gordon Zahn, "Pacifism and the Just War," in *Catholics and Nuclear War*, ed. William Murnion, with a foreword by Theodore Hesburgh (New York: Crossroad, 1983), pp. 119–31.

19. U.S. Catholic Bishops, *The Challenge of Peace*, par. 20.

20. Ibid., par. 78.

21. Ibid., pars. 203–30.

22. Gordon Zahn, *An Alternative to War* (New York: Council on Religion and International Affairs, 1963), p. 13; cf. Gordon Zahn, *War, Conscience and Dissent* (New York: Hawthorn, 1967), pp. 101, 113, 262.

23. Zahn, *An Alternative to War*, p. 22.

24. For a discussion of Catholic pacifists in the Civilian Public Service camp, see Zahn, *War, Conscience and Dissent*, chaps. 9, 10.

25. Zahn, *An Alternative to War*, p. 23.

26. Gordon Zahn, "Afterword," in *War or Peace?* ed. Shannon, p. 244.

27. Ibid., p. 241.

28. Zahn, "Pacifism and the Just War," in *Catholics and Nuclear War*, ed. Murnion, p. 123.

29. See, for example, Dorothy Day, *By Little and By Little: The Selected Writings of Dorothy Day*, ed. and with an introduction by Robert Ellsberg (New York: Alfred A. Knopf, 1983), p. 265.

30. Zahn, "Pacifism and the Just War," in *Catholics and Nuclear War*, ed. Murnion, p. 125.

31. For an instructive discussion of socialist pacifism of the twenties and thirties, see Brock, *Twentieth Century Pacifism*, pp. 10–12, 34–40, and passim.

See also William D. Miller, *A Harsh and Dreadful Love: Dorothy Day and the Catholic Worker Movement* (Garden City, N.Y.: Doubleday, 1974), 162–72.

32. Patricia F. McNeal, *The American Catholic Peace Movement, 1928–1972* (New York: Arno Press, 1978), p. 40. See also David J. O'Brien, *American Catholics and Social Reform: The New Deal Years* (New York: Oxford University Press, 1968), chap. 8; William D. Miller, *Dorothy Day: A Biography* (San Francisco: Harper & Row, 1982), pp. 314–15.

33. Day, *By Little and By Little*, p. 262.

34. Mel Piehl, *Breaking Bread: The Catholic Worker and the Origin of Catholic Radicalism in America* (Philadelphia: Temple University Press, 1982), p. 197.

35. See Tom Cornell, "The Catholic Church and Witness against War," in *War or Peace?* ed. Shannon, pp. 201–2.

36. Zahn, *War, Conscience and Dissent*, p. 153.

37. Cited in ibid., p. 154.

38. Day, *By Little and By Little*, p. 15.

39. See Zahn, *An Alternative to War*, pp. 21–22.

40. See Peter Maurin, *Catholic Radicalism: Easy Essays for the Green Revolution* (New York: Catholic Worker Books, 1949).

41. For a fine study of the anarchist currents in the Worker, see Mary C. Segers, "Equality and Christian Anarchism: The Political and Social Ideas of the Catholic Worker Movement," *Review of Politics* 40 (1978): 196–230.

42. Day, *By Little and By Little*, p. 94.

43. Ibid., pp. 91–94, 245–51, 269, 330, and passim.

44. For a useful discussion of the differences between liberal and radical wings of the movement, and the problems posed to the Catholic Worker in the 1940s by the pacifist question, see Piehl, *Breaking Bread*, pp. 155–59.

45. Day, *By Little and By Little*, p. 262.

46. Piehl, *Breaking Bread*, pp. 197–98.

47. McNeal, *The American Catholic Peace Movement*, p. 103.

48. Cited in Miller, *Dorothy Day: A Biography*, p. 331.

49. Paul Hanly Furfey, *Fire on the Earth* (New York: Macmillan, 1937), p. vii.

50. Ibid., p. 136; cf. Paul Hanly Furfey, *The Mystery of Iniquity* (Milwaukee, Wis.: Bruce, 1944), chaps. 5, 12.

51. Childress, *Civil Disobedience and Political Obligation*, p. 16.

52. Day, *By Little and By Little*, pp. 277–79. See also Miller, *A Harsh and Dreadful Love*, pp. 283–86. In the 1970s, moreover, Day spoke approvingly to Daniel Berrigan about the practice of nonviolent resistance. See Day, *By Little and By Little*, p. 347.

The ambiguity of nonresistance and nonviolent resistance continues to find a way into Catholic pacifism. In a recent essay, Catholic Worker Eileen Egan approvingly cites numerous examples of nonresistant pacifism and voluntary suffering in early Christianity, suggesting a method of nonresistance as appropriate to the pacifism derived from the Sermon on the Mount. Yet she also states that in a proper return to Christian origins, "training for the skills of reconciliation, for nonviolent resistance, and for civil disobedience as responses to injustice and oppression, would become the necessary constituents of gospel teaching." Both Day and Egan suggest a two-tiered approach, in which nonresistance is appropriate to individual morality and nonviolent resistance is appropriate to civil action in response to unjust laws. See Eileen Egan, "The Beatitudes, the Works of Mercy, and Pacifism," in *War or Peace?* ed. Shannon, pp. 175–80, 186.

53. Day, *By Little and By Little*, p. 279.

54. Piehl, *Breaking Bread*, p. 142.

55. Day, *By Little and By Little*, p. 98.

56. Even in the 1980s, Catholic Worker Tom Cornell writes that the capacity for Catholics to provide a powerful witness for peace "depends on how successfully Catholics continue to resist assimilation to the dominant WASP culture." See Tom Cornell, "The Catholic Church and Witness against War," in *War or Peace?* ed. Shannon, p. 211.

57. For a helpful contrast between the Worker and the Social Gospel movement, see Piehl, *Breaking Bread*, pp. 45–46, 134–39.

58. Ibid., p. 133.

59. About the dangers of anti-intellectualism in anarchism, see Segers, "Equality and Christian Anarchism," p. 217, n. 39.

60. Piehl, *Breaking Bread*, p. 90.

61. For an analysis of Douglass's views, see Charles E. Curran, *American Catholic Social Ethics: Twentieth Century Approaches* (Notre Dame, Ind.: University of Notre Dame Press, 1982), chap. 6. Curran's focus is largely on Douglass's theology and its relation to his ethics; I will focus instead on the shape of Douglass's pacifism as a social ethic in light of the elements defined in the first section of this chapter.

62. Douglass, *The Non-Violent Cross*, p. 6 (see chap. 1, n. 85); James Douglass, *Lightning East to West: Jesus, Gandhi, and the Nuclear Age*, with a foreword by Raymond Hunthausen (New York: Crossroad, 1980), pp. 3–4; cf. Zahn, *An Alternative to War*, pp. 8, 11, 13.

63. Douglass, *Non-Violent Cross*, p. 21.

64. Douglass, *Lightning East to West*, p. 59 and passim.

65. Douglass, *Non-Violent Cross*, pp. 61–62.

66. Douglass, *Lightning East to West*, p. 3 and passim.

67. Ibid., p. 43. Cf. Douglass, *The Non-Violent Cross*, chap. 3.

68. Douglass, *Lightning East to West*, p. 21 and passim.

69. James Douglass, *Resistance and Contemplation: The Way of Liberation* (Garden City, N.Y.: Doubleday, 1972), p. 61.

70. Douglass, *Lightning East to West*, pp. 41–55.

71. Douglass, *Resistance and Contemplation*, p. 178.

72. Ibid., p. 179.

73. Ibid.

74. Douglass, *Lightning East to West*, p. 5. Elements of realism are likewise traceable in the work of the Berrigans, who occasionally speak of the futility of violence and the effectiveness of nonviolence as a means of change. See, for example, Daniel Berrigan, *Consequences: Truth and . . .* (New York: Macmillan, 1965), p. 116. But the Berrigans have remained inconsistent about the relation between nonviolence and effectiveness, as I shall discuss below.

75. Douglass, *Non-Violent Cross*, pp. 171–72.

76. Ibid., pp. 267–70.

77. Ibid., p. 191.

78. Douglass, *Lightning East to West*, p. 24.

79. Ibid., p. 28.

80. Ibid., pp. 28–29.

81. Ibid., p. 9.

82. Ibid., pp. 9–10.

83. Cited in John J. Conley, "Catholic Pacifism in America," *America* 131 (December 14, 1974): 381–83.

84. For a brief historical account of the Catholic Left, see Charles A. Meconis, *With Clumsy Grace: The American Catholic Left, 1961–1975* (New York: Seabury Press, 1979).

85. D. Berrigan, *Consequences: Truth and . . .*, p. 85 (see n. 74).

86. Daniel Berrigan, *No Bars to Manhood* (Garden City, N.Y.: Doubleday, 1970), p. 98.

87. Griffiss Plowshares trial brief, quoted in "On Obedience to God and God's Law," in *For Swords into Plowshares, the Hammer Has to Fall*, ed. D. Berrigan, p. 12 (see chap. 2, n. 71); emphasis in original.

88. D. Berrigan, *No Bars to Manhood*, p. 97.

89. Daniel Berrigan, *America Is Hard to Find* (Garden City, N.Y.: Doubleday, 1972), p. 104; D. Berrigan, *No Bars to Manhood*, p. 46; see also Douglass, *Lightning East to West*, p. 77.

90. Daniel Berrigan, *The Trial of the Catonsville Nine* (Boston: Beacon Press, 1970), p. 29.

91. D. Berrigan, *No Bars to Manhood*, p. 92.

92. D. Berrigan, *Consequences: Truth and . . .*, p. 62.

93. Ibid., p. 105.

94. Ibid., pp. 62, 105.

95. D. Berrigan, *Trial of the Catonsville Nine*, pp. 35, 104; see also D. Berrigan, *Consequences: Truth and . . .*, p. 59.

96. Philip Berrigan, *Prison Journals of a Priest Revolutionary*, with an introduction by Daniel Berrigan (New York: Holt, Rinehart & Winston, 1967), p. 118.

97. For Merton's criticisms of the use of coercion by the Catholic Left, see Meconis, *With Clumsy Grace*, pp. 36–37.

98. D. Berrigan, *Consequences: Truth and . . .*, p. 35.

99. D. Berrigan, *Trial of the Catonsville Nine*, pp. 34, 104; cf. P. Berrigan, *Prison Journals*, p. 198.

100. D. Berrigan, *America Is Hard to Find*, p. 108.

101. Daniel Berrigan, "Oedipus and the Daring Seven: An Introduction," in *For Swords into Plowshares*, ed. D. Berrigan, pp. 3, 4.

102. P. Berrigan, *Prison Journals*, pp. 11–12.

103. D. Berrigan, *America Is Hard to Find*, p. 47; D. Berrigan, *No Bars to Manhood*, pp. 143–44. Cf. Douglass, *Lightning East to West*, pp. 73–74.

104. D. Berrigan, *No Bars to Manhood*, p. 49.

105. See, e.g., D. Berrigan, *Consequences: Truth and . . .*, p. 60.

106. D. Berrigan, *No Bars to Manhood*, p. 51; P. Berrigan, *Prison Journals*, p. 105.

107. P. Berrigan, *Prison Journals*, p. 19.

108. Ibid., p. 150.

109. Ibid., pp. 80–81.

110. See chap. 1, n. 14.

111. For a similar point, see Richard A. McCormick, *Notes on Moral Theology, 1965–1980* (Washington, D.C.: University Press of America, 1981), pp. 272, 275.

112. D. Berrigan, *No Bars to Manhood,* p. 156.

113. H. Richard Niebuhr, *The Kingdom of God in America* (New York: Harper & Row, 1937), chap. 1.

114. See also Paul Ramsey, *Christian Ethics and the Sit-In* (New York: Association Press, 1961), pp. 104–22; Childress, *Civil Disobedience and Political Obligation,* pp. 203–6.

115. In the ethics of civil disobedience, as in war, this criterion must be applied flexibly. In war it may be necessary to act with self-defensive, preemptive force before all peaceable measures have been tried. Similarly, as Rawls observes, there may be some cases in domestic politics that are so extreme that we cannot expect victims to seek legal recourse first, e.g., when a legislature forbids the religion of a weak and defenseless minority. See Rawls, *A Theory of Justice,* p. 373 (see Introduction, n. 4).

116. As I remark in n. 2 above, several elements of a pacifist ethic are relevant not only to pacifists but also to selective conscientious objectors who engage in political protest. This relevance likewise holds when considering the ethics of civil disobedience: The use of just-war criteria to shape such an ethic pertains to pacifists and selective objectors alike.

Chapter 4

1. James Turner Johnson, "On Keeping Faith: The Use of History for Religious Ethics," *Journal of Religious Ethics* 7 (1979): 113.

2. James Finn, "Pacifism and Justifiable War," in *War or Peace?* ed. Shannon, p. 3.

3. Hehir, "The Just-War Ethic and Catholic Theology," p. 18 (see chap. 2, n. 41).

4. Charles E. Curran, *Critical Concerns in Moral Theology* (Notre Dame, Ind.: University of Notre Dame Press, 1984), pp. 163–64. Curran rightly argues that traditional Catholic theology does not elevate religious vocation to a higher status of Christian life, and warns against this tendency in pacifist circles today.

5. United Methodist Council of Bishops, *In Defense of Creation,* p. 13; cf. pp. 33, 35 (see chap. 1, n. 87). I do not mean to suggest, however, that the views of Johnson, Finn, Hehir, Curran, and the U.S. Methodist bishops are identical or that they all cohere with the views I set forth in chap. 1 concerning the convergence of pacifism and just-war criteria. I only wish to identify the fact that these authors speak as if pacifism and just-war criteria share significant common ground or at least a close relation.

6. Reinhold Niebuhr, *Christianity and Power Politics* (New York: Charles Scribner's Sons, 1940), p. 7.

7. Ibid., pp. 5, 31.

8. John Howard Yoder, *Nevertheless: Varieties and Shortcomings of Religious Pacifism* (Scottsdale, Pa.: Herald, 1971).

9. John Howard Yoder, *The Original Revolution: Essays on Christian Paci-*

fism (Scottsdale, Pa.: Herald, 1971), pp. 134–35; Yoder, *The Politics of Jesus: Vicit Agnus Noster* (Grand Rapids, Mich.: Eerdmans, 1972), pp. 21–22. Just-war theorists who wish to meet this objection might argue that, within recent developments of transcendental Thomism, orders of creation cannot be separated clearly from orders of redemption. Thus, "natural" moral imperatives are derived from indicatives of a gracious order. For a discussion of this development in Roman Catholic theology, see James M. Gustafson, *Protestant and Roman Catholic Ethics,* pp. 114–19 (see chap. 1, n. 42). For an example of pacifist thought which draws upon traditional natural law claims, see Zahn, *War, Conscience and Dissent,* p. 34 (see chap. 3, n. 22); Douglass, *The Non-Violent Cross,* pp. 209–11 (see chap. 1, n. 85).

10. Stanley Hauerwas, *The Peaceable Kingdom,* chap. 1 (see Introduction, n. 6).

11. Ibid., pp. 23–29. However, one consequence of Hauerwas's critique of foundationalism is that he must also reject non-Christian pacifism, because it is not tied to the particularity of the Christian story.

12. Ibid., pp. 32–33; Yoder, *The Politics of Jesus,* pp. 15–18; Yoder, *The Original Revolution,* p. 72.

13. Yoder, *The Politics of Jesus,* pp. 115–34.

14. G. H. C. Macgregor, *The New Testament Basis of Pacifism* (London: Fellowship of Reconciliation, 1952), pp. 37–39, 46–50.

15. Yoder, *The Politics of Jesus,* p. 238.

16. Stanley Hauerwas, *Should War Be Eliminated? Philosophical and Theological Investigations* (Milwaukee, Wis.: Marquette University Press, 1984), pp. 50–54.

17. Ibid., p. 50.

18. Ibid., p. 56.

19. Martin Luther King, Jr., *Strength to Love* (Philadelphia: Fortress Press, 1963 and 1981), p. 70.

20. Martin Luther King, Jr., *Why We Can't Wait* (New York: New American Library/Mentor, 1964), chap. 7; Martin Luther King, Jr., *Where Do We Go from Here: Chaos or Community?* (New York: Harper & Row, 1967), chap. 6.

21. King, *Strength to Love,* p. 70.

22. See chap. 3, n. 51.

23. King, *Where Do We Go from Here?* pp. 61–63; King, *Strength to Love,* pp. 147–55.

24. John Howard Yoder, *The Christian Witness to the State* (Newton, Kans.: Faith & Life Press, 1964), pp. 36–37; Yoder, *Politics of Jesus,* p. 203.

25. Yoder, *Christian Witness,* p. 38; Yoder, *The Original Revolution,* p. 157.

26. Hauerwas, *Should War Be Eliminated?* p. 53; Hauerwas, *The Peaceable Kingdom,* pp. 96–115; Yoder, *The Original Revolution,* pp. 60–61; Yoder, *The Politics of Jesus,* p. 63.

27. Yoder, *The Original Revolution,* pp. 28, 30, 107–9; Zahn, *War, Conscience and Dissent,* p. 279.

28. Zahn, *War, Conscience and Dissent,* p. 289.

29. Yoder, *Christian Witness,* pp. 16–28; Hauerwas, *Should War Be Eliminated?* p. 56.

30. Douglass, *The Non-Violent Cross,* p. 204. See also Stanley Hauerwas, *The*

Community of Character: Toward a Constructive Social Ethic (Notre Dame, Ind.: University of Notre Dame Press, 1981), pp. 84–85.

31. Yoder, *The Original Revolution*, p. 51; Macgregor, *The New Testament Basis of Pacifism*, p. 12.

32. Douglass, *Lightning East to West*, p. 13 (see chap. 3, n. 62).

33. Ibid., pp. 14, 18, 42, 48, 53–54.

34. King, *Strength to Love*, p. 50.

35. Zahn, *War, Conscience and Dissent*, p. 105; King, *Strength to Love*, p. 49.

36. Zahn, *War, Conscience and Dissent*, p. 105.

37. Merton, *Faith and Violence*, p. 26. Merton never abdicated just-war tenets, at least at the level of theory. Thus, it is difficult to assign him to pacifism in a strict sense. For a discussion of Merton and moral canons of war, see Gordon Zahn, "Original Child Monk: An Appreciation," in *Thomas Merton on Peace* (New York: McCall, 1971), pp. xvii–xviii.

38. James F. Childress, *Moral Responsibility in Conflicts: Essays in Nonviolence, War, and Conscience* (Baton Rouge, La.: Louisiana State University Press, 1982), p. 25.

39. Hauerwas, *Should War Be Eliminated?* p. 53.

40. Zahn, *War, Conscience and Dissent*, pp. 49–50; Zahn, "Afterword," in *War or Peace?* ed. Shannon, p. 235.

41. Douglass, *The Non-Violent Cross*, pp. 156, 171, 175; King, *Strength to Love*, p. 153. King admits that he once saw war as the lesser of two evils, but that later he changed his views in light of the new destructive capacities wrought by nuclear technology.

42. Douglass, *The Non-Violent Cross*, pp. 5–6; Douglass, *Lightning East to West*, p. 3 and passim.

43. Zahn, *War, Conscience and Dissent*, pp. 35–50, 79; Zahn, "Afterword," in *War or Peace?* ed. Shannon, pp. 239–40.

44. James Turner Johnson argues that restraint in recent warfare serves as evidence that just-war tenets are viable today. See Johnson, *Can Modern War Be Just?* pp. 50–52 (see chap. 1, n. 29). However, the presence of restraint is necessary but not sufficient to support the claim that just-war tenets are operative. Nations may restrain themselves out of self-interest, not moral rectitude or adherence to "just" imperatives. On this issue of self-interest and restraint in war, see Thomas Schelling's extremely influential work, *Arms and Influence* (New Haven: Yale University Press, 1966).

45. John Howard Yoder, *When War Is Unjust: Being Honest in Just-War Thinking*, with an introduction by Charles Mutz (Minneapolis: Augsburg Press, 1984), p. 33.

46. Ibid., pp. 36–39.

47. Ibid., pp. 61–62.

48. Ibid., pp. 64–67, 82.

49. Zahn, War, *Conscience and Dissent*, pp. 246–61.

50. Ibid., p. 43.

51. Ibid., p. 252.

52. Ibid., p. 253.

53. Ibid., p. 261.

54. Mulford Sibley, *The Political Theories of Modern Pacifism* (Philadelphia: Pacifist Research Bureau, 1944; rev. 1970), p. 54, cited in Paul Deats, "Protestant Ethics and Pacifism," in *War or Peace?* ed. Shannon, p. 80.

55. Hauerwas, *The Peaceable Kingdom,* pp. 17–49, 99–101, 135–52.

56. Deats, "Protestant Ethics and Pacifism," p. 84.

57. Gibson Winter, "Hope for the Earth: A Hermeneutic of Nuclearism in Ecumenical Perspective," 1983 William Henry Hoover Lecture on Christian Unity (Chicago: Disciples Divinity House of the University of Chicago, 1983), p. 3.

58. Ibid., p. 8. Similarly, Jonathan Schell argues that pathological conditions and disordered passions are likely to characterize members of a culture in which the future is uncertain. See Jonathan Schell, *The Fate of the Earth* (New York: Alfred A. Knopf, 1982), pp. 156–58.

59. Winter, "Hope for the Earth," p. 9. For a theoretical development of the foundations of Winter's argument, see his *Liberating Creation: Foundations of Religious Social Ethics* (New York: Crossroad, 1981).

60. Douglass, *The Non-Violent Cross,* pp. 28–31.

61. Merton, *Faith and Violence,* p. 22.

62. Macgregor, *The New Testament Basis of Pacifism,* p. 77; Douglass, *The Non-Violent Cross,* pp. 18, 71.

63. Yoder, *When War Is Unjust,* p. 61.

64. Macgregor, *The New Testament Basis of Pacifism,* p. 77, n. 1.

65. Ryan, "Self-Defense, Pacifism, and the Possibility of Killing," p. 521 (see chap. 3, n. 11).

66. Ibid., p. 523.

67. Ibid.

68. Macgregor, *The New Testament Basis of Pacifism,* p. 11; Yoder, *The Politics of Jesus,* pp. 115–34; p. 204 n. 3; Yoder, *The Original Revolution,* pp. 51, 55–57, 80–81; Merton, *Faith and Violence,* p. 16; Hauerwas, *The Peaceable Kingdom,* p. 80; Douglass, *The Non-Violent Cross,* pp. 53–55, 62–65, 191–214, 234–54 and passim.

69. Hauerwas, *Should War Be Eliminated?* p. 56.

70. Niebuhr, *Christianity and Power Politics,* pp. 14–15.

71. Hauerwas, *The Peaceable Kingdom,* pp. 142–45.

72. King, *Where Do We Go from Here?* pp. 59–62. Although King's discussion of global warfare was less developed than his defense of nonviolence in the civil rights movement, he could have extended his argument beyond the movement to the global situation given his understanding of the interdependence of reality.

73. See, e.g., William V. O'Brien, *War and/or Survival* (Garden City, N.Y.: Doubleday, 1969), pp. 62–63.

74. Douglass, *The Non-Violent Cross,* pp. 257–82.

75. Zahn, *War, Conscience and Dissent,* pp. 117, 304–6; Douglass, *The Non-Violent Cross,* pp. 8, 275.

76. For a discussion of Barth on the exceptional nature of war, see chap. 1.

77. Ramsey, *Christian Ethics and the Sit-In,* p. 102 (see chap. 3, n. 114).

78. See Joseph Kunkel, "Just War Doctrine and Pacifism," *Thomist* 47 (October 1983): 501–12, for a similar inference drawing on Aquinas's view of charity.

79. See also James Finn, "Pacifism and Justifiable War," p. 13.

80. For a discussion, see chaps. 1 and 2.

81. Brock, *Twentieth Century Pacifism*, p. 258 (see chap. 1, n. 113).

Chapter 5

1. Tillich, *The Protestant Era*, p. 163 (see chap. 1, n. 38).

2. "The Grace of Doing Nothing," *Christian Century* 49 (March 23, 1932): 378–80; "A Communication: The Only Way into the Kingdom of God," *Christian Century* 49 (April 6, 1932): 447; "War as the Judgment of God," *Christian Century* 59 (May 3, 1942): 630–33; "Is God in the War?" *Christian Century* 59 (August 5, 1942): 953–55; "War as Crucifixion," *Christian Century* 60 (April 28, 1943): 513–15.

3. I have in mind the following helpful studies, all of which fail to give systematic treatment to these articles: Bainton, *Christian Attitudes toward War and Peace* (see chap. 1, n. 19); Johnson, *Just War Tradition and the Restraint of War* (see Introduction, n. 13); Holmes, ed., *War and Christian Ethics* (see chap. 2, n. 42); Childress, *Moral Responsibility in Conflicts* (see chap. 4, n. 38).

4. Niebuhr, "The Grace of Doing Nothing," p. 380 and passim.

5. Niebuhr, "War as the Judgment of God," p. 632.

6. Niebuhr, "The Grace of Doing Nothing," p. 378.

7. Niebuhr, "A Communication," p. 447.

8. H. Richard Niebuhr, "The Inconsistency of the Majority," *World Tomorrow* (January 18, 1934): 43–44. As I pointed out in the previous chapter, Reinhold Niebuhr came to embrace this same criticism of nonviolent resistant pacifism.

9. Niebuhr, "War as Crucifixion," p. 513.

10. Ibid.

11. Ibid., p. 515.

12. Ibid., p. 513.

13. Niebuhr, "War as the Judgment of God," p. 631.

14. My reading of Niebuhr's ethics, and especially his use of metaphor, has been instructed by Harold Bloom's notion of a "strong poet" as developed in recent pragmatic philosophy. See Rorty, *Contingency, Irony, and Solidarity*, pp. 24–25 (see chap. 1, n. 104); Harold Bloom, *The Anxiety of Influence* (New York: Oxford University Press, 1973).

15. For an emphasis on Niebuhr's dispositionalism as the key feature in the war articles, see C. David Grant, *God the Center of Value: Value Theory in the Theology of H. Richard Niebuhr* (Fort Worth: Texas Christian University Press, 1984), pp. 26–27.

16. H. Richard Niebuhr, *The Responsible Self: An Essay in Christian Moral Philosophy* (New York: Harper & Row, 1960), chap. 1.

17. Niebuhr, "A Communication," p. 447; cf. H. Richard Niebuhr, "The Social Gospel and the Mind of Jesus," *Journal of Religious Ethics* 16 (Spring 1988): 123, in which Niebuhr remarks, "It is impossible for man to take the kingdom by violence, by self-assertion; he has no means adequate to this purpose. But it is possible for him, in repentance, to anticipate the judgment, to give up the attempt to preserve or extend the dying system and so to hasten its destruction." Emphasizing one theme of the war articles, Niebuhr goes on to say, "The suffering of innocence for guilt is the only strategy possible if there is to

be any cessation of the ceaseless round of self-interests arousing self-interests, of judgments without acceptance of the Kingdom of God." Niebuhr delivered this paper in 1933, about a year after the exchange with his brother about the merits of nonintervention in the Manchurian crisis.

18. Niebuhr, "A Communication," p. 447.

19. Ibid. For a brief discussion of the debate between the Niebuhr brothers in the 1930s over the subject of war, see Richard Fox, *Reinhold Niebuhr: A Biography* (San Francisco: Harper & Row, 1985), pp. 132–34.

20. Niebuhr, "War as the Judgment of God," p. 631.

21. Niebuhr, *Responsible Self,* p. 60.

22. Ibid., p. 63; see also Niebuhr, "War as the Judgment of God," p. 630.

23. Niebuhr, *Responsible Self,* p. 151.

24. See ibid., pp. 149–60; Niebuhr, *Meaning of Revelation,* pp. 90–93 (see chap. 1, n. 43).

25. Niebuhr, "The Grace of Doing Nothing," p. 380.

26. Niebuhr, "War as Crucifixion," p. 514.

27. Niebuhr, "War as the Judgment of God," p. 631; Niebuhr, "Is God in the War?" p. 954; Niebuhr, "War as Crucifixion," pp. 513–14.

28. Niebuhr, "War as Crucifixion," p. 513.

29. Niebuhr, "The Grace of Doing Nothing," p. 379.

30. H. Richard Niebuhr, "Man the Sinner," *Journal of Religion* 15 (1935): 279. Niebuhr first publicly embraces a nonpacifist position in this essay.

31. H. Richard Niebuhr, *Radical Monotheism and Western Culture, with Supplementary Essays* (New York: Harper & Row, 1943), pp. 11, 24, and passim.

32. Ibid., p. 32.

33. Ibid., p. 27.

34. Ibid., pp. 49–63, 68–77, 84–88; cf. Niebuhr, *The Responsible Self,* pp. 86–89.

35. Niebuhr, *Radical Monotheism,* pp. 49–63.

36. Niebuhr, "A Communication," p. 447; cf. n. 17 above.

37. Niebuhr, *Social Sources of Denominationalism,* passim; Niebuhr, *Radical Monotheism,* pp. 53–56.

38. Niebuhr, *Social Sources of Denominationalism,* p. 264.

39. H. Richard Niebuhr, "Reformation: Continuing Imperative," *Christian Century* 77 (March 2, 1960): 249.

40. Niebuhr, *Social Sources of Denominationalism,* p. 25.

41. Niebuhr, *The Meaning of Revelation,* pp. 57, 59.

42. John Calvin, *Institutes of the Christian Religion* 1: 17, 1. In contrast to Calvin's supernaturalism, however, Niebuhr's notion of God as sovereign and immanent precludes the notion of divinity as "sometimes contrary to every intermediary."

43. Niebuhr, *The Responsible Self,* p. 126; Niebuhr, "War as the Judgment of God," p. 630.

44. Niebuhr, "Is God in the War?" p. 954; Niebuhr, "War as the Judgment of God," p. 631.

45. Niebuhr, "Is God in the War?" p. 954.

46. Niebuhr, *The Meaning of Revelation,* p. 82.

47. Niebuhr, "A Communication," p. 447.

48. Niebuhr, "Is God in the War?" p. 954.

49. Niebuhr, *The Responsible Self,* p. 126; Niebuhr, "War as the Judgment of God," p. 630.

50. Niebuhr, *The Responsible Self,* p. 166.

51. Niebuhr, "Is God in the War?" p. 954.

52. Niebuhr, "A Communication," p. 447; cf. Niebuhr, "The Social Gospel and the Mind of Jesus," pp. 121–22.

53. Niebuhr, "Grace of Doing Nothing," pp. 379–80.

54. Niebuhr, "War as the Judgment of God," p. 632.

55. Ibid.

56. Niebuhr, "War as Crucifixion," p. 515.

57. Ibid.

58. Niebuhr, "War as the Judgment of God," p. 630.

59. Ibid., p. 631.

60. Niebuhr, "War as Crucifixion," p. 513.

61. Niebuhr, *The Meaning of Revelation,* p. 97.

62. Ibid., p. 99.

63. Niebuhr, "War as Crucifixion," p. 514.

64. Niebuhr, *The Meaning of Revelation,* p. 61.

65. Ibid., pp. 132–33.

66. Ibid., p. 133; cf. Niebuhr, *Radical Monotheism,* p. 54.

67. Niebuhr, *The Meaning of Revelation,* p. 122.

68. Ibid.; cf. Niebuhr, *Radical Monotheism,* pp. 33–34, 122–26.

69. Calvin, *Institutes* 1: 16, 1 (see n. 42 above).

70. For a discussion of the problem of religion and ethics in Catholic pacifism, see chap. 3.

71. John Barbour, "Niebuhr versus Niebuhr: The Tragic Nature of History," *Christian Century* 101 (November 21, 1984): 1096–99, at 1099.

72. Niebuhr, *The Responsible Self,* p. 123.

73. Niebuhr, "War as Crucifixion," p. 514.

74. Niebuhr, "War as the Judgment of God," p. 630.

75. Niebuhr, "War as Crucifixion," p. 515.

76. Niebuhr, "War as the Judgment of God," p. 632.

77. Ibid.; cf. Paul Ramsey, *Basic Christian Ethics* (New York: Charles Scribner's Sons, 1950), pp. 166–71.

78. Niebuhr, "War as the Judgment of God," p. 632.

79. Ibid.

80. U.S. Catholic Bishops, *The Challenge of Peace,* pars. 92–94 (see Introduction, n. 14); cf. Ramsey, *War and the Christian Conscience,* p. 32 (see chap. 2, n. 1).

81. Niebuhr, "War as the Judgment of God," p. 632.

82. Ibid., p. 633.

83. See chap. 1, n. 39.

84. See chaps. 1 and 4.

85. For a discussion of the jeremiad, see Sacvan Bercovitch, *The American Jeremiad* (Madison: University of Wisconsin Press, 1978).

86. Ibid., p. 62.

Chapter 6

1. U.S. Catholic Bishops, *The Challenge of Peace*, par. 178; Hollenbach, *Nuclear Ethics*, p. 63; Finnis et al., *Nuclear Deterrence, Morality, and Realism*, pp. 79–81, 104–31, and passim (see chap. 1, n. 37).

2. O'Brien, *Just and Limited War*, p. 196 (see chap. 2, n. 72); Johnson, *Can Modern War Be Just?* p. 183 (see chap. 1, n. 29).

3. Robert A. Gessert and J. Bryan Hehir, *The New Nuclear Debate* (New York: Council on Religion and International Relations, 1976), pp. 47–55; Hollenbach, *Nuclear Ethics*, p. 65.

4. Ramsey, *Basic Christian Ethics*, pp. 92–103 (see chap. 5, n. 77).

5. Ibid., p. 94.

6. Ibid., p. 115.

7. Ibid., pp. 130, 133–51; cf. Paul Ramsey, *The Patient as Person: Explorations in Medical Ethics* (New Haven: Yale University Press, 1970), pp. xii–xiv.

8. Paul Ramsey, *The Just War: Force and Political Responsibility* (New York: Charles Scribner's Sons, 1968), p. 142; cf. Ramsey, *Basic Christian Ethics*, p. xvii.

9. Ramsey, *War and the Christian Conscience*, chap. 2.

10. David H. Smith, "Paul Ramsey, Love and Killing," in *Love and Society: Essays in the Ethics of Paul Ramsey*, ed. Smith and James T. Johnson (Missoula, Mont.: Scholars' Press, 1974), p. 6.

11. Ramsey, *Basic Christian Ethics*, p. 177.

12. Ramsey, *War and the Christian Conscience*, p. xviii.

13. Ramsey, *Basic Christian Ethics*, pp. 10, 12, 16, and passim.

14. Ramsey, *The Just War*, p. 143.

15. Paul Ramsey, *Speak Up for Just War or Pacifism: A Critique of the United Methodist Bishops' Pastoral Letter "In Defense of Creation,"* with an epilogue by Stanley Hauerwas (State Park: Pennsylvania State University Press, 1988), p. 54; cf. pp. 108–10.

16. See Ramsey, *Christian Ethics and the Sit-In*, p. 102. The idea that the use of force can be an expression of care suggests that pacifism is deficient, or requires compromises, because it overlooks the duties of love required in third-party relations. Yet Ramsey later came to regard pacifism in what appears to be a more positive light than this criticism suggests. In his last work (*Speak Up for Just War or Pacifism*, p. 123), Ramsey argues that both pacifism and just-war ideas eschew references to consequences, effectiveness, and making history "come out right"; both moralities, in short, are generally deontological. On this basis he concludes that, while pacifism cannot be recommended for the morality of statecraft, both pacifism and just-war morality "are equally Christian discipleships."

This embrace of something like a convergence between pacifism and just-war tenets is noteworthy not because it signals an embrace of pacifism at the level of individual morality. Rather, it is notable because it makes explicit Ramsey's belief that the ethics of individual self-defense is acceptable along with the ethics of pacifism for individual Christians. As I shall show below, this embrace of individual self-defense harks back to Ramsey's early discussions of the ethics of killing. Whatever Ramsey may suggest in *Speak Up for Just War or Pacifism*, neither his embrace of individual pacifism nor his idea that just-war morality can be a "discipleship" for individual Christians is new.

17. Ramsey, *The Just War,* chap. 6.

18. Ibid., pp. 145–46; cf. Paul Ramsey, "A Political Ethics Context for Strategic Thinking," in *Strategic Thinking and Its Moral Implications,* ed. Morton A. Kaplan (Chicago: University of Chicago Center for Policy Study, 1971), p. 133.

19. Ramsey, *The Just War,* pp. 153–54.

20. I owe this analogy to Jeffrey Stout.

21. Ramsey, *The Just War,* p. 294; cf. Ramsey, "A Political Ethics Context," p. 144.

22. Ramsey, *War and the Christian Conscience,* pp. 6–8.

23. Ibid., pp. 25–26; cf. Ramsey, *Christian Ethics and the Sit-In,* p. 75.

24. Ramsey, *The Just War,* p. 152.

25. Ibid., pp. 153–55; cf. Ramsey, "A Political Ethics Context," p. 144.

26. Ramsey, *Basic Christian Ethics,* p. 116; Ramsey, *War and the Christian Conscience,* pp. 4–8.

27. Ramsey, *War and the Christian Conscience,* p. 6.

28. Ibid., p. 8.

29. Ramsey, *Basic Christian Ethics,* p. 387.

30. Ibid., p. 177.

31. Ramsey, *War and the Christian Conscience,* p. 205.

32. Ramsey, *Basic Christian Ethics,* p. 387.

33. Ramsey, *The Just War,* p. 11; cf. Paul Ramsey, *Deeds and Rules in Christian Ethics* (New York: Charles Scribner's Sons, 1967), pp. 115–17.

34. Ramsey, *The Just War,* pp. 260–78; cf. Ramsey, "A Political Ethics Context," pp. 121–25.

35. Ramsey, "A Political Ethics Context," p. 125.

36. Ramsey, *Basic Christian Ethics,* p. 100.

37. Ramsey, *The Just War,* pp. 147, 250–51; cf. Ramsey, "A Political Ethics Context," pp. 134–35.

38. Ramsey, *The Just War,* chaps. 7, 8.

39. Ramsey, *War and the Christian Conscience,* pp. 162–66, 269–72, 306; cf. Ramsey, *The Just War,* p. 147; Ramsey, "A Political Ethics Context," p. 141.

40. Ramsey, *The Just War,* pp. 236–41; cf. Ramsey, *Speak Up for Just War or Pacifism,* p. 58.

41. Ramsey, *The Just War,* pp. 237–38.

42. Ibid., pp. 242–43.

43. Ibid., pp. 247–48.

44. Ibid., pp. 248–58, 314–66; Ramsey, "A Political Ethics Context," pp. 130–47.

45. Ramsey, *The Just War,* pp. 251–56, 294, 314–21. In this work Ramsey includes a fourth possible deterrent, based on a "cultivated ambiguity" about one's intentions. He later abandoned this notion, so I will exclude discussion of it here. Compare Ramsey, *The Just War,* pp. 254–58, 299–302, and 333–36, with Ramsey, "A Political Ethics Context," p. 144, n. 44, and Ramsey, *Speak Up for Just War or Pacifism,* pp. 206–7.

46. Ramsey, *The Just War,* p. 317.

47. Ibid., p. 252.

48. Ibid., p. 320.

49. Ibid., p. 303; cf. Ramsey, "A Political Ethics Context," p. 145.

50. Ramsey, *The Just War,* p. 303.

51. Ibid., p. 304.

52. Ibid., p. 305.

53. For Ramsey on the relevance of nuclear blackmail in the "proportion" to which deterrence is ordered, see *Speak Up for Just War or Pacifism,* pp. 95–96.

54. Ramsey, *The Just War,* p. 323; emphasis in original.

55. Ibid., p. 294; cf. Ramsey, "A Political Ethics Context," p. 144; Ramsey, *Speak Up for Just War or Pacifism,* p. 93.

56. Ramsey, *The Just War,* pp. 253, 330.

57. Schelling, *Arms and Influence* (see chap. 4, n. 44); Robert Jervis, *The Illogic of American Nuclear Strategy* (Ithaca, N.Y.: Cornell University Press, 1984).

58. Ramsey, *The Just War,* p. 254.

59. Ibid.; cf. p. 244.

60. Ramsey, *Speak Up for Just War or Pacifism,* p. 109; emphasis in original.

61. Ibid., p. 110; emphasis in original.

62. Ibid., p. 83; emphasis in original.

63. Ramsey, *The Just War,* p. 252.

64. Again, Ramsey's discussion of medical ethics reveals his problem. In a separate essay about the ethics of fetal experimentation, Ramsey is quite emphatic that it is immoral to gain some forms of beneficial knowledge about neonatal development from elective abortions. Even if the procurement of fetuses for research is a foreseen but unintended by-product of elective abortion, Ramsey contends, such procurement nonetheless remains complicit in evil practices. For Ramsey it is immoral to benefit from immoral practices, like killing the defenseless. For Ramsey on fetal research, see Paul Ramsey, *The Ethics of Fetal Research* (New Haven: Yale University Press, 1975).

65. The implications of a thick theory of intention for the principle of double effect are correctly summarized by Michael Walzer: "The intention of the actor is good, that is, he aims narrowly at the acceptable effect; the evil effect is not one of his ends, nor is it a means to his ends, *and, aware of the evil involved, he seeks to minimize it, accepting costs to himself.*" See Walzer, *Just and Unjust Wars,* p. 155 (see chap. 1, n. 66); emphasis mine.

66. U.S. Catholic Bishops, *The Challenge of Peace,* par. 181.

67. Ibid., par. 182.

68. Ibid., par. 193.

69. Without entering into the debate about whether the rule of double effect is explicitly and thoroughly formulated by Thomas Aquinas, it is still possible to ground the bishops' effort to assess the morality of foreseen, unintended death in Thomistic sources. In *Summa Theologiae,* II-II, Q. 64, A. 8, Thomas raises the question, "Whether One Is Guilty of Murder through Killing Someone by Chance?" He answers this question by noting that, strictly speaking, no one can be accounted sinful for chance happenings. He then qualifies his answer by citing instances in which one can be guilty of sin, the last of which bears directly on the discussion of thin and thick renditions of intention and foreseen, collat-

eral destruction. According to Thomas, one is guilty of an accidental death if one "does not take sufficient care" to prevent such a death. He concludes: "If a man pursue a lawful occupation and take due care, the result being that a person loses his life, he is not guilty of that person's death. Whereas if he be occupied with something unlawful, or even with something lawful, but without due care, he does not escape being guilty of murder, if his action results in someone's death."

70. Ramsey, "A Political Ethics Context," p. 144.

71. Ramsey, *The Just War*, p. 303.

72. The bishops, as I will show in the next chapter, do not reject nuclear deterrence unconditionally. It is possible to read this refusal to reject nuclear deterrence as likewise symptomatic of the pressures of self-preservation on their moral logic. However, this fact, *taken by itself,* should not be construed as problematical for the bishops' argument, for they do not construct their version of just-war ideas along the lines of Ramsey's protection paradigm.

73. Ramsey seeks to supplement his argument that "the threat of something disproportionate is not necessarily a disproportionate threat" with two brief arguments, which merit discussion here. First, Ramsey holds that the "issuance of threats of disproportionate destruction is ever the nature of deterrence under any conditions of warfare. One has to reject deterrence in general or in any war in order to reject this account of justifiable deterrence in a nuclear age" ("A Political Ethics Context," p. 145). Whether such an assertion stands within the realm of competence of a Christian ethicist, in Ramsey's terms, is difficult to say. But in reply to Ramsey it is possible to retort that the issuance of threats of disproportionate destruction is not "the nature of deterrence under any conditions of warfare." Or, if it is, Ramsey has not shown how or why this issuance *must* be so in the *nature* of a moral deterrent. In fact, conventional deterrence rests simply on the premise that the costs of war would, for the enemy, outweigh the gains. But such cost/benefit considerations of war need not entail disproportionate damage as a *necessary* component. Hence, the task of the just-war theorist is to construct a theory of deterrence that may presume the prospect of "unacceptable damage" as integral to deterrence, without embracing the notion that unacceptable damage must necessarily include disproportionate damage. For a discussion of conventional deterrence, see John Mearsheimer, *Conventional Deterrence* (Ithaca, N.Y.: Cornell University Press, 1983).

Second, Ramsey notes that "there is an obligation never to mean to do and accept damage disproportionate to political goals; but I suppose no military commander would calculate on actually doing any such thing" ("A Political Ethics Context," p. 145). But it is not damage disproportionate to *political* goals that is at issue in his discussion of war and deterrence, but damage disproportionate to *military* objectives. By referring to the cautions that may surround political considerations, Ramsey thus only diverts our attention away from the terms that are fundamental to the structure of deterrent strategy. And, it should be added, at the military level Ramsey's theory leaves open, or permits, disproportionate damage—whether or not a "military commander would calculate on actually doing any such thing."

Chapter 7

1. One notable exception is Douglas Lackey's consequentialist critique of nuclear deterrence. See Lackey, *Moral Principles and Nuclear Weapons* (Totowa, N.J.: Rowman & Allanheld, 1984).

2. In public policy, plans to enhance deterrence include the development of the Strategic Defense Initiative (SDI). For discussions of the SDI and its relation to nuclear deterrence, see United Methodist Council of Bishops, *In Defense of Creation: The Nuclear Crisis and a Just Peace,* pp. 49–52 (see chap. 1, n. 87); James R. Schlesinger, "Rhetoric and Realities in the Star Wars Debate," in *The Star Wars Controversy: An International Security Reader,* ed. Steven E. Miller and Stephen Van Evera (Princeton, N.J.: Princeton University Press, 1986), pp. 15–24, esp. pp. 17–18; and Joseph Nye, Jr., *Nuclear Ethics* (New York: Free Press, 1986), p. 125. All of these sources note how the rationale for the Strategic Defense Initiative has shifted from "rendering nuclear weapons obsolete" (in order to move away from the immorality of deterrence) to *enhancing* deterrence. Obviously the shift in rationale entails a shift in the moral evaluation of deterrence. For a trenchant critique of the SDI, see Steven Lee, "Morality, the SDI, and Limited Nuclear War," *Philosophy and Public Affairs* 17 (Winter 1988): 15–43.

3. Johnson, *Can Modern War Be Just?* p. 1 (see chap. 1, n. 29).

4. Caspar Weinberger, "A Rational Approach to Nuclear Disarmament," in *The Ethics of Nuclear War and Deterrence,* ed. James P. Sterba (Belmont, Calif.: Wadsworth, 1985), p. 117. See also the essay by Charles Krauthammer, "On Nuclear Morality," in the same volume, p. 150.

5. Richard Wasserstrom, "War, Nuclear War, and Nuclear Deterrence: Some Conceptual and Moral Issues," *Ethics* 95 (April 1985): 440.

6. O'Brien, *Just and Limited War,* p. 138 (see chap. 2, n. 72).

7. Johnson, *Can Modern War Be Just?* p. 103.

8. Solly Zuckerman, *Nuclear Illusion and Reality* (New York: Vintage Books, 1983), p. 48.

9. Leon Wieseltier, "The Great Nuclear Debate," *New Republic* 188:1–2 (January 10–17, 1983): 35. Wieseltier subsequently published this extended essay as *Nuclear War, Nuclear Peace* (New York: Holt, Rinehart & Winston, 1983).

10. Robert McKim, "An Examination of a Moral Argument against Nuclear Deterrence," *Journal of Religious Ethics* 13 (Fall 1985): 279–97, at 283–85.

11. Hollenbach, *Nuclear Ethics,* p. 83 (see chap. 1, n. 80).

12. The French Catholic Bishops, *Winning the Peace,* in *Out of Justice, Peace* and *Winning the Peace,* ed. with an introduction by James V. Schall (San Francisco: Ignatius Press, 1984), par. 33.

13. United Methodist Council of Bishops, *In Defense of Creation,* p. 49 (see chap. 1, n. 87).

14. *Encyclopedia of Philosophy,* 1st ed., s.v. "Fallacies" by J. L. Mackie. That this is an inductive fallacy, one which pertains to the relation of facts to themselves, means that it is also vulnerable to the charge that it issues in a falsehood. That is, the fallacy obscures other nonnuclear accounts for the absence of war (see n. 15).

15. For a brief discussion of nonnuclear factors contributing to the absence of war, see McGeorge Bundy, "Existential Deterrence and Its Consequences," in

The Security Gamble: Deterrence Dilemmas in the Nuclear Age, ed. Douglas MacLean (Totowa, N.J.: Rowman & Allanheld, 1984), pp. 6–8; cf. James P. Sterba, "How to Achieve Nuclear Deterrence without Threatening Nuclear Destruction," in *The Ethics of War and Nuclear Deterrence,* ed. Sterba, pp. 155–68, to be discussed below.

16. Sissela Bok, "Distrust, Secrecy, and the Arms Race," *Ethics* 95 (April 1985): 716.

17. See, e.g., Johnson, *Can Modern War Be Just?* chaps. 5, 6, 8; O'Brien, *Just and Limited War,* pp. 127–28. In more recent writings, O'Brien has placed tighter restraints on the use of nuclear force than he did in his previous writings. See William V. O'Brien, "The Failure of Deterrence and the Conduct of War," in *The Nuclear Dilemma and the Just War Tradition,* ed. William V. O'Brien and John Langan (Lexington, Mass.: Lexington Books, 1986), pp. 153–97, at 158, 176.

18. Wasserstrom, "War, Nuclear War, and Nuclear Deterrence," p. 440; see also Schell, *The Fate of the Earth,* pp. 197–208 (see chap. 4, n. 58). The problem of introducing notions of successful and unsuccessful deterrence into the same overall account is particularly acute for O'Brien. O'Brien's argument on behalf of a counterforce war-fighting strategy as essential to a credible deterrent begins with the assumption "that the nuclear deterrent has failed, aggression has occurred, and a nuclear response of some kind is under consideration." See O'Brien, *Just and Limited War,* p. 129, and, more recently, "The Failure of Deterrence," in *The Nuclear Dilemma,* ed. O'Brien and Langan, pp. 153, 156.

19. Appeals on behalf of using nuclear weapons are not altogether denied, however, since use is necessary to render deterrence credible, at least according to the U.S. Catholic bishops' treatment of use and deterrence. The point to be emphasized in the just-war thesis is that use must conform to just-war tenets.

20. U.S. Catholic Bishops, "Building Peace: A Pastoral Reflection on the Response to 'The Challenge of Peace,'" *Origins* 18 (July 21, 1988): 137.

21. U.S. Catholic Bishops, *The Challenge of Peace,* pars. 146–61. It should be noted, moreover, that the bishops are considering "the *real* as opposed to the *theoretical* possibility of a 'limited nuclear exchange.'"

22. U.S. Catholic Bishops, "A Pastoral Reflection on the Response to 'The Challenge of Peace,'" p. 137.

23. Ibid., p. 138. I should add that the bishops wish to distinguish between levels of authority in their letter. Such distinctions bear directly on the weight to be assigned to their treatment of use and deterrence. As they state in their introduction, "not all statements in this letter have the same moral authority. At times we state universally binding moral principles found in the teaching of the Church; at other times the pastoral letter makes specific applications, observations and recommendations which allow for diversity of opinion on the part of those who assess the factual data of situations differently." See *The Challenge of Peace,* p. i.

24. U.S. Catholic Bishops, *The Challenge of Peace,* par. 2, in "Summary."

25. Ibid., par. 186.

26. Ibid., par. 188.

27. For a discussion of the incentives to compete for superiority in a counterforce world, see Barry R. Posen and Stephen Van Evera, "Defense Policy and the

Reagan Administration: Departure from Containment," *International Security* 8 (Summer 1983): 3–45, at 12–14.

28. This same problem of reconciling the proscription of a nuclear first strike with the permission of second-strike counterforce warfare plagues the famous "gang of four" article in *Foreign Affairs*. See McGeorge Bundy, George F. Kennan, Robert McNamara, and Gerard Smith, "Nuclear Weapons and the Atlantic Alliance," *Foreign Affairs* 60 (Spring 1982): 753–68.

29. Hollenbach, *Nuclear Ethics,* pp. 47–62.

30. Ibid., p. 65.

31. Douglas MacLean, "Introduction," in *The Security Gamble,* p. xvii.

32. Hollenbach, *Nuclear Ethics,* p. 57.

33. Ibid., p. 74.

34. Ibid., p. 75.

35. French Catholic Bishops, *Winning the Peace,* par. 29.

36. West German Catholic Bishops, *Out of Justice, Peace,* par. 150.

37. The French bishops, it should be noted, seem to recognize this problem of credibility. They opt for a view of deterrence linked to countercity targeting as the lesser of possible evils in the present international order. See *Winning the Peace,* pars. 28–30.

38. Hollenbach, *Nuclear Ethics,* p. 83.

39. Lawrence Freedman, *The Evolution of Nuclear Strategy* (New York: St. Martin's Press, 1983), esp. chaps. 4–9, 14–16, 25; cf. Desmond Ball, "U.S. Strategic Forces: How Would They Be Used?" *International Security* 7 (Winter 1982–83): 31–60, esp. 33–40.

40. Paul Bracken, *The Command and Control of Nuclear Forces* (New Haven: Yale University Press, 1983), chap. 6, passim.

41. For a similar point, see Anthony Kenny, *The Logic of Deterrence* (Chicago: University of Chicago Press, 1985), pp. 50, 53–54.

42. James Sterba, "How to Achieve Nuclear Deterrence without Threatening Nuclear Destruction," in *The Ethics of Nuclear War and Deterrence,* ed. Sterba, p. 159.

43. Ibid., p. 164.

44. James P. Sterba, "Moral Approaches to Nuclear Strategy: A Critical Appraisal," *Canadian Journal of Philosophy,* suppl. vol. 12, ed. David Copp (Calgary: University of Calgary Press, 1986), p. 107.

45. Sterba, "How to Achieve Nuclear Deterrence without Threatening Nuclear Destruction," p. 165.

46. See, for example, Stephen Van Evera, "The Cult of the Offensive and the Origins of the First World War," *International Security* 9 (Summer 1984): 58–107.

47. Walzer, *Just and Unjust Wars,* pp. 269–83 (see chap. 1, n. 66). For a retrieval of the supreme emergency as analogous with Vitoria's application of just-war ideas, see Johnson, *Can Modern War Be Just?* pp. 185–90. See also the recent discussions of Walzer's notion of the supreme emergency by Gerald Mara (to be discussed below), Hollenbach, and O'Brien in *The Nuclear Dilemma and the Just War Tradition,* ed. O'Brien and Langan, pp. 15–18, 49–78, 227–28.

48. Walzer, *Just and Unjust Wars,* pp. 270, 282.

49. Ibid., p. 273.

50. Ibid., pp. 273–74.

51. Ibid., p. 252.

52. Ibid.

53. Ibid., p. 260.

54. Ibid., p. 274.

55. Ibid.

56. Ibid., p. 253.

57. Ibid., p. 282.

58. Gerald M. Mara, "Justice, War, and Politics: The Problem of Supreme Emergency," in *The Nuclear Dilemma,* ed. O'Brien and Langan, pp. 49–78.

59. Ibid., p. 65.

60. Ibid., p. 70. I hasten to add that Walzer's views may be more salvageable along Mara's lines than Mara himself suggests. For if, as Walzer claims, a supreme emergency must be understood in terms of the *nature* as well as the imminence of a threat to one's existence, then it may well be that Walzer can argue that nefarious enemies cannot appeal to the conditions of a supreme emergency. If Western polities are relatively more just than totalitarian regimes, then the nature of the Western deterrent threat does not satisfy one of Walzer's two criteria. It seems intuitively implausible to suggest that Western threats are morally equivalent to the *nature* of a threat like that posed by Nazism to the West in World War II, or so one might argue.

The trouble with this defense, however, lies in presupposing that Walzer's theory enables us to make qualitative distinctions between different polities. Walzer's inchoate political theory in *Just and Unjust Wars,* drawing on social contract philosophy, makes it difficult to speak in terms of virtuous and vicious polities. There is a tension, in short, between Walzer's references to human rights, which make it easier to think in terms of virtuous and vicious polities, and his contract theory, which is developed with an eye to justifying state sovereignty, and which appears morally neutral to questions of collective virtue. See Walzer, *Just and Unjust Wars,* pp. 54–56.

61. Ibid., p. 67.

62. Ibid.

63. See, for example, the U.S. Catholic Bishops, *The Challenge of Peace,* par. 237, where they affirm the "real but relative" value of national sovereignty. The relativity of national sovereignty precludes reference to national survival as an ultimate value or principle, even within the present international order.

64. One such example is Jerram Barrs, *Who Are the Peacemakers? The Christian Case for Nuclear Deterrence,* with an introduction by Francis A. Schaeffer (Westchester, Ill.: Crossway Books, 1983).

65. MacIntyre, *After Virtue,* pp. 236–37 (see chap. 2, n. 35).

66. Mara, "Justice, War, and Politics," in *The Nuclear Dilemma,* ed. O'Brien and Johnson, p. 71.

67. For a critique of nuclear deterrence in light of its moral and historical connection with the nation-state, see Michael J. Quirk, "Just War Theory, Nuclear Deterrence, and Reason of State," *International Journal of Applied Philosophy* 3 (Fall 1986): 51–59. Quirk goes beyond MacIntyre by arguing that deterrence is linked inexorably to the rise of "reasons of state" and that such reasons furnish the ultimate rationale for survivalism. Thus, in the modern context na-

tion-states are especially disposed to suspend the kinds of limits imposed by just-war criteria in order to legitimate nuclear deterrence. Quirk's argument is premised on a distinction between communities and nation-states, although he fails to define the salient features of communities beyond the presence of practical rationality. His argument has the merit of calling attention to the social theory presupposed by deterrent debates. Yet without a fuller account of what comprises a community, his claim that a community formed around pacifist or just-war principles "would rather see itself dissolved than contradict its convictions concerning the strictly limited character of permissible warfare" remains open to doubt. Surely the systematic violation of moral principles of limited warfare in the name of survival predates the birth of the nation-state.

Chapter 8

1. Geuss, *The Idea of a Critical Theory,* p. 5 (see Introduction, n. 4).

2. Ibid., p. 10.

3. James Turner Johnson, "Historical Tradition and Moral Judgment: The Case of Just War Tradition," *Journal of Religion* 64 (July 1984): 302.

4. Johnson, *Just War Tradition,* p. 167 (see Introduction, n. 13).

5. See, e.g., Johnson, "On Keeping Faith: The Use of History for Religious Ethics," pp. 98–115 (see chap. 4, n. 1); Alasdair MacIntyre, *A Short History of Ethics* (New York: Macmillan, 1966), chap. 1; Jonsen and Toulmin, *The Abuse of Casuistry* (see chap. 1, n. 3); Michel Foucault, *The Use of Pleasure,* trans. Robert Hurley (New York: Vintage Books, 1986), chap. 3; Walzer, *Just and Unjust Wars* (see chap. 1, n. 66)—although elsewhere Walzer has suggested ways to address problems surrounding historicism, ethics, and ideology, as I shall indicate below.

6. This is not to suggest that Johnson is wholly unaware of ideology, only that it plays little role in his use of history. When Johnson uses the word *ideology,* he tends to equate it with theology, especially Christian theology. Thus, charting the de-ideologization of just-war tenets is his way of talking about the secularization of just-war vocabulary. See James Turner Johnson, *Ideology, Reason, and the Limitation of War: Religious and Secular Concepts, 1200–1740* (Princeton, N.J.: Princeton University Press, 1975).

7. See Leland D. Baldwin, *The American Quest for the City of God* (Macon, Ga.: Mercer University Press, 1981); Loren Baritz, *City on a Hill: A History of Ideas and Myths in America* (New York: John Wiley & Sons, 1964); Sacvan Bercovitch, *American Jeremiad* (see chap. 5, n. 85); Edward McNall Burns, *The American Idea of Mission: Concepts of National Purpose and Destiny* (New Brunswick, N.J.: Rutgers University Press, 1957); Conrad Cherry, ed., *God's New Israel: Religious Interpretations of American Destiny* (Englewood Cliffs, N.J.: Prentice-Hall, 1971); William A. Clebsch, *From Sacred to Profane America: The Role of Religion in American History* (New York: Harper & Row, 1968); Sam B. Girgus, ed., *The American Self: Myth, Ideology, and Popular Culture* (Albuquerque: University of New Mexico Press, 1981); Norman A. Graebner, ed., *Manifest Destiny* (Indianapolis: Bobbs-Merrill, 1968); Winthrop Hudson, ed., *Nationalism and Religion in America: Concepts of American Identity and Mission* (New York: Harper & Row, 1970); William R. Hutchinson, *Errand to the World: American Protestant Thought and Foreign Missions* (Chi-

cago: University of Chicago Press, 1987); Martin Marty, *Righteous Empire: The Protestant Experience in America* (New York: Dial Press, 1970); Perry Miller, *Errand into the Wilderness* (Cambridge: Harvard University Press, 1975); Reinhold Niebuhr, *The Irony of American History* (New York: Charles Scribner's Sons, 1952); Russel B. Nye, *This Almost Chosen People: Essays in the History of American Ideas* (East Lansing: Michigan State University Press, 1966); Edward Said, "Representing the Colonized: Anthropology's Interlocutors," *Critical Inquiry* 15 (Winter 1989): 205–25; and Ernest Lee Tuveson, *Redeemer Nation: The Idea of America's Millennial Role* (Chicago: University of Chicago Press, 1968). The idea of exceptionalism and its related tropes are treated more generally in several discussions: cf. Sydney E. Ahlstrom, *A Religious History of the American People* (New Haven: Yale University Press, 1972); Catherine Albanese, *America: Religions and Religion* (Belmont, Calif.: Wadsworth, 1981), chaps. 10–12; Robert Bellah, *The Broken Covenant: American Civil Religion in Time of Trial* (New York: Seabury, 1975), chap. 2; Alan Geyer, *Piety and Politics: American Protestantism in the World Arena* (Richmond: John Knox Press, 1963); Robert Handy, *A Christian America: Protestant Hopes and Historical Realities*, 2d ed. (New York: Oxford University Press, 1984).

8. Alexander Whitaker, "Good Newes from Virginia," in *God's New Israel*, ed. Cherry, pp. 32–33.

9. Cited in Winthrop S. Hudson, *Religion in America* (New York: Charles Scribner's Sons, 1965), p. 20; Handy, *A Christian America*, p. 7.

10. Cited in Ahlstrom, *A Religious History*, p. 302.

11. Jonathan Edwards, "The Latter-Day Glory Is Probably to Begin in America," in *God's New Israel*, ed. Cherry, p. 59.

12. Cited in Ahlstrom, *A Religious History*, pp. 310–11.

13. Cited in Nye, *This Almost Chosen People*, p. 190.

14. Ezra Stiles, "The United States Elevated to Glory and Honour," in *God's New Israel*, ed. Cherry, p. 86.

15. Lyman Beecher, *Plea for the West* (Cincinnati: Truman & Smith, 1835), pp. 9, 11.

16. Ibid., pp. 11, 23.

17. Cited in Baldwin, *The American Quest for the City of God*, p. 170.

18. Cited in Burns, *The American Idea of Mission*, p. 14.

19. Abraham Lincoln, "Letter to Thurlow Weed," in *Abraham Lincoln: His Speeches and Writings*, ed. Roy Basler, with a preface by Carl Sandburg (New York: World Publishing Co., 1946), p. 794.

20. Lincoln, "Second Inaugural Address," in *Abraham Lincoln: His Speeches and Writings*, ed. Basler, p. 793.

21. Benjamin Palmer, "National Responsibility before God," in *God's New Israel*, ed. Cherry, pp. 181–93.

22. Cited in Marty, *Righteous Empire*, p. 6.

23. Cited in Hutchinson, *Errand to the World*, p. 29.

24. Cited in Marty, *Righteous Empire*, p. 12.

25. Ibid., p. 25. For a biblical authorization of slavery, see, e.g., John England's letter to Secretary of State John Forsyth, excerpted in H. Shelton Smith, Robert T. Handy, and Lefferts A. Loetscher, eds., *American Christianity: An Historical Interpretation with Representative Documents*, vol. 2, 1820–1960

(New York: Charles Scribner's Sons, 1963), pp. 201–5. England was the Catholic bishop of Charleston, South Carolina.

26. Cited in Marty, *Righteous Empire*, p. 23.

27. Walt Whitman, "Either Back Out Entirely or Establish Our Permanent Power," in *Manifest Destiny*, ed. Graebner, p. 208.

28. Albert Gallatin, "The Mission of the United States," in *Manifest Destiny*, ed. Graebner, p. 196.

29. Cited in Handy, *Christian America*, pp. 90–91.

30. Cited in Geyer, *Piety and Politics*, p. 61.

31. Albert Beveridge, "The Star of the Empire," in *God's New Israel*, ed. Cherry, p. 142.

32. Washington Gladden, "Migrations and Their Lessons," *Publications of the Ohio Archaeological and Historical Society* 3 (1891): 180, cited in Tuveson, *Redeemer Nation*, p. 128.

33. Cited in Handy, *Christian America*, p. 109.

34. William Lawrence, "The Relation of Wealth to Morals," in *God's New Israel*, ed. Cherry, p. 248.

35. Cited in Leslie Berlowitz, Denis Donoghue, and Louis Menand, eds., *America in Theory* (New York: Oxford University Press, 1988), pp. 232, 258.

36. Cited in Paul Boyer, *By the Bomb's Early Light: American Thought and Culture at the Dawn of the Atomic Age* (New York: Pantheon, 1985), p. 224.

37. Ibid., pp. 211–12.

38. William Hard, "The Road Ahead in the Light of the H-Bomb," *Reader's Digest* 65 (August 1954): 8.

39. Cited in Nye, *This Almost Chosen People*, p. 40.

40. Cited in Martin Marty, *Religion and Republic: The American Circumstance* (Boston: Beacon Press, 1987), p. 85.

41. Harvey Cox, *The Secular City: Secularization and Urbanization in Theological Perspective*, rev. ed. (New York: Macmillan, 1966), p. xi.

42. Ibid., pp. 21–23.

43. Ibid., p. 28.

44. So pronounced is this first trope that even historical surveys are controlled by providential beliefs. H. Richard Niebuhr's survey of American Protestantism, *Kingdom of God in America*, is organized in a trinitarian way, using the categories of "The Sovereignty of God," "The Kingdom of Christ," and "The Coming Kingdom" as organizing rubrics; George Bancroft's *History of the United States* seeks "to follow the steps by which a favoring Providence . . . has conducted the country to its present happiness and glory." And even during the American bicentennial a group of scholars, sponsored by the Moody Bible Institute, met to discuss the relation between biblical prophecy and American history. See Niebuhr, *Kingdom of God in America* (see chap. 3, n. 113); George Bancroft, *History of the United States*, vol. 1 (London: George Routledge & Sons, 1834), p. 4; Thomas McCall, ed., *America in History and Bible Prophecy* (Chicago: Moody Press, 1976).

45. John Winthrop, "A Modell of Christian Charity," in *God's New Israel*, ed. Cherry, p. 43.

46. Cited in Bercovitch, *American Jeremiad*, p. 72.

47. George Bancroft, cited in Nye, *This Almost Chosen People*, p. 169.

48. Stiles, "The United States Elevated to Glory and Honour," in *God's New Israel*, ed. Cherry, p. 90.

49. Cited in Tuveson, *Redeemer Nation*, p. 119.

50. See Cherry, ed., *God's New Israel*, p. 114.

51. John O'Sullivan, "The Great Nation of Futurity," in *Manifest Destiny*, ed. Graebner, p. 21.

52. Cited in Nye, *This Almost Chosen People*, p. 174.

53. Isaac Wise, "Our Country's Place in History," in *God's New Israel*, ed. Cherry, p. 225.

54. Gallatin, "Mission of the United States," in *Manifest Destiny*, ed. Graebner, p. 192.

55. Ibid., pp. 192, 194.

56. Gladden, "The Nation and the Kingdom," in *God's New Israel*, ed. Cherry, pp. 264, 269.

57. C. F. Thomas, "Patriotism," in *God's New Israel*, ed. Cherry, p. 281.

58. Woodrow Wilson, "Presenting the Treaty for Ratification," in *God's New Israel*, ed. Cherry, p. 294.

59. Cited in Nye, *This Almost Chosen People*, p. 170.

60. Arthur M. Schlesinger, Jr., *Political and Social Growth of the American Peoples, 1865–1940*, 3d ed. (New York: Macmillan, 1941), p. v.

61. George F. Kennan, "America and the Russian Future," in Loren Baritz, ed., *Sources of the American Mind*, vol. 2 (New York: John Wiley & Sons, 1966), p. 356.

62. Ronald Reagan, "First Inaugural Address," *Vital Speeches of the Day* 47 (February 15, 1981), p. 260.

63. Jacques Maritain, *Reflections on America* (New York: Charles Scribner's Sons, 1958), pp. 83–85.

64. Cited in Marty, *Righteous Empire*, p. 9.

65. Miller, *Errand into the Wilderness*, p. 6.

66. Cited in Tuveson, *Redeemer Nation*, p. 142.

67. Edwards, "Latter Day Glory," in *God's New Israel*, ed. Cherry, pp. 55–57; emphasis in original.

68. Stiles, "The United States Elevated to Honour and Glory," in *God's New Israel*, ed. Cherry, p. 92.

69. Cited in Tuveson, *Redeemer Nation*, p. 25.

70. Cited in Hutchinson, *Errand to the World*, p. 61.

71. Cited in Bercovitch, *American Jeremiad*, p. 141.

72. Cited in Nye, *This Almost Chosen People*, pp. 173–74.

73. *Ralph Waldo Emerson: Essays and Journals*, ed. Lewis Mumford (Garden City, N.Y.: Doubleday, 1968), p. 670.

74. Orestes A. Brownson, "Mission of America," in Aaron I. Abell, ed., *American Catholic Thought on Social Questions* (Indianapolis: Bobbs-Merrill, 1968), p. 25.

75. Ibid., p. 35.

76. Ibid., p. 29.

77. Ibid., pp. 30–31.

78. Robert Stockton, "Redeem Mexico from Misrule and Civil Strife," in *Manifest Destiny*, ed. Graebner, p. 214.

79. Cited in Nye, *This Almost Chosen People*, p. 174.

80. Cited in Hutchinson, *Errand to the World*, p. 99.

81. Ibid., p. 65.

82. Ibid., p. 116.

83. For a further discussion, see Handy, *Christian America*, chap. 5.

84. Washington Gladden, "The Nation and the Kingdom," in *God's New Israel*, ed. Cherry, p. 260.

85. Cited in Nye, *This Almost Chosen People*, p. 83.

86. Lincoln, "Letter to Mrs. Eliza P. Gurney," in *Abraham Lincoln: His Speeches and Writings*, ed. Basler, p. 757.

87. Horace Bushnell, "Our Obligations to the Dead," in *God's New Israel*, ed. Cherry, pp. 200, 204–5.

88. Ibid., p. 202.

89. Cited in Nye, *This Almost Chosen People*, pp. 199–200.

90. Ibid., p. 199.

91. Ibid., pp. 83, 176.

92. Cited in Berlowitz et al., eds., *America in Theory*, p. 258.

93. Franklin D. Roosevelt, "Annual Message to Congress," in *God's New Israel*, ed. Cherry, p. 301.

94. For a discussion, see chap. 1.

95. Excerpted as "Principles of a Durable Peace," in *American Christianity: An Historical Interpretation with Representative Documents*, vol. 2, ed. Smith et al., p. 526 (see n. 25).

96. Fulton J. Sheen, *God and War* (New York: P. J. Kenedy & Sons, 1942), pp. 94–95.

97. Ibid., pp. 95–96.

98. Ibid., p. 91.

99. Ibid., p. 98.

100. Richard John Neuhaus, *The Naked Public Square: Religion and Democracy in America* (Grand Rapids, Mich.: Eerdmans, 1984), p. 72.

101. Thomas Jefferson, "First Inaugural Address," in *God's New Israel*, ed. Cherry, p. 107.

102. Cited in Hutchinson, *Errand to the World*, p. 56; emphasis in original.

103. Cited in Nye, *This Almost Chosen People*, p. 185.

104. Frederick Stanton, "Justification of American Claims by Higher Law," in *Manifest Destiny*, ed. Graebner, p. 94.

105. John O'Sullivan, "The True Title," in *God's New Israel*, ed. Cherry, pp. 128–29.

106. Beveridge, "Star of the Empire," in *God's New Israel*, ed. Cherry, pp. 145, 148, 153.

107. Cited in John Morton Blum, *Woodrow Wilson and the Politics of Morality* (Boston: Little, Brown, 1956), p. 101.

108. "Between War and Peace," *Catholic Action* 27 (December 1945): 27–28, cited in *American Christianity*, vol. 2, ed. Smith et al., pp. 527–29.

109. These citations are from Boyer, *By the Bomb's Early Light*, p. 211.

110. Niebuhr, *Irony of American History*, p. 131.

111. See Emerson, "Self-Reliance," in *Emerson: Essays and Journals;* Dale

Carnegie, *How to Win Friends and Influence People* (New York: Simon & Schuster, 1936); Bloom, *The Anxiety of Influence* (see chap. 5, n. 14); Rorty, *Contingency, Irony, and Solidarity* (see chap. 1, n. 104).

112. Emerson, "Self-Reliance," in *Emerson: Essays and Journals*, pp. 92, 101, 103.

113. Aquinas, *Summa Theologiae*, II-II, Q. 40, A. 1.

114. O'Brien, *Just and Limited War*, p. 29 (see chap. 2, n. 72).

115. Ibid., pp. 21–22.

116. Ibid., p. 21.

117. Ibid., p. 47.

118. Cited in Paul Ramsey's introduction to O'Brien, *War and/or Survival*, p. xv (see chap. 4, n. 73); cf. William V. O'Brien, "Just War Doctrine in a Nuclear Context," *Theological Studies* 44 (June 1983): 211.

119. King, *Why We Can't Wait*, p. 94 (see chap. 4, n. 20).

120. Speech recorded in the television series for the Public Broadcasting System, *Eyes on the Prize: America's Civil Rights Years*, "Awakenings: 1954–1956."

121. King, *Why We Can't Wait*, p. 93.

122. Cited in Taylor Branch, *Parting the Waters: America in the King Years, 1954–63* (New York: Simon & Schuster, 1988), p. 197; cf. James M. Washington, ed., *A Testament of Hope: The Essential Writings of Martin Luther King, Jr.* (San Francisco: Harper & Row, 1986), p. 88.

123. King, *Strength to Love*, p. 154 (see chap. 4, n. 19).

124. King, *Why We Can't Wait*, p. 36.

125. Ibid., p. 44.

126. Cited in Branch, *Parting the Waters*, p. 276.

127. King, *Why We Can't Wait*, p. 45.

128. Ibid., p. 125.

129. Martin Luther King, Jr., "A Mighty Army of Love," *SCLC Newsletter* 2 (October–November 1964): 7–8.

130. Cited in Branch, *Parting the Waters*, p. 363.

131. King, *Strength to Love*, p. 25.

132. Ibid., p. 154.

133. Cited in *A Testament of Hope*, ed. Washington, p. 151; cf. p. 208.

134. Ibid., p. 209.

135. Quoted from *The Words of Martin Luther King*, selected by Coretta Scott King (New York: Newmarket Press, 1983), p. 47.

136. Ibid., p. 94.

137. Tuveson, *Redeemer Nation*, pp. 198–99.

138. Martin Luther King, Jr., "Hammer on Civil Rights," in *A Testament of Hope*, ed. Washington, p. 169.

139. King, *Where Do We Go from Here?* pp. 133–34 (see chap. 4, n. 20).

140. King, *Why We Can't Wait*, p. 82.

141. Martin Luther King, Jr., *Trumpet of Conscience* (New York: Harper & Row, 1967), p. 5.

142. King, *Strength to Love*, p. 25.

143. Bercovitch, *American Jeremiad*, p. 180 (see chap. 5, n. 85).

144. Walzer, *Interpretation and Social Criticism*, chap. 2 (see Introduction, n. 8).

Chapter 9

1. Childress, "Just-War Criteria," p. 40 (see Introduction, n. 9).
2. Ibid., p. 51. For a discussion of pacifists and just-war theorists in Catholicism during the 1960s, see David J. O'Brien, "American Catholic Opposition to the Vietnam War: A Preliminary Assessment," in *War and Peace?* ed. Shannon, pp. 119–50.
3. Aquinas, *Summa Theologiae*, II-II, Q. 40, A. 1.
4. O'Brien, *Just and Limited War*, pp. 37–55 (see chap. 2, n. 72).
5. Ramsey, *The Just War*, pp. 141–47 (see chap. 6, n. 8); U.S. Catholic Bishops, *The Challenge of Peace*, pars. 107–9 (see Introduction, n. 14).
6. Childress, "Just-War Criteria," p. 50.
7. Ibid., p. 51.
8. Ramsey, *The Just War*, pp. 145, 273.
9. Ibid., p. 510.
10. MacIntyre, *After Virtue*, chap. 1 (see chap. 2, n. 35).
11. Hans-Georg Gadamer, *Reason in the Age of Science*, trans. Frederick G. Lawrence (Cambridge, Mass.: MIT Press, 1981), p. 49.
12. For recent discussions of virtue and duty in religious ethics, see Frederick S. Carney, "The Virtue-Obligation Controversy," *Journal of Religious Ethics* 1 (Fall 1973): 5–19; Arthur J. Dyck, "A Unified Theory of Virtue and Obligation," *Journal of Religious Ethics* 1 (Fall 1973): 37–52; and Stanley Hauerwas, "Obligation and Virtue Once More," *Journal of Religious Ethics* 3 (Spring 1975): 27–44.
13. Aristotle, *Nicomachean Ethics* (hereafter *NE*) 1140b20.
14. Ibid., 1142b27.
15. For a discussion of the relation between prudence and choice, see Christopher Lasch, "The Communitarian Critique of Liberalism," *Soundings* 69 (Spring/Summer 1986): 60–76.
16. Aquinas, *Summa Theologiae*, I-II, Q. 57, A. 6. See also Thomas Aquinas, *Commentary on the Nicomachean Ethics*, vol. 2, trans. C. I. Litzinger (Chicago: Henry Regnery, 1964), p. 581.
17. Aristotle, *NE*, 1143b14.
18. Ibid., 1144a30.
19. Ibid., 1143a31–35.
20. Here I am following two helpful studies: Martha Nussbaum, *The Fragility of Goodness: Luck and Ethics in Greek Philosophy and Tragedy* (Cambridge: Cambridge University Press, 1986), p. 305; David Wiggins, "Deliberation and Practical Reason," in *Essays on Aristotle's Ethics*, ed. Amélie Oksenberg Rorty, (Berkeley: University of California Press, 1980), pp. 235–37.
21. Aquinas, *Summa Theologiae*, II-II, Q. 47, A. 3, ad 3.
22. Wiggins, "Deliberation and Practical Reason," p. 237.
23. Aristotle, *NE*, 1144b30.
24. Aquinas, *Summa Theologiae*, II-II, Q. 47, A. 3, ad 3.
25. MacIntyre, *After Virtue*, pp. 174–78.
26. Robert Bellah et al., *Habits of the Heart: Individualism and Commitment*

in American Life (Berkeley: University of California Press, 1985), p. 153.

27. For a helpful discussion of practical reason and memory as the appropriation of custom, see Gadamer, *Truth and Method,* pp. 16–17 (see chap. 1, n. 98).

28. Bellah et al., *Habits of the Heart,* p. 153.

29. Howard Zinn, *A People's History of the United States* (New York: Harper & Row, 1980), p. 9; cf. Johann Baptist Metz, *Faith in Society and History: Toward a Practical Fundamental Theology* (New York: Seabury, 1977), p. 109.

30. Hauerwas, *Should War Be Eliminated?* p. 33 (see chap. 4, n. 16). For a similar set of views, developed with an appeal for reconstructing civic virtue rather than pacifism, see Jean Bethke Elshtain, *Women and War* (New York: Basic Books, 1987).

31. Charles W. Allen, "The Primacy of *Phronesis:* A Proposal for Avoiding Frustrating Tendencies in Our Conceptions of Rationality," *Journal of Religion* 69 (July 1989): 359–74.

32. See Gadamer, *Truth and Method,* p. 17.

33. For a discussion of the memory of suffering as a corrective of historical distortion, see Metz, *Faith in Society and History,* pp. 115, 213–14, 229, 231, and passim.

34. A similar question is posed by Tracy, *Plurality and Ambiguity,* p. 77 (see Introduction, n. 11).

35. See chap. 5.

36. Gutierrez, *A Theology of Liberation,* pp. 213–50 (see chap. 2, n. 73).

37. Paul Tillich, *Dynamics of Faith* (New York: Harper & Row, 1957), pp. 97–98.

38. See, e.g., Ramsey, *The Just War,* chaps. 1, 6.

39. Tracy, *Plurality and Ambiguity,* pp. 67–68.

40. Reinhold Niebuhr, *Christian Realism and Political Problems* (New York: Charles Scribner's Sons, 1953), p. 120.

41. Ibid., p. 131.

42. O'Brien, *Just and Limited War,* p. 329 (see chap. 2, n. 72); O'Brien, *War and/or Survival,* pp. 62–63 (see chap. 4, n. 73).

43. O'Brien, *Just and Limited War,* pp. 38–48.

44. Ibid., p. 47.

45. O'Brien, "Just War Doctrine in a Nuclear Context," pp. 211–20 (see chap. 8, n. 118).

46. Ibid., p. 220.

47. Yoder, *The Priestly Kingdom,* chap. 1 (see Introduction, n. 6).

48. Ibid., p. 44.

49. Ibid., p. 40.

50. Ibid., p. 42.

51. Ibid. One problem with this account is that Yoder fails to reckon with the Thomistic notion that the divine law and the natural law exist under the unity of the eternal law. Since truth is one, differences between the divine and natural law are not so grave as to fracture the overall unity of divine reason, as that is defined, for example, in Thomas's *Treatise on Law.* Thus, in suggesting that the theory of natural law was part of two separate codes (one for "everyone" and the other for Jews alone), Yoder overlooks the general structure of law as emanating

from the unity of divine wisdom, the eternal law. See Thomas Aquinas, *Summa Theologiae*, I-II, Qq. 90–97.

52. See Tracy, *Plurality and Ambiguity*, p. 19.

Epilogue

1. Rorty, *Contingency, Irony, and Solidarity*, p. 78 (see chap. 1, n. 104).

Index

Abbott, Lyman, 199
Adams, John, 205
Adams, John Quincy, 202
Agape, 92–94, 112, 118, 121; in Paul
 Ramsey, 148–55, 242
Aiken, Henry David, 9, 39
American jeremiad, 142–43, 220, 221
Analogy, 247n.11
Aquinas, Saint Thomas. *See* Thomas
 Aquinas, Saint
Aristotle, 60, 186–88, 227, 228–30
Augustine, Saint, 18–23, 47, 54, 60, 81,
 109, 141, 150, 154, 162, 215,
 249nn.17, 18; 250nn.19, 20; 251n.29;
 on individual self-defense, 19–20; on
 peace, 21, 150; on private and public
 morality, 22; on war, 21. Works: *On
 Christian Doctrine,* 19; *City of God,*
 60; *Freedom of the Will* ("De Libero
 Arbitrio"), 19, 249n.18

Bainton, Roland, 27, 30
Baird, Robert, 198
Bancroft, George, 202, 282n.44
Barbour, John, 139
Barth, Karl, 31–35, 45, 48, 49, 121, 239;
 on individual self-defense, 32–33; on
 war, 33–35
Beecher, Lyman, 197. Works: *Plea for the
 West,* 197
Bellah, Robert, et al., 230, 231
Berrigan, Daniel, 97–99, 263n.74
Berrigan, Philip, 97, 99, 100; on destruc-
 tion of property, 100
Beveridge, Albert, 199, 207–8, 211
Bias against violence. *See* Presumption
 against harm
Bloom, Harold, 212, 269n.14
Bok, Sissela, 172
Boyer, Paul, 199

Bracken, Paul, 180
Brackenridge, Hugh Henry, 198
Brock, Peter, 123
Brody, Bernard, 200
Brownson, Orestes, 205–6
Burrell, David, 6
Bushnell, Horace, 125, 207

Calhoun Commission, 27–31, 48, 142, 208
Calvin, John, 134, 138
Carnegie, Dale, 212
Catholic Left, 97–101
Catholic Worker (newspaper), 87
Catholic Worker (movement), 86–88, 90,
 91, 117
Challenge of Peace, The (1983), 35, 62,
 65, 86, 161; on just-war tenets, 66,
 225; on nuclear deterrence, 67–68,
 174–77; on nuclear war, 67, 173–74;
 on relative justice, 66. *See also* U.S.
 Catholic bishops
Charity, order of, 23–25, 61. *See also* Jus-
 tice; Order; Thomas Aquinas, Saint
Childress, James, 7, 16, 17, 18, 44, 66,
 106, 121–22, 162–63, 224–25, 248n.4,
 250n.19, 261n.10
Civic friendship, 60, 74–75
Civil disobedience, 78, 80–82, 89–91, 94–
 96, 97–101, 110–11, 210, 260n.2,
 265nn.115, 116; in terms of exceptionalist counterideology, 217–22
Comparative justice, 214, 237; contrasted
 with relative justice, 216; and just-war
 criteria, 216
Compton, Arthur, 200
Connected criticism, 222, 241–43
Consequences, 15, 119, 151–52, 155–61,
 163–66, 168, 170–71, 184, 214–15.
 See also Double effect, Intention, Proportionality

Convergence of pacifism and just-war tenets, 7, 8, 120–24; in Augustine, 18–23; in contemporary Catholicism, 35–38, 48; in modern Protestantism, 27–35; practical, 38–39, 48; in recent ethical theory, 106–7; rejected by Paul Ramsey, 150; in Thomas Aquinas, 23–27. *See also* Barth, Karl; Calhoun Commission; Hollenbach, David; U.S. Catholic bishops

Counterideology, 217–24, 234–36

Cox, Harvey, 200–201

Crucifixion, 29, 130, 233

Curran, Charles, 106, 263n.61, 265nn.4, 5

Day, Dorothy, 86–91 passim

Deats, Paul, 116

Deterrence. *See* Nuclear deterrence

Discrimination, principle of, 14–15, 64, 150–51, 161, 166, 173–74, 178, 215. See also *Jus in bello*

Double effect, 24, 151, 274n.65

Douglass, James, 91–97, 98, 102, 112, 114, 117, 139; on civil disobedience, 94–96; and eschatological realism, 91, 93

Duties: negative and positive, 41, 161; and rights, 35, 36, 43–44, 80–83. *See also* Nonmaleficence, duty of; Prima facie duties

Edwards, Jonathan, 196, 204

Egan, Eileen, 262n.52

Eisenhower, Dwight, 200

Elshtain, Jean Bethke, 287n.30

Emerson, Ralph Waldo, 205, 212–13

Emmons, Nathaniel, 205

Ethics: and confessionalism, 5–6, 239–41; and disinterested rationality, 5, 43; and intertextuality, 6–7, 49, 73, 217–22, 241–43; and nature, 4–5, 43–44; and public discourse, 221–23, 224–43 passim; and self-reflexivity, 3–4, 49. *See also* Historicism in ethics; Natural law; Practical reasoning; Religion and morality; Theology and ethics

Exceptionalism, 141, 186–88, 195–222 passim; exemplarism, 201–4, 218–19; higher law, 209–13, 220–21; providential election, 196–201, 217–18; redemptive suffering, 204–9, 219–20. *See also* Ideology; King, Martin Lu-

ther, Jr.; Mara, Gerald; O'Brien, William V.

Federal Council of Churches, 208

Finn, James, 106, 265n.5

Finnis, John; Boyle, Joseph; and Grisez, Germain, 148, 252n.37

Flynn, Eileen P., 255n.113

Foucault, Michel, 53

Freedman, Lawrence, 180

French Catholic bishops, 171, 179, 278n.37

Furfey, Paul Hanly, 87, 89

Gadamer, Hans-Georg, 227, 232–33, 254n.98

Gallatin, Albert, 199, 202

Geuss, Raymond, 193, 247n.4

Gewirth, Alan, 5, 43

Gladden, Washington, 199, 203, 207

Guest, Edgar, 212

Gunnemann, Jon, 72–73

Gustafson, James, 28

Gutierrez, Gustavo, 60–74, 233, 258nn.73, 74, 259nn.77, 82, 85, 89; on acts of omission, 74; on implication in evil, 72; on radical difference, 69–70, 71. Works: *A Theology of Liberation,* 69

Handy, Robert, 196

Harris, Samuel, 199

Hauerwas, Stanley, 6, 108–9, 111, 113, 115, 118, 119, 232, 266n.11; and biblical narrative, 109; eschatological themes, 110

Hehir, J. Bryan, 63, 106, 148, 265n.5

Hermeneutics, 229–36, 239; in the Calhoun Commission report, 28–30; in H. Richard Niebuhr's ethics, 130–31, 142–43

Historicism in ethics, 28, 143, 194–95, 222–23

Hollenbach, David, 36–38, 110, 148, 171, 183; on nuclear deterrence, 178–81; on pacifism and pluralism, 37

Howe, Julia Ward, 219, 220

Human rights, 13, 35–36, 37, 80–84, 103

Humphreys, David, 202

Hunthausen, Raymond, 68

Ideology, 193–95, 217, 222, 230–34. *See*

also Counterideology; Exceptionalism; Memory

Institutional violence, 72, 259n.88

Intention, 14, 104, 155, 158–59, 160, 164–66, 178–79, 224, 274n.65

Ironism, 245–46

Jefferson, Thomas, 210

Jewish Record, 200

Johnson, Edmund, 196

Johnson, James Turner, 106, 148, 169, 170, 194–95, 222, 251n.29, 265n.5, 267n.44, 278n.47, 280n.6

John XXIII, 62–63, 65. Works: *Peace on Earth*, 62–64

Jus ad bellum, 13; in terms of *agape*, 149–51; in terms of comparative justice, 214–15, 237

Jus in bello, 13, 14–15, 226; in ethics of nuclear deterrence, 164–65; in terms of *agape*, 150, 161; in William O'Brien, 215, 237

Justice: and *agape*, 152–53; and charity, 25–27, 251nn.33, 36; and order, 53, 58–69, 71, 74–75, 76, 256n.27

Just-war tenets: applied to war, 224–25; defined, 12–13; as framework for civil disobedience, 104–5; limits of, 235–36; and nationalism, 123–24; and prima facie duties, 41; in Ramsey's ethic, 149–52. See also *Jus ad bellum*; *Jus in bello*; Nonmaleficence, duty of

Kennan, George, 203

King, Martin Luther, Jr., 6, 110–11, 112–13, 217–22, 219, 267n.41, 268n.72. Works: *Strength to Love*, 218; *Where Do We Go from Here: Chaos or Community?* 220; *Why We Can't Wait*, 220. See also Civil disobedience, Counterideology

Langan, John, 251n.27, 258n.73

LaPorte, Roger, 97

Lawrence, William, 199

Levels of moral discourse, 39–46, 254n.93

Liberation theology, 54, 69–74. See also Gutierrez, Gustavo

Life, 200

Lincoln, Abraham, 197–98, 207

McClintock, Samuel, 196

Macgregor, G. H. C., 112, 117

MacIntyre, Alasdair, 8, 60, 68, 188, 226–27

McIntyre, Carl, 200

Mackie, J. L., 171

McKim, Robert, 171

Mara, Gerald, 186–88, 193, 216, 240

Mariana, 62

Maritain, Jacques, 204

Mather, Cotton, 198

Maurin, Peter, 86, 87, 117

Memory, 230–34

Merton, Thomas, 113, 117, 264n.97, 267n.37

Methodist Review, 199

Miller, David, 97

Miller, Perry, 204

Miller, Samuel, 210

Moral ambiguity, 30, 141–42, 234–45, 256n.27

Moral equivalence, axiom of, 67, 155, 174–75, 178, 183

Narrative, 230–32

National Catholic Welfare Conference, 211–12

Natural law, 4, 24, 55–56, 108, 206, 213–17, 221, 236, 240, 265n.9

Necessity, 185–86, 237–38

Neuhaus, Richard John, 209

New York Journal American, 212

Niebuhr, H. Richard, 11, 27, 28, 29, 49, 102, 125–43 passim, 153, 197, 233–34, 239, 269n.17, 270nn.30, 42; 282n.44; and cross, 130, 135, 136–37, 140, 141, 143, 233; implications for casuistry, 140; nonpreferentialism, 141; radical monotheism, 128, 131–32, 134; repentance, 127, 133–35, 139, 140, 141, 143. Works: "The Grace of Doing Nothing," 126; "Man the Sinner," 131; *The Meaning of Revelation*, 130, 133, 136–37, 239; *Radical Monotheism and Western Culture*, 131–32; *The Responsible Self*, 128, 129, 140; *Social Sources of Denominationalism*, 132. See also "Protestant principle"

Niebuhr, Reinhold, 27, 107, 118, 125, 126, 212, 236–37, 269n.8; on pacifism, 107; on realism, 236–37

Noncombatant immunity. See Discrimination, principle of

Nonmaleficence, duty of, 7, 16, 17, 161–63; as absolute, 16, 41; in Augustine, 19–21, 162; as counterideological principle, 235–36, 242; insufficient for pacifism, 120; overridden, 17, 41; postethical level, 42–46, 227–28; theological resonances, 45–46; as "weak premise" for pacifism and just-war tenets, 46

Nonpreferential duty: in H. Richard Niebuhr, 141; and nonmaleficence, 46, 234–35, 254n.111; in Paul Ramsey, 150, 152–53

Nonresistance, 19, 35, 47, 77, 80, 82–83, 262n.52

Nonviolent resistance, 77, 82–83, 89–90, 110–11, 262n.52; and American ideology, 217–22

Nuclear deterrence, 147–89 passim, 275n.73; anticipatory thesis, 181–83; exceptionalist thesis, 186–88; just-war thesis, 173–81; success thesis, 169–73, 179–80, 184; and "supreme emergency," 183–86. See also Hollenbach, David; Mara, Gerald; Ramsey, Paul; Sterba, James; U.S. Catholic bishops; Walzer, Michael

Nuclear pacifism, 38, 177–78

Nuclear war, 156–57, 174, 178. See also Just-war tenets

Oakes, Uriam, 201

O'Brien, William V., 148, 170, 213–17, 224–25, 237–39, 258n.72, 277nn.17, 18; on noncombatant immunity, 215; on realism, 237–39

Order: in Augustine, 18, 21–23; in modern Roman Catholic ethics, 62–74; Paul Ramsey's ethics, 153–54, 165–66; in Thomas Aquinas, 58–62, 64, 66–67, 68, 71, 72. See also Charity, order of; Justice

O'Sullivan, John, 197, 202, 211

Otherness, 54, 59–60, 64, 65, 69, 71, 73, 74–75, 235

Pacifism: and *agape*, 112, 118; as "antiwarism," 12; and Christian discipleship, 109, 118; ecclesiology, 112; elements of, 77–78; eschatological, 76, 86–97 passim; "failure motif," 114–16; iconoclastic, 97–101, 260n.6; on militarism, 116–17; on peace, 77, 120; positive virtues, 12; Ramsey on, 150, 272n.16; rights-based, 35, 76, 79–86; suspicions of statecraft, 111; theology of creation, 110–11; theology of history, 109–10; on tragedy, 119; on "witness," 112. See also Berrigan, Daniel; Berrigan, Philip; Catholic Worker (movement); Day, Dorothy; Douglass, James; Hauerwas, Stanley; King, Martin Luther, Jr.; Ryan, Cheyney; Yoder, John Howard; Zahn, Gordon

Palmer, Benjamin, 198

Parker, Theodore, 218

Pastoral Constitution of the Church in the Modern World (Second Vatican Council), 35, 36, 62, 64, 70, 79, 82, 84; and human rights, 80; and nonviolent resistance, 80; and self-defense, 80, 82

Paul VI, 70

Personalism, 87–88, 91, 113, 221

Phronesis. See Practical reasoning

Piehl, Mel, 90, 91

Pierson, Arthur, 206–7

Pius XII, 62, 66

Pluralism, 3, 37, 224–25, 245–46; in Catholic pacifism, 76–77, 103; in Christian ethics of war, 124; in H. Richard Niebuhr's ethics of war, 142

Practical reasoning, 12, 224, 227–43 passim, 256n.24

Presumption against harm, 7–8, 13, 16–18, 23–26, 31–35, 36, 41–42, 65, 76, 106–7, 150, 161–62, 241–42, 257n.39. *See also* Convergence of pacifism and just-war tenets; Nonmaleficence, duty of; Prima facie duties

Prima facie duties, 16–17, 41, 161–62, 166; leaving "moral traces," 17, 41, 162; rejected by Paul Ramsey, 150. *See also* Just-war tenets; Nonmaleficence, duty of

Proportionality, 15, 58; applied to war and deterrence, 64, 151–52, 157–60, 163, 166, 173–74, 178, 214, 225–26

"Protestant principle," 27, 125, 131, 139, 143, 234

Public discourse, 143, 221–23, 224–43 passim

Quirk, Michael, 279n.67

Radical difference. *See* Otherness

Ramsey, Paul, 11, 49, 117, 121, 141, 143,

168, 173, 174, 175, 178, 225–26, 272n.18, 273n.45, 274n.64, 275n.73; on consequentialism, 151–52; on individual self-defense, 149, 153; on intention, 155, 158–59, 160, 164–66; on nuclear deterrence, 157–61; on nuclear war, 155–57; on order, 153–54; on pacifism, 150, 272n.16; on presumption against harm, 150, 161–62; on realism, 154; on third-party relations, 159–60

Rawls, John, 4, 46, 260n.94, 265n.115

Reader's Digest, 200

Reagan, Ronald, 203

Realism, 65, 236–39, 263n.74; in eschatological pacifism, 91–97

Relative justice, 14, 66–67, 141–42

Religion and morality, 88, 95–96, 101, 138–42

Repentance, 127, 133–35, 139, 140, 141, 143. *See also* Niebuhr, H. Richard

Revelation, 31, 136–38

Revolution, 69–74

Rights. *See* Duties; Human rights

Roosevelt, Franklin D., 208

Roosevelt, Theodore, 207, 208

Rorty, Richard, 44, 212, 246, 254n.111

Ross, W. D., 16. *See also* Prima facie duties

Ryan, Cheyney, 117–18, 119

Schell, Jonathan, 268n.58

Schelling, Thomas, 160, 267n.44

Schlesinger, Arthur, Jr., 203

Secular City, The, 200

Seward, William, 206

Sheen, Fulton J., 208–9

Smith, David H., 46, 149

Stanton, Frederick, 210–11

Sterba, James, 181–83

Stiles, Ezra, 197, 202, 204

Stockton, Robert, 206

Strategic Defense Initiative (SDI), 276n.2

"Supreme Emergency," 34, 142, 183–87, 278n.47. *See also* Walzer, Michael

Theology and ethics, 28–30, 31, 45–46, 99, 138–42, 234–35, 256n.27. *See also* Ethics; "Protestant principle"; Religion and morality; Revelation

Thomas, C. F., 203

Thomas Aquinas, Saint, 23–27, 54–61, 214, 221, 224, 228, 229, 251nn.33, 36; 255n.3, 256nn.24, 27; 275n.69; on just war, 58–59, 64; on the order of charity and killing, 24–25, 61; presumption against harm, 24–25, 53; on private self-defense, 24–25, 251n.36; on publicly authorized killing, 25–26; on structure of moral acts, 58–59; on tyrannicide, 55–58, 64. Works: *Commentary on the Sentences of Peter Lombard,* 56; *On Princely Government,* 57; *Summa Theologiae,* 57. *See also* Charity, order of; Natural law; Presumption against harm

Tillich, Paul, 125, 233–34

Tracy, David, 235–36, 240–41, 247n.11

Tradition, 102–5, 226–27, 230–32

Truman, Harry, 203, 212

Tuveson, Ernest, 220

Typology, in ethics, 76–77, 260n.1

U.S. Catholic bishops, 83, 110, 119, 122, 142, 148, 161, 164–65, 171, 173–77, 183, 225, 275n.72, 277nn.21, 23; 279n.63; contrasted with Paul Ramsey, 164–65; on nuclear deterrence 174–77; on nuclear war, 173–74, 176–77; on selective conscientious objection, 83. See also *Challenge of Peace, The*

U.S. Methodist bishops, 38, 106, 171, 265n.5. Works: *In Defense of Creation,* 38

Veatch, Henry, 44

Virtue, 226, 228–36

Vitoria, 61, 278n.47

Walzer, Michael, 6, 34, 183–86, 222, 274n.65, 279n.60, 280n.5; on connected criticism, 222; on "supreme emergency," 183–86

Wasserstrom, Richard, 170, 172

Weinberger, Caspar, 170, 172

West German Catholic bishops, 179

Whitaker, Alexander, 196

Whitman, Walt, 198, 210

Wieseltier, Leon, 170

Wiggins, David, 229

Wilder, Royal, 206

Willson, Marcius, 205

Wilson, Woodrow, 199, 203, 208, 211

Winter, Gibson, 116–17

Winthrop, John, 201

Wise, Isaac, 202

Worcester, Samuel, 206

Yarrow, Thomas, 205
Yoder, John Howard, 6, 108, 111, 239–41, 287n.51; on failure of just-war tenets, 114–15; on practical reasoning, 239–41

Zahn, Gordon, 85–86, 87, 111, 113, 117; human dignity, 85; eschatological themes, 86; on failure of just-war tenets, 115–16
Zinn, Howard, 231–32
Zukerman, Solly, 170

Bross Prize Winners

1990   David S. Cunningham, *Faithful Persuasion: In Aid of a Rhetoric of Christian Theology*
Richard B. Miller, *Interpretations of Conflict: Ethics, Pacifism, and the Just-War Tradition*
Diane H. Lobody, *Lost in the Ocean of Love: The Mystical Writings of Catherine Livingston Garrettson*

1980   James C. Livingston, *Matthew Arnold and Christianity: His Religious Prose Writings*

1970   Dean Claude Welch, *Protestant Thought in the 19th Century*

1960   John A. Hutchison, *Language and Faith: Studies in Sign, Symbol and Meaning*

1950   Amos N. Wilder, *Modern Poetry and the Christian Tradition*

1940   Harris Franklin Rall, *Christianity*

1925   Douglas Clyde MacIntosh, *The Reasonableness of Christianity*

1915   Thomas J. Thoburn, *The Mystical Interpretation of the Gospels*

1905   James Orr, *The Problem of the Old Testament*

1880   Mark Hopkins, *Evidences of Christianity*